Questioning Sexuality

Questioning Sexuality

From Psychoanalysis to
Gender Theory and Beyond

GAVIN RAE

EDINBURGH
University Press

Edinburgh University Press is one of the leading university presses in the UK.
We publish academic books and journals in our selected subject areas across the
humanities and social sciences, combining cutting-edge scholarship with high
editorial and production values to produce academic works of lasting importance.
For more information visit our website: edinburghuniversitypress.com

© Gavin Rae, 2024

Edinburgh University Press Ltd
The Tun – Holyrood Road
12(2f) Jackson's Entry
Edinburgh EH8 8PJ

Typeset in 10/13 ITC Giovanni Std by
IDSUK (DataConnection) Ltd, and
printed and bound in Great Britain

A CIP record for this book is available from the British Library

ISBN 978 1 3995 3509 0 (hardback)
ISBN 978 1 3995 3511 3 (webready PDF)
ISBN 978 1 3995 3512 0 (epub)

The right of Gavin Rae to be identified as the author of this work has been
asserted in accordance with the Copyright, Designs and Patents Act 1988, and the
Copyright and Related Rights Regulations 2003 (SI No. 2498).

CONTENTS

Preface vi

Introduction: The Problem of Sex(uality) 1

Part I. Psychoanalysis and Phenomenology

1. Freud on Sexuality and the Feminine 29
2. Heidegger, Fundamental Ontology, and Sexuality 52
3. Merleau-Ponty on the Sexed Body 74

Part II. Feminism and (Post)Structuralism

4. Beauvoir and the Question of "Woman" 101
5. Lacan, the Symbolic Phallus, and Sexual Difference 130
6. Irigaray on Sexual Difference: Jamming the Patriarchal Machine 154

Part III. Gender Theory and Queer Materialities

7. Butler and Performativity: Thinking Sex through Gender 187
8. Barad, Agential Realism, and Queer Theory 214

Conclusion: Sexuality as Constellation 253

Bibliography 282
Index 302

PREFACE

This book engages with the questioning of sexuality that occupies much twentieth-century Western philosophy, especially its psychoanalytic, phenomenological, and feminist trajectories. The basic contention is that these heterogeneous traditions are united by their participation in an often subterranean debate regarding what I will call the essentialist-patriarchal model; a model that has historically dominated Western thinking on sexuality and that is defined by three premises: (1) there is a natural division between two sexes; (2) this division is based on "essential" differences between the masculine and the feminine; and (3) the masculine is and should be privileged over the feminine. From this contention, I outline a particular *historical* trajectory charting a variety of critical responses to this model within the three traditions previously mentioned, which, in turn, develops a number of *conceptual* claims: (1) the twentieth century witnessed a growing aversion to thinking of sexuality in terms of a straightforward ahistoric, biological determinism. Instead, it was increasingly recognised that sexuality was constructed, with the question of the means and ways of this construction being one of contestation. However, (2) in attempting to undercut both the logics of essentialism and patriarchy, critics tended to undermine one but rely on the other. This occurred in different ways depending on the critical position involved, but it meant that the patriarchal binary sexual opposition inherent in the essentialist-patriarchal conception of sexuality continued to be affirmed. (3) To overcome this, there was a gradual realisation that a more radical critical approach was needed. This was based on two premises: first, focusing on how to overcome the foreclosure inherent in the essentialist-patriarchal model was insufficient; heteronormativity also had to be combated. To achieve this, it was (second) held to be insufficient to simply rethink the coordinates of sexuality; instead, the fundamental concept engaged with had to alter away from "sexuality" to "gender" understood in terms of non-binary socio-linguistic performative becoming. Only this permitted "sexuality" to be thought in terms of fluidity, ambiguity, and constant open-ended alteration. However, (4) although the move to gender pointed to and depended upon a renewed conception of embodiment, its perceived over-reliance on social-linguistic performativity brought forth the charge that it gave too much weight to socio-linguistic processes to the detriment of material ones. Correcting this required, so it was affirmed, a direct engagement with the non-linguistic processes through which matter becomes; a position that brought forth the queer nature of materiality to deconstruct *any* foreclosing of "sexuality" by showing that such foreclosure contradicts "nature". I argue, however, that, although queer theory, at least in its agential realist form, demonstrates that the foreclosure of sexuality has no material basis, its lack of engagement with other dimensions (symbolic, political, and juridical, for example) of sexuality means that it is unable to adequately explain why "sexuality" continues to be foreclosed within exclusionary frameworks despite there being no material foundation for such action.

While the contestation resulting from these debates might be thought to lead us to the antinomy of either abandoning the problem of sexuality as a "false" one that disappears the moment we try to get a handle on it *or* continuing to search for a singular and substantive meaning for "it", I appeal to Walter Benjamin's notion of concepts as constellations to argue for a refocusing of the problem away from the *meaning* of sexuality – which implicitly depends upon the notion that sexuality is "something" substantial or identifiable – to its re-classification as an open-ended, perpetually problematic, empty, and indeterminate field where the term "sexuality" describes the inflection point or *nexal function* through which a particular constellation expresses itself conceptually. Understood in this way, questioning "sexuality" both depends upon and permits interrogation into the host of questions – at the individual level, often of identity, and, at the collective level, juridical-political issues regarding, for example, acceptable and ideal social norms, each of which is also tied to a range of ontological, metaphysical, and epistemological questions – and the relation between them, that "it" is tied to and, indeed, depends upon. This accounts for the contestation that has marred critical discussions of the topic, highlights the complexity of the issue, and points to how the questioning of sexuality can be reinvigorated to maintain its relevance.

This is developed throughout the text, but, at this stage, I would like to acknowledge that this project forms part of the activities for the following research projects: (1) "Agency and Society: An Inquiry through Poststructuralism" (PR108/20–26; PI: Gavin Rae), funded by the Universidad

Complutense de Madrid–Banco Santander; (2) "Differential Ontology and the Politics of Reason", PI: Gavin Rae, funded by the Government of the Region of Madrid, as part of line 3 of the multi-year agreement with the Universidad Complutense de Madrid: V PRICIT Excellence Program for University Professors (Fifth Regional Plan for Scientific Investigation and Technological Innovation); (3) "The Crossroads of the Sexed Body: Cultural Matter and Material Cultures of Sexuality", PI: Emma Ingala, financed by the Government of the Region of Madrid, as part of the multi-year agreement with the Universidad Complutense de Madrid: V PRICIT (Regional Plan for Scientific Investigation and Technological Innovation) program for Incentivizing Young PhDs (PR27/21-020); and (4) "The Politics of Reason" (PID2020-117386GA-I00; PI: Gavin Rae), financed by the Ministry of Science and Innovation, Government of Spain.

Rewritten aspects of Chapters 1 and 2 appear in "Freud and Heidegger on the 'Origins' of Sexuality", *Human Studies*, vol. 42, n. 4, 2019, pp. 543–563; an earlier version of Chapter 3 was published as "Merleau-Ponty on the Sexed Body", *Journal of Phenomenological Psychology*, vol. 51, n. 2, 2020, pp. 162–183; aspects of Chapter 5 appear in "Questioning the Phallus: Jacques Lacan and Judith Butler", *Studies in Gender and Sexuality*, vol. 21, n. 1, 2020, pp. 12–26; and parts of Chapter 6 appear in "Strategies of Political Resistance: Agamben and Irigaray", in *Historical Traces and Future Pathways of Poststructuralism: Aesthetics, Ethics, Politics*, edited by Gavin Rae and Emma Ingala (Abingdon: Routledge, 2021), pp. 223–245. I thank the publishers for permission to include that material here.

I also once again thank Carol Macdonald and her assistant, Sarah Foyle, for supporting this project and marshalling it through the unusually lengthy (caused in part by the COVID-19 pandemic) peer-review process. I also thank the anonymous reviewers for their support for the project and helpful comments to improve it. Iciar L. Yllera (https://iciaryllera.com/), an award-winning local artist from San Lorenzo de El Escorial just outside of Madrid (and my fantastically patient Spanish teacher), was kind enough to provide the original artwork for the cover. Emma was once again a source of inspiration, critique, and help during the completion of this project (*muchas gracias!*), while Toran continues to make sure that no day is dull. Finally, Aurora (Rora) entered our scene in the final stages of this project to cause many sleepless nights and much joy; this book is dedicated to her.

Introduction: The Problem of Sex(uality)

In everyday thought, it is often, if not usually, taken for granted that the meanings and significance of "sex" and "sexuality"[1] are obvious, clear-cut, and determined. Certainly, those who affirm "traditional" moral values or rally against "gender ideology"[2] maintain so. From this viewpoint, there really is not much to think about conceptually. The topic is a simple and resolved one: sex refers to a binary biological division between "males" and "females", each of which is defined by fixed *a priori* (biological) characteristics, while sexuality develops at the (often undefined but nevertheless definitive) moment of entry into adulthood, mirrors the biological sex of each individual, and is defined by predetermined and non-changeable heterosexual and legally sanctioned forms of legitimate expression. Put simply, according to this tradition, a man is defined by a penis and must develop the sexuality that affirms "masculine" traits, which more often than not are taken to entail aggression, virility, honour, protection of women, and so on. Women in contrast are defined by a vagina and must develop the sexuality affirming "feminine" traits: care, compassion, love, and, ultimately, children. The aim politically is to reaffirm this viewpoint against those who mistakenly criticise it and so want to overturn the natural or divinely ordained order.

While this understanding has a long historical trajectory and, indeed, has been the historically dominant one within Western thought and culture, this book challenges it by showing that its philosophical presuppositions – in particular the ontological claims that it is built on; that is, its assumptions regarding what fundamentally *is*, which delineates what a thing, in this case "sexuality", entails – are simply not as clear-cut or obvious as claimed. To do so, I argue that a variety of distinct contemporary and critical theoretical trajectories, from psychoanalysis, Husserlian-inspired phenomenology, and feminist theory, have engaged with and so been united in an often subterranean critique of the traditional conception of sexuality as part of a rethinking of this issue more generally; one that involves an ongoing process of ever-more radical deconstructions of the ontological premises supporting the traditional conception of sexuality to undermine its foreclosing within predetermined boundaries. How this plays out is developed across the book, but, at this stage, one way to delve into the issue is to note that a large part of the problem emanates from questions relating to and arising from the etymology of "sex". Emanating from "scission" and the Latin *sextus*, *secare*, meaning "to divide or cut",[3] "sex" points to the idea of an originary androgynous unity that is split or divided, with the parts subsequently reunited through the sexual act. The nature of the *secare* has, however, always been a difficult one for Western philosophy: Is the division a "natural" one? Into how many segments does the division divide? And can one cross the sex divide to become the other sex and, indeed, what happens if one does?

Although all relevant questions, the history of Western philosophy is, generally speaking, marred by significant aversion to the debates surrounding them. There are many reasons for this but two stand out. First, the Platonic rejection of the body appears to be a particularly fundamental to this foreclosure. In the *Phaedo*, for example, Socrates associates the philosopher – the lover of wisdom – with the soul divorced from the body, whose temptations, needs, and distractions are held to be an impediment to the search for the truth.[4] If the philosopher is the friend of wisdom who searches dispassionately wherever reason takes him, and the body is an impediment to that search, it is not surprising to find that that which is associated with the body is also disparaged. Sex and related questions to do with sexuality and sexual relations are, as a consequence, subsequently downplayed and ignored, with long-standing prejudices, norms, and structures simply accepted.

Second, the institutionalisation of Christianity – itself dependent upon and tied to Platonic thought[5] – further impeded the open questioning of sexuality. Based on a natural sexual division between two distinct sexes, with the relation between them premised on increasingly restrictive prescriptions, and the notion that sex is a source of wickedness and sin, albeit one that is necessary for the propagation of the species, Christian thinking tended to foreclose open analyses of sexuality and, indeed, turned it into something sinful to be avoided.[6] Offering an alternative conception of sexuality to that deemed legitimate by the established authorities required considerable courage, especially because those authorities often vigorously defended the orthodox position and suppressed alternative conceptions through a variety of political (exclusion), juridical (imprisonment or worse), and normative (prescriptions as to how to act) means. Perhaps not surprisingly the result was both a conceptual and cultural (fore-)closing of thinking on the topic. From Ancient Greece, through Christianity, up to the so-called Enlightenment and beyond, Western philosophers from diverse geographies and "schools" of thought have expressed strikingly similar views on the question of sexuality and, by extension, sexual relations that, more often than not insist on a natural binary masculine/feminine division supported by an ontology of fixed essence, all the while extolling the masculine to denigrate, often in extremely harsh terms, the feminine.

So, while Plato's *Republic* is often seen as an early – Martha Nussbaum even suggests it offers some of the first feminist arguments[7] – upholder of sexual equality because of its insistence that what counts when choosing rulers is the capacity to rule, rather than the particular biological sexual traits of the individuals involved,[8] once we turn from the *Republic* to the later *Timaeus*, the story of the sexes becomes far more complicated as we are informed that "all male-born humans who lived lives of cowardice or injustice were reborn in the second generation as women".[9] While this obviously relies upon a theory of rebirth,[10] there is a clear hierarchy established between the sexes, so that men who do not live up to the ideals of bravery and justice are reborn in the secondary state of "woman".

The ambiguity that marks Plato's comments on the nature and role of women in society, in particular whether to affirm a fundamental potential equality between the sexes or whether to structure them hierarchically to the detriment of the feminine, was quickly resolved in favour of the latter. We see this clearly once we turn to Aristotle, who, in the *Politics*,[11] written just one generation later, first praises the novelty of Plato's thinking on women and children before clarifying that it is an aberration that, far from improving the state, would imperil it. This is premised on the claim, made in the *History of Animals*, that woman is fundamentally unequal to man:

> The female is softer in disposition, is more mischievous, less simple, more impulsive, and more attentive to the nurture of the young; the male, on the other hand, is more spirited, more savage, more simple and less cunning. The traces of these characteristics are more or less visible everywhere, but they are especially visible where character is the more developed, and most of all in man.[12]

Furthermore, woman is held to be "more void of shame, more false of speech, more deceptive, and of more retentive memory. She is also more wakeful, more shrinking, more difficult to rouse to action, and requires a smaller quantity of nutriment."[13] In contrast, "the nature of man is the most rounded off and complete".[14]

This natural sexual difference feeds through to and forms the basis for Aristotle's account of the relationship between woman and politics, one that sharply contrasts with Plato's and, in so doing, quickly closes any consideration of sexual equality that may have been opened by the *Republic*. Aristotle notes, for example, that "[j]ust as husband and wife are parts of the family, so it is clear that a city should also be considered as divided almost equally into the male and female populations".[15] However, although Aristotle recognises that women comprise around half the population, he explains that they cannot be considered free and responsible citizens. Their frivolity must be controlled because too much "indulgence permitted to women is damaging both to the purpose of the constitution and to the happiness of the city".[16] The ones to do the controlling are men, who, it just so happens, are ontologically suited to the task by virtue of being naturally superior to women: "the male is by nature superior, and the female inferior; and the one rules, and the other is ruled".[17] As a consequence, "the head of the household rules over both wife and children . . . His rule over his wife is like that of a statesman over fellow citizens; his rule over his children is like that of a monarch over subjects."[18] The rationale for such a division is simply that "The male is naturally fitter to command than the female."[19]

Aristotle's views on women might surprise and, indeed, shock the contemporary Western reader – a reaction that I would suggest is due to the significant engagements with "sexuality" that have marked the twentieth century – but they were the dominant form of understanding of sexuality and sexual relations for almost two millennia. While the understanding of sexuality and the morality surrounding it underwent substantial alterations as the paganism of Ancient Greece was gradually replaced with a Christian metaphysics and morality, these alterations did not change the role and place of the sexes. Indeed, as noted, in many respects, the institutionalisation of Christianity led to far greater institutional and moral rigidity on the question of sexual expression, which exacerbated the division between the sexes and the Aristotelian valorisation of the masculine over the feminine. Perhaps Tertullian, writing in the second century, exhibits this misogyny to the greatest extent by castigating women for bringing sin to man and, in so doing, ultimately killing God's son:

> The sentence of God on this sex of yours lives in this age: the guilt must of necessity live too. *You* are the devil's gateway: *you* are the unsealer of that (forbidden) tree: *you* are the first deserter of the divine law: *you* are she who persuaded him whom the devil was not valiant enough to attack. *You* destroyed so easily God's image, man. On account of *your* desert – that is, death – even the Son of God had to die.[20]

Although it might be thought that such views were a consequence of the follies of youth that would fall out of fashion as Christianity developed, the opposite was the case. Not only does the logic of patriarchy continue but comments regarding women's defectiveness were increasingly emphasised. Augustine, for example, writing in *On the Trinity*, explains that "the woman together with her husband is the image of God, so that that whole substance is one image. But when she is assigned as a helpmate, a function that pertains to her alone, then she is not the image of God."[21] Rather, "the man . . . is by himself alone the image of God, just as fully and completely as when he and the woman are joined together into one".[22] Note that it is not just that women is subordinate to man, as Tertullian, Aristotle, and Plato (at times) maintain; Augustine goes further by associating man with the divine.

As Christianity cemented its dominance within Europe up through the Middle Ages, its views on women became shriller. Writing in the *Summa Theologiae* in the twelfth century, for example, Aquinas explains that "[w]oman is defective and misbegotten".[23] Based on an active/passive division which is associated with masculinity and femininity respectively, Aquinas holds that "the active force in the male seed tends to the production of a perfect likeness in the masculine sex; while the production of woman comes from defect in the active force or from some material indisposition".[24] Again, this ontological defect has political consequences, in so far as we are informed that "[g]ood order would have been wanting in the human family if some were not governed by others wiser than themselves. So by such a kind of subjection woman is naturally subject to man, because in man the discretion of reason predominates."[25] On Aquinas's telling, therefore, women are not only naturally passive; they also lack the capacity for reason that marks the active male and which makes him alone suitable to rule.

A strong misogynistic streak runs then right through the history of early and medieval Christian thinking. Not only are the sexes naturally divided, but the masculine is privileged over the feminine and, indeed, is often associated with the divine itself. Although it might be thought that such conclusions are simply based on the arationality of religious scripture, dogma, and disputes that have little relevance for contemporary critical thought standing as it does at the "end" of a long process of secularisation that has led to the privileging of rational, critical, and often empirically orientated thought that marks Enlightenment and post-Enlightenment thought,[26] this is not so. The Enlightenment's appeal to rational, naturalist premises does not fundamentally alter the dominant perception of the sexes, in so far as the supposed enlightened figures of the Enlightenment continue to espouse the same views on the sexes as their illustrious albeit supposedly unenlightened philosophical forbearers. While there was a definitive rejection of the metaphysical premises of Christianity, Enlightenment and post-Enlightenment thinkers continued to depend upon and affirm prejudices regarding sexuality and women, including the binary opposition, essentialism, and patriarchal positions, found within the traditional rejected.

The rather strange disjunction between professed belief in reason to enlighten and the continuing dependence upon the arational patriarchal logic historically dominant comes to the fore in the infamous fifth chapter of Jean-Jacques Rousseau's *Emile*, where he explains that, while men and women share certain things in common by virtue of belonging to the human species, this does not mean that they are the same: "The only thing we know with certainty is that everything man and woman have in common belongs to the species, and that everything which distinguishes them belongs to the sex."[27] The difference between them is natural – "Women possess their empire not because men wanted it that way, but because nature wants it that way"[28] – and results in significant differences in the ethics appropriate to each. Specifically, "woman is made specially to please man",[29] whereas "[i]f man ought to please her in turn, it is due to a less direct necessity. His merit is in his power; he pleases by the sole fact of his strength."[30] While accepting that this "is not the law of love",[31] Rousseau explains that nevertheless "it is that of nature, prior to love itself. If woman is made to please and to be subjugated, she ought to make herself agreeable to man instead of arousing him."[32] Furthermore, man is naturally more independent and self-sufficient, whereas women need man to survive: "Woman and man are made for one another, but their mutual dependence is not equal. Men depend on women because of their desires; women depend on men because of both their desires and their needs. We would survive more easily without them than they would without us."[33] Lest women wish to criticise this inequality, Rousseau falls back on the natural sexual difference, explaining that

> [w]hen woman complains on this score about unjust man-made inequality, she is wrong. This inequality is not a human institution – or, at least, it is the work not of prejudice but of reason. It is up to the sex that nature has charged with the bearing of children to be responsible for them to the other sex.[34]

As a consequence, while Rousseau agrees with Plato that women should be educated, he disagrees that the sexes should undergo the same type of education: "Once it is demonstrated that man and woman are not and ought not to be constituted in the same way in either character or temperament, it follows that they ought not to have the same education."[35] Each sex must be educated differently, as befits their respective natures. Doing otherwise, risks, on Rousseau's telling, folly: "To cultivate man's qualities in women and to neglect those which are proper to them is obviously to work to their detriment."[36] For this reason, he advises the "judicious mother"[37] to "not make a decent man of your daughter, as though you would give nature the lie. Make a decent woman of her, and be sure that as a result she will be worth more for herself and for us."[38]

While wildly influential, Rousseau's thinking was premised on a number of unacknowledged and unexamined theoretical affirmations and foundations. The philosophical revolution instantiated by Immanuel Kant in *The Critique of Pure Reason*[39] aimed to undo the logic supporting, amongst others, Rousseau's position by questioning the basis of knowledge. Rather than grounding it in metaphysical speculation, Kant insists that knowledge has to be grounded in autonomous reason, which, by insisting on a division between the unknowable noumenal and phenomenal world of appearance, brought him to conclude that reason had to be limited to knowledge of the phenomenal realm. This rejected the pre-critical stance of claiming absolute status for knowledge based in unsubstantiated and unsubstantiable metaphysical speculations, to instead ground knowledge from empirical "data", in combination with autonomous rationality and the limitations of human cognition. However, while based on significant methodological alterations, Kant's later speculations regarding the sexes in the *Anthropology from a Pragmatic Point of View* repeat the conclusions affirmed in much pre-critical thinking:

> When nature entrusted to woman's womb its dearest pledge, namely the species, in the fetus by which the race is to propagate and perpetuate itself, nature was frightened so to speak about the preservation of the species and so implanted this *fear* – namely fear of *physical* injury and *timidity* before similar dangers – in woman's nature; through which weakness this sex rightfully demands male protection for itself.[40]

Woman is held therefore to be naturally timid and fearful and so needs and seeks out masculine protection from potential harm, not only for her own well-being but also for that of the propagation of the species.

It might be thought that it is rational, or at least understandable, that both partners, expecting a child, would wish to protect the child by offering a minimum degree of care and protection for the woman carrying the child, meaning that, being charitable, Kant's comments here could be rationalised and explained away as making a rather banal point. However, he then goes on to make a number of comments that undermine such a reading and, indeed, affirm the absolute unequal division between the two sexes to the detriment of the feminine. As a consequence, we are told that "[i]n marriage the man *woos* only his *own* wife, but the woman has an inclination for *all* men; out of jealousy, she *dresses up* only for the eyes of her own sex, in order to outdo other women in charm or fashionableness".[41] Indeed, whereas "man is jealous *when he loves*; . . . woman is jealous even when she does not love, because every lover won by other women is one lost from her circle of admirers".[42] To women's innate jealousy and vanity is added her unforgiving judgement posited against the leniency of men: "The man judges feminine mistakes leniently, but the women judges them very strictly (in public)."[43] Such is the difference between the two and the severity of female judgement that Kant assures us that even "young women, if they were allowed to choose whether a male or female tribunal should pass judgement on their offences, would certainly choose the former for their judge".[44] "As concerns scholarly women: they use their *books* somewhat like their *watch*, that is, they carry one so that it will be seen that they have one; though it is usually not running or not set by the sun."[45] However, while being innately jealous, vain, stupid, and marked by vicious judgement, Kant explains that women are just as wishful and desiring as men; the difference is that social convention dictates that she be demure so that she limit her actions and desire. Kant warns, however, that this goes against her nature to the extent that, if honest, a woman would make "no secret of wishing that she might rather be a man, so that she could give her inclinations larger and freer latitude; no man, however, would want to be a woman".[46]

Whereas Kant attempted to describe the inclinations and natural constitution of women, Georg Hegel engages with the issue from a different direction by describing the role of the sexes within ethical life; that is, within the social configuration, comprising the institutional structures and ethical (= cultural) norms necessary to realise a fully rational and by extension free social existence. Outlined in *Elements of the Philosophy of Right*, Hegel explains that ethical life is conditioned by three inter-linked social spheres: the family, civil society, and the constitutional state.[47] The discussion of the role of women in ethical life is found within the section on the family, which is composed of a union of two sexes that finds its true expression through the creation of a third – the child – who "breaks" the insular duality of the couple and, by eventually going out into the world, binds the couple to the universality of the whole of ethical life.[48] On the one hand, Hegel accepts that women have an important role to play in the realisation of ethical life, in so far as the family and, by extension, men and women are needed equally for its perpetuation and realisation. But, on the other hand, he is clear that the relationship between the two sexes is one of equality in difference, with women finding her freedom in the private sphere of the household and man realising his in the public sphere of civil society. Both must fulfil their roles, but each has a distinctive role based solely on his/her sex. For this reason, Hegel explains that

> Man . . . has his actual substantial life in the state, in learning [*Wissenschaft*] etc., and otherwise in work and struggle with his external world and with himself, so that it is only through his division that he fights his way to self-sufficient unity with himself . . . Woman, however, has her substantial vocation [*Bestimmung*] in the family, and her ethical disposition consists in this [family] *piety*.[49]

As a consequence, "[w]omen are not to partake in public affairs, her vocation [*Bestimmung*] consists essentially only in the marital relationship".[50] Although Hegel accepts that women "may well be educated",[51] he insists that "they are not made for higher sciences, for philosophy and certain artistic productions which require a universal element".[52] This is premised on the particularities of his philosophy: "Women may have insights [*Einfälle*], taste, and delicacy, but they do not possess the ideal",[53] and so cannot cultivate access to the truth necessary for participation in public affairs. Indeed, Hegel warns that such is their unsuitability for public life that "[w]hen women are in charge of government, the [S]tate is in danger, for their actions are based not on the demands of universality but on contingent inclination and opinion".[54]

Although Kant and Hegel clearly accept a logic of patriarchy and, indeed, a certain sexual essentialism, they do attempt to give women a role within a wider ethical whole. In contrast, Arthur Schopenhauer, who extolled Kant and hated Hegel, removed the ambiguity inherent in their positions by expressing visceral hatred and misogynistic views towards women, explaining on one occasion that "throughout their lives women remain children, never see anything but what is closest to them, cleave to the present, take the appearance of things for their reality and prefer trivialities to the most important affairs".[55] As a consequence, "they are inferior to men in the matter of justice, honesty, and conscientiousness",[56] with this originating "primarily from [their] want of reasonableness and reflection and is further supported by the fact that, as the weaker, they are by nature dependent not on force but cunning; hence their instinctive artfulness and ineradicable tendency to tell lies".[57] Schopenhauer concludes that women's lack of rationality and general stupidity means that they

> are qualified to being the nurses and governesses of our earliest childhood by the very fact that they themselves are childish, trifling, and short-sighted, in a word, are all their lives grown-up children; a kind of intermediate stage between the child and the man, who is a human being in a real sense.[58]

Schopenhauer's misogyny has long been noted,[59] and given his influence on Friedrich Nietzsche it is perhaps not surprising to find that Schopenhauer's views on women and sexuality are mirrored in a number of statements that Nietzsche makes. This is not however straightforward. Nietzsche's views on women are highly ambiguous and have given rise to a significant literature.[60] After all, he explains – in a way that Schopenhauer and, indeed, those philosophers quoted, never would – that "[t]he perfect woman is a higher type of human being than the perfect man: also something much rarer".[61] Far from being equal to man, the perfect woman is, for Nietzsche, more valuable. But lest we think that Nietzsche leaves it here, we find him explaining in *Beyond Good and Evil* that

> [w]hat inspires respect and, often enough, fear of women is their *nature* (which is 'more natural' than that of men), their truly predatory and cunning agility, their tiger's claws insider their glove, the naiveté of their egoism, their inner wildness and inability to be trained, the incomprehensibility, expanse, and rambling character of their desires and virtues.[62]

It should be noted that while the West's Christian heritage holds characteristics such as cunningness, wildness, and incomprehensibility to be negatives, for Nietzsche's particular ethics they do have positive connotations. His description of women is then, *on his terms*, not wholly negative. The problem, however, is that in offering such a (backhanded) compliment, he merely repeats the association between woman and the irrational (opposed to the rational male) that has long underpinned Western views on sex, sexuality, and sexual relations. Even if we read Nietzsche charitably and on his own terms, we see that, in his comments on femininity, he appears to be committed, however unintentionally, to the logic of patriarchy, binary opposition, and essentialism inherent in the Christian tradition that he otherwise criticises.

The Argument Developed

I do not pretend that this snapshot – both of the number of philosophers mentioned or, indeed, the content of the individual philosophers themselves – covers the entire history of thinking on sexuality in Western philosophy.[63] The perception of sexuality and, indeed, women has, of course, been far more nuanced than this picture portrays. Not only have there been philosophers, such as Mary Wollstonecraft[64] and John Stuart Mill,[65] who have strongly supported sexual equality, but there is also much contestation in the secondary literature regarding the views of those philosophers mentioned, with much of it showing that their respective positions are far more nuanced than presented.[66] Nevertheless, my guiding contentions are that (1) the various positions described are united by a common essentialist-patriarchal logic based on three claims: (a) there is a natural division between two sexes; (b) this division is based on "essential" differences between the masculine and the feminine; and (c) the masculine is and should be privileged over the feminine; (2) this essentialist-patriarchal model long-dominated Western thinking on sexuality,[67] and, indeed, (3) was the conception of sexuality that formed the basis for the critiques of sexuality found throughout twentieth-century critical theory.

From these contentions, I aim to develop a particular *historical* trajectory to show that in the twentieth century the Western world experienced significant changes in terms of social attitudes to sexuality that were accompanied by tremendous theoretical debates regarding the nature of sexuality, which, in turn, brought forth substantial conceptual alterations. I aim to offer *a* history of this period, rather than *the* history of it, with the consequence that I do not aim or claim to represent all traditions or viewpoints. This is particularly apparent in relation to feminist theory, which is limited to aspects of Francophone feminist theories (Beauvoir and Irigaray). Even within the landscape of twentieth-century French feminism, this limited focus is admittedly problematic. Nevertheless, beyond a famous and well-worn appeal to space constraints, there are two reasons why I have undertaken this hermeneutic approach. First, a direct historical and conceptual trajectory can be drawn between Beauvoir, Irigaray, and Butler (and Barad) given that Irigaray discusses Beauvoir, and Butler explicitly engages with and, indeed, was influenced by Beauvoir and Irigaray. There are in other words clear links (historical and conceptual) that justify the rationale for the movement between these authors, which would be broken up by discussing other trends within French feminism. Second, one of the benefits of the book is that it does not reduce critical engagements with sexuality to feminism. Although feminist discourse is of course important to contemporary discussions of sexuality, one of the aims of the book is to show that a substantial questioning of sexuality also occurs outside of feminism. That however requires that I devote space to alternative traditions/thinkers, which obviously reduces the amount of space that can be devoted to feminist thinkers/the feminist tradition. As such, I limit the analysis to what I consider to be some of the more significant theories within twentieth-century Western philosophy. By significant, I mean either that they initiated a new way of thinking about the topic and/or were important for the development of subsequents theories. This allows me to offer a detailed treatment of each theory within the confines of a single volume and demonstrate that the historically dominant model was subject to critique from distinct angles.

I start by suggesting that, in the twentieth century, it was Freudian psychoanalytical theory[68] that brought the questioning of sexuality to the fore to move the discussion of sexuality away from natural or biological causes to the (psychic and, in its Lacanian variant, symbolic) processes that take place to create the meaning of sexuality, as a precursor to outlining the pathologies that revolve around sexuality. This was subsequently complemented by Husserlian-inspired phenomenology – in particular, that of Martin Heidegger,[69] and especially Maurice Merleau-Ponty[70] – that accentuated the lived body as a means of undermining the binary mind/body logic inherent in modernity. In turn, this led to radical questioning of the nature and meaning of sexuality, emphasising its temporal and constructed "nature", and undercutting the essentialism that had long dominated Western thinking on the topic. While there are significant differences between Heidegger's and Merleau-Ponty's analyses, I argue that by affirming the importance of the lived body and the notion of a presuppositionless methodological stance, both undercut the notion that the body is defined by an ahistoric sex in ways that come to be important for feminist thinking on embodied subjectivity.

For example, Simone de Beauvoir focuses on the constructed nature of the category "woman",[71] whereas Luce Irigaray[72] takes up insights from Heidegger to affirm a fundamental and primordial sexual difference. Although both, in different ways, privilege a feminine perspective or emphasis to overcome patriarchy, subsequent feminist thinkers sought to go further by focusing on undermining the binary opposition between the masculine and feminine that had continued to structure much (feminist) thought. Instead of merely inverting the privileged term, they – inspired by the deconstruction of Jacques Derrida[73] – sought to undermine the logic upon which patriarchy depends to instantiate a new conceptual apparatus to engage with the problem, one that introduced a number of conceptual innovations, including the distinction between "sex" and "gender".[74] The importance of the latter concept to thinking on sexuality was substantial, in so far as it permitted the removal of all essentialist premises from thinking on sexuality, all the while ensuring that sexuality does not have to adhere to a binary logic. Sexuality can be cut or divided in many more ways or, indeed, just expressed differently without being foreclosed within a prior schema; a conclusion that not only permits those excluded from the binary heteronormative sexual division long established and depended upon to be included, but that also paves the way for the movement to queer theory where the multidimensional, fluid, and inherently singular "nature" of sexual emergence comes to the fore.

From and through this historical trajectory, I develop a number of *conceptual* claims: (1) the twentieth century witnessed a growing aversion

Introduction / 13

to thinking of sexuality in terms of a straightforward ahistoric, biological determinism. Instead, it was increasingly recognised that sexuality was constructed, with the question of the means and ways of this construction being one of contestation. However, (2) in attempting to undercut both the logics of essentialism and patriarchy, critics tended to undermine one by relying on the other. While essentialism was increasingly rejected, those who did so often continued to implicitly affirm a binary sexual division that was usually underpinned by the implicit affirmation of the masculine perspective. This occurred in different ways depending on the critical position involved, but it meant that the patriarchal binary sexual opposition inherent in the essentialist-patriarchal conception of sexuality continued to be affirmed.

(3) To overcome this, there was a gradual realisation that a more radical critical approach was needed. This was based on two premises. First, focusing on how to overcome the foreclosure inherent in the essentialist-patriarchal model was insufficient; not only had previous thinking tended to (implicitly) rely on one aspect (essentialism or patriarchy) to overcome the other, but such enquiries continued to be grounded in a troubling binary heteronormative binary opposition that constrained sexuality within a masculine/feminine opposition and/or took this type of relationship as the prototype for others. Thus, it was gradually realised that it wasn't enough to overcome the foreclosure emanating from ontological essentialism and the logic of patriarchy; heteronormativity also had to be combated. To achieve this, it was (second) held to be insufficient to simply rethink the coordinates of sexuality; instead, the fundamental concept engaged with had to alter away from "sexuality" to "gender" – manifested most clearly in the thought of Judith Butler[75] – and understood in terms of non-binary socio-linguistic performative becoming. Only this permitted sexuality to be thought in terms of fluidity, ambiguity, and constant open-ended alteration.

(4) However, although Butler's gender theory pointed to and depended upon a renewed conception of embodiment, its apparent reliance on a socio-linguistic account of performativity brought forth the charge that it gave too much weight to socio-linguistic processes to the detriment of material ones. Correcting this required, so it was affirmed, a direct engagement with the non-linguistic processes through which matter becomes; a position that brought forth the queer nature of materiality – outlined most substantially through the agential realism of Karen Barad[76] – to deconstruct *any* foreclosing of sexuality by showing that such foreclosure contradicts "nature". In turn, this depends upon and feeds into a debate – one that has a tendency to operate through a troubling and not particularly satisfactory binary opposition – that has long adhered to critical engagements

with the essentialist-patriarchal model, pitching those (Lacan, Butler) who insisted on the symbolic "nature" of sexuality against those (to a degree Freud and Heidegger, Merleau-Ponty, Beauvoir, and Irigaray) who affirmed its "material" base. The "gender" theory versus "queer" theory debate brings this conceptual fault line to the fore to show that the former (is held to) affirm(s) a predominantly symbolic account while the latter re-instantiates a return to "nature", albeit one that rejects the tendency to think of "nature/materiality" in static terms (as underpinned the essentialist-patriarchal model) to instead affirm the ongoing, intra-active becomings constitutive of materiality (= nature), and undermine clear-cut divisions and identities. In so doing, Barad's queer materialism aims to show that matter is constitutively queer; a position that leads to the conclusion that it is non-binary sexual identities that are expressive of actual reality and so might be called "natural". In turn, it is the binary heteronormativity so often affirmed by Chritsian thought as being "natural" that distorts reality and so must be considered to be "un-natural". With this, Barad provides a sophisticated theoriestical framework from which to justify the primacy of non-binary sexual/gender identities, including intersexuality, trans*, queer, and so on. I argue, however, that, although queer theory, at least in its agential realist form, demonstrates that the foreclosure of sexuality has no material basis, its lack of substantial engagement with others dimensions (the symbolic, political, and juridical, for example) of sexuality and sexual expression means that it is unable to adequately explain why "sexuality" continues to be foreclosed within exclusionary frameworks despite there being no material foundation for such action.

Although the contestation resulting from these debates might be thought to lead us into the antinomy of either abandoning the problem of sexuality as a "false" one that disappears the moment we try to get a handle on it *or* continuing to search for a singular and substantive meaning for "it", albeit one that depends upon a return to the foundationalism rejected by the psychoanalytic, phenomenological, and feminist frameworks, I appeal to Walter Benjamin's notion of concepts as constellations to argue that there is another, far more satisfactory, option that respects the afoundationalism, heterogeneity, and complexity that (the phenomenological, psychoanalytic, and feminist critiques reveal) surround the problem of sexuality, all the while continuing to treat "it" as a "real" conceptual problem. To do so, however, it is necessary to refocus the problem away from the *meaning* of sexuality – which implicitly depends upon the notion that sexuality is "something" clearly identifiable – to instead reclassify "it" as an open-ended, perpetually problematic, empty, and indeterminate *nexal function* that is structured around and permits interrogation into the host of questions – at the individual level, often of identity, and, at the collective level, juridical-political issues regarding, for example, acceptable and ideal social norms, each of which is also tied to a range of ontological, metaphysical, and epistemological questions – and the relation between them, that "it" is tied to and, indeed, depends upon.

Structure of the Book

To outline this, the book is split into three parts: Part I is composed of three chapters that explore the responses to the problem of sexuality within Freudian psychoanalysis and Husserlian-inspired phenomenology. Chapter 1 starts with Sigmund Freud's engagement with the question of sexuality to argue that he posits an originary bisexuality to reject the central premise underpinning the essentialist model of sexuality that holds that sexuality is biological, unitary, and fixed. Freud goes on to explore the ways in which, through the combination of biological, social, and psychic processes, this bisexuality finds expression through individual bodies. While this rejects sexual essentialism and, indeed, points to the complexity of the processes through which an individual's sexuality is created, I appeal to Freud's later work on femininity to show that he continues to foreclosure sexuality within a binary heteronormative and patriarchal logic. As a consequence, he undermines the essentialist premise of the essentialist-patriarchal model, but at the expense of depending upon and re-instantiating the logic of patriarchy.

Chapter 2 moves from Freudian psychoanalysis to Husserlian-inspired phenomenology and the fundamental ontology of Martin Heidegger. I first outline the general parameters of Heidegger's engagement with the question of the meaning of Being in *Being and Time*, before responding to the long-standing charge that his ontological difference – between Being and its ontic expressions – is premised on an affirmation of the former to the detriment of the latter, with the consequence that the question of sexuality is ignored. To do so, I show that in the following year's lecture series, translated as *The Metaphysical Foundations of Logic*,[77] Heidegger explicitly engages with the relationship between his fundamental ontology and ontic sexuality to reject Freud's affirmation of an originary bisexuality for needlessly constraining ontic sexual expression within a binary opposition, to instead insist on an originary indeterminacy. However, while Heidegger's thinking on sexuality questions its ontological importance to thereby account for its place "within" human being specifically and Being more generally, he does not aim to offer an ontic analysis of sexuality. The result is a radical, if truncated, critique of sexual essentialism that rejects the notion that sexuality is ontologically foreclosed but does not go further to explain or engage with ontic determinations or the question of patriarchy.

Chapter 3 shows how Husserlian-inspired phenomenology developed once it was transposed to France by arguing that, in contrast to Heidegger, Maurice Merleau-Ponty insists on the need to forego ontological analyses to engage with the phenomenological becoming of sexed bodies. I first outline his notion of the sexual schema to show that, contrary to a number of contemporary feminist critiques, it does not (1) posit a neutral body over-coded by culturally-contingent sexual determinations or (2) erase the feminine body, but is informed by Merleau-Ponty's particular version of the phenomenological reduction whereby factic determinations are "bracketed" to permit the object under study to reveal itself as it is rather than as we wish it to be or have been conditioned to think it. From this, I defend Merleau-Ponty against the long-standing claim that entwining sexuality with existence prevents an analytic and by extension positive conception of sexuality by arguing that he rejects the monadic logic that this charge is premised on to instead challenge us to think of sexuality in terms of its integration with an individual's entire embodied and embedded existence. The result is an analysis that emphasises the ambiguity, afoundationalism, individuality, and open-ended immanent expressivity of embodied sexuality.

Merleau-Ponty's position is important to the historical development of critical thinking regarding the essentialist-patriarchal model of sexuality because he explicitly brings to the fore the relationship between sexuality and the body in a way that emphasises the continuous becoming of both. This opening becomes increasingly important to subsequent feminist theory. Part II takes this up by engaging with feminist, structuralist, and poststructuralist theories regarding the question of sexuality generally and the essentialist-patriarchal model specifically. Chapter 4 starts with Simone de Beauvoir's attempt to answer the question "what is woman?" By responding that "she" is created, Beauvoir aims to undermine both essentialism and patriarchy; the former by rejecting the notion that the body is, in some way, fixed and determined, and the latter by showing that, as a construction, a patriarchal division is not necessary. Beauvoir's solution to the status of woman is to argue for equality with men; a position that, for a number of subsequent feminist thinkers, makes woman dependent upon a privileged masculine position, ignores the specific differences between the two sexes, and implicitly re-instantiates the logic of patriarchy to be overcome. Although this points to the heterogeneous ways in which the logic of patriarchy can be manifested and, by extension, the difficulty faced by those attempts who try to overcome it, I argue that Beauvoir's claim that sexuality is constructed from lived experience means that "it" cannot be thought in terms of clear-cut categories or divisions but must be understood in terms of the ambiguity that marks lived experience. For this reason, she pushes us to forego clear-cut sexual divisions to instead recognise, accept, and even affirm the ambiguity inherent in lived embodied forms of sexuality; a conclusion that not only marks her connection to Merleau-Ponty, but is a precursor to and feeds into the conceptual coordinates subtending subsequent queer theory (Chapter 8).

Chapter 5 charts how from the 1940s to 1950s, the French intellectual scene was marked by a significant theoretical movement from phenomenologically inspired analyses to structuralist ones. Jacques Lacan utilises the latter's logic of differential relations to reinvigorate Freudian psychoanalysis and show that sexuality is a symbolic construct. In so doing, he rejects the notion that sexuality is defined by a fixed, unitary meaning or essence to instead claim that the meaning of each sexual position is premised on its relation to other symbolic positions. While this appears to also undermine any necessary privileging of one sex over the other, Lacan nevertheless reintroduces such a logic by maintaining that each position is orientated to and gains meaning from a "third" term: the symbolic phallus. The masculine is constructed to "have" the phallus and so is the central point from which signification emanates, whereas femininity is positioned to "be" the phallus and so is removed from the "power" of the phallus all the while perpetuating it through this removal. By virtue of not being the phallus, woman looks outside herself – to the phallus – to gain meaning. Her meaning is then dependent upon and defined from the masculine phallus, a position that confirms her inferior status. Although the reception of Lacan's phallic account of sexuality has been contested, I point out that Lacan could defend himself from this charge by insisting that this conclusion results from concrete (clinical) analysis – the discussion of the phallus mirrors the patriarchal structures found in his society and from which is derived his theory – but because he is not sufficiently clear regarding the continuing role of the phallus, it is not obvious whether (1) the phallus must remain, or (2) another principle fulfilling the same founding role can take its place. If (1), the logic of patriarchy continues; if (2), the argument moves away from sexuality towards a meta-principle and/or debates regarding whether language is based in foundational points, what function the anchoring principle fulfils, and what options can fill it; a movement that turns us away from the study of sexuality *per se* to make it derivative of the structure of language. As a consequence, Lacan's symbolic account undermines the essentialism underpinning the essentialist-patriarchal model of sexuality but is ambiguous regarding the patriarchal aspect.

Not surprisingly, this elicited a critical response. Chapter 6 shows that Luce Irigaray's work on (material) sexual difference aims to correct the ambiguities thrown up by Lacan's symbolic account of sexuality. By affirming the fundamental material differences between, rather than equality of, the sexes, Irigaray departs from Beauvoir and opens up a new line of thinking on sexuality generally and within feminist theory specifically. Although her affirmation of the primordiality of sexual difference was almost immediately criticised for implicitly attributing to each sex distinct essential features, I defend Irigaray against this charge by arguing that she actually develops a far more sophisticated account of how the logic of patriarchy must be combated from "within" its own parameters that adopts, while subverting, the essentialist representation underpinning that model. I then go on to show that this "negative" project is accompanied by a positive one, wherein having undermined the dominant phallogocentric logic from within its own premises, Irigaray constructs an alternative from a position that respects and affirms the fundamental differences between the sexes. Although these differences are grounded in an expressive ontology of rhythmic becomings and styles, rather than ahistoric substantial ontological essential features, I conclude that the fundamental problem with Irigaray's notion of sexual difference is that it remains structured around a binary biological division which forecloses sexual expression within heteronormative parameters and implicitly depends upon and perpetuates the hierarchal logic of exclusion – namely against non-heteronormative forms of sexuality – inherent in the patriarchal system to be overcome.

Part III examines the radical, albeit heterogeneous, conceptual reforms proposed by proponents of gender theory and queer theory to overcome the problems identified within Irigaray's affirmation of sexual difference. Chapter 7 shows that Judith Butler claims that if sexuality is not to be foreclosed within predetermined schemas and so is to be opened up to heterogeneous forms, a radical conceptual alteration is required that moves the terms of the debate away from a primordial questioning of sexuality towards gender. For Butler, gender is performatively constructed from power and symbolic relations, which because these are not foreclosed means that their forms of expression are open-ended. With this, Butler *explicitly* criticises both aspects of the essentialist-patriarchal model to question and undermine any attempt to foreclose sexual/gender expression, while, in so doing, also explicitly questioning heteronormativity to open up and respect non-heteronormative forms of gender sexuality. This is important because it brings an added problem into the discussion relating to the way in which thinking on sexuality has tended to assume a heteronormative division between the sexes that also takes this model as *the* model for all forms of sexual relation. By showing that sex is based on the construction of gender performativity, Butler argues that this presumption has no basis and, in so doing, reveals that, if the foreclosure of sexuality that has marked both the essentialist-patriarchal model itself and criticisms of it is to be overcome, any critical questioning of Western thinking on the topic must also explicitly question its long-held, if often implicit, privileging of heteronormativity.

While this appears to deconstruct all foreclosing of gender and by extension sexuality, the problem with Butler's thinking was its reception, especially the claim that their[78] performative account reduces gender to a symbolic construction that is unable to account for non-discursive forms of materiality. In response, I show that Butler argues that the problem with this charge is that it is implicitly premised on a straightforward signification/materiality opposition, where one is held to be foundational for the other. Instead, Butler argues for a particularly innovative position that maintains the fundamental importance of symbolic meaning for our understanding of embodiment, but rejects the linguistic foundationalism often attributed to their theory by recognising that there is always an excess to symbolic construction. As such, the body and, by extension, gender-sexuality is always marked by a fundamental open-ended mysteriousness that undermines all attempts to capture or identify it.

Despite this, however, the radicality of Butler's position on the body was often ignored or reduced to a(n) (idealist) symbolic construction. Although a caricature of Butler's position, this not only brought to the fore the conceptual fault line between symbolic and material analyses that runs through contemporary critical thinking on sexuality, but also permitted the conceptual development that brings us from gender to queer theory. Chapter 8 takes up this issue through Karen Barad's agential realist account of materiality. Having criticised Butler's gender theory, Barad develops an ontology from contemporary scientific theory and, in particular, Niels Bohr's quantum physics that rejects Cartesian dualism, monadism, and epistemic representationalism, to instead insist on the ontological entanglement of matter. By appealing to the notion of intra-action, Barad explains that, rather than existing as monadic entities that subsequently inter-act with one another, things come to be through their ontological entangled becoming. This undercuts ontological essentialism because it shows that matter is purely relational and so defined by an ongoing process of materialisation. Each form of matter is also never single, but always composed of multiple competing aspects, all of which are multiple. It also undermines the logic of purity underpinning patriarchy because it shows that there never is a "pure" masculine that can be privileged over a "debased" feminine. Sexuality is always a hybrid singularity of ever-changing material configurations.

Importantly, Barad argues that such alterations are never the consequence of human intentional agency; the human is held to be an effect of material agency, which Barad develops by appealing to the notion of quantum leaps to argue that they reveal the ways in which materialisations constantly undergo random, non-linear, and radical alterations. Matter is considered to be inherently queer, a nomenclature that Barad uses to not only insist on the absolute lack of any and all forms of identity but also to point to radically complex and heterogeneous forms of material expression. While this undermines the premises of essentialism, patriarchy, and heteronormativity by showing that none can be supported ontologically, I conclude by pointing out that Barad's account fails to explain how and why these logics nevertheless continue to exist. Such an explanation would require engagements with the juridical and political aspects of sexuality that structure its normative expression, as well as an explanation as to how these aspects can either exist apart from materiality or be expressions of materiality while contradicting materiality's queerness. Those, however, are absent from Barad's onto-epistemological-ethical account.

The conclusion ties the various strands together to argue that the question of sexuality has been an ongoing if, at times, subterranean one for thinkers associated with psychoanalysis, phenomenology, and feminist theory. In their different ways, each takes issue with the essentialist-patriarchal (and heteronormative) model long dominant in the Western philosophical and political imaginary to, in combination, reveal an ongoing historical deconstruction of its parameters and forms. While sexuality is often thought to delineate a specific, definitive, and definable aspect of human existence, the contestation inherent in these critical debates reveals this to be fallacious. Every time that a position claims to resolve the issue, that "resolution" is, in turn, revealed to depend upon contestable metaphysical, ontological, and/or epistemological assumptions. Although it is tempting to continue to insist on a unitary response to the issue, I appeal to Walter Benjamin's notion of concepts as constellations to argue for a refocusing of the problem away from the *meaning* of sexuality – which implicitly depends upon the notion that sexuality is "something" clear, identifiable, and/or substantial – to its reclassification as an open-ended, perpetually problematic, empty, and indeterminate field where the term "sexuality" describes the inflection point or *nexal function* through which a particular constellation expresses itself conceptually. On the one hand, this prevents a definitive response to the question of sexuality and, indeed, even makes it difficult to get a handle on "it" – hence the difficulty that commentators have had in nailing it down and the contestation that has resulted – but, on the other hand, it reveals sexuality to be a remarkably rich concept that not only binds a variety of questions and issues, but, as a consequence, also acts as the lens through which to engage them.

Notes

1. As I show, the meaning of these terms, including whether they are in fact employed, depends upon the framework utilising them. Therefore, at this stage, I avoid providing an ahistoric, formal definition of them. Instead, I simply use them as something of an empty placeholder to establish the problematic motivating this enquiry.
2. "Gender ideology" is something of a catch-all phrase that has come to be used mainly, but not exclusively, by a variety of so-called Christian groups (Catholic, Protestant, Eastern Orthodox) and, indeed, right-wing political ideologues, to designate those who question what these groups claim are the traditional/natural/divinely ordained ontological structures and moral values governing the relations between the two natural sexes. See, for example, the teaching document released by the Vatican's Congregation for Catholic Education in June 2019 challenging gender theory along these lines: Giuseppe Cardinal Versaldi and Archbishop Angelo Vincenzo Zani, *Male and Female He Created Them: Towards a Path of Dialogue on the Question of Gender Theory in Education* (Vatican City: 2019): http://www.educatio.va/content/dam/cec/Documenti/19_0997_INGLESE.pdf (accessed 10 June 2019).
3. Alejandro Cerda-Rueda, "Introduction", in *Sex and Nothing: Bridges from Psychoanalysis to Philosophy*, edited by Alejandro Cerda-Rueda (London: Karnac, 2016), pp. xi–xx (p. xiii).
4. Plato, *Phaedo*, trans. G. M. A. Grube, in *Complete Works*, edited by John M. Cooper (Indianapolis, IN: Hackett Publishing, 1997), pp. 50–100 (65b–c).
5. For a recent multidimensional discussion of this relationship, see the essays collected in Panagiotis G. Pavlos, Lars Fredrik Janby, Eyjólfur Kjalar Emilsson, Torstein Theodor Tollefsen, *Platonism and Christian Thought in Late Antiquity* (Abingdon: Routledge, 2019).
6. For a discussion of this, see Kyle Harper, *From Shame to Sin: The Christian Transformation of Sexual Morality in Late Antiquity* (Cambridge, MA: Harvard University Press, 2013).
7. Martha Nussbaum, "Plato and Affirmative Action", *New York Review of Books*, 12 April 1984: https://www.nybooks.com/articles/1985/01/31/plato-affirmative-action/ (accessed 21 November 2018).
8. Plato, *Republic*, trans. G. M. A. Grube and Rev. C. D. C. Reeve, in *Complete Works*, edited by John M. Cooper (Indianapolis, IN: Hackett Publishing, 1997), pp. 971–1223 (456a–b).
9. Plato, *Timaeus*, trans. Donald J. Zeyl, in *Complete Works*, edited by John M. Cooper (Indianapolis, IN: Hackett Publishing, 1997), pp. 1225–1291 (90e).
10. Specifically, it depends upon what has come to be known as Plato's "affinity argument", which is outlined most famously in Plato, *Phaedo*, 78b–84b.
11. Aristotle, *Politics*, trans. Ernest Baker, revised by R. F. Stanley (Oxford: Oxford University Press, 1995), 1266a36–39.
12. Aristotle, *History of Animals*, trans. d'A. W. Thompson, in *The Complete Works of Aristotle*, edited by Jonathon Barnes (Princeton. NJ: Princeton University Press, 1984), pp. 1702–2174 (608b1–5).

13. Ibid., 608b5–10.
14. Ibid., 608b5.
15. Aristotle, *Politics*, 1269b14–16.
16. Ibid., 1269b12–14.
17. Ibid., 1254b12–14.
18. Ibid., 1259b41–47.
19. Ibid., 1259b47–48.
20. Tertullian, *On the Apparel of Women*, 16 August, 2003, I: I. Accessed from http://www.tertullian.org/anf/anf04/anf04-06.htm (accessed 21 November 2018).
21. Augustine, *On the Trinity, Books 8–15*, edited by Gareth B. Mathews, trans. Stephen McKenna (Cambridge: Cambridge University Press, 2002), Book 12, chapter 7, pp. 89–90.
22. Ibid., p. 90.
23. Thomas Aquinas, *Summa Theologiae*, trans. Fathers of the English Dominican Province (Einsiedeln: Benziger Bros, 1947), PI, Q92, A1, RO1.
24. Ibid., PI, Q92, A1, RO1.
25. Ibid., PI, Q92, A1, RO2.
26. While noting that "[t]here has been heated debate over just what the 'Enlightenment' was, when and where it occurred, and whether it was one or many" (*The Enlightenment and Why it still Matters* [Oxford: Oxford University Press, 2013], p. vii), Anthony Pagden explains that the Enlightenment describes "that period of European history between, roughly, the last decade of the seventeenth century and the first of the nineteenth" (p. vii) that is typically associated "with an exalted view of human rationality and of human benevolence, and with a belief, measured and at times skeptical, in progress and in the general human capacity for self-improvement" (p. vii). A large aspect of this is the belief in the power of education to overcome superstitious belief, affirm the power of rationality, and so enlighten. For a discussion of this secularisation thesis, see Gavin Rae, *Evil in the Western Philosophical Tradition* (Edinburgh: Edinburgh University Press, 2019).
27. Jean-Jacques Rousseau, *Emile, or On Education*, trans. Alan Bloom (New York: Basic Books, 1979), p. 356.
28. Ibid., p. 360.
29. Ibid., p. 356.
30. Ibid., p. 356.
31. Ibid., p. 356
32. Ibid., p. 356.
33. Ibid., p. 364.
34. Ibid., p. 361.
35. Ibid., p. 363.
36. Ibid., p. 364.
37. Ibid., p. 364.
38. Ibid., p. 364.
39. Immanuel Kant, *Critique of Pure Reason*, edited and translated by Paul Guyer and Allen Wood (Cambridge: Cambridge University Press, 1998).

40. Immanuel Kant, *Anthropology from a Pragmatic Point of View*, edited and translated by Robert B. Louden (Cambridge: Cambridge University Press, 2006), p. 207.
41. Ibid., pp. 208-209.
42. Ibid., p. 209.
43. Ibid., p. 209.
44. Ibid., p. 209.
45. Ibid., p. 209.
46. Ibid., p. 209.
47. Georg W. F. Hegel, *Elements of the Philosophy of Right*, edited by Allen W. Wood, trans. H. B. Nisbet (Cambridge: Cambridge University Press, 1991), §142-365. Following convention, references to this text will be to the aphorism, followed, where applicable, by (R) for Remarks referring to that aphorism, or (A) referring to any addition comments to that particular aphorism.
48. Ibid., §173.
49. Ibid., §166.
50. Ibid., §164A.
51. Ibid., §166A.
52. Ibid., §166A.
53. Ibid., §166A.
54. Ibid., §166A.
55. Arthur Schopenhauer, "On Women", in *Parerga and Paralipomena, volume 2*, trans. E. F. J. Payne (Oxford: Clarendon Press, 1974), pp. 614-626 (§366).
56. Ibid., §366.
57. Ibid., §366.
58. Ibid., §364.
59. See, for example, David E. Cartwright, *Schopenhauer: A Biography* (Cambridge: Cambridge University Press, 2010), pp. 403-408.
60. See, for example, Lawrence Hatab, "Nietzsche on Women", *The Southern Journal of Philosophy*, vol. 19, n. 3, 1981, pp. 333-345; Ruth Abbey, "Beyond Misogyny and Metaphor: Women in Nietzsche's Middle Period", *Journal of the History of Philosophy*, vol. 34, n. 2, 1996, pp. 233-256; Katrin Froese, "Bodies and Eternity: Nietzsche's Relation to the Feminine", *Philosophy and Social Criticism*, vol. 26, n. 1, 2000, pp. 25-49; Julian Young, "Nietzsche and Women", in *The Oxford Handbook of Nietzsche*, edited by Ken Gemes and John Richardson (Oxford: Oxford University Press, 2013), pp. 46-62.
61. Friedrich Nietzsche, *Human, All too Human*, trans. R. J. Hollingdale (Cambridge: Cambridge University Press, 1996), §377.
62. Friedrich Nietzsche, *Beyond Good and Evil*, edited by Rolf-Peter Horstmann and Judith Norman, trans. Judith Norman (Cambridge: Cambridge University Press, 2002), §239.
63. For a more extensive history, see Thomas Laqueuer, *Making Sex: Body and Gender from the Greeks to Freud* (Cambridge, MA: Harvard University Press, 1990); Kim M. Phillips and Barry Reay, *Sex before Sexuality: A Premodern History* (Cambridge: Polity, 2011); and Sarah Toulalan and Kate Fisher (eds), *The Routledge History of Sex and the Body: 1500 to the Present* (Abingdon: Routledge, 2013); Leah DeVun,

The Shape of Sex: Nonbinary Gender from Genesis to the Renaissance (New York: Columbia University Press, 2021).

64. Mary Wollstonecraft, *A Vindication of the Rights of Woman* and *A Vindication of the Rights of Men*, edited by Janet Todd (Oxford: Oxford University Press, 2009).
65. John Stuart Mill, *On the Subjection of Women*, in *The Collected Works of John Stuart Mill, Volume XXI*, edited by John Robson (Toronto: University of Toronto Press, 1985), pp. 259–340.
66. For example, in relation to Plato and Aristotle, see, respectively, Stella Sandford, *Plato and Sex* (Cambridge: Polity, 2010) and the essays collected in Cynthia Freedland (ed.), *Feminist Interpretations of Aristotle* (University Park, PA: Pennsylvania State University Press, 1998); in relation to Augustine, see the essays collected in Judith Clark (ed.), *Feminist Interpretations of Augustine* (University Park, PA: Pennsylvania State University Press, 2007); and Aquinas, see Susanne DeCrane, *Aquinas, Feminism, and the Common Good* (Washington, DC: Georgetown University Press, 2004). Susan Moller Okin's *Women in Western Political Thought* (Princeton, NJ: Princeton University Press, 2013) has a good discussion of Rousseau on women; the essays in Robin Schott (ed.), *Feminist Interpretations of Kant* (University Park, PA: Pennsylvania State University Press, 2007) offer interesting accounts of Kant's views on women, while a defence of Hegel's view of the sexes, especially as it relates to the family structure, is found in my own *Realizing Freedom: Hegel, Sartre, and the Alienation of Human Being* (Basingstoke: Palgrave Macmillan, 2011). For discussions of Schopenhauer on women, see Angelika Hübscher, "Schopenhauer und 'die Weiber'", *Schopenhauer-Jahrbuch*, 1977, pp. 187–203; while reconsiderations of Nietzsche's ambiguous status towards women are found in Frances Nesbitt Oppel, *Nietzsche on Gender: Beyond Man and Woman* (Charlottesville, VA: Virginia University Press, 2005), and Kelly Oliver and Marilyn Pearsall (eds), *Feminist Interpretations of Nietzsche* (University Park, PA: Pennsylvania State University Press, 1998).
67. For an extended discussion, see Patricia Murphy Robinson, "The Historical Repression of Women's Sexuality", in *Pleasure and Danger: Exploring Female Sexuality*, edited by Carol S. Vance (Abingdon: Routledge, 1984), pp. 251–266; and the texts collected in Beverley Clack, *Misogyny in the Western Philosophical Tradition* (Basingstoke: Palgrave Macmillan, 1999). For a discussion of the ways in which this logic is manifested, supported, and affirmed by contemporary scientific discourse, see Anne Fausto-Sterling, *Sexing the Body: Gender, Politics, and the Construction of Sexuality* (New York: Basic Books, 2000); and Cordelia Fine, *Delusions of Gender: The Real Science behind Sex Differences* (London: Icon, 2010).
68. Sigmund Freud, *Three Essays on Sexuality*, in *The Standard Edition of the Complete Psychological Works of Sigmund Freud: Volume 3*, edited and translated by James Strachey (New York: Basic Books, 2000).
69. Martin Heidegger, *Being and Time*, trans. John Macquarrie and Edward Robinson (Oxford: Blackwell, 1962); Martin Heidegger, *The Metaphysical Foundations of Logic*, trans. Michael Heim (Bloomington, IN: Indiana University Press, 1984).

70. Maurice Merleau-Ponty, *Phenomenology of Perception*, trans. Colin Smith (Abingdon: Routledge, 1962).
71. See, for example, Simone de Beauvoir, *The Second Sex*, trans. Constance Borde and Sheila Malovany-Chevallier (New York: Vintage, 2011).
72. For example, Luce Irigaray, *Speculum of the Other Woman*, trans. Gillian C. Gill (Ithaca, NY: Cornell University Press, 1985).
73. Jacques Derrida, "*Geschlecht I:* Sexual Difference, Ontological Difference", trans. Ruben Bevezdivin and Elizabeth Rottenberg, in *Psyche: Inventions of the Other*, volume 2, edited by Peggy Kamuf and Elizabeth Rottenberg (Stanford, CA: Stanford University Press, 2008), pp. 7–26.
74. Gayle Rubin, "The Traffic in Women: Notes on the 'Political Economy' of Sex", in *The Second Wave: A Reader in Feminist Theory*, edited by Linda Nicholson (Abingdon: Routledge, 1997), pp. 27–62. For an overview and critical discussion of the turn to gender, see Tina Chanter, *Gender* (London: Continuum, 2006).
75. Judith Butler, *Gender Trouble: Feminism and the Subversion of Identity*, Second edition (Abingdon: Routledge, 1999).
76. Karen Barad, *Meeting the Universe Halfway: Quantum Physics and the Entanglement of Matter and Meaning* (Durham, NC: Duke University Press, 2007).
77. Heidegger, *The Metaphysical Foundations of Logic*.
78. Butler (and Barad) have expressed a preference for using the pronouns "they/their" rather than "he/him" or "she/her". This (1) supports the notion that language plays a constutive role in "constructing" material reality, (2) highlights the multidimensionality of gender, (3) undercuts the traditional heteronormative gender binary opposition, and (4) performs a remaking of the norms that define the parameters of gender assignation and the forms of gender that are considered socially acceptable. For these reasons, I use those pronouns when referring to Butler and Barad.

Part I

Psychoanalysis and Phenomenology

CHAPTER 1

Freud on Sexuality and the Feminine

As the twentieth century began, questions regarding the meaning and place of sexuality quickly came to the fore. Sigmund Freud had previously announced the importance of the unconscious and the dream-world, but in 1905 he published *Three Essays on the Theory of Sexuality*;[1] a text that would revolutionise the study of sexuality. Whereas I noted in the Introduction that there had, of course, been previous discussions of sexuality, these had tended to play a relatively minor role within a philosopher's system of thought. In contrast, Roger Horrocks points out that "Freud's own work is marked by a veritable 'discursive explosion' – perhaps no-one else has written so much about sex".[2] Horrocks adds, however, that Freud is important not just for the sheer quantity of writings on sexuality, but also because of the substantial – Horrocks identifies six – innovations he brought to the issue. First, Freud "separated [sexuality] from reproduction, and argued that the sexual instincts are driven by the need for pleasure".[3] In so doing, he rejected reductionist biological accounts, all the while taking aim at the restrictive and puritanical teachings of Christianity. Second, "he described human infants as sexual beings, who pursue pleasure not genitally, but all over their body. Thus, the genital aim in adult sexuality is a much delayed development, and many people retain many pre-genital desires."[4] Third, "Freud opposes civilization to sex in a quite dramatic fashion, arguing as he does that culture must carry out a massive repression of the sexual drives, which cannot be allowed immediate satisfaction, if cultural and social life is to have any stability".[5] Fourth, "sexuality is closely tied to the unconscious, since many repressed desires are retained there, in a 'forgotten' state, but still exerting a pressure on the individual".[6] Fifth,

> Freud is able to connect ... 'frozen' sexual wishes and fixations with the development of character itself so that one can speak of the anal character,

the phallic character, the oral character, and so on. In this way, a whole characterology becomes possible, based on the various types of underlying sexual interest shown by individuals.[7]

Finally, "in the Oedipus complex he postulates a family drama in which sexual desires and prohibitions are played out in painful, even tragic, ways".[8] In so doing, sexuality is tied to wider social and familial relationships; it is never simply an individual and biological phenomenon. For this reason, Gayle Rubin concludes that

> [p]sychoanalysis contains a unique set of concepts for understanding men, women, and sexuality. It is a theory of sexuality in human society. Most importantly, psychoanalysis provides a description of the mechanisms by which the sexes are divided and deformed, of how bisexual, androgynous infants are transformed into boys and girls.[9]

Freud's thinking on sexuality is not, however, outlined in one place, but occurs across his *oeuvre*. This poses, at least, two problems for any commentator who wishes to engage with it: first, the sheer volume of writing on the topic, and, second, the fact that Freud's views on sexuality undergo significant revision as his wider metapsychology develops and changes. As a consequence, a number of commentators have noted that Freud's thinking on sexuality appears to be marked by two approaches or moments. Juliet Mitchell, for example, argues that from around 1890 to 1920 the fundamental issue motivating the analysis is that of childhood sexuality, itself marked by an analysis of the fundamental structures that construct sexuality as it develops through to puberty. However, from 1920, the question of the division between the sexes comes to the fore, with a clear distinction established based around the object-relations constitutive of each sex.[10] Bertram Cohler and Robert Galatzer-Levy agree on the fundamental temporal division, but disagree with Mitchell's assessment of what the temporal alteration refers to, instead claiming that it points to a division in Freud's *oeuvre* regarding the role of feminine sexuality. On this reading, Freud's thought up to 1920 maintains that the question of feminine sexuality merely mirrors that of the masculine, whereas after 1920 Freud insists on the strict division between the two sexes, albeit one in which the female is collapsed into the male to be seen as a defect of the latter.[11]

Rather than maintain a fundamental rupture within Freud's thinking, I will focus, somewhat controversially, on Freud's comments on sexuality, as opposed to those "merely" on feminine sexuality, to argue that there is continuity across his *oeuvre* on this issue, in so far as he consistently rejects the notion that sexuality is grounded in a fixed biological essentialism. To defend this, I first provide an overview of Freud's account of sexuality as outlined in the early *Three Essays on a Theory of Sexuality* to argue that, within this text, Freud undermines the claim underpinning the essentialist-patriarchal model that there is a natural, sexual essentialism. By positing an originary bisexuality and distinguishing between sexuality and genitality – where, very generally, "sexuality" refers to a wider notion of bodily pleasure and "genitality" refers to pleasure received through the genitals – Freud not only undermines the claim that the sexual division is natural or essential to the human species to instead argue that this difference is the result of a particular developmental process – with biological, psychical, and social aspects – but also claims that sexuality is not limited to the stimulation of a body part; it refers to the pleasure derived from the entire body that only with puberty comes to be orientated from and around the genitals.

However, it will be remembered that the essentialist-patriarchal model is composed of three aspects: sexual essentialism, a natural division between two sexes, and a logic of patriarchy where the masculine is privileged over the feminine. For Freud to undermine sexual essentialism does not then mean that he fully departs from the essentialist-patriarchal model; he must also reject its other two conditions. Although I will suggest that the positing of an originary bisexuality points to the conclusion that sexuality does not have to be divided into two sexes, thereby allowing Freud to overcome this charge, I will also argue that Freud's analysis of sexuality continues to be marked by a logic of patriarchy wherein the masculine is privileged over the feminine. To defend this, I move from his early writings on sexuality to his post-1920 writings on femininity. While these are famously centred around three essays – "Some Psychical Consequences of the Anatomical Distinction between the Sexes"[12] from 1925, "Female Sexuality"[13] from 1931, and "Femininity"[14] from 1933 – I will focus on the final 1933 essay, not only because it is the most extensive analysis of the three, but also because it is the last one written and so, I contend, can be taken to be Freud's considered view on the topic.[15] Having revealed the logic of patriarchy inherent therein, I conclude that Freud's rejection of sexual essentialism but continuing dependence on a logic of patriarchy not only reveals the problems inherent in his own critique of the essentialist-patriarchal model, but also instantiates an ambiguous critical stance that will be repeated throughout much subsequent twentieth-century critical thinking on sexuality wherein one aspect of the essentialist-patriarchal model is rejected while, oftentimes, the other aspect is (implicitly) relied upon, repeated, and so perpetuated.

The Origins of Sexuality

Three Essays on the Theory of Sexuality, first published in 1905, has become one of the fundamental texts for understanding Freudian psychoanalytical theory. Juliet Mitchell calls it "the revolutionary founding work for the psychoanalytic concept of sexuality",[16] while Arnold Davidson points out that its importance extends beyond the internal dynamics of psychoanalytical theory, in so far as it marks a fundamental break with the conceptual apparatus that previously underpinned Western thinking about sexuality.[17] This is not to say that it is a complete, polished text. It changed substantially throughout its various versions written over a twenty-year period, with Freud rewriting, removing, and/or adding material as his thinking developed. This is reflected in its fragmentary and somewhat disjointed nature. Indeed, Freud was aware of this, noting in the Preface to the third edition that "It is . . . out of the question that [the essays] could ever be extended into a complete 'theory of sexuality,' and it is natural that there should be a number of important problems of sexual life with which they do not deal at all."[18] Specifically, Freud notes that he offers a primordially *psychoanalytic* account of sexuality that "avoid[s] introducing any preconceptions, whether derived from general sexual biology or from that of particular animal species, into this study".[19] The aim is to not to ground psychoanalysis in biology, but "to discover how far psychological investigation can throw light upon the biology of the sexual life of man".[20] From this, Freud produces a highly nuanced, if at times problematic, critique of the notion of an innate sexuality: the idea that an individual's sexuality is defined and/or determined by an essential ahistoric sexed "core". Instead, Freud insists on an initial bisexuality, before showing that this is gradually expressed through a developmental process as a unitary heteronormative – male or female – sexual division at the point of puberty. Crucially, the initial bisexuality remains implicit to the actual sex developed to both undermine any straightforward binary heteronormative division and offer the possibility of reconstructing an individual's sexuality.

To start, Freud notes that sexuality is generally understood to (1) "be absent in childhood",[21] (2) "[be] set in at the time of puberty in connection with the process of coming to maturity",[22] (3) "[be] revealed in the manifestations of an irresistible attraction exercised by one sex upon the other",[23] while (4) "its aim is presumed to be sexual union, or at all events actions leading in that direction".[24] His hypothesis is, however, that "these views give a very false picture of the true situation".[25] This leads Freud to distinguish between the "*sexual object*",[26] describing "the person from whom sexual attraction proceeds",[27] and the "*sexual aim*",[28] which describes "the act towards which the instinct tends".[29] Far from a straightforward, linear relationship between the two or a unitary meaning to each, "numerous deviations occur in respect of both of these".[30]

This contradicts the then commonly held view, one that continues to adhere to a certain contemporary conservative (religious) discourse, that sexuality is divided between a male and female, who come together to produce a harmonious whole aimed at procreation. Freud notes, however, that this is not always the case: "there are men whose sexual object is a man and not a woman, and women whose sexual object is a woman and not a man".[31] On the basis of the "commonly held" view, such occurrences are an abomination and so are marked as "'inversions'"[32] of "natural" sexual feelings. Rather than simply confirm or deny this nomenclature, Freud engages with the heterogeneity inherent in it to distinguish between "*absolute* inverts",[33] wherein an individual's sexual object is exclusively of their own sex, "*amphigenic* inverts",[34] who have both their own and the opposite sex as their sexual object, and "*contingent* inverts" who, under "certain external conditions . . . are capable of taking as their sexual object someone of their own sex and of deriving satisfaction from sexual intercourse with him [or her]".[35]

Freud goes on to point out that the earliest assessment of these inversions tended to be negative, based on (1) "the attribution of degeneracy",[36] which he rejects claiming that such a label should only be used in a number of very specific circumstances; namely, when "several serious deviations from the normal are found together"[37] and "the capacity for efficient functioning and survival seem to be severely impaired";[38] and/or (2) the existence of some "innate character",[39] which he also rejects because it, at best, only has explanatory value for absolute inverts. He then goes on to engage with whether inversions can be adequately thought from the premises of an epistemological constructivism. The problem, however, is that he notes that "many people are subjected to the same sexual influences . . . without becoming inverted or without remaining so permanently".[40] In other words, appealing to a constructivist argument does not explain why some become inverts whereas others do not when both are subjected to similar experiences.

The fundamental issue with both innate essentialist and constructivist accounts of sexuality is that they are grounded in a singular foundation and, indeed, are premised on a binary heteronormative opposition so that individuals are innately destined or constructed to be either a male or female. Freud undermines both by pointing to the existence of hermaphrodites "in which the sexual characteristics are obscured, and in which it is consequently difficult to determine the sex [because] [t]he genitals of the individuals concerned combine male and female characteristics".[41] While it might be objected that these are relatively rare cases, Freud responds that their importance lies

> in the unexpected fact that they facilitate our understanding of normal development. For it appears that a certain degree of anatomical hermaphroditism occurs normally. In every normal male or female individual, traces are found of the apparatus of the opposite sex. These either persist without function as rudimentary organs or become modified and take on other functions.[42]

From this, he explains that the separation of the sexes into a binary opposition is premised on "an originally bisexual physical disposition [that] has, in the course of evolution, become modified into a unisexual one, leaving behind only a few traces of the sex that has become atrophied".[43]

While it is tempting to mirror this *physical* bisexuality with a *psychical* one, Freud rejects this by holding that each inversion of the sexual object would have to entail both a mental and physical inversion: a male desiring a male sexual object would also have to be accompanied by an inversion in his masculine character so that the inverted male would automatically take on feminine characteristics; whereas, an inverted female with a female sexual object would have to automatically take on masculine characteristics. Freud dismisses this, claiming that "it is only in inverted women that character-inversion of this kind can be looked for with any regularity. In men the most complete mental masculinity can be combined with inversion."[44]

Two related aspects stand out from this. First, Freud is implicitly prefiguring Gayle Rubin's[45] distinction between "sex", defining an individual's biological make-up, and "gender", describing something like the (socially) constructed norms that define sexual roles, characteristics, and mannerisms, to explain that biological sex is not determinant for gender: a biological woman can take on the gendered masculine role and vice versa. Evidence for this emanates from Freud's claim that while the sexual instinct – defined provisionally as "the psychical representative of an endosomatic, continuously flowing source of stimulation, as contrasted with a 'stimulus,' which is set up by *single* excitations coming from *without*"[46] – and sexual object are normally tied tight so that, for example, the masculine sexual instinct has as its object the feminine, such a correspondence is not only artificial, entailing a needless restriction of the sexual instinct, but also reduces "the object [to] part and parcel of the instinct".[47] Instead, Freud maintains that "[i]t seems probable that the sexual instinct is in the first instance independent of its object; nor is its origin likely to be due to its object's attractions".[48] His conclusion is that "[w]e are thus warned to loosen the bond that exists in our thoughts between instinct and object"[49] and recognise that "[u]nder a great number of conditions and in surprisingly numerous individuals, the nature and importance of the sexual object recedes into the background".[50] An individual's sexual instinct is not then necessarily tied to a single, universal object.

Second, the terms "masculine" and "feminine" do not describe physical characteristics, but functions. Freud clarifies this latter in the third essay, when he first notes that the terms "masculine" and "feminine" "are among the most confused that occur in science",[51] before distinguishing between biological, sociological, and logical senses of the terms, claiming that the latter is structured around an active aspect representing masculinity and a passive aspect tied to femininity, and concluding that this active/passive division "is the essential one and the most serviceable in psycho-analysis".[52] On the one hand, by thinking of relationships in terms of an active/passive dichotomy tied to masculinity and femininity respectively, Freud continues to affirm a division that has long re-enforced a patriarchal division. On the other hand, however, tying masculinity and femininity to activity and passivity respectively reveals them to be positions, rather than actors, which, in turn, undermines any straightforward sexual essentialism or division: as a position, a biological women can play the active masculine role in the relation, and vice versa. Indeed, Freud goes further by claiming that regardless of whether there is an explicit identification with the supposed alternative sex/gender role, the individual is *always* bound up with it. There is no such thing as a "pure" masculinity or femininity. Rather, "[e]very individual on the contrary displays a mixture of the character-traits belonging to his own and to the opposite sex; and he shows a combination of activity and passivity whether or not these last character-traits tally with his biological ones".[53]

Given that the original physical inversion is not automatically accompanied by a psychical one, Freud maintains that we need a far more nuanced and sophisticated account of the process(es) through which the originary physical bisexuality is manifested psychically. It is here that psychoanalysis and, in particular, Freud's theory of the libido, steps in to analyse the psychical processes that emanate from and accompany the individual's physical sexual development. Whereas this leads Freud to a detailed discussion of a variety of sexual behaviours, the key point for the current discussion is the claim that there is a non-causal relation between the somatic and psychic aspects of the individual, meaning that any questioning of individual sexuality must occur along these two distinct but related lines.

The Sexuality of Children

Freud engages with the sexuality of children to show how the initial bisexuality is manifested as and developed into an apparent unitary sexuality; a questioning that also reveals how the somatic and psychical aspects relate without determining each other. There are two principle and related ways in which this engagement is orientated: (1) an enquiry into the role that sexuality plays in the life of children, the aim of which is to show that sexuality is a condition of human being generally and so integral to individual life; it is not something that is initially missing before becoming manifest at a particular point in an individual's life; and (2) a discussion of the developmental processes through which an individual's sexuality crystallises.

To start, Freud once more contrasts his analysis to the commonly held view that maintains that childhood is asexual and "the sexual instinct . . . only awakens in the period of life described as puberty".[54] Not only does this fail to explain the onto-genesis of individual sexuality – that is, the way in which the initial bisexuality is manifested in a physically unisexual manner – but it is also unable to adequately explain the psychic life of children. As a consequence, Freud insists that sexuality is inherent in human being from birth, although it only becomes explicit "to observation round about the third or fourth year of life".[55] This is not, however, to say that this development proceeds in a linear or homogeneous manner. Rather,

> germs of sexual impulses are already present in the new-born child and that these continue to develop for a time, but are then overtaken by a progressive process of suppression; this in turn is itself interrupted by periodical advances in sexual development or may be held up by individual peculiarties.[56]

It is important to note, however, that when Freud talks of sexuality in relation to children, he has a very particular understanding in mind. In the chapter "The Development of the Sexual Function", published in *The Outline of Psycho-Analysis*, Freud explains that "[i]t is necessary to distinguish sharply between the concepts of 'sexual' and 'genital.' The former is the wider concept and includes many activities that have nothing to do with the genitals."[57] Specifically, "[s]exual life includes the function of obtaining pleasure from zones of the body – a function which is subsequently brought into the service of reproduction".[58] As a consequence of the sexual/genitals distinction, sexuality is not synonymous with genitalia nor does "[s]exual life begin only at puberty, [it] starts with plain manifestations soon after birth".[59]

Freud engages with the nature of childhood sexuality from a variety of angles. Noting that the child undergoes a profound process of discipline and sublimation wherein his sexual instinct is either repressed or transferred to other outlets, he maintains that the child's behaviour and sexuality is not tied to procreation but to "self-preservation",[60] autonomy, and "auto-eroticism".[61] The reason for the latter is bound to the lack of sexual object inherent in the child's initial sexuality; an object only becomes apparent much later in puberty. Freud outlines the relationship between self-preservation, autonomy, and auto-eroticism via the famous analysis of thumb-sucking, which is taken to mimic the pleasure that the child gains from the breast. Whereas the breast is frequently absent and so beyond the child's control, the child substitutes his own body part for the breast, thereby separating his "sexual satisfaction ... from the need for taking nourishment",[62] while also, in so doing, allowing the child to obtain autonomy from the external world he does not yet control. In other words, the example of thumb-sucking is taken to reveal "the three essential characteristics of an infantile sexual manifestation. At its origin it attaches itself to one of the vital somatic functions; it has as yet no sexual object, and is thus auto-erotic."[63]

The key issue here is that childhood sexuality is not object-orientated, but is auto-erotic, tied to "the excitations of the sensory surfaces – the skin and the sense organs – and, most directly of all, by the operation of stimuli on certain areas known as erotogenetic zones".[64] This excitation is not initially bound to one body part; "any part of the skin and any sense-organ – probably, indeed, *any* organ – can function as an erotogenic zone, though there are some particularly marked erotogenic zones".[65] Furthermore, "sexual excitation is not the primary motivation for the child's action, but "arises as a by-product ... of a large number of processes that occur in the organism, as soon as they reach a certain degree of intensity".[66] The notion of sexuality at play in Freud's analysis of childhood sexuality is then expansive, tied to any form of pleasure, with this usually initially being found through unintended sensory stimuli.

This pre-genital stage of childhood sexual development gradually morphs into a genital one at puberty, wherein sexuality is tied to "the primacy of a single erotogenic zone, [and] form[s] a firm organization directed towards a sexual aim attached to some extraneous sexual object".[67] The transition from childhood auto-eroticism to adult genital sexuality is transitional, based on a continuum and constituted by the child's movement through various stages: First, the oral stage, manifested through, for example, thumb-sucking, where the child obtains pleasure from its own body without this being primarily orientated to a single body part or the satisfaction of its sexual instinct. Second, the later anal stage in which the child comes to associate pleasure with its control over its bowel movements. Here, the child starts to identify pleasure with a particular body part, an alteration that will be taken further in puberty when pleasure is tied explicitly to the genitals. "These phases of sexual organization are normally passed through smoothly, without giving more than a hint of their existence"[68] and are usually "completed" "between the ages of two and five",[69] when it is brought "to a halt or to a retreat by the latency period"[70] characterised by "the infantile nature of sexual aims".[71] It is at this point that the child enters the phallic stage. I will return to this in a later section.

This initial phase is supplemented by a "second wave [that] sets in with puberty and determines the final outcome of sexual life".[72] Specifically, with "the arrival of puberty, changes set in which are destined to give infantile sexual life its final, normal shape".[73] Whereas the sexual instinct was up to this moment auto-erotic, it now settles on an object, whereas the disparate and dispersed manifestations of the sexual instinct found in the pre-puberty stage focus on and "become subordinated to the primacy of the genital zone",[74] which, in turn, is orientated to a singular aim: in the case, of males, "the discharge of the sexual products",[75] whereas in women a more complicated "kind of involution"[76] takes place that Freud has great difficulty identifying or describing. He is clear however that the divergence between men and women is, at this stage, significant.

From an initial bisexuality, individuals come, through a developmental process, to distinguish themselves into one of two sexes. This is not, however, to say that the process is linear so that the initial bisexuality turns into a simple unisexuality. Freud makes this clear when he mentions the possibility of, what will come to be known as, transgender/sexual reassignment: "It has become experimentally possible . . . to transform a male into a female, and conversely a female into a male".[77] When he offers some biological speculations as to why this is so, they return us to his postulation of an original bisexuality, which appears to continue to subtend individual "actual" sexual development ready to disrupt any sexual identity and permit a reconfiguration of it (both physically and psychically). The original bisexuality is then fundamental to Freud's insistence that sexuality not premised on an ahistoric innate essentialism, nor is it ever fully determined. Although it is expressed via a seeming heteronormative division, this division is plastic, fluid, and marked by the initial bisexuality; at no point does it coalesce into a simple unity with a singular structure, aim, or object.

There is obviously far more to Freud's discussion of sexuality, both in the *Three Essays on the Theory of Sexuality* and other works, but this brief engagement suffices for the current purpose of showing how he appeals to an original bisexuality to undermine any sexual innate essentialism, holds that sexuality is a condition of human being – it does not simply develop at a certain point – and outlines some of the developmental stages through which children pass as they move towards a genitally-orientated (adult) sexual life. Sexuality is, for Freud, a process of continuous becoming, so that at no point in the process does it manifest itself as a straightforward unity: the initial bisexuality does not simply become constricted to a unisexuality at puberty; the original bisexual indeterminateness continues to subtend the sexuality that crystallises at puberty disrupting all manifestations of sexuality to, in so doing, both complicate an individual's sexuality and offer the possibility to change it.

Freud on Femininity

Having outlined the basic parameters of Freud's early thinking on sexuality, paying particular attention to his notion of an originary bisexuality that morphs into a heterogeneous sexuality at puberty, I now move beyond the *Three Essays on a Theory of Sexuality* to Freud's later text "Femininity" (from 1933). Here, Freud builds on his earlier analysis by focusing on the way in which one sex – the female sex – is generated from the originary bisexuality, while, at the same time, going on to engage with, what he calls, "the riddle of the nature of femininity".[78] It has been questioned why, given the originary bisexuality, Freud focuses on femininity to the exclusion of masculinity; in other words, if the originary bisexuality is both masculine and feminine, why only focus on the feminine.[79] This has led to the charge that the masculine, manifested through a privileging of the phallus, structures Freudian theory. Indeed, the entire psychoanalytic edifice is, in a strong sense, premised on the masculine perspective as Freud makes clear in his famous comment in *The Question of Lay Analysis* (published in 1926) that "[w]e know less about the sexual life of little girls than of boys. But we need not feel ashamed of this distinction; after all, the sexual life of adult women is a 'dark continent' for psychology".[80] The text on "Femininity" is an attempt – albeit one that as Freud subsequently recognised does not quite succeed – to illuminate that darkness.

Freud starts by explaining that the analysis "brings forth nothing but observed facts, almost without any speculative additions".[81] It is therefore meant as an empirical study, part of an ongoing analysis of the topic. From this, Freud explains that the male/female division is one that we make in every encounter and, indeed, do so "with unhesitating certainty".[82] The question arises as to the ground for such certainty. While the perhaps obvious response would be that the division is anatomical, Freud points out that the issue is not as clear-cut as one would think. In particular, he notes that modern science affirms two points that undermine the notion of a straightforward male/female division. First, whereas "[t]he male sexual product, the spermatozoon, and its vehicle are male [and] the ovum and the organism that harbors it are female",[83] there have been cases in both sexes where opposing "organs have been found which serve exclusively for the sexual functions; they were probably developed from the same [innate] disposition into two different forms".[84] That they emanate from an originary unified source, where both are present, undermines the notion that male/female anatomies are completely distinct. Furthermore, Freud explains that "in both sexes the other organs, the bodily shapes and tissues, show the influence of the individual's sex, but this is inconstant and its amount variable; these are known as the secondary sexual characteristics".[85] In other words, an individual's sexuality is not fixed and determined, but fluid and changing. There is no such thing, biologically speaking, as a pure male or pure female: "portions of the male sexual apparatus also appear in women's bodies, though in atrophied state, and vice versa in the alternative case".[86] The meanings of "masculine" and "feminine" are then based on a continuum that is always attached to the other sex, while the individual manifestation of this hybrid sexuality is fluid and specific to each individual. As a consequence, each individual is not unisexual, but a different configuration of the originary bisexuality; "not a man or a woman but always both – merely a certain amount more the one than the other".[87] The problem, however, is that this contradicts everyday perception wherein it appears that "only one kind of sexual product – ova or semen – is nevertheless present in one person".[88] For this reason, Freud concludes that "you are bound to have doubts as to the decisive significance of those elements and must conclude that what constitutes masculinity or femininity is an unknown characteristic which anatomy cannot lay hold of".[89]

If anatomy cannot settle the question of the sexes, Freud turns to psychology. The basic premise is that "[w]e are accustomed to employ[ing] 'masculine' and 'feminine' as mental qualities [and so] have transferred the notion of bisexuality to mental life".[90] As a consequence, "we speak of a person, whether male or female, as behaving in a masculine way in one connection and in a feminine way in another".[91] In other words, rather than sexuality referring to anatomical parts, psychological conceptions understand "sexuality" to refer to modes of behaviour or action. Rather than these being unitary, each individual can act in both masculine and/or feminine ways at different times.

Freud notes, however, that this does not resolve the issue because it simply generates the question of what constitutes masculine/feminine ways of acting, which invariably returns us to anatomy or to convention; that is, the roles that the masculine and feminine currently fulfil.[92] For this reason, he notes that "when you say 'masculine,' you usually mean 'active', and when you say 'feminine', you usually mean passive".[93] Freud identifies two problems with this logic. First, activity and passive are not exclusively traits of masculinity or femininity: "Women can display great activity in various directions, men are not able to live in company with their own kind unless they develop a large amount of passive adaptability."[94] To simply insist on the masculine–active/feminine–passive dichotomy is then to have decided in advance on those associations and so imposed those categories onto the sexes. Even if it is objected that femininity is not associated with passivity *per se*, but with a preference for "passive aims",[95] Freud objects that, even if correct, there is no guarantee that this is essential to her character. It could simply be the case that it is a consequence of social convention, wherein the feminine is associated with certain behaviours that were subsequently imparted to and adopted by "her" as a child.

Having rejected purely biological and psychological accounts of femininity, Freud proposes to examine the issue from a psychoanalytic viewpoint that "does not try to describe what a woman is – that would be a task that it could scarcely perform – but sets about enquiring how she comes into being, how a woman develops out of a child with a bisexual disposition".[96] He starts the enquiry from two premises: "The first is that here once more the constitution will not adapt itself to its function without a struggle. The second is that the decisive turning-points will already have been prepared for or completed before puberty."[97] Freud claims that both of these are confirmed by experience. However, he notes that the sexes experience the change from childhood to adulthood differently with "the development of a little girl into a normal woman [being] more difficult and more complicated, since it includes two extra tasks, to which there is nothing corresponding in the development of man".[98]

While noting the physical differences between boys and girls – none of which is determinate for the development of sexuality – Freud mentions that "[d]ifferences emerge in the instinctual disposition which give a glimpse of the later nature of women".[99] Specifically, "[a] little girl is as a rule less aggressive, defiant and self-sufficient; she seems to have a greater need for being shown affection and on that account to be more dependent and pliant".[100] Freud notes that, far from being simply negative characteristics, this pliancy permits the female to develop her bladder and excrement control faster than in males. Furthermore, he suggests that "little girls are more intelligent and livelier than boys of the same age; they go out more to meet the external world and at the same time form stronger object-cathexes".[101] However, once the child passes into the phallic phase of development, "which is . . . a forerunner of the final form taken by sexual life and already much resembles it",[102] "the differences between the sexes are completely eclipsed by their agreements".[103] Very basically, the phallic stage denotes the stage of a child's development that occurs relatively early and entails the fixation on the male phallus.[104] In contrast, "[t]he female genitals long remain unknown".[105] Controversially, that both sexes focus on the phallus means, for Freud, that there is a convergence in the psychic development of both sexes, albeit one that is orientated from and around the masculine phallus. As he puts it, "the little girl is a little man".[106]

Freud continues that, in the phallic stage, boys and girls learn that their genitalia are sources of pleasure. Whereas boys learn "how to derive pleasurable sensations from their small penis and connect its excited state with the ideas of sexual intercourse",[107] girls "do the same thing with their still smaller clitoris".[108] There are two issues of importance here. First, the clitoris is understood to be a "penis-equivalent",[109] once again confirming Freud's privileging of the masculine over the feminine (it is not the case that the penis is the clitoris-equivalent, for example). Second, at this stage, "the truly feminine vagina is still undiscovered by both sexes".[110] This discovery takes place later during puberty. A girl's sexual development is more complicated as she has to learn to transfer the site of sexual satisfaction from the clitoris to the vagina; a transference not necessary in boys, whose sexuality is always orientated around the "same" body part: the phallus.

Additionally, Freud argues that female development is further complicated by a second issue not found in the development of the masculine. For boys, the mother is the first object of love and she remains such during the formation of his Oedipus complex and after. The Oedipus complex is, put very schematically, the stage in the child's psychic development wherein he or she experiences an initial *unconscious* desire for his or her opposite-sex parent and *unconscious* jealousy and anger towards his or her same-sex parent: a boy desires his mother and fears his father; whereas a girl desires her father and hates her mother. The implications of the child's experience of the Oedipus complex do, however, take different forms in boys and girls; in the former, it gives rise to the castration complex, while in girls it generates penis envy.

To understand this, it is necessary to note that, while a girl depends upon her mother for "the major and simple vital needs",[111] "the girl's father . . . becomes her love object".[112] In time, she will have to replace the father with another love object, presumably another male. So, a women has to change her love object from the mother to the father, female to male, whereas boys always have a women as their love object; it is a women that initially provides pleasure through providing food to the baby boy and it is a woman who will, if he develops "normally" – that is, heterosexually – provide him with genital pleasure. As a consequence, female sexual development is far more complicated than men's: she not only has to change her erotic zone – from the clitoris to the vagina – but also her love object from one sex to the other.

The question that arises relates to "how this happens: in particular, how does a girl pass from her mother to an attachment to her father? Or, in other words, how does she pass from her masculine phase to the feminine one to which she is biologically destined?"[113] Besides the troubling heteronormativity inherent in Freud's analysis and, indeed, the questionable notion of a biologically determined notion of femininity, which contradicts his previous rejection of sexual essentialism, Freud explains that the transition is not only fantastically complicated but also one that is fundamental to any attempt to "understand women".[114] It is therefore necessary to engage with "the girl's libidinal relations to her mother".[115]

Freud is quick to note that these take different forms and entail a mixture of active and passive stances towards the mother – which, despite warning that "we should avoid doing so as far as possible",[116] he problematically calls masculine (active) and feminine (passive) and so repeats a longstanding division of the sexes. Furthermore, the girl is both affectionate and hostile to the mother, although the latter only arises as a consequence of anxiety.[117] Nevertheless, Freud explains that it is the mother who is initially responsible for providing the baby girl with pleasure, both through the provision of food but also through simply touching the baby's body as the mother cleans her.[118] The question arises as to how this initial pleasurable identification with the mother is broken.

Freud notes that it "usually"[119] ends up with an attachment to the father, which, in turn, is accompanied by an alteration in the girl's relationship to the mother: the girl develops hostility towards the mother so that "the attachment to the mother ends in hate".[120] Freud's explanation for this transition is drawn from the biological differences between the genitalia of the sexes. However, rather than simply appealing to a naturalist argument to the effect that a girl's specific biological form leads her to a certain mode of behaviour, he suggests that "the anatomical distinction [between the sexes] must express itself in psychical consequences".[121] From this premise, he claims "that girls hold their mother responsible for their lack of a penis and do not forgive her for their being thus put at a disadvantage".[122]

So, while both sexes suffer from a castration complex, it takes different forms for both. Boys remember the threats received when he fondled his genitals – for example, "if you keep playing with that [the penis], it"ll fall off", or "if you keep playing with that, I"ll cut it off" – "begins to give credence to the threat . . . and falls under the influence of fear of castration, which will be the most powerful motive force in his subsequent development".[123] In girls, however, while the start of the castration complex also results from seeing the boy's penis, it is complicated by the recognition that she lacks one. With this, girls "feel seriously wronged, often declar[ing] that they want to 'have something like it too,' and [so] fall victim to 'envy for the penis,' which will leave ineradicable traces on their development and the formation of their character".[124]

Penis envy gives rise to certain consequences: whereas boys fear castration and so actively seek to resolve the Oedipus complex to overcome that threat, girls, already castrated, lack the motivation to surmount that complex. As a consequence, "[g]irls remain in [the Oedipus complex] for an indeterminate length of time; they demolish it late and, even so, incompletely".[125] Freud concludes that their "formation of the super-ego must suffer; it cannot attain the strength and independence which give it its cultural significance".[126] Girls are unable to develop sufficiently strong means of self-control; they continue to passively accept external authority to determine what to do. This has dramatic consequences for female behaviour; a conclusion that has, as Freud points out, drawn the ire of "feminists".[127]

That girls cannot obtain a penis is interpreted by them as being inherently unjust. For this reason, Freud explains that "envy and jealousy play an even greater part in the mental life of women than of men".[128] Again, this has been a long-standing claim made within Western philosophy, normally used to denigrate women. That Freud repeats it here and then towards the end of the essay – "The fact that women must be regarded as having little sense of justice is no doubt related to the predominance of envy in their mental life".[129] – reaffirms and reiterates the extent to which his thinking remains tied to the logic of patriarchy inherent in the Western philosophical tradition. It also brings him to "attribute a larger amount of narcissism to femininity"[130] and, indeed, "physical vanity",[131] both of which lead to the conclusion that "women [are] weaker in their social instincts and [have] less capacity for sublimating their instincts than men".[132] In short, women are more deferential, self-centered, vain, and instinctual than men; claims that again have a long heritage within Western philosophy.

Nevertheless, Freud explains that "[t]he discovery that she is castrated is a turning point in a girl's growth".[133] There are three possible lines of response: One leads "to normal femininity",[134] which is understood to entail the adoption of appropriately feminine characteristics and roles and sexual desire for the male object; again revealing that there is a strong heteronormativity to Freud's conception of normalcy. Alternatively, it can lead to "the development of a powerful masculinity complex"[135] wherein "the girl refuses, as it were, to recognise the unwelcome fact [that she lacks a penis], and defiantly rebellious, even exaggerates her previous masculinity, clings to her clitoral activity and takes refuge in an identification with her phallic mother or her father".[136] In short, she aims to overcompensate for her lack of penis by identifying fully with masculinity. The third possibility "leads to sexual inhibition or to neurosis".[137] The girl, having lived up to this point in a masculine way – which presumably equates to an active life – and obtained sexual satisfaction through the stimulus of the clitoris as this was related through the mother, "now, owing to the influence of her penis-envy . . . loses her enjoyment in her phallic sexuality".[138] More specifically, "[h]er self-love is mortified by the comparison with the boy's far superior equipment and in consequence she renounces her masturbatory satisfaction from her clitoris, repudiates her love for her mother and at the same time not infrequently represses a good part of her sexual trends in general".[139] Her repression of clitorial stimulation is also accompanied by the renouncement of a certain amount of activity.[140] As a consequence, whereas each individual is a combination of activity and passivity, masculinity and femininity, "[p]assivity now has the upper hand, and the girl's turning to her father is accomplished principally with the help of passive instinctual impulses".[141] According to Freud, "the wish with which the girl turns to her father is no doubt originally the wish for the penis which [she understands that] her mother has refused her and which she now expects from her father".[142]

Importantly, and not uncontroversially, Freud insists that the girl's identification with the phallic father can be overcome "if the wish for a penis is replaced by one for a baby, if, that is, a baby takes the place of the penis in accordance with an ancient symbolic equivalence".[143] While any baby can act as the symbolic penis that provides her with fulfilment, women find it to be especially fulfilling "if the baby is a little boy who brings the longed-for penis with him".[144] Having answered "the enigma of women"[145] by claiming that femininity is marked by a castration complex that makes her envious of masculinity, more deferential to (male) authority, self-centered, vain, and unjust, Freud now posits the creation of a male baby as the solution.

Conclusion

There is obviously far more to Freud's thinking generally and on sexuality specifically, but this outline is sufficient to demonstrate his continuing privileging of masculinity when thinking about femininity; or, put differently, his attempt to think femininity from masculinity. By insisting that both sexes look to the male phallus, Freud's thinking continues to be clouded by the patriarchal logic dominant in Western philosophy and his cultural milieu. Freud subsequently recognised this charge, and responded, dismissively and condescendingly, that "the ladies, whenever some comparison seemed to turn out unfavourable to their sex, [tended] to utter a suspicion that we, the male analysts, had been unable to overcome certain deeply-rooted prejudices against what was feminine, and that this was being paid for in the partiality of our researches".[146] He attempts to defend himself by explaining that because he stands "on the ground of bisexuality . . . [he] only ha[s] to say: 'This doesn't apply to *you*. You're the exception; on this point you're more masculine than feminine.'"[147]

Sarah Kofman delves into this defence to point out that it is premised on "[t]he thesis of bisexuality [which] implies that Sigmund Freud himself could not have been *purely and simply* a man *(vir)*, that he could not have had *(purely)* masculine prejudices".[148] That Freud, like all men, is, on his telling, a combination of masculine and feminine aspects means that he cannot simply privilege one over the other. This, however, fails to remember that the originary bisexuality, while continuing to adhere to individuals, does not determine behaviour or attitudes, which are a consequence of a long process of socio-psychic maturation. As a consequence, Kofman concludes with the strong claim that

> [t]he thesis of bisexuality . . . allows Freud to repeat the most tenacious, the most traditional, the most metaphysical phallocratic discourse: if you women are as intelligent as men, it is because you are really more masculine than feminine. Thus it allows him to shut women up, to put an end to their demands and accusations.[149]

Kofman doubts that Freud actually believes the theory of originary bisexuality and, indeed, points out that he certainly does not remain consistent with it. Her conclusion is that Freud's positing of an originary bisexuality is a construction to hide and provide intellectual cover for the perpetuation of the logic of patriarchy. In short, the theory of bisexuality permits Freud to *appear* to be "enlightened", when, in actuality, it "is in the last analysis used only as a strategic weapon in connection with women".[150]

While I am sympathetic to Kofman's basic point, which I take to be that there is a tension between Freud's theory of an originary bisexuality – which holds that both sexes are ontologically "equal" – and his subsequent patriarchal claims regarding individual (sexual) development, I disagree with her apparent claim that this is because Freud is engaging in an *intentional* sleight of hand where he aims to affirm the latter under the cover of the former. Rather, I think there is something far less sinister occurring, which is simply that Freud's thinking and analysis *unintentionally* continues to be shaped and informed by the logic of patriarchy that has long defined Western philosophy and was prevalent in his cultural milieu. As his own theory postulates, the social setting through which a child is brought up continues to shape his or her unconscious values throughout his or her life. Applying this insight to Freud, it is possible to conclude that the logic of patriarchy defining his social setting continued to unconsciously affect his thinking. Although he was aware of the important historical role that the logic of patriarchy has played in shaping Western thought and sought to undermine it, Freud continued to be guilty of unconsciously repeating it.

Freud might, of course, defend himself by claiming that his conclusion is not premised on an assumption regarding the nature of femininity, but is gleaned from empirical (clinical) experience, but such an argument would, at best, provide a description of what femininity means within Viennese society at the beginning of the twentieth century; it would not, as Freud insists it does, reveal the structures of femininity (or masculinity) *per se*. As a consequence, it would confirm rather than reject the charge that Freud's analysis of femininity is based on prejudices and assumptions.

That Freud's thinking on femininity continues to implicitly affirm the logic of patriarchy, even as he explicitly undermines the notion of sexual essentialism, reveals, so I want to suggest, the influence that this logic has on the unconscious. This logic has been so ingrained in Western thinking on the subject for so long that even when it is directly challenged, it is all too easy to implicitly repeat it. This confirms the continuing power of the unconscious to shape thought – thereby affirming one of the central insights of Freud's metapsychology – demonstrates how the logic of patriarchy imperceptibly shapes thinking on sexuality, and shows just how difficult it is to overcome it and, by extension, the essentialist-patriarchal model long dominant. Even when sexuality is identified as a problem – as it is with Freud – the long-standing privileging of the masculine means that it is all too easy to unconsciously repeat and so perpetuate the logic of patriarchy inherent in that model. So, whereas Freud undermines the essentialist premises, he nevertheless continues to perpetuate the patriarchal aspect, meaning that he is not capable of fully overcoming the essentialist-patriarchal model. I will argue that this is a problem that is repeated, albeit in slightly different form, throughout many of the critical analyses of the essentialist-patriarchal model found in post-Freudian thinking.

Notes

1. Sigmund Freud, *Three Essays on Sexuality*, in *The Standard Edition of the Complete Psychological Works of Sigmund Freud: Volume 3*, edited and translated by James Strachey (New York: Basic Books, 2000).

2. Roger Horrocks, *Freud Revisited: Psychoanalytic Themes in the Postmodern Age* (Basingstoke: Palgrave Macmillan, 2001), p. 113.
3. Ibid., p. 113.
4. Ibid., p. 113.
5. Ibid., p. 114.
6. Ibid., p. 114.
7. Ibid., p. 115.
8. Ibid., p. 115.
9. Gayle Rubin, "The Traffic in Women: Notes on the 'Political Economy' of Sex", in *The Second Wave: A Reader in Feminist Theory*, edited by Linda Nicholson (Abingdon: Routledge, 1997), pp. 27–62 (p. 43).
10. Juliet Mitchell, "Introduction – I", in *Feminine Sexuality: Jacan Lacan and the école freudienne*, edited by Juliet Mitchell and Jacqueline Rose, trans. Jacqueline Rose (London: Macmillan, 1982), pp. 1–26 (p. 9).
11. Bertram J. Cohler and Robert M. Galatzer-Levy, "Freud, Anna, and the Problem of Female Sexuality", *Psychoanalytic Inquiry*, vol. 28, n. 1, 2008, pp. 3–26 (p. 4).
12. Sigmund Freud, "Some Psychical Consequences of the Anatomical Distinction between the Sexes", in *The Standard Edition of the Complete Psychological Works of Sigmund Freud: Volume 19*, edited and translated by James Strachey (London: Vintage, 2001), pp. 248–258.
13. Sigmund Freud, "Female Sexuality", in *The Standard Edition of the Complete Psychological Works of Sigmund Freud: Volume 21*, edited and translated by James Strachey (London: Vintage, 2001), pp. 223–243.
14. Sigmund Freud, "Femininity", in *The Standard Edition of the Complete Psychological Works of Sigmund Freud: Volume 22*, edited and translated by James Strachey (New York: W. W. Norton, 1989), pp. 139–167.
15. For a critical overview of all three essays, see Teresa Brennan, *The Interpretation of the Flesh: Freud and Femininity* (Abingdon: Routledge, 1992), pp. 39–65.
16. Mitchell, "Introduction – I", p. 10.
17. Arnold I. Davidson, *The Emergence of Sexuality: Historical Epistemology and the Formation of Concepts* (Cambridge, MA: Harvard University Press, 2001), p. 92.
18. Mitchell, "Introduction – I", p. xxvi.
19. Sigmund, *Three Essays on Sexuality*, p. xxvii.
20. Ibid., p. xxvii.
21. Ibid., p. 1.
22. Ibid., p. 1.
23. Ibid., p. 1.
24. Ibid., p. 1.
25. Ibid., p. 1.
26. Ibid., pp. 1–2.
27. Ibid., p. 1.
28. Ibid., p. 2.
29. Ibid., p. 2.
30. Ibid., p. 2.

31. Ibid., p. 2.
32. Ibid., p. 2.
33. Ibid., p. 2.
34. Ibid., p. 2.
35. Ibid., p. 3.
36. Ibid., p. 4.
37. Ibid., p. 4.
38. Ibid., p. 4.
39. Ibid., p. 5.
40. Ibid., p. 5.
41. Ibid., p. 7.
42. Ibid., p. 7.
43. Ibid., p. 7.
44. Ibid., p. 8.
45. Gayle Rubin, "Thinking Sex: Notes for a Radical Theory of the Politics of Sexuality", in *Pleasure and Danger: Exploring Feminist Sexuality*, edited by Carol S. Vance (Abingdon: Routledge, 1984), pp. 267–319 (p. 308).
46. Sigmund, *Three Essays on Sexuality*, p. 34.
47. Ibid., p. 14.
48. Ibid., p. 14.
49. Ibid., p. 14.
50. Ibid., p. 15.
51. Ibid., p. 85fn1.
52. Ibid., p. 85.
53. Ibid., p. 86.
54. Ibid., p. 39.
55. Ibid., p. 43.
56. Ibid., p. 42.
57. Sigmund Freud, *The Outline of Psycho-Analysis: The Standard Edition of the Complete Psychological Works of Sigmund Freud: Volume 23*, edited and translated by James Strachey (New York: W. W. Norton, 1989), p. 23.
58. Ibid., p. 23.
59. Ibid., p. 23.
60. Freud, *Three Essays on Sexuality*, p. 48.
61. Ibid., p. 47.
62. Ibid., p. 48.
63. Ibid., p. 48.
64. Ibid., p. 70.
65. Ibid., p. 98.
66. Ibid., p. 99.
67. Ibid., p. 63.
68. Ibid., p. 64.
69. Ibid., p. 64.
70. Ibid., p. 66.

71. Ibid., p. 66.
72. Ibid., p. 66.
73. Ibid., p. 73.
74. Ibid., p. 73.
75. Ibid., p. 73.
76. Ibid., p. 73.
77. Ibid., p. 81.
78. Freud, "Femininity", p. 140.
79. Janine Chasseguet-Smirgel, "Freud and Female Sexuality: The Consideration of Some Blind Spots in the Exploration of the 'Dark Continent'", *International Journal of Psychoanalysis*, vol. 57, 1976, pp. 275–286, (p. 275).
80. Sigmund Freud, *The Question of Lay Analysis*, in *The Standard Edition of the Complete Psychological Works of Sigmund Freud: Volume 20*, edited and translated by James Strachey (New York: W. W. Norton, 1990), pp. 177–258 (p. 211).
81. Freud, "Femininity", p. 140.
82. Ibid., p. 141.
83. Ibid., p. 141.
84. Ibid., p. 141.
85. Ibid., p. 141.
86. Ibid., p. 141.
87. Ibid., p. 141.
88. Ibid., p. 141.
89. Ibid., p. 142.
90. Ibid., p. 142.
91. Ibid., p. 142.
92. Ibid., p. 142.
93. Ibid., p. 142.
94. Ibid., p. 143.
95. Ibid., p. 143.
96. Ibid., p. 144.
97. Ibid., p. 145.
98. Ibid., p. 145.
99. Ibid., p. 145.
100. Ibid., p. 145.
101. Ibid., p. 146.
102. Freud, *The Outline of Psycho-Analysis*, p. 25.
103. Freud, "Femininity", p. 146.
104. Freud, *The Outline of Psycho-Analysis*, p. 25.
105. Ibid., p. 25.
106. Freud, "Femininity", p. 146.
107. Ibid., p. 146.
108. Ibid., p. 146.
109. Ibid., p. 146.
110. Ibid., p. 146.

111. Ibid., p. 147.
112. Ibid., p. 147.
113. Ibid., p. 147.
114. Ibid., p. 148.
115. Ibid., p. 148.
116. Ibid., p. 149.
117. Ibid., p. 149.
118. Ibid., pp. 149–150.
119. Ibid., p. 151.
120. Ibid., p. 151.
121. Ibid., p. 154.
122. Ibid., p. 154.
123. Ibid., p. 155.
124. Ibid., p. 155.
125. Ibid., p. 160.
126. Ibid., pp. 160–161.
127. Ibid., p. 161.
128. Ibid., p. 156.
129. Ibid., p. 166.
130. Ibid., p. 164.
131. Ibid., p. 164.
132. Ibid., p. 166.
133. Ibid., p. 156.
134. Ibid., p. 156.
135. Ibid., p. 161.
136. Ibid., p. 161.
137. Ibid., p. 156.
138. Ibid., p. 157.
139. Ibid., p. 157.
140. Ibid., p. 158.
141. Ibid., p. 159.
142. Ibid., p. 159.
143. Ibid., p. 159.
144. Ibid., p. 159.
145. Ibid., p. 162.
146. Ibid., p. 145.
147. Ibid., p. 145.
148. Sarah Kofman, *Women in Freud's Writings*, trans. Katherine Porter (Ithaca, NY: Cornell University Press, 1985), p. 15.
149. Ibid., pp. 14–15.
150. Ibid., p. 15.

CHAPTER 2

Heidegger, Fundamental Ontology, and Sexuality

Writing at around the same time as Freud, Edmund Husserl developed an alternative philosophical methodology that forewent the creation of speculative (meta)-physical schemas as a means to explain what something is, to instead emphasise a detailed and patient analysis of particular concrete things. While Husserl's thinking underwent various changes and revisions, very generally, the basic premise is that, rather than start from a preconceived idea of what something is or what thought entails, philosophical enquiry has to focus on an immediate concrete phenomenon and let it appear as it is.[1] This is not an easy endeavour and, indeed, as Husserl was at pains to stress, is an activity that requires a certain preparation and orientation, which he termed the "phenomenological reduction".[2]

While this concept is a complex one and, indeed, changes throughout Husserl's writings, the basic premise is that in normal, everyday life, we exist a *"natural attitude"*[3] that delineates consciousness of a spatio-temporal given imbued with value-characteristics. Because this attitude imposes meaning onto objects, it reveals objects as we want them to appear or are accustomed to seeing them, rather than as they actually are. To correct this, Husserl *"propose[s] to alter [our cognitive standpoint] radically"*[4] by bracketing factual determinations to *"put out of action the general positing which belongs to the essence of the natural attitude"*.[5] Through this, Husserl insists that he will be *"completely [shut] off from any judgement about spatiotemporal factual being"*.[6] This will remove (= bracket) the everyday presuppositions of the natural attitude to permit an enquiry into the object's transcendental conditions purified of the determinations of factual being; a methodological manoeuvre that will permit an enquiry into "things themselves".[7]

The impact of Husserl's thinking was substantial in the early decades of the twentieth century, spawning a number of debates and conceptual innovations. Some of the most important of these were tied to and arose from the thinking of Husserl's one-time assistant: Martin Heidegger. In 1927, Heidegger published *Being and Time*[8] in which he dismisses what he takes to be the implicit dependence on and affirmation of an other-worldly metaphysics inherent in Husserl's affirmation of the primary importance of a pure transcendental realm, to instead affirm the fundamental importance of ontology. From this, Heidegger introduces the ontological difference between ontology, constituted by a questioning of the meaning of Being, and its ontic expression in spatio-temporal entities. To fully understand the latter requires that the Being of each entity be investigated.[9]

The issue that Heidegger immediately encounters is how to prevent such a study from falling into empty universal abstractions. In *Being and Time*, he aims to overcome this by insisting on the need to engage with one type of entity – the human one, termed Dasein for reasons that will be subsequently explained – and use the revelation of the Being of Dasein to reveal characteristics of Being *per se*. However, in so doing, Dasein must be initially posited as ontically/ontologically neutral; only this permits it to reveal itself as it is rather than as how we, the phenomenologists, desire it to be or have been conditioned to think it is.

While Heidegger's emptying out of all factual determinations accords with Husserl's affirmation of the importance of the phenomenological reduction, it does lead to the question of the ontological importance of factual determinations, such as sexuality. Whereas Heidegger's insistence that Being is "nothing" other than pure open-ended becoming undermines the notion that sexuality is fixed or ahistoric, it seems to simply remove sexuality from the equation. The question of Heidegger's relationship to the question of sexuality has, therefore, been a contentious one within the secondary literature. While, in the 1983 essay "*Geschlecht I: Sexual Difference, Ontological Difference*",[10] Jacques Derrida belatedly recognised that Heidegger's fundamental ontology is intimately tied to the question(ing) of sexual difference, there is a long history, mainly within feminist and sexuality studies, that agrees with Jean-Paul Sartre's earlier assessment (from 1943) that "Heidegger . . . doesn't make the slightest allusion to [sexuality] in his existential analysis with the result that his 'Dasein' strikes us as sexless".[11]

Patricia Huntington[12] provides a detailed overview of these positions, but, put schematically, they centre around two lines of attack. The weaker line[13] argues that whereas, on its own, Heidegger's thinking on sexuality is unhelpful, when it is combined with the insights of other feminist writers, it can be reconstructed to offer helpful insights into sexuality. However, while this position takes seriously Heidegger's fundamental ontology and, indeed, the analysis of sexuality permitted by it, it suffers from two problems. First, it aims to "rescue" Heidegger's thinking on sexuality by combining aspects of his analyses with psychoanalytic theory, especially its post-Lacanian (feminist) variant; a manoeuvre that ends up bypassing Heidegger's critique of psychoanalysis to significantly distort his thought. Second, it uses Heidegger's thought for another predetermined end and so examines how Heidegger can be reconfigured (or combined with another perspective) to contribute to our understanding of (a prior notion of) sexuality. This not only instrumentalises Heidegger's thinking, thereby ignoring his critique of instrumental rationality,[14] but also fails to concentrate on what Heidegger actually says about sexuality.

The stronger line of critique maintains that once we do in fact pay attention to what Heidegger says on the topic, we find that he has, in fact, nothing appropriate nor useful to say either because his analysis is held to depend upon a number of implicit, unexplained patriarchal privilegings that bring him to implicitly analyse issues from a supposedly masculine perspective[15] or because his fundamental ontology cannot say anything about actual physical bodies.[16] The fundamental point behind this strong line of critique is a methodological one: instead of depending upon the neutering principle inherent in Husserl's phenomenological reduction, "sexuality" must simply be understood through the study of concrete actual beings and, crucially, that these are always sexed. Whereas Heidegger dismisses this for producing merely ontic studies based on everyday prejudices, his critics argue that it is his affirmation of an *ontological* analysis that permits the prejudices suffered everyday by women to be covered over or ignored. In other words, this critique maintains that the affirmation of an originary neutrality does not reveal a dispassionate prejudice-free notion of what sexuality really is, but actually perpetuates prejudices by imposing a veneer of neutrality that masks the ways in which the logic of patriarchy is subtly reintroduced into the analysis; an introduction that turns socially contingent determinations into fundamental ontological ones.

The question driving this dispute relates to the "correct" way to study sexuality and indeed combat, what I have called, the essentialist-patriarchal model; a dispute that will become increasingly apparent as we move through feminist theory in later chapters. Whereas his critics insist on the importance of immediate concrete analyses of already sexed beings, Heidegger maintains that the primordial question is an ontological one that necessitates the adoption of a neutral mentality towards the object of study specifically and ontic determinations more generally; only this will prevent us from imposing ideas onto the object and, instead, let the object appear to us as it is.

As a consequence, from a Heideggerian perspective, his critics make two conceptual errors. First, the claim that the affirmation of neutrality masks the implicit affirmation of the logic of patriarchy seems to confuse the affirmation of the principle of neutrality with its implementation. In other words, Heidegger's critics identify moments of what they take to be a dependence on the logic of patriarchy within his thought and, based on his affirmation of the originary neutrality inherent in the phenomenological reduction, conclude that *all* affirmations of neutrality regardless of their content actually depend upon, are committed to, and are infected by that logic. However, even if it is accepted that Heidegger's thought contains traces of patriarchy – an argument which itself seems to be based on certain prejudices regarding what is patriarchal – it is not clear that this undermines the affirmation of neuturality inherent in the phenomenological reduction. It could simply be that Heidegger failed to implement it properly. As befits the becoming of Being, new configurations of Being will require ongoing original phenomenological analyses to undercover and combat existing prejudices.

Second, the claim that Heidegger's fundamental ontology fails to produce sufficiently empirical or ontically focused studies radically distorts his thinking and/or judges it against a purpose that it was never intended to fulfil. As Jesus Escudero explains:

> One must not forget that the original purpose of Heidegger's analytic is none other than to articulate the foreunderstanding that Dasein has of Being and not to develop a philosophical or ethical anthropology. For this reason, Heidegger does not use the word 'man' or 'person' but the neutral German term 'Dasein.'[17]

Rather than aim to offer an ontic analysis, Heidegger's fundamental ontology is orientated to the conditions, manifested from a questioning of the meaning of Being, that generate ontic understandings. Instead of aiming to use Heidegger's thinking to develop a predetermined conception of sexuality and, indeed, judging it in accordance with that end, his thinking must be examined on its own ontologically orientated terms. When read in this manner, Heidegger's thinking on sexuality questions its ontological importance and aims to account for its place "within" human being specifically and Being more generally; it does not aim to offer an ontic analysis of sexuality, but undercuts that issue by engaging with the more primordial question of the role and place of "sexuality" in relation to Being. This results in a radical, if truncated, critique of sexual essentialism that challenges us to question our prejudices about sexual determinations.

Heidegger, Fundamental Ontology, and the Sexuality of Dasein

Heidegger's early, incomplete work *Being and Time*, published in 1927, aims to "raise anew *the question of the meaning of being*"[18]; a question that concerns "[e]verything we talk about, everything we have in view, everything towards which we comport ourselves in any way, is Being; what we are is Being, and so is how we are".[19] This questioning occupied the Ancient Greeks, but has been largely ignored or forgotten as a particular understanding – based on the notion of a fixed substance, or presence – has been settled on and come to dominate Western thought. In contrast, Heidegger tentatively affirms "*time* as the possible horizon for any understanding whatsoever of Being",[20] with the consequence that Being and its manifestations are to be thought, not in terms of a fixed substance or presenting ground, but as pure, open-ended becoming.

From here, Heidegger enquires into the "nature" of Being to, in so doing, dismiss long-held prejudices that insist that the question of Being is the most universal question – after all, everything is a manifestation of Being – and therefore the most vacuous. Because it relates to everything that exists, Heidegger holds that it is the most important concept, although he accepts that "this cannot mean that it is the one which is clearest or that it needs no further discussion. It is rather the darkest of all."[21] Indeed, Heidegger notes that, although it is universal and transcends entities, Being does not exist in a separate, transcendent realm. Rejecting a two-world metaphysical understanding that posits a true, essential, but hidden, world against an inessential world of appearance, he explains that "Being . . . is no class or genus of entities; yet it pertains to every entity. Its 'universality' is to be sought higher up. Being and the structure of Being lie beyond every entity and every possible character which an entity may possess. *Being is transcendens pure and simple.*"[22] That Being is different to entities and always transcends them but is never transcendent to them, leads to the famous notion of the ontological difference.

The first thing to note is that, while different, "Being is always the Being of an entity"[23] but yet "cannot . . . be conceived as an entity".[24] As a consequence, Being is non-conceptual, although "it" is that from which and upon which entities depend for their existence. For this reason, "we cannot apply to Being the concept of 'definition' as presented in traditional logic, which itself has its foundations in ancient ontology and which, within certain limits, provides a quite justifiable way of defining 'entities.'"[25] Such a definition depends upon a particular conception of Being, wherein "it" is understood to present itself as what it is, take on objective conceptual form to do so, and, crucially, not change: the entity *is* what is presented and nothing else. The question that Heidegger's re-raising addresses is whether such an assumed conception of Being is accurate or whether, as he postulates, Being (and its manifestations) must be understood in terms of time. It is for this reason that "[o]ntological inquiry is . . . more primordial, as over against the ontical inquiry of the positive sciences. But it remains naïve and opaque if in its researches into the Being of entities it fails to discuss the meaning of Being in general."[26] There is therefore a distinction between an *ontological* level of analysis concerned with Being and an *ontic* one that limits the discussion to entities. Because, for Heidegger, Being expresses itself in entity form, the ontological level is far more important than the ontic one. An ontological analysis can however take two forms: a "naïve"[27] approach that focuses on an entity to reveals its particular Being; and *"fundamental ontology"*[28] which draws general conclusions regarding Being from the ontological analysis of an entity.

However, if Being is different to entities and so non-conceptual, how are we to understand (= conceptualise) it? Heidegger's response is twofold. First, he asks for nothing other than a fundamental alteration in how we think, away from a conceptual focus to a more ineffable, flowing, and changing mode of thought.[29] As a consequence, Being must "be asked about, exhibited in a way of its own essentially different from the way in which entities are discovered".[30] While this changes after his *Kehre* in 1933 when an unmediated study of Being is affirmed, Heidegger, in *Being and Time*, returns to the ontological difference to suggest that if Being is always the Being of an entity, perhaps enquiring into an entity can reveal Being. In particular, he insists that one entity, Dasein, can fulfil this role because "it is ontically distinguished by the fact that, in its very Being, that Being is an *issue* for it".[31] In other words, Dasein is the only entity for whom "asking this question is [the] entity's mode of *Being*".[32] Importantly, the analysis of Dasein is used, not as an end in itself, but as a means to raise the question of the meaning of Being.

"Dasein" is a neologism of "Da", meaning "there", and "sein", meaning "is", and so literally gives us "there-is". There are at least two issues that need to be unpacked for this nomenclature to make sense. First, "Dasein" is employed because it reveals the particular understanding of the ontological difference that Heidegger has in mind. Dasein, as an entity, has a Being of its own but, crucially, it also signifies the way in which entities relate to Being: against the temporal flux of Being, Dasein stands out so that "there-is" something with spatio-temporal form. Because it exists from a temporal flow, Dasein is never defined by a substance; "it" is defined by the possibility that is always created from the changing configurations made possible by the temporality of Being. In *Being and Time*, Heidegger terms this "existence" and claims that "Dasein always understands itself in terms of its existence – in terms of a possibility of itself: to be itself or not itself. Dasein has either chosen these possibilities itself, or got itself into them, or grown up in them already."[33] How it understands this ontological possibility shapes its ontic possibilities and, indeed, comportment. In short, if Dasein denies the subtending ontological possibility, it will tend to take itself to be a fixed thing and so, on Heidegger's terms, will be inauthentic. Authenticity requires that it recognise, accept, and affirm its ontological possibility throughout its ontic existence.[34]

Second, when engaging with the preliminary ontic analysis of Dasein, Heidegger returns to the basic premise of Husserl's phenomenological reduction where the phenomenologist "let[s] that which shows itself be seen from itself in the very way in which it shows itself from itself".[35] As a consequence, Heidegger explains that, in contrast to other branches of knowledge that already know the object to the studied, "'[p]henomenology' neither designates the object of its researches, nor characterizes the subject-matter thus comprised. The word merely informs us of the *'how'* with which *what* is to be treated in this science gets exhibited and handled."[36] From these premises, the preliminary ontic analysis of Dasein cannot be undertaken from preconceptions regarding Dasein. Instead of starting from a predetermined understanding that is imposed onto it, Dasein – and by extension Being – must be allowed to reveal "itself" as "it" actually is, and not as how we want it to be. This requires that the analysis initially bracket all factual determinations, adopt a neutral stance, and, from this, permit Dasein and by extension Being to reveal itself.

It should, however, be noted that Heidegger's affirmation of the importance of an originary neutral "Dasein" is not a synonym for the disembodied, abstract, unencumbered self that has marked Western modern philosophy. This line of critique will feed through into a number of later feminist criticisms, which suggest that Heidegger's analysis both ignores and is unable to conceptualise concrete, embodied, and differentiated entities. In contrast, Heidegger maintains that Dasein is inherently embodied and embedded within a world. Dasein is not defined by an "inner" innate core, but by its "*'existence'*"[37] which, very generally, describes both the world it inhabits and how it comports itself. These are not two distinct aspects but intertwine to create Dasein: as a manifestation of Being, Dasein is not and cannot be a fixed substance, thing, or object;[38] it is inherently historical and changing. Furthermore, as a situated, worldly entity, there is entwinement between the Being of Dasein, Dasein's understanding and comportment, and the concrete world: "In Dasein itself, and therefore in its own understanding of Being, the way the world is understood is . . . reflected back ontologically upon the way in which Dasein itself gets interpreted."[39] Contrary then to the mind/body dualism that has long conditioned Western philosophy, Dasein is not separated from its world or body; it is factical being, with its facticity (including its actions and understanding) entailing and defined by an intimate and co-constitutive understanding of the world. As Heidegger warns,

"Being-in is not a 'property' which Dasein sometimes has and sometimes does not have, and *without* which it could *be* just as well as it could with it. It is not the case that man 'is' and then has, by way of an extra, a relationship-of-Being towards the 'world.'"[40] Dasein is not a disembodied entity that may choose how to interact with its world; "it" is a worldly embodied entity that cannot be separated or distinguished from its facticity from and through which it acts.

It must be remembered, however, that the preliminary enquiry into Dasein aims not to elicit the meaning of Dasein *per se*, but to determine the meaning of Being. For the pre-*Kehre* Heidegger, all enquiries must concern themselves with a questioning of the meaning of Being – not entities – through a prior analysis of one entity: Dasein. This analytic of Dasein is not however the end of the process, but the first stage to understanding the meaning of Being. For this reason, he criticises disciplines such as anthropology, biology, and psychology for not only undertaking purely ontic analyses, but also conceptualising human being as an enclosed monadic entity to be studied in isolation from its worldliness.[41] Based on this, we can surmise that, from a Heideggerian perspective, Freud's approach is too limited and ontic, in so far as it focuses on providing an ontic analysis of human consciousness that not only locks the enquiry within a predetermined ontological schema, but is unable to appreciate that it has done so. To truly understand human being, Freud's ontic analysis must be turned into an ontological one regarding the meaning of Being. It is this insight that underpins the critique of psychoanalysis and the development of Daseinanalysis in the *Zollikon Seminars*.[42] In turn, Heidegger's fundamental ontology has radical implications for the questioning of sexuality.

Dasein, Sexuality, and Fundamental Ontology

The use of the term neutral term "Dasein" as a means of signifying the human entity prior to its ontic determinations leaves the question of sexuality open. For this reason, Sartre's claim that "Heidegger . . . doesn't make the slightest allusion to [sexuality] in his existential analysis with the result that his 'Dasein' strikes us as sexless"[43] is, strictly speaking, accurate in so far as the analysis of Dasein goes, but it fails to recognise that (1) this must be so to permit Dasein to reveal itself without being constrained by prior imposed ontic determinations, (2) the analysis of Dasein is part of a wider strategy that uses this analysis to question the meaning of Being, and (3) Heidegger does, in fact, discuss the relationship between Dasein and sexuality one year later in his lecture course from 1928, translated as *The Metaphysical Foundations of Logic*.

Heidegger starts by clarifying that the analysis is bound to the premises of fundamental ontology, outlined the previous year in *Being and Time*. For this reason, "[t]he issue is . . . neither one of anthropology nor of ethics but of . . . being as such, and thus one of a preparatory analysis concerning it".[44] Importantly, to ensure that Being reveals itself through the entity under analysis, "[t]he term 'man' was not used . . . Instead the neutral term *Dasein* was chosen."[45] The problem with using the determination "man" or "human" is that it comes loaded with conceptual baggage from the history of Western thinking. Rather than simply assuming an understanding of Dasein or take over the historically dominant conception, Heidegger maintains that it is necessary to re-engage with Dasein on its own terms. It might turn out that the way in which "human" has been thought historically is accurate, but unless an investigation takes place that critically challenges long-held nomenclature and, by extension, thinking on the topic, it will not be possible to confirm this. For this reason, Heidegger explains that, rather than simply assume an understanding of Dasein, "the interpretation of this being must be carried out prior to every factual concretion".[46] As a consequence, it must be accepted and affirmed that initially "Dasein is neither of the two sexes".[47]

Whereas this appears to remove sexual considerations from the analysis, Heidegger goes on to make the crucial claim that "here sexlessness is not the indifference of an empty void, the weak negativity of an indifferent ontic nothing. In its neutrality Dasein is not the indifferent nobody and everybody, but the primordial positivity and potency of the essence."[48] The neutrality of Dasein does not, somewhat paradoxically, neuter it, rendering it an abstract, empty void, but points to and describes "the potency of the *origin*";[49] the ever-changing, non-determinate "power" that "bears in itself the intrinsic possibility of every concrete factual humanity".[50]

Crucially, Heidegger holds that, technically, "[n]eutral Dasein is never what exists; Dasein exists in each case only in its factical concretion".[51] Neutral Dasein must nevertheless be posited to explain the transition from the temporal becoming of Being to its manifestation in ontic form. Only by positing an originary neutrality is it possible to ensure that Being's open-ended becoming and the possibility that defines it is not foreclosed within factic determinations. For this reason, Heidegger explains that neutral Dasein is "the primal source of intrinsic possibility that springs up in every existence and makes it intrinsically possible".[52]

The positing of an originary neutral Dasein does not however imply that ontic Dasein is split between an ontologically essentially "free" neutrality and a factical world of appearance. Neutral Dasein – tied to Being's becoming – is immanently expressed factically and always subtends its factic expression. Heidegger links this to the question of sexuality, noting that it ensures that

"Dasein harbors the intrinsic possibility for being factically dispersed into bodiliness and thus into sexuality".[53] Factical being is not annihilated by neutrality, but is, in fact, only possible because it is "grounded" in neutrality. Reiterating that this neutrality is not an empty void, but a potency, Heidegger explains that "[t]he metaphysical neutrality of the human being, inmost isolated as Dasein, is not an empty abstraction from the ontic, a neither-nor; it is rather the authentic concreteness of the origin, the not-yet of factical dispersion [*Zerstreutheit*]".[54] As such, and starting from a non-determined metaphysical neutrality, "Dasein is, among other things, in each case dispersed in a body and concomitantly, among other things, in each case disunited [*Zwiespältig*] in a particular sexuality".[55] From an initial, non-determined "ground", Dasein is disseminated into factical being; a process that requires that its initial indeterminateness be broken up and multiplied to take on ontic form. For this reason, this breaking-up is not negative, but the "positive" process whereby an initial indeterminate neutrality is distinguished into different parts to permit ontic individuated existence. It is, in other words, the moment when Dasein is thrown into a factical body.

This does not simply entail a "split[ting] into many individuals";[56] each individuated entity is itself defined by "the intrinsic possibility of multiplication which ... is present in every Dasein and for which embodiment presents an organizing factor".[57] It is not the case then that having been divided into different ontic beings, each entity created is singular and determined. Neutrality continues to subtend it, providing the possibility that the ontic determination will take on different forms. As such, ontic sexuality is created from a well-spring of indeterminate (ontological) neutrality and is expressed through processes of differentiation that, rather than coalescing into a determinate being, create a multiplicity that is not and cannot be defined in terms of a defined totality, fixed unity, or a whole with multiple parts. Instead, it is demarcated by the openness that expresses the possibility inherent in its neutral "ground". The original neutrality does not disappear in the process of ontic expression but continues to subtend it, thereby ensuring that ontic sexuality is never determined or fixed and is and can be reactivated in a different manner.

For this reason, Heidegger rejects the notion that factical being is determinate for either Dasein or sexuality:

> [F]actical bodiliness and sexuality are in each case explanatory only – and even then only within the bounds of the essential arbitrariness of all explanation – to the extent that a factical Dasein's being-with is pushed precisely into this particular factical direction, where other possibilities are founded out or remain closed.[58]

Sexuality and factic being more generally are not determinate for Dasein, but an additional layer of complexity to its becoming. They limit the expression of Dasein's becoming, but do not annihilate Dasein's becoming or, indeed, predetermine its meaning.

Heidegger outlines this through a discussion of the essential structure of being-with. This is a key feature of *Being and Time* that rejects the Cartesian notion of an isolated self by insisting that Dasein always exists in relation to others, but is never determined by them: "Even in our Being 'among them' they are *there with us*; their Dasein-with is encountered in a mode in which they are indifferent and alien."[59] Dasein does not form a seamless, harmonious relationship with others; "it" must live with others, but always encounters them as, in some way, an imposition or awkward occurrence. That it exists with others but is never determined by them ensures that Dasein must choose the type of relationship it will have with others. In this it can either follow the dictates of the "they" and be determined by what others define it as and by or it can strive to develop an authentic relationship with others wherein it affirms itself in spite of the dictates of others.

There is far more to Heidegger's analysis of the notion of being-with,[60] but it is important in relation to the question of sexuality because it brings forth the issue of how Dasein's being-with others shapes and structures Dasein's factical sexuality. More specifically, it highlights the question of the relationship between "nature", or ontic determinations, and "freedom". After all, if neutral Dasein is thrown into a factical body and a world populated with others who act on it and its freedom, but yet must choose its relationship to its possibility and indeed others, the issue arises as to "how Dasein can exist as essentially free in the freedom of the factical ties with being-with-one-another".[61] In other words, how can the open-ended possibility that defines metaphysical, neutral Dasein remain and be compatible with factical Dasein?

Heidegger does not so much respond to this issue, as simply affirm the primordial importance of metaphysical, neutral Dasein: "Insofar as being-with is a basic metaphysical feature of dissemination, we can see that the latter ultimately has its ground in the freedom of Dasein as such."[62] It is from freedom that factical Dasein arises and, indeed, always depends. For this reason, factical being is never determined; Dasein must always choose how it will live its facticity. Although Heidegger never says this explicitly, this gives rise to the conclusion that while individual factical sexuality emanates from the thrownness of neutral metaphysical Dasein, what sexuality means and how it is lived is an open question, based on how the individual comports itself towards its factical being generally and sexuality more specifically.

Heidegger's fundamental ontology therefore rejects the notion that sexual determinations are essential to Dasein. Sexual determinations emanate from a prior ontological neutrality that is thrown into a particular body. Dasein's factical being is however always subtended by the open-ended possibility inherent in its metaphysical neutrality, with the consequence that "Dasein always exists as itself, and being-a-self is in every case only in its process of realization, as is also existence".[63] Dasein must choose how to live its existence, which means how to live its facticity, with this choice defining its existence and, indeed, what it will be. For this reason, factical being – sexuality – is not fixed or a limitation of Dasein's possibilities; it is the arena on, through, and from which Dasein chooses itself.

With this, Heidegger undermines the notion of sexual essentialism by arguing that sexuality is a secondary phenomenon dependent upon the continuous becoming that defines Being. Furthermore, once created, Dasein's metaphysical neutrality is thrown into physical ontic form, the factical determinations created are not fixed and ahistoric. Not only do these factical determinations continue to change, but the *meaning* of them is dependent upon the choices that Dasein makes regarding them; choices that are dependent upon and permitted because its neutrality continues to subtend its facticity. By insisting that sexuality is an expression of Being's becoming, Heidegger rejects the notion of an ahistoric substantial essence that underpins the essentialist-patriarchal model of sexuality. An individual's existence is not defined by a fixed essence that truly defines him or her; it is defined by the way in which each Dasein lives its temporal existence, meaning, generally speaking, how it chooses to comport itself to and through its facticity and relationship with others. This opens sexuality to different manifestations, expressions, and ways of living, thereby indicating that, for Heidegger: (1) an individual is never determined by its sexual facticity, and (2) sexuality is one aspect of human being but is never the fundamental one. Dasein must be thought from the freedom that defines and is made possible by its metaphysical neutrality.

Neutrality and Patriarchy

A number of subsequent feminist thinkers have however questioned Heidegger's affirmation of an originary neutrality when thinking about sexuality, arguing that rather than being neutral it actually masks and so re-enforces a particular cultural or patriarchal value system. In other words, while the affirmation of an originary ontological neutrality undermines sexual essentialism, it does so at the expense of concrete analyses of sexuality and the perpetuation of Western sexual binary oppositions through an *implicit* dependence on the logic of patriarchy.

Tina Chanter, for example, "aims to 'expose' a normative bias that is built into Heidegger's ontological method in such a way as to cover over its prejudice".[64] Only once these prejudices are brought to light will it be possible "to see not only that Heidegger neglects feminist concerns when treating certain topics, but also how his philosophy is formulated in such a way as to render such concerns irrelevant".[65] Chanter's fundamental claim is that the basic problem resides with Heidegger's dependence on neutrality, which far from being neutral actually depends upon and perpetuates a particular Western masculine stance that "exhibits a systematic blindness not only to its own gender bias, but also to a range of other normative assumptions it makes".[66] In particular, she identifies at least three moments where this occurs: first, in the privileging of ontological analysis over ontic ones; a methodological move that "rules out in advance any serious consideration of significant differences between individuals (whether those differences are specified in terms of gender, race, class, ethnicity, sexuality, or some other culturally loaded difference)".[67] By abandoning the study of ontic determinations for the generality of ontology, Chanter charges that Heidegger is led "to posit, almost by default, a culturally specific version of Dasein that he takes to be exemplary, but whose exemplarity is never made available for critical interrogation".[68] Interestingly, Trish Glazebrook supplements Chanter's point by arguing that while Heidegger affirms Dasein's concreteness, his insistence on the fundamental importance of Dasein's originary neutrality reveals that he "think[s] transcendentally . . . in a gender-neutral way",[69] which is "precisely to transcend the world [and so] be worldless".[70] With this, Glazebrook argues that Heidegger's affirmation of the neutrality of Dasein not only contradicts his own insistence regarding the embodiment and embeddedness of Dasein, but also threatens to re-inscribe the Western autonomous, unencumbered subject; a conclusion that ties her position, and so returns us, to that of Chanter.

A Heideggerian response to this line of critique would be to insist that it fails to properly note that the appeal to "neutrality" is based on a particular methodological manoeuvre that aims to allow Dasein to reveal itself; neutrality is not privileged in itself. Furthermore, Glazebrook's criticism appears to confuse "transcendent", meaning to escape the world, with "transcendental", describing the conditions that make possible an entity. Whereas Glazebrook correctly holds that to posit Dasein as neutral is to posit an existence that transcends its ontically gendered expression, she reads this moment of "transcendence" as entailing a "transcendent world" and so reintroduces a two-world metaphysics into Heidegger's schema that his notion of worldliness explicitly rejects. This conflation of "transcends" with "transcendent" is however not part of Heidegger's positing of a metaphysical neutrality.

Heidegger's fundamental ontology engages with the meaning of Being that makes possible (knowledge of) the Being of entities. Being transcends entities but is never transcendent to them; it is the transcendental condition for entities. As he explains, "[e]very disclosure of Being as the *transcendens* is *transcendental* knowledge".[71] Neutral Dasein is not transcendent to ontic being, in the same way that Being is not transcendent to ontic entities; it is bound to, but differentiated from, ontic being as the fundamental premise that permits an ontic analysis to take place. Because "the 'there' exists *before* we interpret ourselves in terms of gender, practices, biological characteristics, religious preferences, and ethnic features",[72] re-raising the question of the meaning of Being requires that ontic determinations are initially removed to permit the entity to reveal itself – and by extension Being – as it is rather than how we wish to see it.[73]

Chanter's second line of critique insists that besides the fact that "it always seems [that Heidegger has] decided in advance in favor of ontology and against the ontic level of experience, another problem is that it is geared almost exclusively to the world of work".[74] More specifically, she claims that his descriptions of Dasein's being-in-the-world are orientated towards "Dasein's involvement with objects and with others are oriented around the equipmental world, with the result that both the picture of Dasein that emerges and the *existentialia* that it yields are largely task oriented".[75] This, however, produces a very one-sided picture that

> either ignores what most would regard as important aspects of experience, for example, sexuality, eroticism, enjoyment, and pleasure, or, at best, treats them as only important as subordinate to Dasein's successful negotiation of its equipmental relations and its ultimate ontological task of clarifying the significance of such dealings.[76]

Chanter's conclusion is not only that Heidegger's account of Dasein is incomplete, but that in affirming the instrumental orientation of Dasein's existence or at least framing Dasein's activity from an instrumental logic he continues to affirm a fundamentally "masculine" perspective; one that fails to adequately conceive and take into account "feminine" characteristics of human existence such as sexuality, eroticism, and the body in its lived being.

The fundamental problem with this line of critique from a Heideggerian perspective is that it is premised on preconceptions regarding the characteristics of the sexes, as evidenced by Chanter's claims that "[t]ypically, women have been more associated with spatiality than temporality"[77] or "[i]n short, women are other-directed, and men are self-directed; women are context-bound, while men strive for objectivity and distance; women, in part because of their privileged relationship to child rearing, are caring and nurturing, while men are rational and abstract".[78] Nowhere is it shown why the sexes are associated with these terms; it is simply assumed and imposed onto Heidegger's analysis, which is then rejected because it does not conform to these preconceptions. For Heidegger, this is precisely the danger to be avoided; one that the positing of an originary neutrality forestalls because it means that we cannot simply presuppose a meaning for the sexes but must let them reveal themselves as they are.

Even if it is objected that Chanter is describing how the sexes have typically been thought in the history of Western philosophy and using that to show how Heidegger repeats those patriarchal conclusions, Heidegger would be able to respond that this misunderstands his intention in describing Dasein. Rather than focus on his ontic analysis of Dasein and show how these repeat well-worn patriarchal tropes, the whole point of his ontic descriptions is to show that they depend upon the way in which Being is understood. The determinations attributed to Dasein are not then taken to be fixed and ahistoric, but simply illustrative for the purposes of exposing the primary importance of the question of the meaning of Being, which, in any case, is a constant becoming and so cannot be described in one singular ahistoric manner.

Alternatively, Heidegger might respond that repeating conclusions derived from or found through the history of Western philosophy does not mean that he accepts all conclusions found therein. As he notes in his discussion of the notion of "destruction",[79] the history of Western philosophy cannot simply be abandoned but must be contended with to determine what is accurate in it and what is inaccurate. If, having posited the originary neutrality to allow Dasein to reveal itself as it is, Dasein reveals itself in ways found in the history of Western thought, we must accept them as true. From a Heideggerian perspective, however, Chanter is unable to do this because she starts her analysis from preconceptions about the sexes. While criticising Heidegger for implicitly perpetuating long-standing stereotypes, Heidegger would be able to respond that not only is she unable to account for her assumptions – he, of course, supposedly can; the phenomenological method reveals them as such – but it is actually Chanter who depends upon the logic of patriarchy to simply invert the privileged moment so that the "feminine" not the "masculine" is privileged. However, as he will later explain in the *Letter on Humanism*, "the reversal of a metaphysical statement remains a metaphysical statement".[80] In other words, Chanter's critique is premised on unaccounted, assumed designations of each sex and the mere inversion of a patriarchal logic that, as an inversion, leaves intact the logic of patriarchy that divides Being into two opposed sexes and privileges one over the other. In contrast, his affirmation of an originary neutrality not only provides a space to question long-standing assumptions about the sexes to determine whether they stand up to scrutiny, but, by insisting that any ontic determination is always subtended by the possibility inherent in the originary neutrality (itself derived from Being's becoming), he rejects the notion that the sexes can be described universally and criticises the binary logic that pits one against the other that underpins Chanter's critique.

Now, of course, Chanter might object that this is all well and good, but Heidegger does not do this, instead simply repeating the logic of patriarchy. In turn, Heidegger would likely point out that, even if true, faulty implication of the principle of neutrality does not negate the principle itself. Insisting that Dasein's ontic sexuality is not predetermined or foreclosed within oppositions or characteristics allows the affirmation of an originary neutrality to remain true to the fundamental methodological principle of Husserlian-inspired phenomenology, all the while offering the *possibility* that sexuality can take on a multiplicity of forms; it does not have to be divided between two sexes or even between masculine and feminine.

Chanter's third general criticism, however, holds that this only results because Heidegger continues to depend upon and affirm a conception of Dasein that is socially unencumbered. While she notes that he insists that Dasein is always "with" others to the extent that "Others thus have an existential privilege akin to Dasein that sets them apart from all other entities",[81] she nevertheless argues, as evidenced by his "concept of world; the distinction between authentic and inauthentic; the 'who' of Dasein; and the role that death plays in Heidegger's analysis",[82] that Heidegger continues to privilege Dasein's individuality over its sociality. Although Dasein lives with and in proximity to others, it is always in some way detached from them; a detachment that permits Dasein to choose itself. As a consequence, Chanter affirms "that Heidegger's account of Dasein remains more consonant with the disembodied transcendental subject that Heidegger claims Kant inherited from Descartes than Heidegger admits".[83] Heidegger therefore once more affirms a "masculine" stance wherein Dasein is always fundamentally detached from and so "against" the world, even as "it" is attached to that world. This confrontational relationship is contrary to the "feminine" one based on care, embeddedness, and "genuine" other-directedness.[84] Chanter's conclusion is that

> [w]hile maintaining that his analysis of Dasein is neutral with respect to sex, gender, race, and class, Heidegger in fact presents us with a picture of a very specific Dasein. Heidegger's Dasein is one who is largely untroubled by its bodily existence (except insofar as bodily needs are subordinated to goal-oriented ends, as in the for-the-sake-of-which), one who assumes the priority of self over other, and one for whom spatiality is subordinated to temporal ordering. Is it accidental that all these facets of Dasein's existence articulate traditionally masculine characteristics?[85]

On Chanter's reading, therefore, the logic of Heidegger's argument regarding the importance of Dasein's originary neutrality does not open up thinking on sexuality; it subtly but definitively closes and restricts it to a particular conception of sexuality that affirms and re-enforces long-standing Western sexual stereotypes. That this privileging is *implicit* in his position makes it all the more dangerous; it is far more difficult to identify and so combat.

The problem, however, is, as Chanter recognises, that Heidegger explicitly addresses this interpretation, and while he agrees that the notion of a neutral Dasein implies a "peculiar isolation",[86] he rejects the suggestion that this implies "the egocentric individual, the ontic isolated individual".[87] Rather than describing an ontic form of neutral isolation or egocentric foundation akin to that offered and defended by modern Cartesian philosophy, it must be thought of as the initial "*metaphysical isolation* of the human being".[88] Heidegger will come to criticise the notion of "metaphysics",[89] but here it is used to indicate a "place" between an ontological and ontic analysis, in so far as it is posited to explain the Being of Dasein "prior" to its manifestation in ontic facticity. In other words, when Heidegger talks of "neutrality", he means it in a very specific, technical sense that is used to explain the process of ontic determination; it is not valued in itself. More specifically, the positing of an originary neutrality has *methodological* importance, in so far as it permits an enquiry into Dasein and by extension Being distinct from preconceptions regarding Dasein; it also has *philosophical* importance for Heidegger, in so far as it ties into his affirmation that "[h]igher than actuality stands *possibility*".[90] As pure flux, Being (and all its manifestations, Dasein included) is/are nothing other than pure becoming. If its ontological flux were shaped from ontic considerations, such as sexuality, the becoming of Dasein would be constrained within the parameters of that ontic description, thereby undermining the pure open-ended possibility that defines Being. Dasein's ontological neutrality is therefore necessary to secure the ontological difference and the possibility that lies at the heart of Heidegger's conflation of Being and time. It is from this ontological neutrality that ontic sexuality springs and must be thought, albeit in ways that are not predetermined or constrained.

Conclusion

We see then that Heidegger's account both undermines any notion of an innate ontological sexuality and reveals that ontic sexuality is never constrained or (pre)determined. Furthermore, the affirmation of an originary neutrality maintains that sexuality is not ontologically fundamental to Dasein; it is only ever of the ontic order, with this arising from an autopoietic process that is never structured around a definitive division, but is fluid, historical, multifaceted, and defined by open-ended possibilities. With this, Heidegger, in agreement with Freud, rejects the notion of a fixed determination to sexuality, but claims, contra Freud, that this is not due to the continuing influence of an originary bisexuality but to an originary ontological indeterminateness that results from Being's temporality.

From the perspective of those looking for an immediate empirical enquiry of sexual inequality or patriarchy, his ontological analysis will, no doubt, appear "far too vacuous and abstract to serve the needs of any radical world-renewing project".[91] But, as I have argued, Heidegger's questioning of sexuality is not premised on an immediate political engagement; prior to that, he insists that we have to step back and ensure that we understand what it is that we are discussing. He thinks that this "pausing" will allow the entity to reveal itself as it is, meaning that we will be less likely to misinterpret it and so act towards it in ways that are contrary to what it "is". Rather than leading to empty abstractions, the benefit of this approach is that instead of simply affirming a particular conception of sexuality, it actually asks us to think about what sexuality means. This is only possible however because Heidegger insists on the fundamental importance of the ontological difference. By bracketing everyday and/or long-standing presuppositions to ask about the Being of the entity, he provides a space and means from and through which to rethink long-held positions, including those that have historically conditioned thinking on sexuality, all the while insisting that any ontic (sexual) determinations identified must be constantly re-engaged to take into consideration the ontological change subtending it.

The disadvantage of his approach, one that very quickly became apparent in subsequent evaluations of his thinking on the topic, is that it requires that we enter into and accept Heidegger's framework and way of thinking and indeed think with him to "fill in the blanks". In short, Heidegger's discussion of sexuality is premised on and from his privileging of the question of the meaning of Being. As a consequence, it is primarily interested in clarifying the relationship between sexual ontic determinations and the temporal flux of Being, showing that the former does not undermine and indeed must be thought from the latter. While this ties into and affirms Heidegger's insistence that entities are never fixed and determined but must be thought from Being's becoming and so constantly engaged with to "capture" their changing configurations, subsequent phenomenological thought insisted that it was not necessary or, indeed, desirable to downgrade ontic descriptions for ontological analyses. Rather than turn away from ontic being to focus on the "abstraction" of the question of the meaning of Being – a topic that Heidegger never managed to satisfactorily resolve – and think sexuality from and in relation to that question, subsequent phenomenologists claimed that revealing the "truth" of facticity required and was simply a matter of refocusing the enquiry on factical being "itself". Only this would fulfil the phenomenological mantra of returning to "things themselves" to let them reveal themselves as they are. For this reason, Maurice Merleau-Ponty focuses on the ways in which sexuality is tied to and expressed through the lived concrete body.

Notes

1. Good overviews of this issue are found in Dagfinn Føllesdal, "Husserl's Reductions and the Role they Play in his Phenomenology", in *A Companion to Phenomenology and Existentialism*, edited by Hubert L. Dreyfus and Mark A. Wrathall (Oxford: Wiley-Blackwell, 2006), pp. 105–113; Sebastian Luft, "Husserl's Theory of the Phenomenological Reduction: Between LifeWorld and Cartesianism", *Research in Phenomenology*, vol. 34, n. 1, 2004, pp. 198–234; Dan Zahavi, *Husserl's Phenomenology* (Stanford, CA: Stanford University Press, 2003), pp. 43–78.
2. Edmund Husserl, *Ideas Pertaining to a Pure Phenomenology and to a Phenomenological Philosophy, First Book*, trans. F. Kersten (Dordrecht: Kluwer, 1983), pp. 56–62.
3. Ibid., p. 51.
4. Ibid., p. 57.
5. Ibid., p. 61.
6. Ibid., p. 61.
7. Edmund Husserl, *Logical Investigations: Volume One*, trans. J. N. Findlay (Abingdon: Routledge, 2001), p. 168.
8. Martin Heidegger, *Being and Time*, trans. John Macquarrie and Edward Robinson (Oxford: Blackwell, 1962).
9. Matheson Russell, "Phenomenological Reduction in Heidegger's *Sein Und Zeit*: A New Proposal", *Journal of the British Society for Phenomenology*, vol. 39, n. 3, 2008, pp. 229–248.
10. Jacques Derrida, "*Geschlecht* I: Sexual Difference, Ontological Difference", trans. Ruben Bevezdivin and Elizabeth Rottenberg, in *Psyche: Inventions of the Other, volume 2*, edited by Peggy Kamuf and Elizabeth Rottenberg (Stanford, CA: Stanford University Press, 2008), pp. 7–26.
11. Jean-Paul Sartre, *Being and Nothingness: An Essay on Phenomenological Ontology*, trans. Sarah Richmond (Abingdon: Routledge, 2018), p. 506.
12. Patricia Huntingdon, "Introduction I – General Background History of the Feminist Reception of Heidegger and a Guide to Heidegger's Thought", in *Feminist Interpretations of Martin Heidegger*, edited by Nancy J. Holland and Patricia Huntington (University Park, PA: Pennsylvania State University Press, 2001), pp. 1–42.

13. Trish Glazebrook, "Heidegger and Ecofeminism", in *Feminist Interpretations of Martin Heidegger*, edited by Nancy J. Holland and Patricia Huntington (University Park, PA: Pennsylvania State University Press, 2001), pp. 221–251; Jean McConnell Graybeal, *Language and 'the Feminine' in Nietzsche and Heidegger* (Bloomington, IN: Indiana University Press, 1990); Patricia Huntington, *Ecstatic Subjects, Utopia, and Recognition: Kristeva, Heidegger, Irigaray* (Albany, NY: State University of New York Press, 1998).
14. For a discussion of Heidegger's critique of instrumental rationality, see Gavin Rae, "Being and Technology: Heidegger on the Overcoming of Metaphysics", *Journal of the British Society for Phenomenology*, vol. 43, n. 3, 2012, pp. 305–325.
15. Tina Chanter, "The Problematic Normative Assumptions of Heidegger's Ontology", in *Feminist Interpretations of Martin Heidegger*, edited by Nancy J. Holland and Patricia Huntington (University Park, PA: Pennsylvania State University Press, 2001), pp. 73–108.
16. S. L. Bartky, "Originative Thinking in the Later Philosophy of Heidegger", *Philosophy and Phenomenological Review*, vol. 30, n. 3, 1970, pp. 368–381; Glazebrook, "Heidegger and Ecofeminism", p. 233.
17. Jesus Adrian Escudero, "Heidegger and the Hermeneutics of the Body", *International Journal of Gender and Women's Studies*, vol. 3, n. 1, 2015, pp. 16–25 (p. 20).
18. Heidegger, *Being and Time*, p. 1.
19. Ibid., p. 26.
20. Ibid., p. 1.
21. Ibid., p. 23.
22. Ibid., p. 62.
23. Ibid., p. 29.
24. Ibid., p. 23.
25. Ibid., p. 23.
26. Ibid., p. 31.
27. Ibid., p. 31.
28. Ibid., p. 34.
29. For a discussion of this, see Gavin Rae, "Overcoming Philosophy: Heidegger on the Destruction of Metaphysics and the Transformation to Thinking", *Human Studies*, vol. 36, n. 2, 2013, pp. 235–257.
30. Heidegger, *Being and Time*, p. 26.
31. Ibid., p. 32.
32. Ibid., p. 27.
33. Ibid., p. 33. In the later *Letter on Humanism* (trans. Frank A. Capuzzi in collaboration with J. Glenn Gray, in *Basic Writings*, edited by David Farrell-Krell [London: Harper Perennial, 1977], pp. 217–266), Heidegger undertakes a self-critique that brings him to abandon the notion of "existence", for two principle reasons: (1) To distinguish his thinking from Sartrean existentialism, which, according to Heidegger, is founded on the human subject and so simply continues the anthropocentric logic of Western metaphysics (p. 232); and (2) The term "existence" has historically been opposed to "essence", with the consequence that his

earlier discussion of "Dasein's existence" ties his thinking to the logic of binary oppositions, inherent in Western metaphysics. To overcome this, Heidegger talks of "ek-sistence" (p. 230), which for etymological reasons he takes to better signify the way in which Dasein stands out from Being.

34. Heidegger, *Being and Time*, pp. 312–315.
35. Ibid., p. 58.
36. Ibid., p. 59.
37. Ibid., p. 32.
38. Ibid., p. 73.
39. Ibid., pp. 36–37.
40. Ibid., p. 84.
41. Ibid., pp. 71–75.
42. Martin Heidegger, *Zollikon Seminars: Protocols–Conversations–Letters*, edited by Medard Boss, trans. Franz Mayr and Richard Askay (Evanston, IL: Northwestern University Press, 2001).
43. Sartre, *Being and Nothingness*, p. 506.
44. Heidegger, *The Metaphysical Foundations of Logic*, p. 136.
45. Ibid., p. 136.
46. Ibid., p. 136.
47. Ibid., p. 136.
48. Ibid., pp. 136–137.
49. Ibid., p. 137.
50. Ibid., p. 137.
51. Ibid., p. 137.
52. Ibid., p. 137.
53. Ibid., p. 137.
54. Ibid., p. 137.
55. Ibid., p. 137.
56. Ibid., p. 138.
57. Ibid., p. 138.
58. Ibid., p. 139.
59. Heidegger, *Being and Time*, p. 157.
60. Good recent discussions are found in Irene McMullin, *Time and the Shared World: Heidegger on Social Relations* (Evanston, IL: Northwestern University Press, 2013), and Antonio Gómez Ramos, "Hegel's Ethical Life and Heidegger's They: How Political is the Self?", in *Subjectivity and the Political: Contemporary Perspectives*, edited by Gavin Rae and Emma Ingala (Abingdon: Routledge, 2018), pp. 197–219.
61. Heidegger, *The Metaphysical Foundations of Logic*, p. 139.
62. Ibid., p. 139.
63. Ibid., p. 139.
64. Chanter, "The Problematic Normative Assumptions of Heidegger's Ontology", pp. 73–74.
65. Ibid., p. 74.

66. Ibid., p. 74.
67. Ibid., p. 74.
68. Ibid., p. 74.
69. Glazebrook, "Heidegger and Ecofeminism", p. 233.
70. Ibid., p. 233.
71. Heidegger, *Being and Time*, p. 62.
72. Escudero, "Heidegger and the Hermeneutics of the Body", p. 21.
73. Heidegger, *Being and Time*, p. 58.
74. Chanter, "The Problematic Normative Assumptions of Heidegger's Ontology", p. 82.
75. Ibid., p. 82.
76. Ibid., p. 82.
77. Ibid., p. 98.
78. Ibid., p. 88.
79. Heidegger, *Being and Time*, p. 44.
80. Heidegger, *Letter on Humanism*, p. 232.
81. Chanter, "The Problematic Normative Assumptions of Heidegger's Ontology", p. 89.
82. Ibid., p. 90.
83. Ibid., p. 80.
84. Ibid., p. 89.
85. Ibid., p. 98.
86. Heidegger, *The Metaphysical Foundations of Logic*, p. 137.
87. Ibid., p. 137.
88. Ibid., p. 137.
89. For example, in the *Letter on Humanism*, from 1947, Heidegger criticises "metaphysics" because it denotes a mode of thinking that (1) is based on and enclosed within a prior assumed conception of Being (p. 226), (2) takes certain truths to be self-evident (p. 225), and (3) is trapped within a logic of binary oppositions (p. 232). For an extended discussion of this text and issue, see Gavin Rae, *Ontology in Heidegger and Deleuze* (Basingstoke: Palgrave Macmillan, 2014).
90. Heidegger, *Being and Time*, p. 63.
91. Bartky, "Originative Thinking in the Later Philosophy of Heidegger", p. 369.

CHAPTER 3

Merleau-Ponty on the Sexed Body

In the hands of its most famous German proponents, Husserlian-inspired phenomenology had an ambiguous relationship to sexuality, in so far as it was either promised as the topic of a future, never completed, study (Husserl),[1] or dealt with in a rather perfunctory way in an obscure lecture course not published until fifty years later (Heidegger). However, once phenomenology was transposed to France in the 1930s and early 1940s, there was an almost immediately explosion in phenomenological interest in sexuality. For example, in *Being and Nothingness*, published in 1943, Jean-Paul Sartre laments the lack of focus on sexuality in Heidegger's *Being and Time* before producing an analysis of love and sexual desire that points to the conflict inherent in those relationships.[2] On the other hand, in the 1946 essay *Time and the Other*, Emmanuel Levinas focuses not on conflict but "th[e] mystery of the feminine"[3] that "bears alterity as an essence"[4] and that forever escapes cognition; a notion that he ties to a wider ethical point regarding the absolute alterity of the other more generally. It is, however, Maurice Merleau-Ponty's *Phenomenology of Perception*, published in 1945, that produces the most extended and sophisticated analysis of the "body in its sexual being".[5]

Importantly, this analysis had a marked impact on Sartre's partner Simone de Beauvoir who recognised that it "presented a viable alternative to Sartre's 'phenomenological ontology' troubled by the problems of solipsism and dualism"[6] and, in so doing, brought Merleau-Ponty's thought into later feminist debates on sexuality. This is not to say that his influence has been welcomed or universally approved. As Elizabeth Grosz points out, "[i]t takes only the slightest shift in perspective to see Merleau-Ponty writings as either profoundly, if unconsciously, misogynist through neutralization ... or as profoundly and unusually useful for feminist purposes".[7] So, whereas de Beauvoir affirms aspects of Merleau-Ponty's analysis, in particular the idea that "man is not a natural species: he is a historical idea",[8] to explain that "[w]oman is not a fixed reality, but rather a becoming; she has to be compared to with man in her becoming, that is her *possibilities* have to be defined"[9] – an intellectual debt supported by a number of recent feminist writers[10] – other feminists have rejected this, claiming that his affirmation of an original sexual neutrality (1) masks a particular masculine normative perspective that downplays or rejects femininity,[11] and/or (2) is "surprisingly rudimentary in that [it] hardly mention[s] the question of sexual difference or consider[s] the gendered body as a significant phenomenological example in itself".[12]

Taking these criticisms in turn, I will argue that, with regards to (1), while Merleau-Ponty does indeed write in the masculine tense and affirms an originary neutrality to the schemas that structure the body, this does not necessarily introduce a masculine perspective that downgrades femininity. Rather, it reveals Merleau-Ponty's commitment to Husserlian phenomenology and, in particular, Husserl's notion of the "phenomenological reduction",[13] which, as noted in the previous chapter, insists on the need to adopt a particular cognitive standpoint that brackets everyday assumptions prior to undertaking an enquiry. This movement is necessary to overcome the presuppositions of the natural attitude to permit the transcendental essence of the object to be revealed. Whereas Husserl offers this as a methodological principle of his transcendental phenomenology, following Joel Smith,[14] I argue that Merleua-Ponty takes off from Heidegger's insistence that the reduction must focus on "being-in-the-world" and maintains that, rather than simply starting with pre-established notions of factic sexual determinations/differences, we have to suspend judgements about the categories or "nature" of concrete beings.[15] Only this will allow those beings to reveal themselves as they are, rather than as we wish them to be or have been conditioned to think of them.

As a consequence, while (2) rejects Merleau-Ponty's position because it does not engage with the sexual difference, I argue that this fails to appreciate that he is making the far more radical claim that, rather than start the enquiry with the binary opposition constitutive of the sexual difference (masculinity versus femininity), we have to distinguish between the bodily schemas that condition factic determinations and those determinations themselves to first enquire into the former (by which Merleau-Ponty means the style of the pre-reflective lived fluid body) before moving to the latter. For Merleau-Ponty, if we are to understand the relationship between embodiment and sexuality "free" of reflective impositions regarding what sexuality is or should be, we cannot simply start from presupposed factic (sexual) determinations – doing so risks essentialising those ontic determinations – but must start from the anonymous bodily schemas that are the condition of and manifested through specific factic sexual determinations.

Having clarified the purpose and role of neutrality in Merleau-Ponty's account, I critically engage with the claim that the resultant analysis is problematic because by tying the sexual schema to existence, Merleau-Ponty is unable to provide an individual analytic of "sexuality" *per se*.[16] Correcting this requires, so it is argued, that we move from a logic of entwinement, where sexuality and existence are mutually constituting, to a foundational logic (expressed through a binary opposition) where sexuality and existence are opposed to one another with one grounding the other. However, whereas this critique maintains that we must look for a single ground and conceive of "objects" as monads capable of individual analysis, I argue that Merleau-Ponty aims to undermine those assumptions by challenging us to rethink the role that sexuality plays in existence from a logic of entwinement whereby sexuality is understood to be a particular ineffable style manifested throughout each individual's embodied, embedded existence; a rethinking that, instead of sterilising sexuality in the name of definite clearcut analytical certainties, recognises, accepts, and engages with the ambiguities and paradoxes of actual concrete (sexual) existence. Indeed, in so doing, Merleau-Ponty lays the theoretical foundations for subsequent queer and trans* theories.

To outline this, the first section provides a brief overview of Merleau-Ponty's project by situating its emphasis on embodiment in contrast to the dominance of Descartes's cogito argument, before going on to outline Merleau-Ponty's understanding of the relationship between embodiment and sexuality. Section two defends Merleau-Ponty against the claim that his analysis of sexuality masks a number of patriarchal and normative assumptions, while section three discusses the relationship between sexuality and existence to engage with the argument that affirming the entwinement of both prevents an analysis of the former. The conclusion brings together the various strands of the argument to demonstrate the continuing relevance of Merleau-Ponty's analysis of sexuality.

Merleau-Ponty on the Sexed Body

Merleau-Ponty's *Phenomenology of Perception* is orientated, generally speaking, against a certain idealism derived from the privileging of the cogito argument in Descartes's second meditation, which Merleau-Ponty holds to have had a malignant influence on subsequent Western thought. While Descartes's outlines his methodological scepticism in the first meditation including the problematic implications it has for knowledge derived from the senses in so far as he recognises that because the senses have previously deceived him they cannot be the ground for epistemic certainty,[17] the second meditation goes on to question whether there is, as a consequence, anything that can be known with certainty. The breakthrough comes when he recognises that the method of doubt provides this, in so far as to doubt requires a being that thinks, which requires a being that exists. From the activity of doubting (= thinking), the enquirer can therefore be sure that he exists.[18] This will subsequently be complicated in the fifth meditation, where it is recognised that the cogito's foundational status depends upon the existence of God,[19] but the lesson of the second meditation establishes a binary opposition between a privileged mind and downgraded body which conditions much subsequent philosophy.

Merleau-Ponty's *Phenomenology of Perception* challenges the fundamental tenets of Descartes's argument, both in relation to the privileging of the mind over the body and, indeed, the binary mind/body opposition it depends upon.[20] In *Signs*, Merleau-Ponty places this task within a larger trend within contemporary (for him) philosophy:

> Our century has wiped out the dividing line between 'body' and 'mind,' and sees human life as through and through mental and corporeal, always based upon the body and always (even in its most carnal modes) interested in relationships between persons. For many thinkers at the close of nineteenth century, the body was a bit of matter, a network of mechanisms. The twentieth century has restored and deepened the notion of flesh, that is, of animate body.[21]

Contributing substantially to this trend, Merleau-Ponty insists that we must move away from tying knowledge to a non-corporeal mind to recognise that knowledge is resultant of a socially embedded living body. There is a substantial secondary literature on Merleau-Ponty's account of the body,[22] but the key aspect of it for current purposes is the discussion of the relationship between sexuality and the body in the chapter "The Body in its Sexual Being".[23] Due to space constraints, I will focus on his analysis of (1) the case of Schneider, and (2) the relationship between sexuality and existence.

Merleau-Ponty starts the chapter on the sexed body by restating that the general aim of his enquiry is "to elucidate the primary function whereby we bring into existence, for ourselves, or take a hold upon, space, the object or the instrument, and to describe the body as the place where this appropriation takes place".[24] He notes that there are two problems or approaches that must be avoided, a division which mirrors the discussion in the opening chapters of *Phenomenology of Perception*, where Merleau-Ponty warns about the dangers of "empiricism", namely that there is a privileging of an objective world of non-qualitative sensation, and "intellectualism" wherein the mind intentionally projects meaning onto an object. The basic problem with each is that, while they privilege a distinct aspect, they both depend upon a foundational atomism that is unable to appreciate or account for the "organic" whole. In short, they are guilty of reading the results of perception (the individual objects of the world) back into perpetual experience *per se* to hold that perceptual experience is composed of and conditioned by atomistic objects that perfectly present themselves. This, however, falsifies perception's *actual* structure, which is defined by "a *phenomenal field*"[25] that entails a constantly altering non-totalised "organic" whole full of ambiguities and indeterminacies that make possible the objective divisions of perception.

Rather than that which appears to perception, Taylor Carmen notes that "the phenomenal field is for Merleau-Ponty a *transcendental* condition of the possibility of our being perceptually open to the world at all".[26] Therefore, if the failures of empiricism and intellectualism are to be avoided, the body must be thought, not as a discrete entity, but as and through its phenomenal field. However, if the phenomenal field is both the genesis of perception and that which eludes objective perception, we have to find another "lens" through which to engage it. For this reason, Merleau-Ponty explains that "[i]f we want then to bring to light the birth of being for us, we must finally look at that area of our experience which clearly has significance and reality only for us, and that is our affective life";[27] through this move, the question of sexuality enters the scene.

Merleau-Ponty notes that "[o]rdinarily affectivity is conceived as a mosaic of affective states, of pleasures and pains each sealed within itself, mutually incomprehensible, and explicable only in terms of the bodily system".[28] This ordinary explanation means, however, that if we are to understand affective bodily sensations, we are implicitly committed to the notion that "emotional life is 'shot through with intelligence'".[29] Specifically, there must be a simple correspondence between (mental) representation and natural stimuli (that gives rise to pleasure or pain). While such a connection permits affectivity to be represented, it means that affectivity is reduced to (mental) representation and so "is not recognized as a distinctive form of consciousness".[30] Merleua-Ponty notes that "[i]f this conception were correct, any sexual incapacity ought to amount either to the loss of certain representations or else to a weakening of the capacity for satisfaction".[31] However, as he dryly notes, "this is not the case".[32]

To show why, Merleau-Ponty turns to the case of Schneider who was injured during the First World War by a shell splinter to the back of his head. From the middle of the war onwards, he was treated by the neurologist Kurt

Goldstein and the gestalt psychologist Adhémar Gelb at the Hospital for Brain Injury in Frankfurt, which was created by the former to rehabilitate soldiers who had received brain injuries. Schneider was important because, as Merleau-Ponty explains, he

> no longer [sought] sexual intercourse of his own accord. Obscene pictures, conversations on sexual topics, the sight of a body do not arouse desire in him. The patient hardly ever kisses, and the kiss for him has no value as sexual stimulation. Reactions are strictly local and do not begin to occur without contact. If the prelude is interrupted at this stage, there is no attempt to pursue the sexual cycle. In the sexual act intromission is never spontaneous. If orgasm occurs first in the partner and she moves away, the half-fulfilled desire vanishes. At every stage it is as if the subject did not know what is to be done. There are no active movements, save a few seconds before the orgasm which is extremely brief. Noctural emissions are rare and never accompanied by dreams.[33]

Merleau-Ponty considers "why in Schneider's case touch stimulation, and not only visual perception, has lost much of its sexual significance".[34] His point is that, simply holding that sexuality is tied to representation, which, when lacking, leads to sexual incapacity, is too general to reveal which representations have been lost and why. "[T]he problem still remains of describing the concrete aspect assumed by this wholly formal deficiency in the realm of sexuality".[35] In response, Merleau-Ponty thinks that Schneider's lack of sexual stimulation is not the consequence of inadequate representation of a stimulus. It is not the case that Schneider fails to get sexually excited because he does not represent something sufficiently well, but that he is not aroused and so does not represent the sexual object. The question is not then why he lacks adequate mental representation, but why he is not capable of arousal; an issue that Merleau-Ponty claims points to a far more radical "change in the character of sexual life itself".[36]

He goes on to question whether this change is simply a consequence of physical impairment; "after all Schneider's troubles spring from a wound of limited extent in the occipital region".[37] The problem with this understanding is, so Merleau-Ponty contends, that such an injury would not necessarily lead to the deterioration of the sexual function. Quite the contrary, "[i]f sexuality in man were an autonomous reflex apparatus, if the object of sexual desire affected some organ of pleasurable sensation anatomically defined, then the effect of the cerebral injury would be to free these automatic responses and take the form of accentuated sexual behavior".[38] In other words, if sexuality were located in single autonomous reflex, damage to that reflex would not necessarily obliterate it; it might merely alter its functioning.

Having rejected representational and physical accounts of sexuality, Merleau-Ponty suggests that "[p]athology brings to light, somewhere between automatic response and representation, a vital zone in which the sexual possibilities of the patient are elaborated".[39] As such, he contends that

> [t]here must be, immanent in sexual life, some function which ensures its emergence, and the normal extension of sexuality must rest on internal powers of the organic subject. There must be an Eros or a Libido which breathes life into an original world, gives sexual value or meaning to external stimuli and outlines for each subject the use he shall make of his objective body.[40]

Shannon Sullivan[41] criticises this by claiming that it subtly reintroduces an essence/culture division, wherein an essential "neutral" body is overlaid with a culturally determined sexuality, but it seems that Merleau-Ponty is actually proposing something more akin to a vitalist immanently genetic account of sexuality. Rather than being grounded in an ahistoric "blank" essence that is over-coded with cultural meaning, Merleau-Ponty holds that sexuality arises immanently to and from the becoming inherent in the individual's living body. Instead of being grounded in a natural stimuli or mental representation, Merleau-Ponty challenges the logical foundationalism upon which such explanations depend to, instead, affirm a logic of (immanent) expressionism: the lived body expresses itself spontaneously and simultaneously in different ways. These manifestations are, however, dependent upon different, but intertwined, bodily schemas, which are the non-objective conditions of factic existence. From this premise, Merleau-Ponty posits that it is the schema through which sexuality is expressed that "has undergone change in Schneider".[42]

Merleau-Ponty explains that "[i]n the case of a normal subject . . . the visible body is subtended by a sexual schema, which is strictly individual, emphasizing the erogeneous areas, outlining a sexual physiognomy, and eliciting the gestures of the masculine body which is itself integrated into this emotional totality".[43] The sexual schema describes the sexual aspect of the body. It is not transcendent to the body, but that which conditions the sexual expression of each individual. Rather than objective, the sexual schema is always particular and delineates something akin to the ineffable style of the body as this is manifested sexually.

Normally, the sexual schema is defined by a particular emotional totality manifested in physical stimulus orientated towards another body. Merleau-Ponty points out however that the problem with Schneider is that, for him, "a woman's body has no particular essence: it is, he says, pre-eminently character which makes a woman attractive, for physically they are all the same".[44] He is not then attracted to the object, with the consequence that "close contact causes only a 'vague feeling,' the knowledge of 'an indeterminate something' which is never enough to 'spark off' sexual behavior and create a situation which require a definite mode of resolution".[45] "What has disappeared from the patient is his power of projecting before himself a sexual world, of putting himself in an erotic situation, or, once such a situation is stumbled upon, of maintaining it or following it through to complete satisfaction."[46]

Crucially, however, Schneider's lack of sexual projection is not a mental activity; "absent mindedness and inappropriate representations are not causes but effects, and in so far as the subject coolly perceives the situation, it is in the first place because he does not live it and is not caught up in it".[47] This calls forth a distinction between two modes of perception: "objective perception",[48] which describes the intentional perception of distinct objects, and "erotic perception",[49] which "is not a *cogitatio* which aims at a *cogitatum*; through one body it aims at another body, and takes place in the world, not in a consciousness".[50] Erotic perception is "not of the order of the understanding, since understanding subsumes an experience, once perceived, under some idea, while desire comprehends blindly by linking body to body".[51] As such,

> [a] sight has significance for me, not when I consider, even confusedly, its possible relationship to the sexual organs or to pleasurable states, but when it exists for my body, for that power always available for bringing together into an erotic situation the stimuli applied, and adapting sexual conduct to it.[52]

Sexuality is not then an objective intentionality orientated around and intended towards a static object, but it is a spontaneous (erotic) upsurge of the body towards another body, itself "experienced" as living rather than inert. The problem is that "Schneider can no longer put himself into a sexual situation any more than generally he occupies an affective or an ideological one".[53] He has lost erotic perception, instead being confined to the emotional neutrality of objective perception, with the consequence that his sexuality is not based on an organic, spontaneous bond with another body but "from a decision made in the abstract".[54] Again, this reliance on abstract decision-making is not because of an objective decision, but because his sexual schema – the way his body spontaneously expresses itself sexually – has been so damaged as to make "organic" erotic perception and, by extension, bodily comportment impossible.

From this, Merleau-Ponty draws a number of conclusions regarding sexuality. First, it is defined by a sexual schema that spontaneously shapes, defines, and conditions the expression of an individual's sexual existence. Second, the sexual schema "is a dimension [of the body] that involves the personal being as a whole, rather than being limited to genitality".[55] It is akin to the style through which the individual expresses himself, with this style being expressed in minute ways of bodily comportment. "Thus sexuality is not an autonomous cycle. It has internal links with the whole active and cognitive being, these three sectors of behavior displaying but a single typical structure, and standing in a relationship to each other of reciprocal expression."[56] Importantly, third, these behaviours are not under volitional control; they occur "prior" to volition as its condition. Because the sexual schema is the fundamental, organic aspect of an individual's being that occurs prior to all forms of volition and objective perception, it is, as Helena de Preester points out, "co-extensive with life".[57]

Patriarchy, Heteronormativity, and the Sexual Schema

I will return to the connection between sexuality and life, but, before doing so, it will be helpful to pause to engage with certain recurrent criticisms of Merleau-Ponty's analysis of the Schneider case to not only clarify his theory but also situate it within contemporary debates. Specifically, two different but ultimately related criticisms have been aimed at Merleau-Ponty's analysis and, by extension, the notion of sexual schema that it points to; namely that it (1) masks a particular masculine normative perspective that downplays or rejects femininity[58] and/or (2) is unable to take into consideration the sexual difference.[59]

Judith Butler, for example, claims that, by assuming that Schneider must desire a women, manifested through terminology regarding what is "normal", Merleau-Ponty depends upon and imposes a particular heteronormative masculine sexuality that "is characterized by a disembodied gaze that subsequently defines its object as mere body".[60] This fragments the female body, turns the masculine subject into "a strangely disembodied voyeur whose sexuality is strangely non-corporeal",[61] and "manages to reify cultural relations between the sexes".[62] In relation to Merleau-Ponty's claim that Schneider is abnormal because he is unable to get aroused by pictures of women, Butler not only notes that this depends upon "the presumption that the decontextualized female body, the body alluded to in conversation, the anonymous body which passes by on the street, exudes a natural attraction",[63] but also wonders "what kind of cultural presumptions would make arousal in such contexts seem utterly normal".[64] Far from describing sexuality *per se*, Merleau-Ponty's analysis is conditioned by a range of "tacit normative assumptions about the heterosexual character of sexuality".[65]

Butler's reading has, however, been challenged. Anna Foultier, for example, objects that "the assumption of Schneider's heterosexuality is not the consequence of a general norm about sexuality, as Butler believes, but of certain known facts about the patient".[66] As a consequence, "the standard of normality that is presupposed in the account of Schneider's sexuality is not 'normal male sexuality' and even less 'normal human sexuality,' but rather a healthy Schneider, as he was before his injury, and as he still sometimes would like to be".[67] Rather than impose a heteronormative schema onto Schneider's case, Merleau-Ponty simply uses Schneider's heterosexual desire prior to his injury as the standard against which his post-injury sexual desire is judged. From the normalcy of his prior sexual desire, his altered sexual behaviour is abnormal. Instead of imposing a heteronormative schema onto Schneider that is then reified to define a "normal" cultural norm, Merleau-Ponty describes the alterations that have taken place to Schneider's particular sexual schema.

However, that Foultier defends Merleau-Ponty against Butler's heteronormative charge does not mean that she accepts his theory in its entirety. Based on the claim that Merleau-Ponty's affirmation of a sexual schema points to a dimension of the body that is abstract prior to being individuated into a particular sexuality, Foultier maintains that his analysis points to a neutral or anonymous aspect of the body that is subsequently over-coded with sexual meaning. For this reason, Foultier concludes that Merleau-Ponty's analysis is "surprisingly rudimentary in that [it] hardly mention[s] the question of sexual difference or consider[s] the gendered body as a significant phenomenological example in itself";[68] a point echoed by Iris Young's insistence that Merleau-Ponty's analysis is too general to consider the "particular style of bodily comportment which is typical of feminine existence".[69]

This criticism is a long-standing one within a certain feminist reception of Merleau-Ponty's thinking and is based on, at least, two premises: by appealing to an anonymous bodily schema to question sexuality, Merleau-Ponty (1) removes the sexual differences that truly define concrete embodied beings; and (2) depends upon and re-enforces a particular masculine analysis that is unable to think the specificity of the female body. The problem, however, is that it is unclear that either premise applies to Merleau-Ponty.

Sonia Kruks, for example, argues that these premises and the argument that they support are based on a particularly reductionist reading of the *Phenomenology of Perception* that focuses on the early chapters alone. This hermeneutical strategy therefore fails to appreciate that the text actually develops a particular narrative wherein "an account of discrete bodies and individual perceptions of things"[70] is gradually supplemented by "an account of social relations as ones of complex interdependence that may involve both connectedness and conflict".[71] Rather than a linear movement, the latter must be read back into the former. As such, "culture, language, politics, and history are shown always and already to imbue the body-subject, and even the simplest and apparently most isolated acts of perception are, Merleau-Ponty demonstrates, inherently social".[72] It is not then the case that Merleau-Ponty affirms a neutral body that is over-coded with meaning; the feminist critique is based on a reductionist reading that fails to recognise and do justice to the complexity of his analysis.

As a consequence, Johanna Oksala explains that whereas his critics maintain that Merleau-Ponty establishes and depends upon a foundational "neutral" body that is subsequently situated and given meaning historically, "his understanding of the body-subject is open to a second reading that is more in line with Butler's insights about the historical constitution of the body".[73] On this alternative reading, "transcendental subjectivity – language, tradition, and community – is understood as the reality-constituting principle providing the conditions of possibility for all forms of subjectivity as well as objective reality".[74] Rather than being added to a foundational layer, Oksala explains that Merleau-Ponty's appeal to "anonymous" bodily schemas aims to identify, not "a foundation, but a constitutive condition: a dimension of sense constitution".[75] Importantly, this must not be understood to entail "ahistorical or universal forms, but as dynamic and developing structures derived from our cultural environment, constantly in a state of changing".[76] According to Oksala, instead of developing an account of a monadic subject who comes to interact and develop socially, Merleau-Ponty points to an analysis of subjectivity that is inherently intersubjective.[77] As a consequence, the body, for Merleau-Ponty, is not structured around a founding–founded structure; it is orientated around an immanent process of social constitution. For this reason, it is not possible to start with sexual differences as if they existed "prior" to the body's social constitution, but neither is it possible to simply deny the differences that are part and parcel of the society through which the body becomes. The body and its sexual expression must be understood as an immanent and ongoing manifestation of the differences inherent in and learned through its process of social constitution.

From this, Sylvia Stoller explains that those who insist on "placing 'differences' at the beginning . . . take for granted without philosophically reflecting upon the conditions of their existence. In taking them for granted [they] see no necessity to call them into question."[78] In contrast, Merleau-Ponty "questions the conditions for the possibility of difference [and so] does not simply presuppose (the existence of) differences".[79] As such, his critics charge Merleau-Ponty with not adequately accounting for the foundational status of factical sexual determinations, whereas Merleau-Ponty argues that that issue depends upon the more fundamental question regarding the conditions that make possible such sexual difference(s).

Furthermore, Stoller maintains that Merleau-Ponty follows Husserl in distinguishing between an "intentionality of act which is that of our judgements and of those occasions when we voluntarily take up a position"[80] and "operative intentionality (*fungierende Intentionalität*), or that which produces the natural and antepredicative unity of the world and of our life".[81] Put simply, there is a fundamental phenomenological distinction between reflective, willed judgement and the intentional unity upon which the former act depends. As Stoller notes, this "is in keeping with Merleau-Ponty's interest in revealing the difference between the pre-predicative and predicative level, between lived experience and reflected attitude".[82] Whereas reflective judgements conceptualise and so objectify the lived pre-reflective experience, the latter is non-conceptual and defined by pure becoming. It is this level of experience that Merleau-Ponty's discussion of the primordial importance of pre-reflective bodily (sexual) schemas is orientated. It is why he maintains that sexuality is not defined by "objective perception" of the body but pre-reflective "erotic perception" wherein the body undergoes a sudden, pre-reflective surge towards the other. Erotic perception subsequently undergoes a modification into objective perception and, as a consequence, the objectification and hence creation of the sexual object. Crucially, because sexuality is premised on erotic perception, it is fundamentally non-conceptual and so cannot be said to be constituted by conceptual categories such as "male" or female"; such determinations are second order reflective phenomena of objective perception.

So, whereas his critics affirm the importance of starting with the sexual difference, doing so, on Merleau-Ponty's telling, undermines the distinction between objective perception and erotic perception to take the secondary status of the former as primary. Not only does this create a methodological and conceptual error, but it risks carrying the presuppositions of reflective judgement into the analysis of pre-reflective erotic perception to turn contemporary understandings of sexuality into the "essential" structures of the human body. Combating this requires that the sexual schema be "understood" as "initially" anonymous or undifferentiated so as to suspend "presuppositions about the nature of subjectivity or objectivity".[83]

Merleau-Ponty outlines what he has in mind most clearly and succinctly in his inaugural address at the Collège de France in 1953 where he first distinguishes between the philosopher and man-of-action, as a precursor to making a distinction between thinking and acting. Rather than simply wading into events with an opinion, the philosopher must keep a certain distance from them to be able to bear witness to them: "One must be able to withdraw and gain distance in order to become truly engaged, which is, also, always an engagement."[84] This is not to affirm a complete detachment of thought from the world, but entails a "pulling-back" that permits a clearer perspective on the issue. Rather than simply adopt a particular stance towards an object, there must be a withdrawal from projecting such assumptions onto the object so that it can reveal itself as it is.

For this reason, (1) the pre-reflective lived body that Merleau-Ponty affirms is neither masculine nor feminine; these are second order reflective judgements about the fundamental pre-reflective lived body. Because reflective judgement introduces determinations into the pre-reflective lived body, the pre-reflective lived body and, by extension, sexual schema must be taken to be originarily determinate-free (= anonymous); and (2) those who insist on starting with sexual differences fail to make the distinction that Merleau-Ponty does between the reflective and pre-reflective levels of perception to instead simply start with the conceptual distinctions found at the reflective level to subsequently attribute that conceptual schema to the pre-reflective, non-conceptual, lived body. Their analyses do not describe the (pre-reflective) lived body *per se* but a reflective judgement about the lived body. They do not then undertake the concrete analysis that they think they do; instead they hypostatize a particular reflective conceptual schema which is taken to describe the lived body when, in fact, it simply presupposes and forecloses the analysis within predetermined conceptual parameters. In contrast, Merleau-Ponty affirms the anonymity of the sexual schema to suspend the conceptual schemas of reflectivity to avoid prejudging the pre-reflective lived body and let the latter reveal itself as it is, not as how we may wish it to be. This, however, brings forth the question of the relationship between sexuality and existence, for, as a "thing" immanently expressed, the sexual schema is only revealed through each (individual) existence.

Sexuality and Existence

The sexual schema is not then a strictly separate "part" of the body, but an immanent non-objective pre-reflective aspect of the living body that is expressed immanently through the existence of the entire body. For this reason, "sexuality is not an autonomous cycle. It has internal links with the whole active and cognitive being, these three sectors of behavior displaying but a single typical structure, and standing in a relationship to each other of reciprocal expression."[85] From this, Merleau-Ponty ties the analysis to what he takes to be the fundamental discovery of psychoanalysis; namely that it affirms "a dialectical process in functions thought of as 'purely bodily' ... to reintegrate sexuality into the human being".[86]

Merleau-Ponty agrees with Freud that sexuality cannot be reduced to a genital part or an instinct that has a definitive teleology; rather, "[i]t is what causes man to have a history".[87] The reason for this is as simple as it is dramatic: "In so far as a man's sexual history provides a key to his life, it is because in his sexuality is projected his manner of being towards the world, that is, towards time and other men."[88] Sexuality is one of the fundamental ways in which each individual becomes what he/she is. Rather than determining existence, sexuality is coterminous to it, shaping, expressing, and revealing the way an individual exists. Instead of being merely a part of a larger bodily existence, sexuality "symbolize[s] a whole attitude"[89] to existence. There is no separation from one's sexuality; one's sexual being reveals, without determining, what one is.

As a consequence of the intimate bond between sexuality and (individual) existence, Merleau-Ponty maintains that "the question is not so much whether human life does or does not rest on sexuality, [but] what is to be understood by sexuality".[90] In response, he identifies a tension within psychoanalytic thought wherein "on the one hand it stresses the sexual substructure of life [while] on the other it 'expands' the notion of sexuality to the extent of absorbing into it the whole of existence".[91] The problem is that this is inherently ambiguous: "do we mean, in the last analysis, that all phenomenon has a sexual significance or that every sexual phenomenon has existential significance?"[92] In other words, do we ground sexuality in existence or existence in sexuality?

In response, Merleau-Ponty questions the logic of foundations implicit in both formulations, noting that because sexuality cannot be thought of as a "separate function definable in terms of the causality proper to a set or organs, there is now no sense in saying that all existence is understood through the sexual life".[93] But neither does this mean that sexuality is simply a reflection of existence. Sexuality must be thought as a particular "current of life ... bearing a special relation to the existence of sex. There can be no question of allowing sexuality to become lost in existence, as if it were no more than an epiphenomenon."[94] Rather than a logic of foundations, Merleau-Ponty suggests that we rethink the sexuality–existence relation as one of entwinement.

It is however precisely this claim that Martin Dillon criticises, claiming that if "sexuality and existence so interpenetrate that they cannot be distinguished ... we could not talk about the one without tacitly referring as well to the other".[95] Whenever we wish to talk of "sexuality", we must immediately talk of "existence" – the body, perception, values, and so on – that is indistinguishable from sexuality. As a consequence, we are unable to actually say anything analytical about sexuality *per se*; it all just melds together into an indeterminate soup. For this reason, Dillon concludes that Merleau-Ponty's approach is unable to provide "a positive account of sexuality".[96]

Putting to one side the question of whether such an endeavour is actually the issue to which Merleau-Ponty's analysis responds, Dillon goes on to propose two remedies for this perceived failing. First, he reaffirms the fundamental analytic and existential distinction between "sexuality" and "existence" to permit the former to be analysed in distinction to the later. Second, he criticises the logic of entwinement inherent in Merleau-Ponty's argument and affirms Husserl's *Fundierung* model, conforming to a founding–founded structure, to reaffirm a logic of foundations where either sexuality grounds existence or vice versa. As he explains:

> The difference between the *Fundierung* model and that of reciprocal expression is crucial in theorizing about the relation of sexuality and existence because on it rests the possibility of defining sexuality in such a way that its meaning does not immediately threaten to be reabsorbed within existence.[97]

Specifically, Dillon asks that we identify a foundational aspect of the body from which to think sexuality. By grounding sexuality in "certain aspects of the phenomenal body",[98] we will be able "to identify or define the ground or origin of existential sexuality and distinguish it from the existential significance of such other global phenomena as history, economics and so forth".[99]

To do so, Dillon rejects what he takes to be Merleau-Ponty's synchronic analysis that, on Dillon's understanding, simply proposes the logical entwinement of sexuality and existence to, instead, recommend the adoption of a diachronic analysis that takes into consideration the way in which layers are gradually added to the body as a consequence of the individual's history.[100] The basic point is that by taking into consideration this diachronic process of body-construction, we will be able to work backwards to strip away the "cultural" additions that have brought the body to its factic determinations. As a consequence of his adoption of the "foundational principle", Dillon claims that such a process will ultimately reveal the "foundational" structures upon which an individual's sexuality actually depends.

There are, however, at least three problems with this. First, Dillon's position appears to affirm and depend upon a logic of binary oppositions, wherein a foundational sexual base is pitted against a historico-cultural inessential appearance. It is this that allows him to claim that a diachronic analysis will strip away the latter to reveal the former. However, as Elizabeth Grosz points out, rather than affirm or depend upon a logic of binary oppositions, Merleau-Ponty's work is premised on a "resumption or reclamation of the space in between binary pairs, that apparently impossible no-man's land of the excluded middle, the gulf separating the one term from its opposite or other".[101]

Second, Dillon's argument depends upon and reaffirms the notion of a singular origin or foundation to an individual's sexuality that, somewhat paradoxically and despite Dillon's affirmation of diachronicity, simply does not accord with the diachronicity inherent in Merleau-Ponty's account of the pre-reflective lived body. Whereas Dillon appears to ground the diachronicity through which the sexual schema is "over-coded" with cultural meaning upon a non-diachronic foundational point that will reveal what "sexuality" truly is divorced from an individual's existence, Merleau-Ponty's notion of the sexual schema points to an "initial" pre-reflective lived unity that is subsequently expressed immanently (and so distorted) into reflective conceptual determinations. Reflective conceptual determinations are not then divorced from the diachronicity of the pre-reflective lived body but entail a particular modification of "it". As a consequence, there is no foundational point; the lived body is inherently and constitutively diachronic. By searching for a foundational body, Dillon ignores what is arguably the fundamental point of Merleau-Ponty's phenomenological analysis of being-in-the-world: there is no fixed foundational point grounding embodied being; "only" a body that continuously transcends itself by projecting itself from, through, and against a conditioned existence. We are not defined by a hidden essential core; we are a continuous historical (= living) projection of an embedded body: "All that we are, we are on the basis of a *de facto* situation which we appropriate to ourselves and which we ceaselessly transform by a sort of *escape* which is never an unconditioned freedom."[102] It is only from the perspective of objective perception that this durational flux is split into the clear-cut conceptual predicates that permit thought to think from a logic of foundations. However, as noted in the discussion of the phenomenal field, Merleau-Ponty's phenomenological method points to a different primordial "form" of perception that is imprecise, non-objective, fluid, and that reveals an object's "living function".[103] By insisting on a fixed foundation to sexuality, Dillon reads the structures of objective perception into this more primordial form of existence to reify them into a fixed foundation. In contrast, Merleau-Ponty claims that the pre-reflective lived body is a constant living flow and so cannot have a singular base; rather, it is bound up with and expressed through the living totality that *is* each individual.

Third, Dillon's affirmation of a logic of binary opposition and foundationalism reveals his dependence on, what I will call, analytic monadism, which holds that each "thing" – sexuality or existence, for example – is fundamentally and existentially separate and distinct from others, with this permitting each to be analysed in distinction on its own terms. Dillon makes this move because he affirms the need for conceptual clarity, but the problem with this demand from Merleau-Ponty's perspective is that it (1) obtains such clarity only by distorting the "prior" lived field of existence to foreclose it within the objective categories of reflective judgement and, in so doing, is unable to appreciate the fluidity and dynamism of the pre-reflective lived field; and (2) means that Dillon ignores what Merleau-Ponty insists is a fundamental aspect of existence: paradox and ambiguity. After all, existence is never static and clearly defined, but always points towards "another existence which denies it, and yet without which it is not sustained".[104] The individual, for example, becomes what he is by projecting himself into the future. He only is by virtue of this projection that cancels out what he previously was. It also means that his existence is never clear-cut but always an uneasy persistence in constant transition and movement.

Because sexuality is intimately entwined with existence, it too shares the indeterminateness of the latter; an idea that Merleau-Ponty tries to capture by explaining that, rather than being distinct or distinguishable from existence, sexuality is "at all times present there like an atmosphere".[105] Just as an atmosphere cannot be objectively defined, nor can sexuality. This does not mean that it does not exist or that we cannot explain it, but that we cannot think about it in objective, clear-cut, and monadic terms. Sexuality must be understood to spread "forth like an odour or like a sound".[106] It therefore requires a different, non-objective form of cognition to capture and analyse it, one that ties sexuality to and reads it through the continuous becoming that marks the pre-reflective lived field and, by extension, the "totality" of individual existence.

Dillon is correct that this makes an analysis of sexuality *per se* difficult, but, rather than a failing, this is the challenge that Merleau-Ponty sets us: we have to learn and accept that "ambiguity is of the essence of human existence and everything we live or think has always several meanings".[107] Instead of being a contingent or compartmentalised aspect of our existence, it is through sexuality that "we commit our whole personal life",[108] with the consequence that sexuality conditions and is caught up in all the ambiguities of our life. With this, Merleau-Ponty not only challenges us to think and constantly engage with this ambiguity, but also undermines the notion that sexuality is defined by clear-cut oppositions and essential structures. Focusing on the pre-reflective lived phenomenal field reveals sexuality to be multidimensional, defined by constant becoming, and, crucially, specific to each existence. With this, Merleau-Ponty establishes the theoretical parameters that will form the basis for much subsequent gender theory, especially its queer and trans* versions.

Conclusion

Merleau-Ponty's account of the sexed body is then far more complicated and nuanced than his critics often recognise. It not only develops Husserlian-inspired phenomenological thinking on this topic, but also introduces an important conceptual innovation, in the form of the notion of a sexual schema, that reveals the key, but not determining, importance that sexuality has for the individual's body and existence. Rather than something fixed and determinate, the sexual schema points to a conception of sexuality as ineffable and fluid. Instead of being reduced to or defined by a fixed essence or body part, sexuality pertains to a style of being, unique to but expressed through each individual's body and, for this reason, is coextensive with each individual's whole existence.

On the one hand, this exacerbates the importance of sexuality, in so far as it makes it a fundamental aspect of individual existence. But, on the other hand, by claiming that it is not possible to distinguish between "sexuality" and "existence", Merleau-Ponty, somewhat paradoxically, undermines its importance by pointing out that it is not the fundamental issue through which an individual can be understood. Of course, this does not mean that we must ignore the question of an individual's sexuality; it is fundamental to an individual's bodily existence and so must be taken into account. But Merleau-Ponty resists the notion that a study of an individual's sexuality somehow explains his "whole" existence. Indeed, this ties into his claim that the sexual schema cannot simply be thought from or through the sexual (male/female) difference. Rather than merely assume and so analyse sexuality from a presupposed sexual (binary) difference, Merleau-Ponty employs a modified version of Husserl's phenomenological reduction to claim that for "sexuality" to be understood requires that we "bracket" everyday assumptions to "return" to the pre-reflective phenomenal field from where such reflective judgements and distinctions arise. Only this will allow an individual's sexual existence to reveal itself as it is and not as we have been conditioned to think about it or might wish it to be.

While this methodological manoeuvre has caused consternation amongst a certain strand of femininst theory, I have argued that it not only points to a particular phenomenological approach to sexuality – thereby revealing Merleau-Ponty's importance to phenomenological theory generally – but, by holding that sexuality is individual and openly expressive, also ensures that Merleau-Ponty undercuts the long-held affirmation of sexual essentialism or determinism in a way that avoids foreclosing sexuality within a predetermined schema, including the logic of patriarchy. By opening sexuality in this manner, Merleau-Ponty shows that "it" does not have to be expressed through a straightforward sexual difference/opposition, but is actually individual, malleable, fluid, and altering/able. Indeed, by insisting that sexuality is expressive and intimately bound to the ambiguities of each individual's existence, he also points to the contradictions and opaqueness of sexuality. Instead of ignoring or seeking to clarify such chaos by imposing unambiguous analytic definitions and categories, Merleau-Ponty pushes us to accept this obscurity and rethink sexuality as embodied and fluidly expressive. Only this will allow sexual existence to reveal itself in all its non-determined glory. Whether we are willing to accept such ambiguity and indeed how we do so is the task that he sets for us, but this challenge is why his thinking on sexuality remains relevant (especially but not only for queer and trans* theories).

However, for all its innovation and originality, Merleau-Ponty's thinking on sexuality has a fittingly ambiguous status within subsequent thought on the topic. Whereas his attempt to undercut the notion of sexual essentialism was widely praised, especially within feminist theory, his methodological neutrality met strong resistance precisely because it rejects, what some held to be, the fundamental importance of the sexual difference; a move that appeared to affirm an abstract universalism that is unable to properly account for the concrete realities of the sexual difference. While I have argued that Merleau-Ponty's position is far subtler than these critics tend to appreciate – indeed, the emphasis of neutrality points to a particular phenomenological approach to the issue – Simone de Beauvoir, writing just after the end of the Second World War, aimed to correct it by focusing on the role of women in Western society to offer an alternative analysis of sexuality that, on the one hand, mirrors the psychoanalytic and phenomenological rejection of sexual essentialism and by extension the notion that there is an essential distinction between the sexes, while, on the other hand, explicitly turning to the ways in which Western forms of representation nevertheless relegate "woman" to secondary status.

Notes

1. Husserl never undertook a detailed study of sex or sexuality although he did accept in the late (1936) *The Crisis of European Sciences and Transcendental Phenomenology* (trans. David Carr [Evanston, IL: Northwestern University Press, 1970]) that "the problem of the sexes" (p. 188) was one for future study. His death in 1938 meant that he never completed that study.

2. Jean-Paul Sartre, *Being and Nothingness: An Essay in Phenomenological Ontology*, trans. Sarah Richmond (Abingdon: Routledge, 2018), p. 506. For a discussion of Sartre's analysis of love, see Gavin Rae, "Sartre on Authentic and Inauthentic Love", *Existential Analysis: Journal of the Society for Existential Analysis*, vol. 23, n. 1, 2012, pp. 75–88.
3. Emmanuel Levinas, *Time and the Other*, trans. Richard A. Cohen (Pittsburgh, PA: Duquesne University Press, 1987), p. 87.
4. Ibid., p. 88.
5. Maurice Merleau-Ponty, *Phenomenology of Perception*, trans. Colin Smith (Abingdon: Routledge, 1962), pp. 178–201.
6. Sara Heinämaa, *Toward a Phenomenology of Sexual Difference: Husserl, Merleau-Ponty, Beauvoir* (Lanham, MD: Rowman & Littlefield, 2003), p. xii.
7. Elizabeth Grosz, "Merleau-Ponty and Irigaray in the Flesh", *Thesis Eleven*, n. 36, 1993, pp. 37–59 (p. 37).
8. Simone de Beauvoir, *The Second Sex*, trans. Constance Borde and Sheila Malovany-Chaveallier (London: Vintage, 2011), p. 46.
9. Ibid., p. 46.
10. Lisa Guenther, "Merleau-Ponty and the Sense of Sexual Difference", *Angelaki*, vol. 16, n. 2, 2011, pp. 19–33 (p. 29); Martha J. Reineke, "Lacan, Merleau-Ponty, and Irigaray: Reflections on a Specular Drama", *Auslegung*, vol. 14, n. 1, 1987, pp. 67–85 (pp. 67, 84); Silvia Stoller, "Reflections on Feminist Merleau-Ponty Skepticism", *Hypatia*, vol. 15, n. 1, 2000, pp. 175–182 (p. 181).
11. Judith Butler, "Sexual Ideology and Phenomenological Description: A Feminist Critique of Merleau-Ponty's Phenomenology of Perception", in *The Thinking Muse: Feminism and Modern French Philosophy*, edited by Jeffner Allen and Iris Marion Young (Bloomington, IN: Indiana University Press, 1989), pp. 85–100 (p. 86).
12. Anna Petronella Foultier, "Language and the Gendered Body: Butler's Early Reading of Merleau-Ponty", *Hypatia*, vol. 28, n. 4, 2013, pp. 767–783 (p. 779); Iris Marion Young, "Throwing Like a Girl: A Phenomenology of Feminine Body Comportment Motility and Spatiality", *Human Studies*, vol. 3, n. 2, 1980, pp. 137–156 (p. 140). Luce Irigaray (*An Ethics of Sexual Difference*, trans. Carolyn Burke and Gillian C. Gill [Ithaca, NY: Cornell University Press, 1993], pp. 151–184) suggests that this masculine bias is nuanced in Merleau-Ponty's later work, namely the chapter "The Intertwining – The Chiasm" found in the unfinished, posthumously, published *The Visible and the Invisible* (edited by Claude Lefort, trans. Alphonso Lingis [Evanston, IL: Northwestern University Press, 1968], pp. 130–155). While still maintaining that he depends upon a privileging of a masculinist privileging, Irigaray holds that this text exhibits a concern with the "feminine" tactile not found in his earlier work. Space constraints mean that I will not discuss this issue here – although I will return to Irigaray's thought in Chapter 6 – but I mention in passing that (1) various commentators (Guenther, "Merleau-Ponty and the Sense of Sexual Difference", pp. 19–33; Reineke, "Lacan, Merleau-Ponty, and Irigaray", pp. 175–182; Mark Sanders, "Merleau-Ponty and the Ethics of Engagement", in *Ethics and Phenomenology*, edited by Mark Sanders

and J. Jeremy Wisnewski [Lanham, MD: Lexington, 2013], pp. 103–116) have suggested that the notion of flesh found in the later work expands and complements, rather than replaces, the earlier analysis found in *The Phenomenology of Perception*, and (2) Irigaray's claim depends upon a strict division between (a) masculine and feminine, and (b) Merleau-Ponty's earlier and later works that falls foul of Merleau-Ponty's rejection of binary logic. Nevertheless, for a discussion of Irigaray's reading of Merleau-Ponty, see Alison Ainley, "The Invisible of the Flesh: Merleau-Ponty and Irigaray", *Journal of the British Society for Phenomenology*, vol. 28, n. 1, 1997, pp. 20–29.

13. Edmund Husserl, *Ideas Pertaining to a Pure Phenomenology and to a Phenomenological Philosophy, First Book*, trans. F. Kersten (Dordrecht: Kluwer, 1983), pp. 56–62.
14. Joel Smith, "Merleau-Ponty and the Phenomenological Reduction", *Inquiry*, vol. 48, n. 6, 2005, pp. 553–571.
15. A number of commentators have recently argued that there are significant overlaps between Heidegger's and Merleau-Ponty's conceptions of the body, although there is disagreement over whether to affirm Heidegger's account (Kevin A. Aho, "The Missing Dialogue between Heidegger and Merleau-Ponty: On the Importance of the *Zollikon Seminars*", *Body and Society*, vol. 11, n. 2, 2005, pp. 1–23) or Merleau-Ponty's account (Douglas Low, "Merleau-Ponty's Criticism of Heidegger", *Philosophy Today*, vol. 53, n. 3, 2009, pp. 273–293). Regardless, this trajectory demonstrates the validity of the historical narrative outlined here, in so far as it confirms my claim that their conceptions of the body and, by extension, sexuality have points of intertwinement.
16. Martin C. Dillon, "Merleau-Ponty on Existential Sexuality: A Critique", *Journal of Phenomenological Psychology*, vol. 11, n. 1, 1980, pp. 67–81.
17. René Descartes, "Meditations on First Philosophy", in *Discourse on Method and Meditations on First Philosophy*, Fourth edition, trans. Donald A. Cress (Indianapolis, IN: Hackett, 1998), pp. 59–103 (p. 60).
18. Ibid., p. 64.
19. Ibid., pp. 87–92.
20. The secondary literature on Merleau-Ponty's contribution to the mind–body problem is extensive. For an overview, see Shaun Gallagher, "Merleau-Ponty", in *Consciousness and the Great Philosophers: What Would They have Said About our Mind–Body Problem?*, edited by Stephen Leach and James Tartaglia (Abingdon: Routledge, 2016), pp. 235–243.
21. Maurice Merleau-Ponty, *Signs* (Evanston, IL: Northwestern University Press, 1964), pp. 226–227.
22. Renaud Barbaras, *The Being of the Phenomenon: Merleau-Ponty's Ontology*, trans. Ted Toadvine and Leonard Lawler (Bloomington, IN: Indiana University Press, 2004); Taylor Carmen, *Merleau-Ponty* (Abingdon: Routledge, 2008); Martin C. Dillon, *Merleau-Ponty's Ontology*, Second edition (Evanston, IL: Northwestern University Press, 1998); Lawrence Hass, *Merleau-Ponty's Philosophy* (Bloomington: Indiana University Press, 2008); Scott Marrato, *The Intercorporeal Self: Merleau-Ponty on Subjectivity* (Albany, NY: State University of New York Press, 2013).
23. Merleau-Ponty, *Phenomenology of Perception*, pp. 178–201.

24. Ibid., p. 178.
25. Ibid., p. 62.
26. Taylor Carmen, "Between Empiricism and Intellectualism", in *Merleau-Ponty: Key Concepts*, edited by Rosalyn Diprose and Jack Reynolds (Abingdon: Routledge, 2014), pp. 44–56 (p. 54).
27. Merleau-Ponty, *Phenomenology of Perception*, p. 178.
28. Ibid., p. 178.
29. Ibid., pp. 178–179.
30. Ibid., p. 179.
31. Ibid., p. 179.
32. Ibid., p. 179.
33. Ibid., p. 179.
34. Ibid., pp. 179–180.
35. Ibid., p. 180.
36. Ibid., p. 180.
37. Ibid., p. 180.
38. Ibid., p. 180.
39. Ibid., p. 180.
40. Ibid., p. 180.
41. Shannon Sullivan, "Domination and Dialogue in Merleau-Ponty's Phenomenology of Perception", *Hypatia*, vol. 12, n. 1, 1997, pp. 1–19 (p. 8).
42. Merleau-Ponty, *Phenomenology of Perception*, p. 180.
43. Ibid., p. 180.
44. Ibid., p. 180.
45. Ibid., pp. 180–181.
46. Ibid., p. 181.
47. Ibid., p. 181.
48. Ibid., p. 181.
49. Ibid., p. 181.
50. Ibid., p. 181.
51. Ibid., p. 181.
52. Ibid., p. 181.
53. Ibid., p. 182.
54. Ibid., p. 182.
55. Patricia Moya and Maria Elena Larrain, "Sexuality and Meaning in Freud and Merleau-Ponty", *The International Journal of Psychoanalysis*, vol. 97, n. 3, 2016, pp. 737–757 (p. 754).
56. Merleau-Ponty, *Phenomenology of Perception*, p. 182.
57. Helena de Preester, "Merleau-Ponty's Sexual Schema and the Sexual Component of Body Integrity Identity Disorder", *Medical Healthcare and Philosophy*, vol. 16, n. 2, 2013, pp. 171–184 (p. 181).
58. Butler, "Sexual Ideology and Phenomenological Description", p. 86.
59. Foultier, "Language and the Gendered Body", p. 779; Young, "Throwing Like a Girl", p. 141.
60. Butler, "Sexual Ideology and Phenomenological Description", p. 86.

61. Ibid., p. 93.
62. Ibid., p. 86.
63. Ibid., p. 92.
64. Ibid., p. 92.
65. Ibid., p. 86.
66. Foultier, "Language and the Gendered Body", p. 774.
67. Ibid., p. 774.
68. Ibid., p. 779.
69. Young, "Throwing Like a Girl", p. 141.
70. Sonia Kruks, "Merleau-Ponty and the Problem of Difference in Feminism", in *Feminist Interpretations of Maurice Merleau-Ponty*, edited by Dorothy Olkowski and Gail Weiss (University Park, PA: Pennsylvania State University Press, 2006), pp. 25–48 (p. 29).
71. Ibid., p. 29.
72. Ibid., p. 30.
73. Johanna Oksala, "Female Freedom: Can the Lived Body be Emancipated?", in *Feminist Interpretations of Maurice Merleau-Ponty*, edited by Dorothy Olkowski and Gail Weiss (University Park, PA: Pennsylvania State University Press, 2006), pp. 209–228 (p. 218).
74. Ibid., p. 218.
75. Ibid., p. 218.
76. Ibid., p. 221.
77. Ibid., p. 221. In a similar vein, Kruks concludes that Merleau-Ponty's account of the sexed body does not "obscure or deny differences" (Kruks, "Merleau-Ponty and the Problem of Difference in Feminism", p. 42), but aims to point to "the tensions of difference and commonality . . . to suggest that embodiment offers a site of *potential* communication and affirmative intersubjectivity" (ibid., p. 42).
78. Stoller, "Reflections on Feminist Merleau-Ponty Skepticism", p. 178.
79. Ibid., p. 178.
80. Merleau-Ponty, *Phenomenology of Perception*, p. xx.
81. Ibid., p. xx.
82. Stoller, "Reflections on Feminist Merleau-Ponty Skepticism", p. 178.
83. Diana Coole, *Merleau-Ponty and Modern Politics after Anti-Humanism* (Lanham, MD: Rowman & Littlefield, 2007), p. 139.
84. Maurice Merleau-Ponty, "In Praise of Philosophy", in *In Praise of Philosophy and Other Essays*, trans. John Wild and James M. Edie (Evanston, IL: Northwestern University Press, 1963), pp. 3–70 (p. 60).
85. Merleau-Ponty, *Phenomenology of Perception*, p. 182.
86. Ibid., p. 182.
87. Ibid., p. 183.
88. Ibid., p. 183.
89. Ibid., p. 183.
90. Ibid., p. 183.
91. Ibid., pp. 183–184.

92. Ibid., p. 184.
93. Ibid., p. 184.
94. Ibid., p. 184.
95. Dillon, "Merleau-Ponty on Existential Sexuality", p. 71.
96. Ibid., p. 67.
97. Ibid., p. 74.
98. Ibid., p. 74.
99. Ibid., p. 74.
100. Ibid., p. 80.
101. Grosz, "Merleau-Ponty and Irigaray in the Flesh", p. 38. Interestingly, one of the fundamental arguments of Dillon's later *Merleau-Ponty's Ontology* is that Merleau-Ponty's ontology critiques and rejects binary oppositions. However, Dillon never relates this to, or indeed renounces, his earlier critique of Merleau-Ponty's analysis of the sexed body.
102. Merleau-Ponty, *Phenomenology of Perception*, p. 198.
103. Ibid., p. 197.
104. Ibid., p. 194.
105. Ibid., p. 195.
106. Ibid., p. 195.
107. Ibid., p. 193.
108. Ibid., p. 198.

Part II

Feminism and (Post)Structuralism

CHAPTER 4

Beauvoir and the Question of "Woman"

In 1949, Simone de Beauvoir published *The Second Sex*,[1] a text that would reorientate the study of sexuality within the phenomenological movement specifically and twentieth-century philosophy more generally. Reportedly selling over 22,000 copies in its first week of release,[2] *The Second Sex* quickly "caused a major outrage because it dealt with a taboo subject – women's sexuality – and contained a harsh critique of patriarchal power structures".[3] Specifically, Beauvoir analyses the ways in which "social institutions, such as marriage, motherhood, and the family, predefine women's and men's roles in a male-dominated society and subsequently denigrate women to the status of secondary citizens",[4] an argument "buttressed . . . by showing how changing ideals of 'femininity' are not essential aspects of women's identity based on biological sex".[5]

Beauvoir's text marks a radical departure from previous psychoanalytical and phenomenological accounts of sexuality. Whereas she praises the former for recognising "that no factor intervenes in psychic life without having taken on human meaning",[6] with the consequence that psychoanalysis permits a huge expansion of our understanding of what constitutes human experience, she goes on to criticise Freud for "not [being] very concerned with woman's destiny; it is clear that he modelled his description of it on that of masculine destiny, merely modifying some of the traits".[7] Interestingly, however, she praises Lacan's account of the mirror stage,[8] thereby revealing not only that she was up-to-date with contemporary (for her) psychoanalytic theory but also that her relationship to psychoanalysis was nuanced.

Her ties to the phenomenological tradition are far stronger, both as a consequence of her own philosophical education and, indeed, her relationship with Jean-Paul Sartre. The specifics of their physical relationship – that they never married, kept other lovers, and so on – have been told multiple times and are of little interest here,[9] but their intellectual bond and influence over one another brings to the fore Beauvoir's intimate relationship to the phenomenological tradition. While Beauvoir always emphasised her philosophical dependence on Sartre, recent scholarship has reopened that issue to show that she was far more fundamental to his thinking that she recognised or is often given credit for.[10] Indeed, it has been suggested that, rather than Sartre, Beauvoir depended upon, engaged with, and was more fundamentally influenced by other figures within the phenomenological tradition, including Hegel,[11] Heidegger,[12] Husserl,[13] and Merleau-Ponty.[14]

Whatever the truth(s) of these connections – and it is, of course, possible that Beauvoir was influenced by all these figures – they reveal that the phenomenological tradition was a key one for Beauvoir. This is not to say, however, that the relationship was uni-directional. Stella Sandford notes that Beauvoir introduced important conceptual innovations into phenomenological thinking:

> First, there is the attempt to make the Other or others necessary to the meaningfulness of my freedom, which thus leads to the centrality of ethical and political questions *within* existentialism [and phenomenology] and to the privileging of the other's freedom. Second, there is the growing insistence on the claims of facticity or the claims of the situation on the subject.[15]

This later focus brought the question of the relationship between sexuality and the body to the fore. As noted, this had been raised by Heidegger and, more specifically, Merleau-Ponty, but, as Anna Alexander notes, both "(on the face of it) theorized a 'body' belonging to no one",[16] in so far as they both affirmed the fundamental importance of the phenomenological reduction to think sexuality in relation to a prior (ontological) neutrality. Beauvoir takes over and focuses on Merleau-Ponty's notion of the lived body, but "reconceptualis[es] . . . the subject *through* the idea of the situation . . . [to] problematize the intelligibility of a metaphysical or ontological concept of freedom divorced from political and social contexts".[17] Rather than strip bodies of their factical determinations, Beauvoir maintains that it is necessary to study the concrete factical determinations of bodies in their socio-political situatedness. From this methodological starting point, she turns to focus on the situation of women, as a precursor to responding to the question "what is a woman?"[18]

Instead of appealing to a definite, ahistoric (biological) essence, Beauvoir posits that "woman", and by extension, sexuality is not a thing or substance, but a process of becoming; a conclusion captured by her famous statement that "[o]ne is not born, but rather becomes, woman".[19] To support this, she not only discusses myths about women, but also biological, psychoanalytic, historical materialist, historical, and sociological accounts of female sexual development. By focusing on her critique of biological essentialism, notion of woman as Other, and *The Second Sex*'s closing section on liberation, I will first outline her critique of the logic of patriarchy that has dominated Western thinking, before (second section) engaging with her critique of the long-held notion that sexuality generally and "woman" specifically are defined by a determining, fixed biological essence. I then (third section) tie her materialist, non-essentialist account of "woman" to her earlier *The Ethics of Ambiguity*[20] – thereby following Toril Moi's claim that this text "remains crucial to an understanding of *The Second Sex*"[21] – to suggest that Beauvoir's point is that sexuality, as a social construct, cannot be thought of in terms of clear-cut categories or divisions, but must be thought of in terms of the ambiguity that marks lived experience. For this reason, she pushes us to recognise, accept, and even affirm the ambiguity of lived sexuality.

Section four engages with the long-standing issue of whether Beauvoir implicitly depends upon a masculine position, so that her supposed affirmation of women continues to depend upon and, indeed, perpetuate the privileging of masculinity that has long marked Western thinking. While noting the ambiguity that has marked contemporary responses to this issue,[22] I argue that the fact that it has been raised at all points to the subtle ways in which a privileging of the logic of patriarchy can continue to adhere to thinking that explicitly seeks to undermine it – a charge that was also levelled, albeit in different ways, against Freud, Heidegger, and Merleau-Ponty – and, in so doing, points to the complexity of the problem faced by those seeking to undermine patriarchy.

Section five complements this by tying Beauvoir's thinking to the contemporary debate regarding whether Beauvoir's account of woman affirms (1) a sex/gender division wherein a biologically passive sexed body is given meaning through fluid, heterogeneous socially-constructed gender norms, and so is understood to prefigure Judith Butler's gender theory (chapter 7);[23] or (2) a new conception of "sex" that cuts across the sex/gender divide by rethinking "sex" from a socially situated body that continuously becomes without becoming anything; a conception that sees Beauvoir as affirming a radical materialist rethinking of the sexed body that figures into what has become known as the new materialisms (Chapter 8).[24] Rather than seek to resolve these interpretative disputes, my aim is to show that Beauvoir fulfils this dual role because her account of sexuality maintains that sexuality must be thought in terms of ambiguity, a position that permits her analysis to be appropriated by distinct positions within subsequent (feminist) thinking.

The Second Sex

Beauvoir's writing career stretches from the 1940s through to her death in 1986, but her reputation as the "mother"[25] of feminism lies on the foundation of her 1949 book *The Second Sex*; a text that has been called "the 'bible' of modern Western feminism".[26] Beauvoir starts by explaining that she "hesitated a long time before writing a book on women".[27] Indeed, she admits that she found the topic "irritating",[28] if only because of the inadequate ways it has been historically treated wherein the question of "woman" has tended to be answered by appeal to an ahistoric essence or an unrealisable (Platonic) ideal, or simply rejected as being irrelevant to the more universal question of "human being". However, while "woman like man is a human being ... such an assertion is abstract; the fact is that every concrete human being is always uniquely situated".[29] Despite her rejection of universal categories, Beauvoir subsequently asks: "If the female function is not enough to define woman, and if we also reject the explanation of the 'eternal function', but ... we accept, even temporarily, that there are women on the earth, we then have to ask: what is a woman?"[30]

Beauvoir notes that the power of the question rests on its peculiarity, in so far as the same question has never been asked of man. She takes this to show that Western thinking has been dominated by a logic of patriarchy, wherein "man" is taken to be synonymous with "human being", with "woman" relegated "to the negative, to such a point that any determination is imputed to her as a limitation".[31] Because "woman" is defined and, indeed, defines herself negatively in relation to the "positive" masculine position,

> she is nothing other than what man decides; she is thus called 'the sex,' meaning that the male sees her essentially as a sexed being; for him she is sex, so she is it in the absolute. She determines and differentiates herself in relation to man, and he does not in relation to her; she is the inessential in front of the essential. He is the Subject; he is the Absolute. She is the Other.[32]

This feeds into a distinction that Beauvoir makes between two types of relation: one based on alterity and the other based on opposition. Regarding the former, she suggests that the logic of alterity is fundamental to the human condition and, indeed "is the fundamental category of human thought".[33] This onto-epistemic claim undermines the primordial claim of monadic ontologies, wherein categories are defined prior to any relationality they might have. For Beauvoir, relationality is ontologically primarily, so that "things" only are by virtue of being distinguished from what they are not. In relation to the sexes, this should lead to both terms – masculine and feminine – being held to be of symmetrical worth: the masculine can only be what it is by virtue of its negative relation to the feminine and vice versa. However, this has not been the case historically; the relation between the sexes has been *oppositional*, so that one aspect of the relation "asserts itself as the essential and sets up the other as inessential, the object".[34] Not only does this turn a relation between two "subjects" into one between a "subject" and an "object", but it leads to an asymmetric relation wherein the "positive" subject is affirmed over the "negative" object; the masculine is privileged over the feminine. Beauvoir wonders how it is "that between the sexes this reciprocity has not been put forward, that one of the terms has been asserted as the only essential one, denying any relationality in regard to its correlative, defining the latter as pure alterity? Why do women not contest male sovereignty?"[35]

Her point is that "[n]o subject posits itself spontaneously and at once as the inessential form from the outset; it is not the Other who, defining itself as Other, defines the One; the Other is posited as Other by the One positing itself as One".[36] Due to the relational symmetry inherent in the process of meaning-generation, each aspect is actually as valuable as the other. If, however, one aspect comes to be more valued within that cultural system than the other, it is not due to a "natural" ontological superiority, but because the originary alterity has been forcibly turned into an opposition. However, force alone is not sufficient to maintain such an asymmetrical relation. Rather, "in order for the Other not to turn into the One, the Other has to submit to this foreign point of view".[37] Where then "does this submission in woman come from?"[38]

While accepting that "[t]he division of the sexes is a biological given, not a moment in human history",[39] Beauvoir notes that the *meaning* of that division is not predetermined but must be constructed. Because women comprise around half the population, a construction that leaves woman in a secondary position can only occur and be sustained with her consent; in other words, women must acquiesce and, indeed, affirm their secondary status. Crucially, Beauvoir rejects the notion that this inequality is a contemporary occurrence; "woman has always been, if not man's slave, at least his vassal; the two sexes have never divided the world up equally; and still today, even though her condition is changing, woman is heavily handicapped".[40]

Writing in France in the late 1940s, Beauvoir notes that there is no country where woman have equal legal rights as men, although she then claims that, even if that formal equality did exist, it would merely mask "long-standing habit[s] [that] keep them from being concretely manifested in customs".[41] After all, men occupy positions of historical prestige, which are re-enforced by an educational system that teaches children, often implicitly, to accept and affirm the subordination of women. This feeds through into later life, so that

> [e]conomically, men and women almost form two castes; all things being equal, the former have better jobs, higher wages and greater chances to succeed than their new female competitors; they occupy many more places in industry, in politics, and so on, and they hold the most important positions.[42]

The chips are, then, stacked against women, which is compounded further by their complicity in perpetuating that system. Again, Beauvoir recognises that there is significant social pressure that supports and perpetuates mechanisms of conformity, but she also highlights that women are not simply helpless victims in the process. This however is tempered by the recognition that "women makes no claim for herself as subject because she lacks the concrete means, because she senses the necessary link connecting her to man within positing its reciprocity, and because she often derives satisfaction from her role as *Other*".[43] Because this inequality is not pre-given, "[i]t remains to be explained how it was that man won at the outset. It seems possible that women might have carried off the victory, or that the battle might never be resolved."[44]

Beauvoir notes that this question has a long history and, indeed, has been met with multiple responses. The fundamental problem with them is that, while they appeal to different sources to justify patriarchy – Beauvoir mentions that "antifeminists . . . draw not only . . . on religion, philosophy and theology, but also on science: biology, experimental psychology, and so on"[45] – all conclusions are underpinned by a common ontological principle: human being is defined in terms of an ahistoric essence, so that, in the case of "woman", she is attributed a definite unchanging essence that "naturally" leads to her subordination.

Beauvoir's rejects this essentialist ontology and, instead, follows Hegel – who at the beginning of the *Science of Logic* argues that the dialectical relationship between "being" and "nothing" gives way to the truth of becoming[46] – in claiming that "*to be* is to have become, to have been made as one manifests oneself".[47] Woman is a construction that is continually constructed; there is nothing "natural" or determined about her. If she is socially inferior to man, it is because the sexes have been conceived and structured in that manner; but, crucially, there is nothing necessary about that construction.

To develop this, Beauvoir adopts the "perspective . . . of existentialist morality",[48] by which she means, generally speaking, the insistence that, rather than being an inert thing, "[e]very subject posits itself as a transcendence concretely, through projects; it accomplishes its freedom only by perpetual surpassing towards other freedom".[49] Importantly, "there is no other justification for present existence than its expansion towards an indefinitely open future".⁵⁰ For Beauvoir, each subject only is what it is as a consequence of an onto-genetic process of projection into the future. There is then a constant surmounting of what one "is" in each moment, with this depending upon and permitting the individual the freedom to become "something" else in the future. This moment of transcendence is not to another world, but is always within a social situation. Emphasising its transcendence-in-situation safeguards and, indeed, depends upon the freedom of the subject. As a consequence, Beauvoir stresses that the subject is always situated, but is never determined by that situation.

Problems arise, however, "every time transcendence lapses into immanence",⁵¹ by which Beauvoir means a lack of becoming. When this occurs, "there is a degradation of existence into 'in itself,' of freedom into facticity".⁵² Rather than project oneself into the future to realise the open-ended possibilities open to the subject based on its lack of ontological essence, the turn to immanence implies an acceptance and, indeed, affirmation of the current state of things. It is, to put it simply, to turn oneself into an unchanging "thing".

Beauvoir ties this to the situation of women by claiming that, while every individual "experiences his [sic] existence as an indefinite need to transcend himself",⁵³ for women, this possibility is stunted. Rather than being able to transcend herself, "she discovers and chooses herself in a world where men force her to assume herself as an Other: an attempt is made to freeze her as an object and doom her to immanence, since her transcendence will be forever transcended by another essential and sovereign consciousness".⁵⁴ Woman therefore finds herself in a "drama",⁵⁵ wherein she is caught between her own self-affirmation as essential (= transcendence) "and the demands of the situation that constitutes her as inessential".⁵⁶

Again, there is no doubt that, for Beauvoir, women participate in this process. As she puts it, "[i]f woman discovers herself as the inessential, and never turns into the essential, it is because she does not bring about this transformation herself".⁵⁷ However, Beauvoir also recognises that such a transformation is never purely voluntarist. The situation that woman finds herself in imposes this normative framework onto her, with the consequence that her decision is made within a social field that restricts her options. Her transcendence is always constrained by her situation, which constantly pressurises her to deny the transcendence that she is ontologically. As a consequence, "frustration and oppression"⁵⁸ are her lot. It must be remembered, however, that, for Beauvoir, this frustration is not an ontological given, but the result of a particular constructed normative value system. The question arises as to whether the normative framework supporting such judgement is sustainable and/or to be sustained.

The Question of Biology

The Second Sex examines how the inferior position of women has been constructed and maintained from a variety of positions – including biology, psychoanalysis, economics, historical narrative, myth, education, and so on – to show that there is not one singular source of her oppression; rather, Western society is structured from and around an imperceptible web of normative structures and meanings that gently but constantly impose themselves onto the sexes to define their possibilities. In the case of women, this leads her to the status of Other and the denial of her transcendence. Beauvoir's identification of this normative construction is also accompanied by its critical interrogation. Given the dominant role it has played in vindicating women's secondary status within Western history, I will briefly focus on her critique of the biological justifications for women's inferior status. This will highlight Beauvoir's materialist, anti-essentialist account of the lived body and, by extension, sexuality, emphasise the crucial role that ambiguity plays therein, and show how her analysis has fed into and stimulated a number of debates within contemporary feminist theory.

Beauvoir notes that responses to the question of "woman" typically aim to reduce her to her biology or biological function: childbirth. In so doing, woman is defined by a lack of transcendence. To explain this, Beauvoir introduces and depends upon a distinction between "woman" and "female". The latter is associated with biology and is "pejorative not because it roots woman in nature, but because it confines her in her sex".[59] "Woman", on the other hand, refers to the *meaning* that "female" has within a particular social setting. Beauvoir's point regarding her discussion of biology is to reject the reduction of "woman" to "female", all the while accepting and recognising that the biological conditions of "female" must be accepted, albeit in a non-determining way, when discussing the construction of "woman". As a consequence, whereas "[m]ales and females are two types of individuals who are differentiated within one species for the purposes of reproduction; they can be defined only correlatively [and] it must be pointed out first that the very meaning of *division* of the species into two sexes is not clear".[60] In other words, although Beauvoir accepts a heteronormative division as in some sense biologically given, she recognises that the *meaning* of that division is open and contested.

Despite this, however, she notes that the history of Western philosophy has tended to treat it homogeneously as a consequence of taking its meaning "for granted without attempting to explain it".[61] Beauvoir backs this up with a quick overview of the topic in Plato, Aristotle, Aquinas, Hegel, Merleau-Ponty, Sartre, and Heidegger, which are shown to presuppose the division, reject it out of hand, or produce analyses that Beauvoir finds to be unacceptable. Specifically, she argues that, while all these thinkers affirm the absolute objective status of woman, their "[o]pinions about the respective roles of the two sexes . . . only reflected social myths".[62] This created and depended upon a vicious circularity where the supposed biological inferiority of woman depended upon and repeated a number of norms about women, which, in turn, created and depended upon the supporting "myth" of the absolute biological inferiority of woman. To correct this, Beauvoir clarifies that she is not interested in proposing a "philosophy of life",[63] nor "tak[ing] sides too hastily in the quarrel between finalism and mechanism".[64] Her analysis will instead be guided by the vitalist premise "that any living fact indicates transcendence, and that a project is in the making in every function".[65] In other words, biology is not static and determined, but fluid, plastic, and continuously becoming.

To outline and defend this, Beauvoir demonstrates an admirable knowledge of contemporary (for her) biological theory to discuss sexual differentiation in mammals and non-mammals. I will however limit the discussion to the former and, in particular, her analysis of the sexual differentiation of humans. She notes that for those species that permit "individual flourishing",[66] it is usually the case that the male is "bigger than the female, stronger, quicker, more adventurous; he leads a more independent life whose activities are more gratuitous; he is more conquering, more imperious: in animal societies, it is he who commands".[67] While this would seem to warrant the conclusion that the male is physically superior, Beauvoir quickly nuances her understanding, explaining that "[i]n nature nothing is ever completely clear: the two types, male and female, are not always sharply distinguished".[68] Nevertheless, she does accept that "as a whole and especially at the top of the animal scale, the two sexes represent two diverse aspects of the species' life".[69] Although rejecting the notion that this relates to the active–male/passive–female dichotomy that has long structured Western thinking, she does accept that the two sexes relate to procreation differently: the male "can affirm himself in his autonomy; he integrates the specific energy into his own life",[70] whereas, for the female, "individuality is fought by the interests of the species; she seems possessed by outside forces: alienated".[71] From this, Beauvoir concludes that, when measured in terms of the capacity for autonomy, "[w]oman, the most individualized of females, is also the most fragile, the one who experiences her destiny the most dramatically and who distinguishes herself the most significantly from the male".[72]

Building on this, Beauvoir claims that male biological development is also relatively simple, in so far as "[f]rom birth to puberty, he grows more or less regularly"[73] until with puberty hormonal and physical changes activate his sexual life. Rather than being something external to him, Beauvoir claims that there is an organic movement that entwines the male's body to his sexual life. As a consequence, the male "*is* his body".[74] On the contrary, "[w]oman's history is much more complex".[75] Not only does she undergo significantly more physical changes as she enters puberty, but these changes are also experienced as an imposition: "[f]rom puberty to menopause [woman] is the principal site of a story that takes place in her and does not concern her personally".[76] For Beauvoir, menstruation is not something that woman is part of or that which she "owns", but is an activity that passes *through* her. For this reason, it is at this moment that "she feels most acutely that her body is an alienated opaque thing; it is the prey of a stubborn and foreign life that makes and unmakes a crib in her every month".[77] Indeed, Beauvoir claims that woman's sense of alienation from her body is magnified once she becomes pregnant, an activity that she calls "tiring work that offers woman no benefit as an individual but that demands serious sacrifices",[78] "exhausting servitude",[79] whereas the child is termed "a hostile element".[80] For this reason, "woman *is* her body as man *is* his, but her body is something other than her".[81]

The question of Beauvoir's views on motherhood have, however, always been a contested issue whose resolution depends upon how her larger project is understood; that is, whether she is taken to be offering a phenomenological critique of how "woman" is treated in patriarchal societies or whether she is undertaking an ahistoric ontological analysis of woman.[82] A "phenomenological" reading would claim that we must read Beauvoir's descriptions in line with her insistence that "woman" is a social construct. On this understanding, Beauvoir is simply explaining how women tend to experience their pregnancy in *patriarchal* societies, where the demands placed upon them are substantial with little care for her freedom. The problem is that her descriptions of the physiological changes that occur to women in pregnancy appear to be asocial,[83] with the consequence that she seems to be making a point about pregnancy that holds for all women regardless of their place or society. Support for this ontological reading is found, for example, from her claim that "[a]ll that a healthy and well-nourished woman can hope for after childbirth is to recoup her losses without too much trouble".[84] From this, it appears that pregnancy is always an imposition suffered by woman; an experience that negates her autonomy and is to be endured and overcome as quickly and, hopefully, as painlessly as possible. Indeed, Beauvoir claims that woman escapes this ordeal only with the onset of menopause, whereupon she obtains "physiological autonomy [that] is matched by a health, balance and vigour [that she] did not previously have".[85] Again, however, if we read this comment in terms of a phenomenological reading, the menopause simply frees her from the demand placed upon her by a patriarchal society to define herself in terms of child-rearing.

Regardless of which approach is adopted, it appears that Beauvoir is making, at least, two claims. First, motherhood is not, as the most biologically reductionist conception of "woman" would maintain, something "natural" to woman, nor is it something to which she is naturally attuned. It is a scary and difficult process that brings about substantial changes that are not within a woman's control. This is part of Beauvoir's critique of the logic of patriarchy and reduction of woman to a biological function: childbirth. However, second, this is not to say that pregnancy must simply be abandoned or rejected. Rather, it is to accept that pregnancy is a biological possibility for woman, with the consequence that any response to the question "what is a woman?" must engage with this issue to take into consideration the biological, physiological, psychological, and social aspects of motherhood and pregnancy. So, rather than affirm the binary opposition that posits pregnancy as natural to and the essential end of woman *or* that which is to be avoided to safeguard her autonomy, Beauvoir offers a compatibilist position that recognises that pregnancy/childbirth is a possibility for woman based on her biological composition, but rejects the notion that it is what essentially defines her. Its meaning is socially constructed and so can take on different forms, giving rise to different experiences.

This, however, feeds into a second issue that arises from Beauvoir's description of the alienation experienced by woman from her body relating to how we are to understand the notion of "body" within Beauvoir's thinking. Adrian Mirvish, for example, argues that Beauvoir's account is premised on a division between two bodies, one passive, the other active.[86] Mirvish's point is that the human body is not defined by a division between a biological substratum which gains means socially; it is better understood through the active/passive opposition wherein the body is sometimes active and sometimes passive. Mirvish concludes that while Beauvoir appears to affirm the active body over the passive one, in actuality she is pointing to the ambiguous status of the body as *both* active *and* passive. It is, however, highly questionable whether, for Beauvoir, the body is ever passive, in the sense of not moving. After all, the body is an organic, vitalistic becoming, and so is always active. At most, it could be true that the body is not always *intentionally* active, but that is a very different argument. Nevertheless, by noting that Beauvoir's notion of the body is a combination of two "different" states, Mirvish highlights the extent to which Beauvoir's account of the lived body as a continuous becoming is not constrained by nor can it be captured by clear-cut dualisms. It is, rather, ambiguity that defines it, with the consequence that a far more fluid conception of the body-as-becoming is required.

To develop this, a number of commentators have argued that Beauvoir's account of the body-as-becoming must be tied to and read through its situatedness. By claiming that Beauvoir always thinks of the subject as situated, thereby escaping both the mind/body dualism and notion of an unencumbered self dominant in Western (modern) philosophy, this perspective holds that Beauvoir points to a notion of the body-subject that is always immersed in, defined by, and active through its situation. Importantly, however, rather than reducing this body-subject to its situation or making the latter a determined effect of the former, Beauvoir is taken to "both acknowledge the weight of social construction . . . in the formation of the self and yet refuse to reduce the self to an 'effect'".[87] Instead of an autonomous or determined subject, Beauvoir is understood to argue for a compatibilist position that recognises that the subject is always situated but, crucially, remains capable of acting within that situation. Such autonomy occurs, however, *within*, not *from*, its situation. Beauvoir therefore rejects the binary logic that pits a passive body acted upon against a voluntarist position that maintains that the body simply chooses its situation, to instead affirm the relational entwinement of both aspects. For this reason, there is, strictly speaking, no hard and fast division between the subject and its situation, nor is one aspect privileged over or more essential than the other; their entwinement ensures a thoroughly ambiguous relation.

This feeds into Beauvoir's earlier affirmation of ambiguity in *The Ethics of Ambiguity* (from 1947), where she notes that, while the default historical position has been to seek clear-cut categories to thought to deny any form of ambiguity, the result has been the creation of a number of "false" oppositions and privilegings: a "free" mind over a constrained body, the "free" self over the constraining other, and so on.[88] Beauvoir's solution, one she attributes to existential philosophy, is to abandon the appeal to an ethics of binary oppositions that allows clarity but does so by rejecting the entwinement of things, to instead recognise and affirm the importance of ambiguity, where "meaning is never fixed [or clear-cut but] must be constantly won".[89] As a consequence, she insists that human being is not clear-cut or easily identifiable; "the human condition is ambiguous".[90]

Beauvoir calls this an "ethics" because she follows the existentialist tradition in holding that the being of an entity is its doing, but this conclusion also implicitly depends upon a particular ontology of entwinement. Rather than being clear-cut and monadic, entities are complex, situated, continuous becomings, and, as such, "are" always in flux and so highly ambiguous. The emphasis placed on (sexual) ambiguity lays the groundwork for later queer and trans* theories, but tying this back to Beauvoir's account of the relationship between biology and woman, we see that her affirmation of an ethics/ontology of ambiguity underpins her rejection of a straightforward ground for the notion of "woman", whether that be biological, psychological, or social-historical. For this reason, it is not possible to reduce "woman" to her biology, which is also not to say that there is no such thing as biology.

Indeed, Beauvoir recognises that "[o]n average, [woman] is smaller than man, lighter; her skeleton is thinner; the pelvis is wider, adapted to gestation and birth; her connective tissue retains fats, and her forms are rounder than man's"[91] and that

> [w]oman has much less muscular force: about two-thirds that of man; she has less respiratory capacity ... Instability is a striking characteristic of [woman's] bodies in general ... More instability and less control make them more emotional, which is directly linked to vascular variations: palpitations, redness, and so on; and they are thus subject to convulsive attacks: tears, nervous laughter and hysterics.[92]

Although these statements affirm many of the stereotypes of woman that have long dominated Western patriarchal thinking – women are naturally weaker than men, more emotional, and so on – Beauvoir immediately calls them into question by explaining that "they do not carry their meaning in themselves".[93] Biological differences ensure that the world is experienced differently by the sexes, but the species is not a static entity; it "realizes itself as existence in a society"[94] and a society is defined by "customs [that] cannot be deduced from biology".[95] As a consequence, "individuals are never left to their nature; they obey this second nature, that is, customs in which the desires and fears that express their ontological attitude are reflected".[96] For this reason, Beauvoir concludes that "woman's body is one of the essential elements of the situation she occupies in the world. But her body is not enough to define her."[97] "We refuse the idea that [biological data] form a fixed destiny for her. They do not suffice to constitute the basis for a sexual hierarchy; they do not explain why woman is the Other; they do not condemn her for ever after to this subjugated role."[98] Instead, woman's biology only gains meaning once it is "taken on by consciousness through actions and within a society";[99] an issue that brings to the fore "the question [of] what humanity has made of the human female".[100]

With this, Beauvoir once again engages with various historical theories that have been proposed to explain the question of "woman", as a precursor to showing that they are either mistaken or one-dimensional. Her overriding point is that, as a situated becoming, "woman" cannot be thought from a singular causal fixed ground, but must be thought from the constellation of a variety of different perspectives – biology, society, psychological, and so on – all of which are in constant entwined alteration. The subject cannot be thought in terms of clear-cut divisions or a foundational principle; the subject is a complicated, ambiguous process. In turn, this feeds through to her response to the question of sexuality more generally, which is and must also be recognised as multidimensional, complex, fluid, and, by extension, ambiguous. Indeed, as noted, it opens the possibility, which will be key to subsequent queer and trans* theories, of being constituted by multiple (sexual) roles and identities or even moving between different roles and identities. If sexuality and sexual expression are not foreclosed but become what they are through an open-ended process of (social) becoming, there is no reason for them to be limited to particular predefined roles or ends.

Ambiguity and the Logic of Patriarchy

To this point, I have argued that Beauvoir's critical discussion of the biological differences between the sexes and, by extension, their implications for the question of woman has been orientated against the logic of patriarchy, in so far as she aims to expose and call into question the bond long held to exist between *female* biology and its implications for *woman*. Whereas those defending a logic of patriarchy tend to maintain that the latter is grounded in the biology of the former, Beauvoir recognises the former but insists that it has no determination for the latter. She therefore rejects the notion that biology determines and justifies woman's secondary status.

The claim that woman is constructed, not biologically given, has been fundamental to the development of feminist theory and, indeed, continues to find expression throughout contemporary debates. In particular, I will focus on two issues that have sprung from it; namely, whether Beauvoir's supposed affirmation of woman is dependent on and so continues to affirm a logic of patriarchy *and* the extent to which *The Second Sex* can be said to offer a theory of gender. I engage with the first charge in this section, and the second in the subsequent section. The aim is to (1) show the continuing relevance of Beauvoir's thinking to contemporary debates around the question of sexuality, and (2) highlight how her affirmation of ambiguity has given rise to distinct positions within the literature, although I will argue that this influence is premised on something of a misreading, in so far as it arises from the attempt to attribute to Beauvoir a single, clear-cut theory which has tended to downplay the fundamental role that ambiguity plays within her thinking on the human condition generally and sexuality specifically.

As noted in previous chapters, although they reject the notion that sexuality can be understood in essentialist terms, Freud's, Heidegger's, and Merleau-Ponty's theories are all subject to the charge – one that I rejected in the case of Heidegger and Merleau-Ponty – that they continue to, at least, implicitly affirm a male perspective. On first appearances, Beauvoir seems to escape this charge; after all, she not only explicitly calls into question the logic of patriarchy but also appears to affirm the importance of questioning "woman" as opposed to man. Such a project appears then to undercut the logic of patriarchy by bringing to the fore and explicitly rejecting many of the traditional theories supporting that logic. However, a number of commentators have argued that Beauvoir's analysis continues to depend upon an implicit privileging of the masculine, as evidenced, most explicitly, by her claim that woman is the second sex, which indicates that she is always defined from the perspective of the masculine.

On this issue, however, it must be noted that Beauvoir's comments are fragmentary and ambiguous, thereby again permitting different interpretations. For example, she claims that "[t]o emancipate woman is to refuse to enclose her in the relations she sustains with man, [but it is] not to deny them".[101] Instead, and "while [woman] posits herself for herself, she will nonetheless continue to exist for hi[m] *as well*: recognizing each other as subject, each will remain an *other* for the other".[102] From this, it could be concluded that rather than aim to mirror masculine transcendence, feminine liberation requires a relationship of mutual recognition between the sexes, one that does not abolish the fundamental division between them: "reciprocity in their relations will not do away with the miracles that the division of human beings into two separate categories engenders".[103]

If, however, this is so, it is not clear what it might entail. For example, when Beauvoir claims that "the phallus is assimilated with transcendence"[104] as is autonomy, both of which woman lacks, does this mean that woman should strive for autonomy and by extension the phallus; a position that would continue to define woman from the masculine perspective. Or, when Beauvoir continues to push for woman's liberation from the structures of patriarchy, does this affirm strict equality (= sameness) with men, thereby undermining the differences that she otherwise claims "will always exist",[105] or, is it the case that she wants to maintain equality in difference, which she otherwise appears to reject when she explains that "those who talk so much about 'equality in difference' would be hard put not to grant me that there are differences in equality".[106]

Such ambiguities have led to wildly different assessments of Beauvoir's thinking: Céline Léon, for example, accuses Beauvoir of taking the status of the masculine as the goal of woman's liberation: "Not only does Beauvoir take her cues directly from Sartre's nauseous distaste of a world whose grasp eludes him, but she indirectly accepts as given the binarities of Oedipal culture – man/woman, activity/passivity, culture/nature."[107] As a consequence, "[n]otwithstanding all protestations to the contrary, [woman's] desire remains based on a lack, a stasis, and [Beauvoir] never moves away from the cultural stereotypes she attacks".[108] For this reason, Léon charges that "[e]ven as Beauvoir rejects the concept of a feminine essence, there sprout, through the crevices that riddle Western man's discourse, the very seedlings she has trampled underfoot".[109] In other words, Beauvoir takes the characteristics that define masculinity as her model of and for feminine liberation and, in so doing, continues to reduce woman to the male perspective to implicitly perpetuate the logic of patriarchy otherwise rejected.

Léon's assessment does however appear to depend upon an "ontological" reading of Beauvoir's thinking, where Beauvoir's description of a number of binary oppositions is taken as both describing and affirming the ontological reality of woman regardless of her social situation. In contrast, a "phenomenological" reading would argue that Beauvoir's identification of those oppositions is not, at the same time, an affirmation of them, but merely describes how the problem presents itself through the logic dominant in contemporary patriarchal society; a description that permits a prescription regarding how to overcome such divisions. Again, however, the ambiguities inherent in the prescriptive aspect of Beauvoir's analysis have given rise to wildly different interpretations.

Nadine Changfoot, for example, argues that, contrary to Léon's assessment, Beauvoir does not try to overcome the logic of patriarchy by modelling women's liberation on masculinity. Rather, Beauvoir challenges the binary logic underpinning patriarchy – wherein the sexes are divided into two opposing sexes structured around a privileging of the masculine – by affirming a future wherein the sexes are structured around a relation of entwinement. However, Changfoot argues that the problem with this is that it can entail, at least, two options. First, that the future appealed to is thought from the present, with the consequence that it continues to depend upon the imagination currently constituted. This does not, however, permit a material alteration to the situation, not only because it entails an "idealistic" alteration that does not actually affect a material change in the status of woman, but also because its grounding in the present means that it will likely continue to implicitly depend upon and affirm the unequal relations between the sexes that structures the present. Second, and for this reason,

Changfoot insists that Beauvoir affirms an alternative understanding of the future, wherein "both genders culminate in a completed transcendence, but this is envisaged as a condition free from the encumbered bodily experience and consciousness of the present".[110]

Changfoot's argument does, however, depend upon the notion that "transcendence" can be "completed",[111] which is an impossibility for Beauvoir, in so far as she follows Heidegger and Sartre in holding that "transcendence" entails a continuous projection into the future. Rather than a state attained, transcendence describes a continuous, open-ended process of becoming. Furthermore, Changfoot's interpretation depends upon the affirmation of unencumbered bodies that is explicitly rejected by Beauvior's insistence that embodiment is always situated. There is no such thing as an unencumbered, trans-historical body or subject for Beauvoir; that is precisely the ontology that she associates with the logic of patriarchy that has dominated Western thinking and which she explicitly criticises.[112] As a consequence, Changfoot's affirmation of unencumbered (sexed) bodies recuperates Beauvoir's thinking within the logic of patriarchy to be overcome.

For this reason, another line of interpretation has claimed that Beauvior's thinking on woman's liberation is not and cannot be based on simply mirroring the characteristics associated with masculinity in patriarchal societies nor, indeed, affirming a flight to an unencumbered future. Rather, as Tom Grimwood argues, Beauvoir insists on a process of indeterminate and open-ended becoming that affirms "the constitutively unstable process that both confirms the position of woman as man's constructed 'other' and also questions the determinacy of this position".[113] "Beauvoir is not arguing that one *is* a woman, in so far as 'woman' is the 'other' constructed by man's One, but that the female sex is one of unrealized futurity".[114] The emphasis on the future as a site of liberation is not premised on an escape to disembodiment, but is based on the notion of projection that Beauvoir ties to (situated) transcendence. While it might be objected that, because Beauvoir ties "transcendence" to masculinity, this recuperates woman's liberation to the male perspective currently dominant, a phenomenological reading would respond that Beauvoir's account of the masculine–transcendence relation is based on how "masculinity" has been historically constructed. Just because "woman" has been historically excluded from "transcendence" does not mean that she must be. The open-ended challenge is for "woman" to alter the social dynamics so that they too will be able to constantly transcend her situation. For this reason, Grimwood explains that "[t]he iconic statement 'that one is not born, but rather becomes, a woman' is both a statement of woman's oppression and her potential freedom".[115] As Susan Hekman puts it, "if . . . the One/Other dichotomy gives woman no way out . . . it is incumbent on woman to develop a new approach to find that way out".[116] On this reading, Beauvoir's affirmation of woman's liberation offers not a blueprint, but a "challenge that women must meet and transcend".[117]

The jury is then still out regarding whether Beauvoir continues to implicitly depend upon and affirm the logic of patriarchy. On the one hand, those who read *The Second Sex* as offering an ontology of woman maintain that, when she describes woman as the Other, Beauvoir is making a universal ontological statement about woman that defines her negatively from the male perspective. On the other hand, a phenomenological reading maintains that she is merely describing the situation of "woman" within the logic of patriarchy that has dominated Western society; a positioning that, due to her affirmation of open-ended becoming, does not necessarily need to structure the future. The former reading lends support to the charge that Beauvoir continues to implicitly affirm the logic of patriarchy, while the latter offers a way to undercut it but leaves open the question regarding the action and type of relationship that would do so. Although I am more inclined to the latter position, as Ulrika Björk notes, Beauvoir's comments are simply too "indefinite"[118] to be conclusive. Again, however, this is perfectly in keeping with her affirmation of ethical and ontological ambiguity and insistence that the future is contingent and defined by open-ended projection that cannot (and so should not be) predetermined.

The Second Sex and Gender Theory

Although Beauvoir's thinking, particularly on the question of woman's liberation, has given rise to a lively contemporary debate regarding whether she continues to depend upon the logic of patriarchy that she aims to undermine, I have argued that this is a consequence of her attempt to affirm the ambiguity of lived experience and, by extension, sexuality. Her thinking has then often frustrated readers precisely because it (purposefully) does not provide definitive answers, but, instead, affirms the heterogeneity of lived experience. Those looking for such answers have fundamentally missed her point that existence cannot be predetermined, nor does it fit neatly into clear-cut boxes or plans. Rather, Beauvoir points out that an individual's lived situation is "messy", fluid, and various. Instead of providing definite answers to be followed, she aims to open up thinking on sexuality by freeing it from the logic underpinning the historically dominant essentialist-patriarchal conception so that individuals can project themselves in their own way based on their particular situation.

While those, such as Mathew Braddock, who demand determined "guidance"[119] for future action in the form of specific norms and principles to be followed have found her thinking to be "vacuous"[120] and frustrating, Beauvoir's point is that such a rule-based form of thinking subjugates our future projections to predetermined rules that both foreclose concrete reality to a predetermined schema, and, in so doing, permit each individual to abrogate responsibility for deciding on how to live their particular concrete situation. Beauvoir does not then aim to provide the final word on sexuality, but argues that thinking on sexuality must be opened so as to prevent it from being forestalled within one-dimensional forms.

Whatever the *conceptual* merits of such a position, it also has *historical* importance, in so far as it has allowed her thinking to act as a stimulus for a variety of positions, as evidence by the way that Beauvoir has been appropriated by different sides in contemporary debates regarding (1) whether feminist theory should tie embodiment to gender (rather than sexuality), and (2) whether to reconfigure sexuality in terms of embodiment understood not in terms of a monadic substance or signification, but as "an" immanent, dynamic, relationally entwined, and open-ended material becoming.

These issues come fully to fore with Judith Butler's claim that Beauvoir's insistence that "one is not born, but rather becomes, woman"[121] "distinguishes sex from gender and suggests that gender is an aspect of identity gradually acquired".[122] The sex/gender division has, as Butler notes, "been crucial to the long-standing feminist effort to debunk the claim that anatomy is destiny".[123] We will also see (Chapter 7) that it is fundamental to Butler's own theory of performative gender. Within the traditional sex/gender division, "*sex* is understood to be the invariant, anatomically distinct, and factic aspects of the female body, whereas *gender* is the cultural meaning and form that that body acquires, the variant modes of that body's acculturation".[124] Butler explains that the power of this division arises from the fact that it makes it "no longer possible to attribute the values or social functions of women to biological necessity, and neither can we refer meaningfully to natural or unnatural gendered behavior: all gender is, by definition, unnatural".[125] Not only does the sex/gender division undermine the notion of a fixed, determinate sex – after all, gender is the more important term – but by decoupling sexuality from gender, "[t]he presumption of a causal or mimetic relation between sex and gender is undermined"[126] for the simple reason that

> [i]f being a woman is one cultural interpretation of being female, and if that interpretation is in no way necessitated by being female, then it appears that the female body is the arbitrary locus of the gender 'woman' and there is no reason to preclude the possibility of that body becoming the locus of other constructions of gender.[127]

As a consequence, Butler reads Beauvoir as offering "a radical heteronomy of natural bodies and constructed genders with the consequence that 'being' female and 'being' a woman are two very different sorts of being".[128]

From this, Butler goes on to identify the prescriptive aspect of Beauvoir's thinking by first exploring the charge that Beauvoir's dependence on the notion of "transcendence" binds her to "the model of freedom currently embodied by the masculine gender",[129] before, second, defending Beauvoir against this charge by reading it through Hegel's master–slave dialectic "to show that, for Simone de Beauvoir, the masculine project of disembodiment is self-deluding and, finally, unsatisfactory".[130] Instead, Butler develops the logic of the constructivism inherent in Beauvoir's notion of "woman" to conclude that, because it involves a continuous process of becoming, "woman" does not (have to) conform to any predetermined models, logics, or universal categories. Indeed, Butler claims that, as a construction, the way in which one exists gender can not only "be the place in which the binary system restricting gender is itself subverted",[131] but also "promises to proliferate into a multiple phenomenon for which new terms must be found".[132]

On Butler's reading, then, the strength of Beauvoir's approach is "the radical challenge she delivers to the cultural status quo",[133] in so far as Beauvoir undermines both any foreclosing of sexual expression and indeed any determination to sexual expression in a way that opens up the possibilities for sexual (gender) expression. The problem, however, is that it is not clear that Beauvoir actually does this. Not only does Butler subsequently reject their previous argument by criticising Beauvoir for continuing to implicitly depend upon a logic of patriarchy,[134] but Butler's claim that Beauvoir's female/woman division is a precursor of the sex/gender one inherent in Butler's gender theory has also been challenged.

Stella Sandford, for example, argues that Butler's position is undermined by Beauvoir's discussion of biology, which, as we have seen, makes it clear that "woman" is not simply a social construction, but must actually contend with biological sex.[135] Sandford's point is that Butler's privileging of gender construction makes biology an effect of that construction, with the consequence that, for Butler, there is no such thing as a "prior" biological component within Beauvoir's thinking. Sandford points out however that Beauvoir does accept that there is a biological bedrock that demarcates the female body. As such, Sandford charges that while Butler operates through the biological/construction, nature/culture oppositions, Beauvoir's account undercuts these by offering a compatibilist account wherein, as Beauvoir puts it, "the woman's body is one of the essential elements of the situation she occupies in this world. But her body is not enough to define her;

it has a lived reality only as taken on by consciousness through actions and within a society."[136] For this reason, Sandford concludes that "the notion of 'woman' in *The Second Sex* is not simply translatable into the category of 'gender,' indeed it cuts across or problematizes the traditional sex/gender distinction".[137] It is, however, significant that although Sandford affirms that "strictly speaking, there is no sex/gender distinction in *The Second Sex*",[138] she also subsequently accepts that "the move from 'woman' to 'gender' in feminist theory was an extraordinarily productive development of Beauvoir's work",[139] thereby confirming the important role that Beauvoir's thinking played in opening up the theoretical movement to gender.

While I will return to this movement and Butler's thinking specifically in Chapter 7, it is important to recognise that Beauvoir's analysis was also significant for the development of the new materialist reception of Butler's gender theory. I will (re)turn to this in Chapter 8, but, very schematically, the new materialist critique argues that Butler's gender theory reduces material bodies to linguistic-social constructions and so fails to understand and account for the material processes constitutive of the lived body. Rather than turn to the constructionism of gender, it is necessary to examine how the lived material body becomes from the queer processes inherent in nature. Crucially, Beauvoir's thinking on the female/woman division, in combination with her affirmation of the becoming of the situated body, has been identified as a precursor to this development. Ruth Groenhout, for example, argues that, according to Beauvoir,

> material embodiment is the very condition of freedom, what freedom can mean for us occurs within the constraints of being a physical being, and that physicality includes sex characteristics. Flesh and freedom are coextensive. Human freedom and transcendence do not remove us from our material existence. Material existence is the situation within which freedom and transcendence are possible. Embodiment is simultaneously the ground and the boundary of our freedom to act and become.[140]

In a similar vein, Sara Heinämaa argues against Butler's reading of Beauvoir to, instead, claim that Beauvoir offers a sophisticated account of the concrete, lived, fluid, and situated body that cannot be captured by universalist terms such as "sex" or "gender". Here, Beauvoir is taken to offer an understanding of the body as it is manifested and experienced through "the feminine and masculine styles of lived experience".[141] Although Heinämaa's reading reaffirms Beauvoir's links to the phenomenological tradition, it also emphasises a fundamental point inherent in contemporary analyses of the body: instead of being reduced to an inert substance opposed to the becoming inherent in the construction of its meaning, Beauvoir permits a rethinking of sexuality and the body in terms of situatedness, fluidity, and processes that undercuts both the substance and essentialist premises and the nature/culture, mind/body, essentialism/constructivism oppositions, that have long defined Western thinking on sexuality.[142] On this reading, Beauvoir prefigures and justifies the need to turn away from gender construction to return to a purely materialist explanation of sexuality that places the body and processes of emergent materialisation as its site of interrogation.

Conclusion

There are, of course, many other facets to Beauvoir's thinking and, indeed, its reception, but I have argued that her raising of and engagement with the question "what is a woman?"[143] offers a particularly innovative and important contribution to the critique of the essentialist-patriarchal model that has long dominated Western thinking on sexuality. *Conceptually*, she not only brings to the fore the question of "woman" to combat the logic of patriarchy inherent in Freud's thinking and the affirmation of ontological neutrality constitutive of the phenomenological analyses of Heidegger and Merleau-Ponty, but also emphasises the ways in which Western thinking has constructed an abstract value schema to evaluate the worth and status of concrete, sexed beings. Indeed, by explicitly recognising the all-pervasive role that the logic of patriarchy plays in constructing the social and sexual roles of men and, in particular, women, Beauvoir brings to our attention the limiting effects that this logic has on the actions and possibilities of the latter.

Second, she explicitly calls into question the premises sustaining arguments that justify the logic of patriarchy in terms of the inherent biological inferiority of woman. Beauvoir does not deny the biological differences between the sexes; she accepts them and so enters onto her opponent's terrain to show that, on their own terms, their arguments do not stand up to scrutiny. Woman may, on average, be physically weaker than men, but this is not determinate for her existence, which is fundamentally defined by socio-cultural norms and values.

Third, by insisting that sexuality generally and "woman" specifically are a constant socio-somatic-symbolic becoming, Beauvoir points to the embedded "nature" of sexuality in a way that undercuts any notion of clear-cut sexual divisions. That the body is tied to and expressed through its situation means that it is inherently ambiguous, being both what it appears to be and that which it does not. This ambiguity is a source of frustration to those seeking clear-cut definitions, but it is perfectly in keeping with Beauvoir's existentialist claim that the lived body is fluid, malleable, relational, and equivocal; any attempt to reduce sexuality to clear-cut definitions, a single ground, or simple determination will only ever offer, at best, reductive analyses that fail to recognise and accept that opacity is both the price to be paid for, and the necessary condition of, the transcendence and freedom that prevents individuals from being pigeon-holed in and limited to predetermined categories.

Finally, I have argued that Beauvoir's affirmation of ambiguity has permitted her thinking to remain relevant because her notion of sexuality-as-ambiguous is sufficiently open to be capable of providing inspiration to a variety of contemporary theoretical positions. Indeed, I briefly showed how this has played out in relation to contemporary debates regarding the turn to gender within feminist theory and the materialist queer response(s) to that turn, both of which have been linked to different aspects of Beauvoir's thinking. Rather than seek to resolve this dispute, I purposefully left it open to show that Beauvoir's continuing relevance is perhaps best understood not in the conclusions that she arrives at, but in terms of the ways in which she works to undermine long-held assumptions to open up the space from and through which sexuality can be rethought through a situated body defined by open-ended becoming. Understood in this way, the ambiguity inherent in her thinking on the question of "woman" becomes (and has been) a continuing and positive resource for engaging with and challenging the essentialist-patriarchal paradigm that has long dominated Western thinking on sexuality.

Unfortunately, however, such a conclusion was not immediately obvious to her contemporaries. Although *The Second Sex* was, upon publication in France, an instant success, its fortunes ebbed rather quickly because of phenomenology's eclipse by structuralism in the 1950s. Rather than give primordial importance to subjectivity, structuralism thought of subjectivity as an effect of social and linguistic structures. Beauvoir's ties to and dependence on the existential-phenomenological framework generally and the primary role that she affords to subjectivity specifically, meant that her work was quickly sidelined.[144] Although her reputation would rise once more, the continuing dominance of poststructuralism on feminist theory in the 1970s and 1980s meant that this did not occur until the 1990s when it was recuperated posthumously; Beauvoir having died in 1986. In the meantime, through the work of Jacques Lacan, structuralism fused with psychoanalytical theory to reinvigorate the latter in a way that would have radical implications for future thinking on sexuality, and, indeed, influence how Beauvoir's analysis would subsequently be evaluated. It is to this that we now turn.

Notes

1. Simone de Beauvoir, *The Second Sex*, trans. Constance Borde and Sheila Malovany-Chevallier (London: Vintage, 2011).
2. This figure is quoted by Ingrid Galster, "'The Limits of the Abject': The Reception of *Le Deuxième Sexe* in 1949", in *A Companion to Simone de Beauvoir*, edited by Laura Hengehold and Nancy Bauer (Oxford: Wiley-Blackwell, 2017), pp. 37–46 (p. 39).
3. Sandra Reineke, "The Intellectual and Social Context of *The Second Sex*", in *A Companion to Simone de Beauvoir*, edited by Laura Hengehold and Nancy Bauer (Oxford: Wiley-Blackwell, 2017), pp. 28–36 (p. 28).
4. Ibid., p. 28.
5. Ibid., p. 28.
6. Beauvoir, *The Second Sex*, p. 50.
7. Ibid., p. 51.
8. Ibid., p. 294n.
9. For a discussion of their relationship, see Hazel Rowley, *Tête-à-Tête: The Tumultuous Lives and Loves of Simone de Beauvoir and Jean-Paul Sartre* (New York: Harper, 2006).
10. For a general discussion of the intellectual relationship between Beauvoir and Sartre, see Christine Daigle, "Unweaving the Threads of Influence: Beauvoir and Sartre", in *A Companion to Simone de Beauvoir*, edited by Laura Hengehold and Nancy Bauer (Oxford: Wiley-Blackwell, 2017), pp. 260–270. For reconstructive accounts that argue that it was Beauvoir who was instrumental to the development of Sartre's thinking and not vice versa as has long been thought, see Karen Vintges, "*The Second Sex* and Philosophy", in *Feminist Interpretations of Simone de Beauvoir*, edited by Margaret A. Simmons (University Park, PA: Pennsylvania State University Press, 1995), pp. 45–48; and Edward Fullbrook and Kate Fullbrook, *Sex and Philosophy: Rethinking de Beauvoir and Sartre* (London: Continuum, 2008).
11. Michèle Le Doeuff, "Simone de Beauvoir: Falling into (Ambiguous) Line", in *Feminist Interpretations of Simone de Beauvoir*, edited by Margaret A. Simmons (University Park, PA: Pennsylvania State University Press, 1995), pp. 59–66; Kimberley Hutchins, "Beauvoir and Hegel", in *A Companion to Simone de Beauvoir*, edited by Laura Hengehold and Nancy Bauer (Oxford: Wiley-Blackwell, 2017), pp. 187–197; Zeynep Direk, "Simone de Beauvoir's Relation to Hegel's Absolute", in *A Companion to Simone de Beauvoir*, edited by Laura Hengehold and Nancy Bauer (Oxford: Wiley-Blackwell, 2017), pp. 198–210.
12. Eva Gothlin, "Reading Simone de Beavoir with Martin Heidegger", in *The Cambridge Companion to Simone de Beauvoir*, edited by Claudia Card (Cambridge: Cambridge University Press, 2003), pp. 45–65; Nancy Bauer, "Beauvoir's Heideggerian Ontology", in *The Philosophy of Simone de Beauvoir: Critical Essays*, edited by Margaret A. Simons (Bloomington, IN: Indiana University Press, 2006), pp. 65–91.

13. Eleanor Holveck, "Can a Woman be a Philosopher? Reflections from a Beauvoirian Housemaid", in *Feminist Interpretations of Simone de Beauvoir*, edited by Margaret A. Simmons (University Park, PA: Pennsylvania State University Press, 1995), pp. 67–78; Sara Heinämaa, "Simone de Beauvoir's Phenomenology of Sexual Difference", in *The Philosophy of Simone de Beauvoir: Critical Essays*, edited by Margaret A. Simons (Bloomington, IN: Indiana University Press, 2006), pp. 20–41.
14. Sonia Kruks, "Simone de Beauvoir: Teaching Sartre about Freedom", in *Feminist Interpretations of Simone de Beauvoir*, edited by Margaret A. Simmons (University Park, PA: Pennsylvania State University Press, 1995), pp. 79–96; Kristina Arp, "Beauvoir's Concept of Bodily Alienation", in *Feminist Interpretations of Simone de Beauvoir*, edited by Margaret A. Simmons (University Park, PA: Pennsylvania State University Press, 1995), pp. 161–178; Sara Heinämaa, "What is a Woman?: Butler and Beauvoir on the Foundations of the Sexual Difference", *Hypatia*, vol. 12, n. 1, 1997, pp. 20–39; Jennifer McWeeny, "Beauvoir and Merleau-Ponty", in *A Companion to Simone de Beauvoir*, edited by Laura Hengehold and Nancy Bauer (Oxford: Wiley-Blackwell, 2017), pp. 211–223.
15. Stella Sandford, "Beauvoir's Transdisciplinarity: From Philosophy to Gender Theory", in *A Companion to Simone de Beauvoir*, edited by Laura Hengehold and Nancy Bauer (Oxford: Wiley-Blackwell, 2017), pp. 15–27 (p. 18).
16. Anna Alexander, "The Eclipse of Gender: Simone de Beauvoir and the *Différance* of Translation", *Philosophy Today*, vol. 41, n. 1, 1997, pp. 112–122 (p. 116).
17. Sandford, "Beauvoir's Transdisciplinarity", pp. 18–19.
18. Beauvoir, *The Second Sex*, p. 5.
19. Ibid., p. 289.
20. Simone de Beauvoir, *The Ethics of Ambiguity*, trans. Bernard Frechtman (New York: Open Road, 2018).
21. Toril Moi, *Simone de Beauvoir: The Making of an Intellectual Woman*, Second edition (Oxford: Oxford University Press, 2008), p. 169.
22. Proponents of the charge that Beauvoir depends upon and perpetuates the logic of patriarchy include Céline T. Léon, "Beauvoir's Woman: Eunuch or Male?", in *Feminist Interpretations of Simone de Beauvoir*, edited by Margaret A. Simmons (University Park, PA: Pennsylvania State University Press, 1995), pp. 137–161; and Nadine Changfoot, "Transcendence in Simone de Beauvoir's *The Second Sex*: Revisiting Masculinist Ontology", *Philosophy and Social Criticism*, vol. 35, n. 4, 2009, pp. 391–410. For a defense of Beauvoir against this charge, see Tom Grimwood, "Re-Reading *The Second Sex's* 'Simone de Beauvoir'", *British Journal for the History of Philosophy*, vol. 16, n. 1, 2008, pp. 197–213; and Susan Hekman, "Simone de Beauvoir and the Beginnings of the Feminine Subject", *Feminist Theory*, vol. 16, n. 2, 2015, pp. 137–151. In contrast to these positions, Ulrika Björk ("Paradoxes of Femininity in the Philosophy of Simone de Beauvoir", *Continental Philosophy Review*, vol. 43, n. 1, 2010, pp. 39–60) notes the ambiguity that marks Beauvoir's thinking on this issue.

23. Judith Butler, "Sex and Gender in Simone de Beauvoir's *Second Sex*", *Yale French Studies*, vol. 72, 1986, pp. 35–49; Heinämaa, "What is a Woman?" p. 32; Stella Sandford, "Contingent Ontologies: Sex, Gender, and 'Woman' in Simone de Beauvoir and Judith Butler", *Radical Philosophy*, vol. 97, September/October, 1999, pp. 18–29; Alexander, "The Eclipse of Gender", p. 117.
24. Sonia Kruks, "Gender and Subjectivity: Simone de Beauvoir and Contemporary Feminism", *Signs: Journal of Women in Culture and Society*, vol. 18, n. 1, 1992, pp. 89–110; Ruth Groenhout, "Beauvoir and the Biological Body", in *A Companion to Simone de Beauvoir*, edited by Laura Hengehold and Nancy Bauer (Oxford: Wiley-Blackwell, 2017), pp. 73–86; and Emily Anne Parker, "Becoming Bodies", in *A Companion to Simone de Beauvoir*, edited by Laura Hengehold and Nancy Bauer (Oxford: Wiley-Blackwell, 2017), pp. 87–98.
25. Carol Ascher, "Simone de Beauvoir – Mother of Us All", *Social Text*, vol. 6, n. 2, 1987, pp. 107–109.
26. Ursala Tidd, *Simone de Beauvoir* (Abingdon: Routledge, 2004), p. 1.
27. Beauvoir, *The Second Sex*, p. 3.
28. Ibid., p. 3.
29. Ibid., p. 4.
30. Ibid., pp. 4–5.
31. Ibid., p. 5.
32. Ibid., p. 6.
33. Ibid., p. 6.
34. Ibid., p. 7.
35. Ibid., p. 7.
36. Ibid., p. 7.
37. Ibid., p. 7.
38. Ibid., p. 7.
39. Ibid., p. 9.
40. Ibid., p. 9.
41. Ibid., p. 10.
42. Ibid., p. 10.
43. Ibid., p. 10.
44. Ibid., p. 10.
45. Ibid., p. 12.
46. Georg Hegel, *The Science of Logic*, trans. George di Giovanni (Cambridge: Cambridge University Press, 2010), p. 59.
47. Beauvoir, *The Second Sex*, p. 13.
48. Ibid., p. 17.
49. Ibid., p. 17.
50. Ibid., p. 17.
51. Ibid., p. 17.
52. Ibid., p. 17.
53. Ibid., p. 17.
54. Ibid., p. 17.

55. Ibid., p. 7.
56. Ibid., p. 17.
57. Ibid., p. 8.
58. Ibid., p. 17.
59. Ibid., p. 21.
60. Ibid., p. 21.
61. Ibid., p. 23.
62. Ibid., pp. 24-25.
63. Ibid., p. 26.
64. Ibid., p. 26.
65. Ibid., p. 26.
66. Ibid., p. 38.
67. Ibid., p. 38.
68. Ibid., p. 38.
69. Ibid., p. 38.
70. Ibid., p. 38.
71. Ibid., p. 39.
72. Ibid., p. 39.
73. Ibid., p. 39.
74. Ibid., p. 39.
75. Ibid., p. 39.
76. Ibid., p. 40.
77. Ibid., p. 43.
78. Ibid., p. 42.
79. Ibid., p. 43.
80. Ibid., p. 43.
81. Ibid., p. 42.
82. For an overview of the debate, see Nancy Bauer, "Simone de Beauvoir on Motherhood and Destiny", in *A Companion to Simone de Beauvoir*, edited by Laura Hengehold and Nancy Bauer (Oxford: Wiley-Blackwell, 2017), pp. 146-159.
83. Beauvoir, *The Second Sex*, p. 42.
84. Ibid., pp. 42-43.
85. Ibid., p. 43.
86. Adrian Mirvish, 'Simone de Beauvoir's Two Bodies and the Struggle for Authenticity", *Journal of French and Francophone Philosophy*, vol. 13, n. 1, 2003, pp. 78-93 (pp. 79-80).
87. Kruks, "Gender and Subjectivity", p. 92.
88. Beauvoir, *The Ethics of Ambiguity*, pp. 6-7.
89. Ibid., p. 139.
90. Simone de Beavoir, "Jean-Paul Sartre", in *Philosophical Writings*, edited by Mary Beth Marder (Urbana, IL: University of Illinois Press, 2004), pp. 229-234 (p. 233).
91. Beauvoir, *The Second Sex*, p. 44.
92. Ibid., p. 44.
93. Ibid., p. 47.

94. Ibid., p. 48.
95. Ibid., p. 48.
96. Ibid., p. 48.
97. Ibid., p. 49.
98. Ibid., p. 45.
99. Ibid., p. 49.
100. Ibid., p. 49.
101. Ibid., p. 782.
102. Ibid., p. 782.
103. Ibid., p. 782.
104. Ibid., p. 739.
105. Ibid., p. 781.
106. Ibid., p. 782.
107. Léon, "Beauvoir's Woman", pp. 145–146.
108. Ibid., p. 146.
109. Ibid., p. 155.
110. Changfoot, "Transcendence in Simone de Beauvoir's *The Second Sex*", p. 393.
111. Ibid., p. 393.
112. Beauvoir, *The Ethics of Ambiguity*, pp. 5–6; Beauvoir, *The Second Sex*, p. 49.
113. Grimwood, "Re-Reading *The Second Sex*'s 'Simone de Beauvoir'", p. 210.
114. Ibid., p. 210.
115. Ibid., p. 210.
116. Hekman, "Simone de Beauvoir and the Beginnings of the Feminine Subject", p. 141.
117. Ibid., p. 141.
118. Björk, "Paradoxes of Femininity in the Philosophy of Simone de Beauvoir", p. 49.
119. Matthew Braddock, "A Critique of Simone de Beauvoir's Existential Ethics", *Philosophy Today*, vol. 51, n. 3, 2007, pp. 303–311.
120. Ibid., p. 308.
121. Beauvoir, *The Second Sex*, p. 289.
122. Butler, "Sex and Gender in Simone de Beauvoir's *Second Sex*", p. 35.
123. Ibid., p. 35.
124. Ibid., p. 35.
125. Ibid., p. 35.
126. Ibid., p. 35.
127. Ibid., p. 35.
128. Ibid., p. 35.
129. Ibid., p. 43.
130. Ibid., p. 43. Very simply, Hegel's master–slave dialectic explores the way in which the logic of domination inherent in a master–slave relation is undermined by the experience of that form of relation. More specifically, as the dialectic unfolds, the logic of domination reveals that the master, who takes himself to be independent and primary in the relation, is actually – as master – dependent upon the slave, who, as such, is revealed to be the master. The

point is that each position is defined relationally, rather than monadically, and that for their relation to survive it must morph from one based on a logic of domination to one based on mutual recognition. Butler discusses this in *Subjects of Desire: Hegelian Reflections in Twentieth-Century France* (New York: Columbia University Press, 1999), pp. 17–60. For an extended discussion of Hegel's thinking, especially as it relates to that of Sartre, see my *Realizing Freedom: Hegel, Sartre, and the Alienation of Human Being* (Basingstoke: Palgrave Macmillan, 2011).
131. Butler, "Sex and Gender in Simone de Beauvoir's *Second Sex*", p. 47.
132. Ibid., p. 47.
133. Ibid., p. 48.
134. In *Gender Trouble: Feminism and the Subversion of Identity*, Second edition (Abingdon: Routledge, 1999), Butler reverses their previous positive assessment, explaining that "[d]espite my own previous efforts to argue the contrary, it appears that Beauvoir maintains the mind/body dualism, even as she proposes a synthesis of those terms" (p. 16), with this being "symptomatic of the very phallogocentrism that Beauvoir underestimates" (pp. 16–17). As a consequence, Butler charges that Beauvoir's thinking continues to implicitly depend upon and so perpetuate the logic of patriarchy that it supposedly aims to escape. Butler uses this assessment to justify their move away from questions of "sex" to those of "gender".
135. Sandford, "Contingent Ontologies", p. 21.
136. Beauvoir, *The Second Sex*, p. 49.
137. Sandford, "Contingent Ontologies", p. 21.
138. Sandford, "Beauvoir's Transciplinarity", p. 24.
139. Ibid., p. 24.
140. Groenhout, "Beauvoir and the Biological Body", p. 77.
141. Heinämaa, "What is a Woman?", p. 32.
142. See also, Parker, "Becoming Bodies", pp. 95–96.
143. Beauvoir, *The Second Sex*, p. 5.
144. Contemporary scholarship has started to re-engage with the structuralism–Beauvoir relationship to challenge this oppositional understanding. See, for example, Eva D. Bahovec, "Beauviour between Structuralism and 'Aleatory Materialism'", in *A Companion to Simone de Beauvoir*, edited by Laura Hengehold and Nancy Bauer (Oxford: Wiley-Blackwell, 2017), pp. 249–259.

CHAPTER 5

Lacan, the Symbolic Phallus, and Sexual Difference

In France, the transition from the 1940s to the 1950s was marked not only by a temporal change, but also a conceptual one wherein the phenomenological-existentialist framework that dominated the former was usurped by structuralism. Whereas this alteration took place primarily through the anthropological theory of Claude Lévi-Strauss and the linguistic theory of Ferdinand de Saussure,[1] it quickly spread and instantiated nothing short of a revolution in philosophical thought. The idea that the individual subject is foundational was replaced with a form of thinking that emphasised the foundational role of linguistic structures. Put differently, philosophies of consciousness were replaced by philosophies of the concept.[2] In turn, this was combined with a resurgence in interest in psychoanalysis, with Jacques Lacan insisting in the famous 1953 essay "The Function and Field of Speech and Language in Psychoanalysis" that

> [w]e must . . . take up Freud's work again starting with the *Traumdeutung* [*The Interpretation of Dreams*] to remind ourselves that a dream has the structure of a sentence or, rather, to keep to the letter of the work, of a rebus – that is, a form of writing, of which children's dreams are supposed to represent the primordial ideography, and which reproduces, in adults' dreams, the simultaneously phonetic and symbolic use of signifying elements found in the hieroglyphs of ancient Egypt and in the characters still used in China.[3]

By affirming the intimate bond between language, manifested through signifiers, and the unconscious, Lacan's return to Freud had radical implications for psychoanalytic theory and the understanding of sexuality.

The question of sexuality pervades Lacan's writings and teachings throughout the 1950s, with *Seminar III*,[4] from 1955–1956, and a number of texts – "The Signification of the Phallus",[5] "Guiding Remarks for a Convention on Female Sexuality",[6] and *Seminar V*[7] – from 1958 being particularly important. While multidimensional, these texts outline a conception of sexuality from Lacan's conception of the symbolic. This, however, requires a word on Lacan's project. According to Lacan, individual experience is composed of three distinct but intertwined aspects: the imaginary, the symbolic, and the real. While Lacan always insisted on their entwinement, methodologically, he focused on them in different periods: from around 1936 to 1953, the emphasis is placed on the "imaginary", which describes the creation of an illusionary identity; while from the 1960s onwards, he focuses on the "real" or that which resists symbolisation. The writings and teachings of the 1950s concentrate on the symbolic, which describes and is composed of the differential relations between signifiers that generate meaning. Crucially, as Lacan explains elsewhere, "it is in the chain of signification that meaning *insists*, but . . . none of the chain's elements *consists* in the signification it can provide at that very moment. The notion of an incessant sliding of the signified under the signifier thus comes to the fore."[8] Extrapolating from this schema, we find that the meaning of the sexes emanates not from an "inner" essentialism or pre-existing monadism, but from the relationship to the other, which, in turn, gains meaning from its relation to the first. As a consequence, the relationship and, indeed, the meaning of each position is purely relational; there is no permanence to either the relation or its aspects.

However, no sooner did Lacan outline this logic than he complicated it by appearing to reintroduce a privileging of patriarchy. Despite insisting that the relationship has no fixed foundation, he maintains that each position is nevertheless orientated to and gains meaning from a "third" term: the phallus. Whereas the "imaginary phallus"[9] is tied to the pre-Oedipal castration complex and designates a part-object that can be castrated, the symbolic phallus is not an object or bodily organ but an empty signifier-function that grounds the economy of signifiers to generate symbolic meaning. While important in relation to the child's psychic development, it is also significant in relation to the issue of sexual difference because Lacan claims that the masculine and feminine take different positions in relation to the phallus: the former is constructed to "have" the phallus and so is the central point from which signification emanates, whereas femininity is positioned to "be" the phallus and so is removed from the "power" of the phallus all the while perpetuating it through this removal. By virtue of not being the phallus, woman looks outside herself – to the phallus – to gain meaning. As such, her meaning is dependent upon and defined from the masculine phallus; a conclusion that *appears* to reach its apogee in *Seminar XX*, where

Lacan explains that "'[w]oman' (*la*) is a signifier, the crucial property (*propre*) of which is that it is the only one that cannot signify anything, and this is simply because it grounds woman's status in the fact that she is not-whole. That means we can't talk about Woman (*La femme*)."[10]

Lacan's symbolic account of the phallus therefore recognises that the meaning of sexuality is relational and so undermines any form of sexual essentialism but continues to define the feminine from the masculine perspective; a position that has meant that the reception of his thinking on sexuality has been contested. Jacqueline Rose, for example, praises Lacan's analysis and argues that because it divorces the phallus from the penis, it undermines the claim that the masculine perspective is the ahistoric ground of meaning. Her position is premised on the argument that Lacan does not so much affirm a patriarchal privileging as enter into the logic of patriarchy to undermine it by showing its "internal" symbolic machinations. Given that the phallus is a contingent, symbolic construction, "the phallus stands at its own expense and any male privilege erected upon it is an imposture".[11] By showing that the phallus is the empty signifier that orientates meaning, Rose argues that Lacan subtly but definitively disrupts the notion of a grounding masculinity upon which the logic of patriarchy depends. Instead, Lacan's argument points to the more fundamental question "as to why that necessary symbolization and the privileged status of the phallus appear as interdependent in the structuring and securing (never secure) of human subjectivity".[12] In other words, he not only internally "deconstructs" the logic of patriarchy but also brings to the fore the issue of whether the symbolic relation does, in fact, need to be anchored by the phallus or an anchoring principle generally.

For other commentators, however, Lacan's account of the symbolic phallus does not go far enough in combating the logic of patriarchy precisely because it continues to simply use the language of "phallus". The basic premise is that, regardless of the intention, the use of the linguistic term "phallus" can only continue to affirm a privileged position for the masculine. Judith Butler, for example, develops this conclusion across three critical points. First, Lacan's account continues to implicitly depend upon and so (needlessly) perpetuates patriarchal structures because – despite his insistence that the phallus is not attached to a biological sex but operates as a symbolic function – the simple use of the term "phallus" always brings the discussion back to the masculine to devalue the feminine perspective.[13] Second, by structuring the discussion of the sexual difference in terms of the binary opposition between "having" or "being" the phallus, Lacan's discussion of sexual difference continues to implicitly affirm a logic of binary sexual division that remains restrictively heteronormative, in so far as it is limited to the heterosexual relation.[14] Finally, Butler points out that if sexuality is symbolically constructed and this construction is not based on *a priori* principles then sexuality does not have to conform to the binary heteronormative division that Lacan affirms.[15]

In response, a number of commentators have recently sought to recuperate Lacan's thinking on sexuality by downplaying his symbolic account of sexuality – with its emphasis on the phallus – to instead focus on his later works, where, as noted, the emphasis is placed on the real. Eve Watson,[16] for example, outlines Lacan's phallic account of sexuality from the 1950s, as a precursor to showing how it is extended, altered, and developed in his later work on the real; Lorenzo Chiesa[17] concentrates on the notion of *jouissance* to show that Lacan uses the example of a number of feminine mystics to offer a far more nuanced conception of the feminine–phallus relation than is usually appreciated; Patricia Gherovici appeals to Lacan's late notion of "sinthome"[18] – the bind linking the Lacanian notions of real, symbolic, and imaginary – to suggest that, through it, "we can rethink sexual difference without the notion of phallus";[19] and Alenka Zupančič argues that Lacan's discussion of the phallus does not point to the privileging of a "thing" but the uncovering of "the *missing link* between the biological and the Symbolic (or between nature and culture) *as the generic point of sexuation*".[20]

Although I do not necessarily wish to reject these authors' conclusions, I also do not wish to simply repeat and affirm the implicit claim subtending their line of interpretation which holds that Lacan's later works correct his earlier symbolic account and so reveal his "true" theory of sexuality. Instead, this chapter is guided by the contention that different approaches to the question of sexuality can be gleaned from Lacan's writings.[21] I take seriously Lacan's earlier, symbolic account of sexuality – taken from the writings and teachings of the 1950s – not only because I wish to argue that these writings are far more nuanced than is often appreciated, but also because Lacan's symbolic account of sexuality forms the basis from which much subsequent (feminist) thought – such as that of Luce Irigaray (Chapter 6) and Judith Butler (Chapter 7) – develops itself by way of contrast. Concentrating on these writings and teachings will allow me to reconsider an often-neglected aspect of Lacan's *oeuvre* and develop the historical narrative of this book. I start by outlining Lacan's analysis of the symbolic division of the sexes in *Seminar III* and "The Signification of the Phallus" to argue that it undermines the notion that the sexes are defined by a (biological) essentialism, but appears to open him to the charge that this rejection is nevertheless premised on the affirmation of a binary patriarchal opposition between a privileged "masculine" and a dependent "feminine" position. In response, I appeal to comments that he makes in *Seminar V* on the "paternal metaphor"[22] to argue that the symbolic law (both prior and subsequent to the resolution of the Oedipus complex) is also transferred through the maternal function. This occurs prior to the resolution of the Oedipus complex, but, given Lacan's reliance on a logic of negative relationality – where A is A because it is not B, meaning that "having" the phallus depends upon it being distinguished from the position of "being" the phallus and vice versa – I argue that the resolution of the Oedipus complex does not lead to the simple affirmation of the paternal law absent the maternal; the paternal law continues to be logically related (and so bound) to the maternal. While the acceptance of the symbolic law is often understood to be underpinned by the simple adoption of the paternal law, it is actually the acceptance of a law that is conditioned by a complex entwinement of the maternal and paternal. This undermines the notion of a strict opposition between the symbolic positions, which, in turn, prevents them from joining together in a unity; a conclusion echoed in his later famous claim that "[t]here's no such thing as a sexual relationship".[23] From this, I claim that Lacan's comments on the "phallic" anchor point that orientates the "two" positions is inherently fragile, with the consequence that far from holding the positions together, it is chimeric, acting as the illusionary point that generates the masquerade of masculine privilege. The phallus is not a "thing" but an empty position; as such, it can be replaced, although the anchoring function it fulfils must always remain. This undermines the *necessity* of the logic of patriarchy, but continues, somewhat strangely, to affirm it by virtue of, at least, positing the issue in terms of a privileging of the foundational logic underpinning the phallic economy.

By way of conclusion, I note that Lacan would probably defend himself by insisting that this conclusion emanates from concrete (clinical) analysis – i.e. the discussion of the phallus mirrors the patriarchal structures found in his society and from which is derived his theory – but because he is not sufficiently clear regarding the continuing role of the phallus, it is not obvious whether (1) the phallus must remain, or (2) another principle fulfilling the same role can take its place. As a consequence, Lacan's symbolic account undermines the essentialism underpinning the essentialist-patriarchal model of sexuality, but is ambiguous regarding the patriarchal aspect. If (1), the logic of patriarchy continues; if (2), the argument moves away from sexuality towards a meta-principle/debates regarding the structure of language and specifically what function the anchoring principle fulfils and what options can fill it; a movement that turns us away from the study of sexuality *per se* to the structure(s) of language.

Lacan on the Symbolic Phallus

One of Lacan's earliest discussions of sexuality occurs in *Seminar III*, given in 1955–1956, where, in lecture thirteen, he offers an analysis of the question

"What is a woman?"[24] through an interpretation of the famous Dora case in Freudian theory.[25] Lacan uses a brief discussion of it to move the discourse from the question of hysteria to that of the asymmetrical ways that the sexes enter into and resolve the Oedipus complex. Arguing that Freud struggled to satisfactorily explain this dissymmetry because he located the difference anatomically, Lacan insists that it must be explained "at the symbolic level".[26] It is not the case that Lacan rejects biology, but that he thinks that it is not capable of explaining the complexity of psychic life. Biology is, to put it one way, merely the undifferentiated stuff from which the differentiation of the symbolic world emanates from and, indeed, whose meaning depends upon how the symbolic is structured. For this reason, Lacan acknowledges that there is a biological difference between the sexes, but in *Seminar XIX* dismisses it as merely "the small difference"[27] before, in *Seminar XX*, explaining that "[t]he body's being (*l'être du corps*) is of course sexed (*sexué*), but it is secondary, as they say".[28] Rather than explain sexuality in naturalist or biological terms, it must be understood psychically, which, for Lacan, means symbolically.

From this premise, Lacan makes the strong claim that "there is no symbolization of woman's sex as such",[29] before weakening it to accept that, while there might be some symbolisation possible, "it doesn't have the same source or the same mode of access as the symbolization of man's sex".[30] The reason for this fundamental symbolic difference is that "the phallus is a symbol to which there is no correspondent, no equivalent".[31] As a consequence, "one of the sexes is required to take the image of the other sex as the basis of its identification".[32] Because masculinity *is* the phallus by virtue of possessing the phallus, and indeed because there are only two sexes, it is femininity that is marked by a lack of its own symbolic status; it "only furnishes an absence where elsewhere there is a highly prevalent symbol".[33] Indeed, Lacan goes further, explaining that because "[t]he female sex is characterized by an absence, a void, a hole . . . it happens to be less desirable than is the male sex for what he has that is provocative".[34] Femininity therefore depends upon the other sex – masculinity – for its significance and, based on its lack and dependence, is simply less desirable than the masculine sex. Dora's problem, according to Lacan, is that she ignores this and by "wondering, *What is a woman?*, [attempts] to symbolize the female organ as such".[35] Her inability to do so, brings her to realise that there is nothing to symbolise and no way to do so. Instead, she identifies "with the man, bearer of the penis, [who] for her on this occasion [is] a means of approaching this definition that escapes her. She literally uses the penis as an imaginary instrument for apprehending what she hasn't succeeded in symbolizing."[36] When that does not turn out to be as she thought, the ground from which she signified herself shifts, with this bringing forth her hysteria.

Regardless of whether this diagnosis of Dora is accurate or not,[37] Lacan's comments on sexuality in *Seminar III* are important because they point, in very schematic form, to a symbolic account of sexuality that rejects biological essentialism and insists on a fundamental symbolic difference between man and woman, all the while privileging the masculine position to think femininity as an absence that is defined from its relation to the masculine phallus. This logic and the positions contained therein are developed in far more conceptual depth three years later in the short dense text "The Signification of the Phallus".

Here, Lacan reiterates his famous return to Freud; this time, in relation to the question of the role that the phallus-function plays within psychoanalytic theory. While noting that Freud emphasises the important role it plays in the castration and Oedipus complexes, Lacan claims that his comments led to a number of unresolved problems including why a girl ever considers herself to be castrated, the reason why both sexes identify the mother with the phallus, why the discovery of the mother's castration is so clinically problematic, and, perhaps most important of all, Freud's exclusion "in both sexes [of] any instinctual mapping of the vagina as the site of genital penetration until ... the dissolution of the Oedipus complex".[38] Having outlined Freud's "ignorance"[39] on these issues, Lacan briefly criticises contemporary attempts, namely those of Helene Deutsch, Karen Horney, and especially Ernst Jones, for having "los[t] their way to a greater or lesser degree".[40]

To start to rectify this, Lacan reiterates that the signifier is the key to any analytic theory and practice.[41] While noting that the theory of the signifier in modern linguistics postdates Freud, Lacan claims that this notion can only be fully understood through and from Freud's thinking. Specifically, with the notion of the unconscious, "the signifier ... becomes a new dimension of the human condition in that it is not only man who speaks, but in man and through man that it speaks".[42] Rather than think of the individual in substantive terms or as a constituting ego, Lacan maintains that the ego is an effect of the unconscious, which is structured like language. Far from being the foundation of knowledge, the conscious ego is "grounded" in the unconscious subject and, for this reason, is always "the ego of the [unconscious] subject".[43] To truly comprehend the subject, therefore, we must move away from the conscious ego to "[t]he true subject – that is, the subject of the unconscious".[44]

To understand why, it is necessary to have a basic knowledge of the linguistic theory of Ferdinand de Saussure and, in particular, his claim that language is composed of signs. These are constituted by a signifier and signified that relate to one another in a particular way. As Lionel Bailly explains, for Saussure,

> the signifier (sound image/acoustic image) is not the *material* sound but the hearer's impression it makes on our senses. Also, the signified (concept) is not the object (the chair in front of you) but *the idea of the object* (any chair – the property of being a chair – of which an example may or may not be before you at the time of speaking).[45]

Because the (immaterial) signifier represents an immaterial signified, Saussure holds that signs are immaterial. Lacan, in contrast, holds that "language is not immaterial. It is a subtle body, but a body it is".[46] The object designated by the signifier "chair" is not a chair apart from its signification – apart from its signification it is simply an object – it becomes a "chair" through being named as such.

Furthermore, Lacan accepts Saussure's[47] claim that meaning arises from the relations between signifiers, but radicalises it by claiming that, if meaning is dependent upon the movement between signifiers, they must take precedence over that which is signified. Meaning is not generated from the movement from signifier to *signified*, but is created from the constant and incessant movement between signifiers. For this reason, "the empty spaces are as signifying as the full ones".[48] Indeed, Lacan defines the chain of signification as "presence in absence and absence in presence"[49]: the (presented) signifiers only attain meaning from the differences (= absence) between them:

> the sun in so far as it is designated by a ring is valueless. It only has a value in so far as this ring is placed in relation with other formalizations, which constitute with it this symbolic whole within which it has its place, at the centre of the world for example, or at the periphery, it doesn't matter which. The symbol only has value if it is organised in a world of symbols.[50]

As such, it is "in the chain of signifier that meaning *insists*, but . . . none of the chain's elements *consists* in the signification it can provide at that very moment. The notion of an incessant sliding of the signified under the signifier thus comes to the fore."[51] This constant sliding is contained by "the laws of a closed order",[52] but even within that order signifiers continue to relate to others in different ways so that meaning is constantly changing. For this reason, "[e]verything that is language proceeds via a series of steps like those of Achilles who never catches up to the tortoise – it aims at re-creating a full sense which, however, it never achieves, which is always somewhere else".[53]

In relation to the subject, the constant sliding of the signifier "under" the signified ensures that the subject is not a unified entity; "it" is defined by a constant process of becoming wherein the signifying chain that subtends the signified (name) undermines the latter to reproduce it. This is not however an act done by the subject to itself; the subject does not act to subvert its own identity in a process of wilful becoming. Rather, "this division stems from nothing other than . . . the play of signifiers",[54] which marks the very structure of the unconscious from which the subject arises.

Importantly, Lacan claims that "the unconscious is structured like a language"[55] rather than by language. If it were structured by language it would be defined by both a signifier *and* signified in the same way that language is: there would be a chain of signification that led to a particular signification of word. The unconscious, however, lacks signifieds; it is pure movement across the signifying chain. "If there were signifieds as well, then the meaning of any particular signifier for a [s]ubject would be quite rigid: a signifier (and its emotional load) would remain immovable, attached forever to one particular thing and not be transferable to another."[56] For this reason, Lacan claims that to understand what the "subject" is requires an analysis of

> the chain of materially unstable elements that constitutes language: effects that are determined by the double play of combination and substitution in the signifier, according to the two axes for generating the signified, metonymy and metaphor; effects that are determinant in instituting the subject.[57]

That the subject is an effect of the chain of signifiers ties it intimately to the differential relations and hence Other that defines that chain.[58]

It is here that the function of the phallus comes to the fore. As Lacan explains: "In Freudian doctrine, the phallus is not a fantasy, if we are to view fantasy as an imaginary effect. Nor is it such an object (part-, internal, good, bad etc.) inasmuch as 'object' tends to gauge the reality involved in a relationship. Still less is it an organ – penis or clitoris – that it symbolizes."[59] Rather, "the phallus is a signifier . . . whose function . . . is destined to designate meaning effects as a whole, insofar as the signifier conditions them by its presence as signifier".[60] Put simply, the phallus is the anchoring point for the symbolic system, which supports and generates meaning for signifiers.

From here, Lacan reaffirms the notion that the subject is an effect of signifiers and, indeed, is only a signifier, before pointing to the relationship between signifier and desire, with the latter resulting from the relationship between need and the demand issued to satisfy that need. Through the demand, the subject reveals not only what it desires but also its dependence upon the Other, who can choose to satisfy or deny the subject's desire. In either case, the Other takes on a privileged role, with this seen most clearly in "love".[61]

Love, in this scenario, is not a "thing" freely given through a wilful act; it is a consequence of the economy inherent in desire wherein the subject desires that the other show the subject love by putting aside its own desire to try to satisfy the subject's demand. Of course, the subject's desire can never be satisfied; it is the lack that distinguishes need from demand, with the consequence that it keeps returning to, in a sense, sustain the love relation. The relationship between love and desire is a crucial one for Lacan, but in "The Signification of the Phallus" the discussion of it is severely underdeveloped.[62] It appears, however, that, rather than desire structuring and sustaining "a sexual relationship",[63] for Lacan, it is love – defined by the lack that binds the lack of social relations and the lack inherent in the desire for the Other – that fulfils this role. Rather than focus on the Other as that desired, love describes a structure developed in relation, and hence lack, to the lack that identifies and distinguishes the object desired. Whereas desire is focused on an object, to love is to sustain the structure of lack (the "in-between") that generates the desire of and for the Other.

Crucially, it is here that the question of the phallus takes on significance. While the phallus does not explicitly appear, it structures and anchors the subject's desire as it is expressed through the demand for/to the Other. For this reason, the emphasis can only ever be on the subject's desire, although such a focus implicitly depends upon and so reveals the subject's relation to the phallus. Lacan explains that "[t]hese relations revolve around a being and a having".[64] To "have" the phallus is to be the signifier for the Other's desire; it is, in other words, to be the anchoring point for the Other. The problem, of course, is that, strictly speaking, the subject that *has* the phallus is a symbolic construction defined by the lack constitutive of the symbolic and its relation to the Other who does not have the phallus and, for this reason, is designated, somewhat paradoxically, as "being" the phallus. To be the phallus is to be in a position that is desired without, somewhat paradoxically, having that which is desired: the phallus.

Importantly, because the sexual difference is symbolically constructed and so constituted by lack, the sexual relation is always based on a play of mirrors: the position of having the phallus depends upon the desire of the Other – the one who "is" the phallus – but the desire of the one who *is* the phallus depends upon the one who *has* the phallus, which, as noted, depends upon the desire of the one who *is* the phallus. There is no foundation grounding this relation; it is one of pure relationality. This afoundationality will be important to my argument that the phallic function cannot simply be reduced to a patriarchal privileging: if the position of having/being the phallus is implicitly dependent on the other then it follows that neither position can simply be privileged over the other in the way that patriarchy demands.

However, rather than leave the relation as one of pure symbolic lack, Lacan maintains that this lack is "covered" through the projection of "the ideal or typical manifestations of each of the sexes' behaviour, including the act of copulation itself".[65] It is not clear if this is a universal claim or one based on the behaviours that Lacan witnessed from his clinical sessions, which were, of course, conducted from and within a particular patriarchal society, but the basic point is that the symbolic phallus is covered over with, sustained by, and associated with the illusion of an imaginary essential identity. As such, the symbolic relation (which is wholly constructed) comes to be interpreted and understood through an imaginary essentialist perspective imposed on it so that the positions – being and having – come to be confined to a particular heteronormative logic: to *have* the phallus is associated with and requires the adoption of typically (socially defined) masculine characteristics, whereas the one who *is* the phallus is associated with and requires the adoption of (socially defined) feminine mannerisms. However, because the relation to the phallus is a symbolic construction, Lacan recognises that, within actual relationships, this positioning is based on playing the role of either sex, which ensures that a biological woman can take the "masculine" position of having the phallus, while a biological man can take up the "feminine" position of being the phallus. Nonetheless, he notes that for a woman to *have* the phallus requires that she "rejects an essential part of femininity";[66] namely, the status of *being* the phallus.

This, however, generates a particularly problematic situation: on the one hand, when woman *has* the phallus, she is the anchor for the Other's desire; but, at the same time, she "finds the signifier of her own desire in the body of the person to whom her demand for love is addressed".[67] She herself desires another and so *is* the phallus for another. This reiterates the point that, because desire is conditioned by lack, even if the individual *has* the phallus, his or her desire for the Other means that he or she always lacks the phallus and so *is* the phallus. The basic idea behind this convoluted logic is that, contrary to initial formulations, the being/having dichotomy is not a zero-sum game; in an actual sexual relation, each position finds itself bound to and defined by the Other so that the position of "having" the phallus is actually (but implicitly), at the same time, a position of "being" the phallus by virtue of the logic of negative relationality that underpins these positions.

Lacan claims, however, that men and women relate to this double bind – being and having the phallus – differently: heterosexual women always privilege "having" the phallus over "being" the phallus (and so affirm the masculine over the feminine), with the consequence that they tend to privilege a relationship of love, which it will be remembered is understood to focus on the *lack* generating desire for that which is desired: the phallus. Heterosexual males also privilege "having" the phallus over "being" the phallus but privilege a relationship based on desire, understood as affirming the desiring of what one already has, i.e. the phallus.

The reason for this conclusion is underdeveloped, but how it is interpreted depends upon which hermeneutical strategy is adopted regarding Lacan's thinking on the sexes. A reading like Judith Butler's is implicitly underpinned by the argument that Lacan's analysis is a "positive" one that describes how the sexes relate to one another symbolically and so understands that while the phallus is symbolically structured, the reaction to the symbolic phallus is determined by the sex of the participants: men *always* prefer to "have" the phallus and so, in a sense, have power over the Other. As such, they privilege a relationship where the phallus is affirmed, and the relationship is structured as desire for what the Other does not have: the phallus. Women, in contrast, do not "have" the phallus, but desire to attain that which has it, with the consequence that their desire is *always* orientated to love in so far as they desire the *relation* with what they do not have. This problematic essentialism comes further to the fore in Lacan's comments on homosexual males and females wherein the former, regardless of the object of desire, continue to affirm the male privileging of "having" the phallus with the consequence that a male homosexual relationship "is constituted along the axis of desire",[68] while female homosexuality is marked by the female privileging of being the phallus in a way that "strengthens the axis of the demand for love".[69]

If, however, we follow Jacqueline Rose, Alenka Zupancic, and Todd McGowan in arguing that Lacan's discussion of sexuality in "The Signification of the Phallus" does not aim to offer a "positive" conception of sexuality *per se*, but undertakes an immanent critique of the logic of patriarchy from the perspective of the differential logic underpinning his symbolic account, then we get a different conclusion wherein, rather than prescribing or lapsing back into essentialist premises, Lacan is showing how such essentialist premises continue to cling to, are imposed on, and/or operate despite being grounded in differential relations.[70]

Lacan's text is notoriously ambiguous regarding its purpose, but my sympathies lie with this latter interpretation for two reasons. First, it better accords with Lacan's previous claim that the play of mirrors resulting from the afoundationality of the differential symbolic relations subtending the sexual relation is covered over with a projected identity.[71] It is not the case that masculinity or femininity must mean "X", but that to be considered masculine/feminine (in a particular society) it must adopt certain characteristics. Failure to do so prevents it from being considered (appropriately) masculine or feminine. Rather than affirming an essentialist understanding of the sexes, Lacan is showing that the lack of essentialism resulting from the differential logic of the symbolic is covered over through the projection of social ideals and mores that bring the sexes to foreclose themselves to predefined modes of behaviour.

Second, this understanding better accords with Lacan's recognition that such divisions need to be "refined through a re-examination of the function of the mask"[72] – by which he means the illusion of sexual identity assumed by each subject – inherent in sexual relations. Rather than simply describing the essential characteristics of both "masculinity" and "femininity", the mask distorts the symbolic relationality subtending the meaning of each so that they *appear* to possess and be defined by that which they really do not: essentialist identity traits. To understand how the logic of identity works and, by extension, to undermine it, we need to better comprehend how the mask works to distort the play of mirrors inherent in the sexual relation so that it appears that each sex is defined in a singular essentialist manner.

Indeed, in another short text from 1958, "Guiding Remarks for a Convention on Female Sexuality", Lacan even wonders whether female sexuality *can*, in fact, be understood through the phallic function.[73] Affirming the absence of *a priori* symbolic determinants, he notes that how "woman" is conceived is not predetermined but is a consequence of each particular symbolic relation. As such, while he had interpreted "woman" in a particular way, it is not necessarily the case that we need to tie "being" and "having" the phallus to the masculine and feminine in the way that he does or, indeed, employ those oppositions. In a certain reading, this endeavour is pointed to in "The Signification of the Phallus", but it becomes more explicit in other texts; namely, *Seminar V*, written in the same year as "The Signification of the Phallus", which undermines the notion that the sexes constitute a binary opposition because they are defined in essentialist "purely" masculine or feminine positions, and his later works, especially *Seminar XX*, where the fragility of the relation between two positions is extensively engaged with to show that there is no substantiality to it.

Symbolic Law and Sexual Division: From Binarity to Entwinement

Seminar V was held in 1957–1958 under the title "Formations of the Unconscious". It is of particular interest to the current discussion because a number of its lectures are orientated to the question of the Name-of-the-Father[74] and the maternal–paternal relation,[75] which work at different, but ultimately complementary, symbolic levels. Whereas the Name-of-the-Father describes the Law that conditions symbolic relations – "This is what I call the Name-of-the-Father, namely the symbolic father. It's a term that subsists at the level of signifiers and that, in the Other as the seat of the law, represents the Other. This is the signifier that gives the law its support, that promulgates the law. It is the Other in the Other"[76] – the paternal metaphor and phallus describe the way in which the infant relates to the Law. The former describes how the meaning of the Law changes as the child develops. More specifically, it is tied to the triadic structure – child, mother, father – of the Oedipus complex, although, technically speaking, it is not part of that structure but "represents" a "dummy"[77] fourth term that, while never present, supports the other three and, indeed, the relation between them. The paternal function is fundamentally "a metaphor"[78] because it "is a signifier that comes to take the place of another signifier".[79] More specifically, the paternal metaphor describes the way in which the perception of the father function changes as the child develops. Lacan notes, for example, that "[t]he father's function in the Oedipus complex is to be a signifier substituted for the first signifier introduced into symbolization, the maternal signifier".[80] While it takes different forms, these all act as a metaphor for the symbolic Law (= Name-of-the-Father). The (symbolic) phallus describes the empty signifier from which the child who has passed into the symbolic anchors all its symbolic relations. Importantly, the Name-of-the-Father, phallus, and paternal metaphor are interrelated: the Name-of-the-Father generates and depends upon the paternal metaphor and phallus to function whereas the paternal metaphor and phallus are anchored in and generated from the Name-of-the-Father. For this reason, Lacan's discussion of the paternal metaphor and Name-of-the-Father sheds light on the structure and function of the phallus.

This is clearly seen from Lacan's remarks on the relationship between the paternal metaphor and phallus. During the Oedipus complex, the child appears to move from its desire for the mother to recognise the Name-of-the-Father. In so doing, the metaphor (and signifier) used to signify the Name-of-the-Father alters from the mother to the father. In turn, the structure of the anchoring point (the phallus) alters away from the mother (who is the phallus) to the father (who has the phallus). With this, the child orientates itself towards the position that *has* the phallus: the masculine. This appears to support Butler's claim that Lacan's schema is inherently patriarchal: not only are the terms that Lacan grounds his theory in related to the masculine (Father, paternal, phallus), but the infant's ability to use meaning depends upon the adoption of the Name-of-the-Father and the movement from the maternal to the paternal so that rather than desire a signifier that "merely" *is* the phallus, he desires one that actually *has* it.

However, Lacan muddies this substantially by pointing out that the place and function of the symbolic phallus (and paternal metaphor) are far more nuanced and unsettled, in so far as the maternal function is also always an implicit "carrier" of the symbolic law. What this entails depends upon whether the examination takes place prior or subsequent to the resolution of the Oedipus complex, but the basic point in both is to complicate and undermine any notion of a straightforward binary opposition between the maternal and paternal. For example, the pre-Oedipal "state" is not based on a straightforward mother–child relation absent the father; while the mother–child relation is dominant, it is conditioned by the presence (through the mother function) of the imaginary father, which is the symbolic father as it is mediated through the actions of the mother who has entered the symbolic and so adopted the paternal law, which she exhibits and transmits through her actions and speech. The mother represents the (symbolic and imaginary) father through her actions because she desires the phallus: "Everyone realizes that many things depend on her relations with the father, especially when ... the father fails to play his role, as they say."[81] As such, the pre-Oedipal mother–child relation is not absent the father. Through the mediation of the mother, the father function takes on an imaginary importance to the child who "has not yet made his entry"[82] into the symbolic.

From this, it is tempting to conclude that Lacan affirms (1) a patriarchal binary opposition between the mother and father, wherein the mother is the phallus because she desires the male who has the phallus, with the consequence that the mother is a mere vassal for the transmission of the paternal symbolic law, and (2) a linear movement to the child's psychic development in which he moves from the desire for the mother to the acceptance of the paternal symbolic law. Lacan, however, rejects such a simplistic binary opposition and linear movement between the maternal and paternal functions by appealing to the work of Melanie Klein to note that "[t]he further back she goes on the imaginary plane, the further back she discovers – very difficult to explain if we cling to a purely historical notion of the Oedipus complex – the appearance of the paternal third term, and this is so from the child's earliest imaginary phases".[83] While the maternal function may be the child's first "historical" relationship, the mother is always implicitly tied to the symbolic paternal law that exists in the background:

> This something extra, which must be there, is precisely the existence behind her of this entire symbolic order on which she depends, and which, since

it's always there more or less, permits a degree of access to the object of her desire, which is already such a specialized object and so marked with the necessity the symbolic system institutes that in its prevalence it's absolutely unthinkable in any other way.[84]

This complicates the maternal function by ensuring that it is never "pure", but always located in and through the paternal function. As Lacan explains, "it's not so much a question of the personal relations between the father and the mother, nor . . . simply of the person of the mother to the person of the father, but of the mother with the father's speech".[85]

While a linear understanding of the resolution of the Oedipus complex would hold that the father's pre-Oedipal spectral appearance through the mother morphs into an explicit affirmation of the paternal phallus once the symbolic law is accepted to, in so doing, "clear-up" the messiness of the pre-Oedipal maternal function by establishing a clear patriarchal binary opposition between the privileged paternal and downgraded maternal functions, Lacan's comments in *Seminar V* point to an alternative conclusion in which the resolution of the Oedipus complex does not establish a straightforward patriarchal binary opposition between the maternal and paternal functions nor does it simply affirm the paternal over the maternal. Whereas in the pre-Oedipal mother–child relation, the father appears spectrally through the mother, Lacan makes it clear that this continues to occur once the symbolic law is accepted. He gives the example of little Hans, "where it's the mother who says 'Put it away, you don't do that.' In general, it's most often the mother who says, 'If you keep on doing that, we will call the doctor who will cut it off.' It's therefore correct to point out that the father, as he who prohibits at the level of the real drive, isn't so essential."[86]

There are, at least, two key issues with this statement. First, it demonstrates that far from simply substituting the father for the mother, the resolution of the Oedipus complex continues to be structured around, albeit in different ways, the complex entwinement of the mother, child, and father triad. There is no straightforward movement from a pre-Oedipal mother–child relation to a post-Oedipal father–child one; the third (whether mother or father) always intervenes to disrupt any linearity to the movement or straightforward affirmation of the maternal (as in the pre-Oedipal stage) or paternal (once the Oedipus complex has reached resolution).

Second, Lacan makes the claim that the symbolic father "isn't so essential"[87] to the transmission of the symbolic law. Rather, the maternal function is the one that often has the crucial role in transmitting it. This can be understood in, at least, two ways, in so far as it can be read as (1) reducing the maternal function to a vassal of the paternal one thereby reinforcing the claim that the maternal "merely" *is* the phallus because she depends upon the paternal who *has* the phallus; this is the reading upon which Butler bases their critique; or (as I maintain) (2) suggesting that, because the maternal function speaks the symbolic law of the father function, she, in a very strong sense, becomes mixed with the father function. Rather than simply being the phallus, she actually comes to *have* and *be* the phallus by virtue of the crossing that occurs when the maternal transmits the Name-of-the-Father through her actions and speech.

This, in turn, depends upon two sub-arguments. First, the phallus and paternal metaphor are empty and so can be constructed in a myriad of different ways, with the consequence that they can take on different meanings. Second, that neither the maternal or paternal functions are pure; rather, having or being the phallus is always tied to the other by virtue of the negative relationality that defines the logic of the symbolic order wherein A only is A by virtue of its distinction from non-A: "having" the phallus implicitly depends upon being distinguished from the position of "being" the phallus, which, in turn, depends upon its distinction from the position of "having" the phallus. Instead of being a one-off event, this distinction between being and having the phallus is diachronic, with the consequence that both positions are always returned to the other and so exist in a relation of entwinement even as this logical entwinement is a condition of their conceptual distinction. Whereas Butler[88] maintains that the maternal and paternal functions are engaged in an endless comedy where each tries, but fails, to be the other; the comedy actually results when each tries to maintain the binary opposition that pits the pure maternal against the pure paternal and fails to recognise and accept the *implicit* entwinement of both. Lacan's point is that because sexual positions are relational, they are coextensive, entwined, and always impure. This undermines the notion of a strict opposition between the symbolic positions, which, in turn, prevents them from joining together in a unity; a conclusion summed up nicely by his later famous claim that "[t]here's no such thing as a sexual relationship".[89] The logic of binarism, upon which patriarchy depends, simply fails to appreciate this, instead imposing "pure" categories that distort the complexity of the positions and, indeed, the relation itself.

Conclusion

There is, of course, far more to Lacan's thinking on sexuality – for example, and as noted, he returns to discuss the sexual difference in *Seminar XIX* and the sexual relation in *Seminar XX* – but reconsidering his earlier (symbolically focused) writings from the 1950s shows that, far from simply discriminating against femininity to privilege the masculine phallus, Lacan's thinking on sexuality is multidimensional, complicated, and open-ended. At no point does it resolve itself into a fixed state, nor was it meant to. Rather, in line with the dynamism inherent in his notion of the symbolic, sexuality is thought from constantly moving differential symbolic relations. To show this, I have moved through a lot of material within Lacan's *oeuvre* and by necessity have been forced to downplay the significant alterations that take place within his schema(s). Such an approach has however allowed me to show that the question of sexuality is a near constant one for him and that he offers a multifaceted and highly original rethinking of it. By insisting that sexuality is not defined by biology or a body part, but is a position taken in relation to a privileged, albeit ultimately empty, point in the symbolic order (= phallus), he continues the rejection of sexual essentialism found in the thinkers engaged with in previous chapters. He does however radicalise their thinking by making sexuality a fundamentally symbolic position conditioned by ever-changing differential relations. This implies that sexual positions are never strictly dual: each position depends upon and is tied to the other, which reveals their hybrid "nature" and shows that sexuality does not necessarily have to be foreclosed within predefined roles or binary logic. If they are held to have a definitive role or nature or be structured within a binary division, it is as a consequence of a symbolic system that, by definition, can be altered.

The fundamental problem with his analysis, however, relates to the role that the phallus plays within the symbolic order. While I have argued that the phallus is an empty signifier that acts as the anchor point of the relationship between the "two" positions, we saw that the differential relations subtending each position mean that the bind that ties them is inherently fragile and illusionary. Whereas this, once again, opens up the configurations that a sexual relationship may take, it does so by actually dissolving the bind between the "two" positions in the relationship and, by extension, the "two" positions themselves, which it will be remembered only are by virtue of the relationship between them. On the one hand, Amy Hollywood notes that, as a consequence, Lacan's schema "refuse[s] the claims to mastery and wholeness on which male-dominant culture, society, and their unconscious rest".[90] But, on the other hand, if the relationship is constantly altering and nothing but an illusionary chimera, it is unclear how the symbolic anchor point operates to bind the positions together.

A Lacanian response might be that this is the challenge posed by Lacan's symbolic account of sexuality; rather than expect fixed and definite answers, it opens up a problematised field wherein "relationality" must be thought as being conditioned by a necessary mirage that has to be constantly rethought.

This undermines the *necessity* of the logic of patriarchy, but continues, somewhat strangely, to affirm it by virtue of, at least, positing the issue in terms of the foundational logic tied to the phallic economy. Why the phallus continues to be privileged despite there being no justification for such privileging is where, according to Lacan, the clinic enters the scene, but, from a *philosophical* perspective, the emptying out that his thinking on sexuality entails causes consternation. It appears to undermine the sexual difference, while insisting that symbolic regimes require an anchoring point which means that it is not obvious what happens to the phallus function from this emptying out: Does (1) the phallus necessarily remain as an empty master-signifier, or (2) another principle that fulfils the same role take its place? If (1), the logic of patriarchy continues; if (2), not only does this risk re-instantiating the *logic* of the phallus under a different name, but it also moves the terms of the debate away from sexuality towards an analysis of the structure of language and specifically to the issue regarding the function that the anchoring principle fulfils and the forms it can take; a movement that risks simply downgrading the feminine perspective once again and/or turns us away from the study of sexuality *per se* to that of the structure(s) of language.

With regards to the essentialist-patriarchal model, therefore, Lacan's grounding of sexuality in differential symbolic relations is strong at undermining the essentialist premise, but weak – based on the ambiguity inherent in it – regarding the patriarchal aspect. This is, as noted, a pattern that has been repeated throughout many of the analyses examined in previous chapters. To correct it, post-Lacanian thinking turned its attention more forcibly to the patriarchal premise; a move that also brings forth various challenges to the emphasis that Lacan places on the symbolic. To start to outline what this entails, the next chapter turns to Luce Irigaray's analysis of the elusive but totalising manner in which the logic of patriarchy has operated historically within Western thought and her subsequent attempt to overcome it through a rethinking of sexual difference.

Notes

1. Good critical overviews of their respective theories are found in Maurice Godelier, *Claude Lévi-Strauss: A Critical Study of his Thought* (London: Verso, 2018); and David Holdcroft, *Saussure: Signs, System, and Arbitrariness* (Cambridge: Cambridge University Press, 2008).
2. For an excellent discussion of the historical development of and conceptual implications inherent in this movement, see Knox Peden, *Spinoza contra Phenomenology: French Rationalism from Cavaillès to Deleuze* (Stanford, CA: Stanford University Press, 2014).

3. Jacques Lacan, "The Function and Field of Speech and Language in Psychoanalysis", in *Écrits*, trans. Bruce Fink in collaboration with Héloïse Fink and Russell Grigg (New York: W. W. Norton, 2006), pp. 197–268 (p. 221).
4. Jacques Lacan, *Seminar III: The Psychoses*, edited by Jacques-Alain Miller, trans. Dennis Porter (New York: W. W. Norton, 1993), pp. 173–182.
5. Jacques Lacan, "The Signification of the Phallus", in *Écrits*, trans. Bruce Fink in collaboration with Héloïse Fink and Russell Grigg (New York: W. W. Norton, 2006), pp. 575–584.
6. Jacques Lacan, "Guiding Remarks for a Convention on Female Sexuality", in *Écrits*, trans. Bruce Fink in collaboration with Héloïse Fink and Russell Grigg (New York: W. W. Norton, 2006), pp. 610–620.
7. Jacques Lacan, *Seminar V: Formations of the Unconscious*, edited by Jacques-Alain Miller, trans. Russell Grigg (Cambridge: Polity, 2017).
8. Jacques Lacan, "The Instance of the Letter in the Unconscious, or Reason since Freud", in *Écrits*, trans. Bruce Fink in collaboration with Héloïse Fink and Russell Grigg (New York: W. W. Norton, 2006), pp. 412–441 (p. 419).
9. Lacan, *Seminar III*, p. 319.
10. Jacques Lacan, *Seminar XX: On Feminine Sexuality, The Limits of Love and Knowledge, 1972–1973*, edited by Jacques Alain-Miller, trans. Bruce Fink (New York: W. W. Norton, 1999), p. 73.
11. Jacqueline Rose, "Introduction – II", in *Feminine Sexuality: Jacques Lacan and the école freudienne*, edited by Juliett Mitchell and Jacqueline Rose (London: Macmillan, 1982), pp. 27–58 (p. 44).
12. Ibid., p. 56.
13. Judith Butler, *Bodies that Matter: On the Discursive Limits of "Sex"* (Abingdon: Routledge, 1993), pp. 42, 51.
14. Judith Butler, *Gender Trouble: Feminism and the Subversion of Identity*, Second edition (Abingdon: Routledge, 1999), p. 74.
15. Ibid., p. 67.
16. Eve Watson, "Some Guiding Remarks for a Convention on Female Sexuality", in *Reading Lacan's Écrits: From "Signification of the Phallus" to "Metaphor of the Subject"*, edited by Stijn Vanheule, Derek Hook, and Calum Neill (Abingdon: Routledge, 1999), pp. 66–91.
17. Lorenzo Chiesa, *The Not-Two: Logic and God in Lacan* (Cambridge, MA: The MIT Press, 2016), pp. 1–6.
18. Jacques Lacan, *Seminar XXIII: The Sintome*, edited by Jacques-Alain Miller, trans. A. R. Price (Cambridge: Polity, 2016), p. 3.
19. Patricia Gherovici, *Transgender Psychoanalysis: A Lacanian Perspective on Sexual Difference* (Abingdon: Routledge, 2017), p. 8.
20. Alenka Zupančič, *The Odd One In: On Comedy* (Cambridge, MA: The MIT Press, 2008), p. 207.
21. Although I do not discuss it here, this feeds into the claim that Lacan's conception of the body is multiple. See Emma Ingala, "Not just *a* Body: Lacan on Corporeality", in *Historical Traces and Future Pathways of Poststructuralism: Aesthetics, Ethics,*

Politics, edited by Gavin Rae and Emma Ingala (Abingdon: Routledge, 2021), pp. 143–159.
22. Lacan, *Seminar V*, pp. 180–196.
23. Lacan, *Seminar XX*, p. 144.
24. Lacan, *Seminar III*, p. 173–182.
25. Very schematically, the Dora case describes a young woman suffering from a variety of physical ailments. Brought to Freud by her father (who had previously been treated by Freud), Freud theorises that her hysteria stems from psychological trauma or problems in the patient's sexual life. To explain this, Freud notes that Dora was particularly close to her father, who, having moved to a new town to treat her tuberculosis, became friends with a couple: Herr and Frau K. Dora became close to Herr K, but their relationship cooled after she alleged that he made an indecent proposal to her on one of their walks and, indeed, on one occasion kissed her by surprise. Dora was disgusted by this act and told her father. Herr K denied the allegations and her father believed him. Furthermore, when Dora demanded that her father end the relationship with Herr and Frau K, her father ignored her, namely because he felt indebted to Frau K for helping him after he was sick. As a consequence, Dora became resentful of her father's relationship with Frau K, which Dora suspected of being a love affair. The case has generated much attention, not only because of its clinical importance – including its unsuccessful conclusion when Dora ended treatment – but also because it highlights the complex interplay between different social relationships and their effect on psychic life. For a detailed and multidimensional discussion of the case, see the essays collected in Daniela Finzi and Herman Westerink (eds), *Dora, Hysteria, and Gender: Reconsidering Freud's Case Study* (Leuven: Leuven University Press, 2018).
26. Lacan, *Seminar III*, p. 176.
27. Jacques Lacan, *Seminar XIX: . . . Or Worse*, edited by Jacques-Alain Miller, trans. Adrian Price (Cambridge: Polity, 2018), p. 5.
28. Lacan, *Seminar XX*, p. 5.
29. Lacan, *Seminar III*, p. 176.
30. Ibid., p. 176.
31. Ibid., p. 176.
32. Ibid., p. 176.
33. Ibid., p. 176.
34. Ibid., p. 176.
35. Ibid., p. 178.
36. Ibid., p. 178.
37. Lacan's comments on the Dora case in *Seminar III* are very brief. A fuller engagement is found in the earlier 1951 paper titled "Presentation and Transference", in *Écrits*, trans. Bruce Fink in collaboration with Héloïse Fink and Russell Grigg (New York: W. W. Norton, 2006), pp. 176–185. For an overview of this paper and, indeed, Lacan's engagement with the Dora case, see Patricia Gherovici, "Where have the Hysterics Gone?: Lacan's Reinvention of Hysteria", *English Studies in Canada*, vol. 40, n. 1, 2014, pp. 47–70.

38. Lacan, "The Signification of the Phallus", p. 576.
39. Ibid., p. 576.
40. Ibid., p. 577.
41. Ibid., p. 578.
42. Ibid., p. 578.
43. Jacques Lacan, *Seminar I: Freud's Papers on Technique*, edited by Jacques-Alain Miller, trans. John Forrester (New York: W. W. Norton, 1991), p. 62.
44. Jacques Lacan, "Introduction to Jean Hyppolite's Commentary on Freud's 'Verneinung'", in *Écrits*, trans. Bruce Fink in collaboration with Héloïse Fink and Russell Grigg (New York: W. W. Norton, 2006), pp. 308–317 (p. 310).
45. Lionel Bailly, *Lacan* (London: OneWorld, 2009), p. 43.
46. Lacan, "The Function and Field of Speech and Language in Psychoanalysis", p. 248. On Lacan's materialism, see Gavin Rae, "The 'New Materialisms' of Jacques Lacan and Judith Butler", *Philosophy Today*, vol. 65, n. 3, 2021, pp. 655–672.
47. Ferdinand de Saussure, *Course in General Linguistics*, edited by Charles Bally, Albert Sechehaye, Albert Riedlinger, trans. Roy Harris (Chicago, IL: Open Court, 1986), p. 118.
48. Jacques Lacan, "Response to Jean Hyppolite's Commentary on Freud's 'Verneinung'", in *Écrits*, trans. Bruce Fink in collaboration with Héloïse Fink and Russell Grigg (New York: W. W. Norton, 2006), pp. 318–333 (p. 327).
49. Jacques Lacan, *Seminar II: The Ego in Freud's Theory and in the Technique of Psychoanalysis*, edited by Jacques-Alain Miller, trans. Sylvana Tomaselli (New York: W. W. Norton, 1991), p. 38.
50. Lacan, *Seminar I*, p. 225.
51. Lacan, "The Instance of the Letter in the Unconscious, or Reason since Freud", p. 419.
52. Ibid., p. 418.
53. Lacan, *Seminar V*, p. 92.
54. Jacques Lacan, "Position of the Unconscious", in *Écrits*, trans. Bruce Fink in collaboration with Héloïse Fink and Russell Grigg (New York: W. W. Norton, 2006), pp. 703–721 (p. 712).
55. Lacan, *Seminar XX*, p. 15.
56. Bailly, *Lacan*, p. 48.
57. Lacan, "The Signification of the Phallus", p. 579.
58. Lacan explicitly distinguishes between "two *others*, at least two – an other with a capital *O*, and an other with a small *o*, which is the ego. In the function of speech, we are concerned with the Other" (Lacan, *Seminar II*, p. 236). In other words, the *other* refers to a particular ego-other, whereas the *Other* refers to the differential relations inherent in language, discourse, norms, and everything that Lacan calls the symbolic order.
59. Lacan, "The Signification of the Phallus", p. 579.
60. Ibid., p. 579.
61. Ibid., p. 580.
62. The heterogeneity of his comments on the topic mean that Lacan's notion of "love" is not easily summarised. Indeed, Bruce Fink explains that that there "is,

in my view, no singular theory of love to be found in Freud's work or in Lacan's work: there are only multiple attempts to grapple with it at different points in their theoretical development" (*Lacan on Love: An Exploration of Lacan's Seminar VIII, Transference* [Cambridge: Polity, 2015], p. 34). For example, the most well-known of Lacan's definitions is found in *Seminar VIII* where he explains that "love is to give what one does not have" (Jacques Lacan, *Seminar VIII: Transference*, edited by Jacques-Alain Miller, trans. Bruce Fink [Cambridge: Polity, 2015], p. 34). Rather than permitting a simple or singular explanation, Fink identifies at least three ways in which it can be interpreted. First, "love" is getting from the other that which it is not easy for them to give: "Giving what you have is easy – anyone can do it. Giving what you do not have is far more meaningful" (Fink, *Lacan on Love*, p. 54). By struggling to give what you do not have, others are able to "see" the significance that they have for you. Second, Finks suggests that it can also mean that love is defined by the acceptance and admittance that one does not have something that the other is taken to have, with the consequence that the other is needed to "fulfil" it. To admit love is then to ask the other to both care for and take care of that which you do not perceive yourself to have (ibid., p. 54). Third, Fink claims another meaning arises if we treat "love" as a noun rather than a verb and link it to the epistemological ignorance of the participants as to what binds each to the other: the lover does not know what he/she desires in the beloved, who in turn does not know what his/her lover wants (ibid., pp. 55–56). The basic idea is that at the "heart" of love is "something" that is fundamental to the functioning of the economy of the relation but that can never be captured symbolically to explain why we are in love or even what brings us to love the other. This ensures that love is defined by a "comical feeling" (Lacan, *Seminar VIII*, p. 33) wherein the participants tie themselves to the other without knowing why they do so. It also means that, rather than being transparent, love is defined by a mysterious and unidentifiable unknowable; a conclusion that ties into and affirms the importance that Lacan attributes to the real within symbolic relations and, by extension, human existence.
63. Lacan, "The Signification of the Phallus", p. 580.
64. Ibid., p. 582.
65. Ibid., p. 582.
66. Ibid., p. 583.
67. Ibid., p. 583.
68. Ibid., p. 583.
69. Ibid., p. 583.
70. Rose, "Introduction – II", p. 44; Zupančič, *The Odd One In*, p. 207; Todd McGowan, "The Signification of the Phallus", in *Reading Lacan's Écrits: From "Signification of the Phallus" to "Metaphor of the Subject"*, edited by Stijn Vanheule, Derek Hook, and Calum Neill (Abingdon: Routledge, 1999), pp. 1–20.
71. Lacan, "The Signification of the Phallus", p. 582.
72. Ibid., p. 583.

73. Lacan, "Guiding Remarks for a Convention on Female Sexuality", p. 613.
74. Lacan, *Seminar V*, pp. 129–180.
75. Ibid., pp. 180–196.
76. Ibid., p. 132.
77. Ibid., p. 143.
78. Ibid., p. 158.
79. Ibid., p. 158.
80. Ibid., p. 159.
81. Ibid., p. 174.
82. Ibid., p. 164.
83. Ibid., p. 149.
84. Ibid., p. 166.
85. Ibid., p. 174.
86. Ibid., p. 156.
87. Ibid., p. 156.
88. Butler, *Gender Trouble*, p. 77.
89. Lacan, *Seminar XX*, p. 144.
90. Amy Hollywood, *Sensible Ecstacy: Mysticism, Sexual Difference, and the Demands of History* (Chicago, IL: University of Chicago Press, 2002), pp. 16–17.

CHAPTER 6

Irigaray on Sexual Difference: Jamming the Patriarchal Machine

Lacan's return to Freud and the subsequent conceptual developments it spawned reinvigorated psychoanalytic accounts of sexuality, while alterations within Lacan's conceptual schema, namely the growing emphasis he placed on the unknowable real within the symbolic realm, contributed to the movement from structuralism to poststructuralism that occurred in France in the 1960s.[1] Very simply, the poststructuralist position rejected what was perceived to be structuralism's continuing dependence on ahistoric foundational structures and/or symmetrical binary relations. Whereas structuralist thought recognised the importance of relationality to the generation of meaning, *post*structuralist thinkers argued that this approach continued to depend upon a restricted economy wherein two positions were defined relationally.[2] As a consequence, structuralism undermined the essentialist premises upon which traditional metaphysics had tended to depend, but was held to continue to implicitly depend upon and emphasise a closed totality that, in so doing, affirmed the importance that traditional metaphysics placed on unity, singularity, and sameness. The key lesson learnt was that the logic of essentialism (= one = totality = foundations) was a subtle and conniving opponent; while it may be *explicitly* rejected, it can all too easily regroup to find expression *implicitly*. As a consequence, poststructuralists argued – in heterogeneous ways – that it was not only important to reject a foundational metaphysical unity or identity; it was also necessary to be ever vigilant to foreclose the implicit recuperation of unity or identity within a closed system of thought. This led to the affirmation of the "foundational" importance of difference, asymmetric relations, heterogeneity, and open-ended becoming; a reorientation that had significant important for the issue of sexuality.[3]

We see this alteration if we turn to Jacques Lacan's late seminars from 1971–1973 on the question of (female) sexuality, which, on first appearance, seem to entail a significant departure from his earlier work on the topic from the 1950s.[4] While we saw in the previous chapter that his earlier work insists that sexual positions are defined from their orientation to the phallus and so depends upon an anchoring principle to give meaning to each sexual position – one that is necessarily restrictive – his later work on the topic focuses, to a much greater degree, on the relationality – or, as Lacan calls it, the *"not-all"*,[5] which, for the sake of clarity, we may designate as the "between-ness" – inherent in sexual positions. Contemporary Lacanian scholarship has focused on this later work to claim that it severs the determining role that Lacan had previously given to the phallus to, in so doing, open up sexuality to heterogeneous forms.[6]

The problem with this line of critique is that it ignores the extent to which Lacan's later work continues to give an important role to the logic of the phallus. For example, he famously claims that "[t]here's no such thing as Woman, Woman with a capital W indicating the universal".[7] On first reading, this appears to indicate that Lacan is simply affirming that individual women cannot be recuperated into a universal essence defining "Woman-as-such". He would then be rejecting the essentialist claim that *all* women are defined by a universal essence to, instead, ask that each particular woman be studied in her sexual particularity. However, as we read on, we see that this is not the case: the reason why women "cannot signify anything"[8] is not because there is no universal *per se*, but because she lacks the phallus;[9] a conclusion that returns Lacan to his earlier privileging of the phallus and the degradation of female sexuality to secondary status.

To correct this, feminist poststructuralist theory turned more forcibly to question the logic of the phallus and, by extension, patriarchy that was held to underpin Lacan's thinking to argue that a radical rethinking of sexuality was needed for the differences between the sexes to be recognised, respected, and thought. Luce Irigaray's work on sexual difference – a topic she calls "one of the major philosophical issues, if not the issue, of our age"[10] – is particularly important in this regard. While trained in Lacanian psychoanalysis, Irigaray calls attention to the continuing role that the logic of patriarchy plays within Freudian, and by extension Lacanian, psychoanalysis. By showing that Freud's discourse of sexuality is infected by and depends upon a privileging of the masculine phallus, Irigaray claims that it is incapable of adequately thinking woman and so either ignores her or reduces her to the masculine: "The enigma that *is* woman will therefore constitute the *target*, the *object*, the *stake*, of a masculine discourse, of a debate among men, which would not consult her, would not concern her. Which, ultimately, she is not supposed to know anything about."[11] Ironically, the Lacanian reaction to Irigaray's critique meant that she was removed from the faculty at the University of Vincennes.[12] While personally difficult, it was a pyrrhic victory of sorts because it demonstrated her theoretical point that Freudian-Lacanian theory was not willing to listen to a (female) perspective that departed from the centrality given therein to the phallus or that aimed to discuss "woman" in alternative (non-masculine) terms.

Importantly, Irigaray does not simply content herself with a critique of Freudian psychoanalysis, but expands her critical stance by claiming that the masculine bias inherent in Freudian psychoanalysis is but the latest manifestation of the logic of patriarchy that has defined Western philosophy and culture: "We can assume that any theory of the subject has always been appropriated by the 'masculine.'"[13] To develop and defend this, she undertakes sweeping and extended engagements with the history of Western philosophy, showing that some of its major figures – Plato, Descartes, Kant, Hegel, and Freud in *Speculum of the Other Woman*; Nietzsche in *Marine Lover of Friedrich Nietzsche*;[14] Heidegger in *The Forgetting of Air in Martin Heidegger*;[15] Aristotle, Spinoza, Levinas, and Merleau-Ponty in *An Ethics of Sexual Difference* – are guilty of perpetuating a system of representation that is incapable of doing justice to the difference of women.[16] From this, she makes the strong claim that the Western system of representation has been unable to accurately describe sexual difference and so has instead affirmed a foundational unity that ignores "femininity" or "hom(m)osexualiz[es] her"[17] by reducing her to the "masculine" (= foundation = one = same).

Irigaray's guiding contention, one that will bring her into the political realm, is not that the sexual difference *per se* must be overcome, but that the patriarchal form of sexual difference must be overcome to re-instantiate the "proper" form of sexual difference, wherein the differences between sexualities are respected on their own terms.[18] With this, Irigaray opens up a new perspective within feminist theory, one that rejects Beauvoir's earlier emphasis on equality, which is held to make the "theoretical and practical error"[19] of continuing to think "women" in relation to her otherness from "men" and, in so doing, reduce "woman" to the vassal status of the "masculine". Rather than affirm "woman's" equality *with* "men", Irigaray demands that "woman" be thought from "her" difference *from* "men".[20]

This also brings to light a fundamental distinction between phenomenological and poststructuralist approaches to sexuality. Whereas I previously (Chapters 2 and 3) pointed out that a key aspect of Heidegger's and Merleau-Ponty's phenomenological accounts of sexuality is their affirmation of an originary neutrality that allows sexuality to be revealed through experience rather than through the imposition of conceptual presuppositions or logic, Irigaray interprets their comments on an originary neutrality as entailing the affirmation of sexual neutrality *per se*. Her poststructuralist account rejects this to affirm the fundamental importance of sexual difference: "The human race is divided into *two genres* which ensure its production and reproduction."[21] Based on this presupposition, she claims that suppressing this distinction in the name of "neutrality" would require the elimination of half the human race and so "invite a genocide more radical than any destruction that has ever existed in History".[22]

In other words, for Irigaray, the affirmation of neutrality does not, in fact, lead to a "neutral" stance. Because she maintains a binary masculine/feminine binary opposition and holds that thought is conditioned by that division, she claims that any investigation located within contemporary Western culture can only ever be taken from the perspective of the "masculine" or "feminine", which, given her analysis of the history of Western systems of representation, Irigaray takes to mean the affirmation of the "masculine" over the "feminine" and, indeed, the collapsing of the later into the former. As a consequence, Irigaray claims that Heidegger's and Merleau-Ponty's phenomenological approaches actually produce a masculine-defined analysis of sexuality that is unable to account for the specificity of female sexuality. To avoid this, Irigaray's poststructuralist account of sexuality insists that any investigation must start from and indeed affirm the pre-existing concrete factual difference(s) between the "masculine" and "feminine" sexes.

To develop this, I first outline the parameters of Irigaray's critique of the logic of patriarchy found within Western philosophy and her conception of sexual difference, before going on to engage with the long-standing question of whether Irigaray's affirmation of a fundamental sexual difference depends upon and so perpetuates ahistoric, essentialist conceptions of sexuality.[23] I agree with those who defend Irigaray against this charge by arguing that, rather than simply and simplistically reaffirming the essentialist thinking underpinning the logic of patriarchy, she actually develops a far more sophisticated account of how the logic of patriarchy must be combated from "within" its own parameters that adopts, and at the same time subverts, the essentialist premises underpinning that model.[24] The means through which this is undertaken are subtle and complex, but I argue that her aim is to bring to light the absurdity of the essentialist justifications for the logic of patriarchy as a means of "jamming the theoretical machinery"[25] supporting it.

From here, I engage with Alison Stone's[26] influential, albeit controversial, claim that Irigaray's early strategic or political essentialism is unable to explain her subsequent development of and dependence on a realist form of essentialism that affirms the foundational importance of an actual – as opposed to mimetic or strategic – binary sexual division between a masculine sex and a feminine sex. While accepting Stone's basic claim that Irigaray relies upon and affirms an actual material difference between (the) two sexes, I question Stone's distinction between an "early/later" Irigaray by (1) arguing that this reads Irigaray's work through a logic of binary opposition that implicitly repeats the fundamental binary structure underpinning the logic of patriarchy ("masculine" versus "feminine"); and (2) claiming that there is no fundamental rupture within Irigaray's *oeuvre*, but a gradual alteration wherein she moves from an initial "negative" focus that criticises the logic of representation historically dominant in Western philosophy and culture to the complementary question of how a "positive" ethical-political programme of sexual difference could be developed and, crucially, justified from an expressive conception of nature.[27] Although this demonstrates the ambition and subtlety of Irigaray's thinking, I conclude that her insistence that sexual difference is structured around a binary heteronormative biological division forecloses sexual expression within heteronormative parameters to implicitly depend upon and perpetuate the hierarchal logic of exclusion – namely against non-heteronormative forms of sexuality – inherent in the patriarchal system to be overcome.

Sexual Difference and the Logic of Patriarchy

Irigaray's thinking starts from the Heideggerian premise that each age is dominated by a single issue. Whereas, for Heidegger, this is the question of the meaning of Being, Irigaray argues that it is the question of sexual difference.[28] Starting from the premise that sexual difference "belongs universally to all humans",[29] Irigaray claims that the world is simply and always divided between two sexes: men and women. Indeed, because this division is universal, sexual difference is held to be "the fundamental paradigm of the difference between us"[30] and, by extension, the difference upon which all other differences – class, race, nationality, and so on – depend.

Importantly, Irigaray maintains that the criteria upon which sexual difference depends cannot be reduced to genitality. Here, she is critiquing Freud's claim that at puberty the genitals come to be the source of (adult) sexuality. This however makes sexual difference derivative of a prior process of development. In contrast, "we need to recall that the girl has a sexualized body different from the boy's well before the genital stage".[31] As a consequence, Irigaray commits herself to the claim that, while sexual difference cannot be reduced to differences in genitalia, there is a fundamental biological difference that distinguishes the sexes.

The danger however of this initial formulation is that it runs the risk of reducing sexuality to a determining biology. I will subsequently show that Irigaray introduces an important modification to how "biology" is understood to avoid this charge, but, at this stage, it is important to note that, although she claims that sexual difference is *the* question grounding all others, she also, somewhat paradoxically, claims that this does not entail a privileging of it over other questions. This conclusion is premised on the idea that "privileging" entails an arbitrary choice to affirm one principle over an equally valid one. Focusing on the question of sexual difference does not do this, however, because sexual difference is, for Irigaray, not one difference amongst others, but *the* difference upon which all others depend. Engaging with it is not therefore to negate other differences or questions but to engage with the conditions upon which all others depend.[32]

From this bedrock, Irigaray moves to question the way(s) in which the sexual difference has been organised and thought in Western culture, which takes her to question the logic of representation inherent in Western thought. To frame her discussion, it is necessary to make a preliminary remark regarding the logic underpinning her analysis, in so far as Irigaray rejects Lacan's claim that sexual difference is premised on a form of negative relationality which holds that something is what it is by virtue of being defined as not another: A is A because it is not B, which is B because it is not A. This can take a weaker form, where two beings pre-exist the relation but their individual *meaning* only results from being defined negatively against the other, or a stronger form, where both the *being* and *meaning* of each aspect depends upon the other. Rather than affirm the weak or strong version of this logic, Irigaray's questions the logic itself by claiming that it implicitly makes each entity dependent on and so subordinate to the other. Not only does this logic necessarily establish a hierarchical relation between the parts, but, in so doing, the danger is that one aspect comes to be continuously privileged over the other. Trying to overcome this imbalance by simply reaffirming the mutual dependence inherent in the logic of negative relationality does not go far enough because there will continue to exist the dangerous possibility that the relation will once again fall into a hypostatised hierarchy.

To fully prevent this possibility requires, on Irigaray's telling, a radical alteration to the logic through which sexual difference is premised, away from one of negative relationality to a logic of difference. There are, at least, two aspects to this. First, although recognising that each sex exists in relation to the other, Irigaray maintains that there is no constitutive bond between them that makes each *dependent* on the other. The sexes are different to one another, defined by their own being. Second, and for this reason, Irigaray depends upon a distinction between the "being" of and "representational meaning" attributed to each sex. This distinction is important because it allows her to (1) undertake a critical analysis of the ways in which representation has failed to respect the difference between the sexes and, in particular, the "being" of women; (2) insist that the "being" of each sex must be engaged with on its own terms; neither can be understood through or from the "being" of the other sex; and (3) argue for a conceptual movement from representationalism to expressivism to undercut any ontology of substances, all the while taking heed of and respecting the difference(s) defining the two sexes.

Irigaray starts by claiming that "[t]o approach the question of sexual difference is to realize that this difference has been forgotten, overlooked by the Western tradition"[33] because "in the West, being is always understood as 'one' or a 'multiple of one'".[34] As a result, Western culture has been defined by "hierarchies and subordinations between One and the other, One and others, One and the multiple".[35] By affirming a single principle, all else has been thought from and as derivative of that foundational point. Irigaray ties this to her affirmation of the primordial importance of the sexual difference to conclude that the masculine has been historically defined as the One and the feminine as that which is subordinate to the former: "Man has been the subject of discourse, whether in theory, morality, or politics".[36] Even when the fundamental premise does not *explicitly affirm* a masculine perspective, Irigaray claims that the masculine is simply recuperated in the "new" anchoring points created to ground the system of representation. For example, she notes that "[t]he Copernican revolution has yet to have its final effects in the male imaginary",[37] in so far as it removes the immediate human male as the locus of the universe only to re-instantiate "him" as "the transcendental (subject)"[38] who rises to a "perspective that would dominate the totality, to the vantage point of greatest power, [and] cuts himself off from the bedrock, from his empirical relationship with the matrix that he claims to survey".[39]

Similarly, psychoanalysis's turn to the unconscious perpetuates a similar exclusion, in so far as it relies upon a logic of "verticality"[40] that returns the discussion to a singular point, which, when combined with Irigaray's claim regarding the dominance of the masculine over the feminine, leads her to conclude that the single foundation is masculine; hence Lacan's (and Freud's) valorisation of the phallus. However, as Irigaray puts it, "[w]oman has no cause to envy the penis or the phallus".[41] This association is simply the clearest and most explicit expression of "the failure to establish a sexual identity for both sexes – man, and the race of men, has transformed the male organ into an instrument of power with which to master material power (*puissance*)".[42] As a consequence, psychoanalysis reduces woman to the masculine perspective – "the clitoris is conceived as a little penis . . . and the vagina is valued for the 'lodging' it offers the male organ"[43] – and defines her "as the necessary complement to the operation of male sexuality, and, more often, as a negative image that provides male sexuality with an unfailingly phallic self-representation".[44]

Even when a privileging of the masculine perspective is *explicitly denied*, Irigaray claims that the logic that supports its privileged status continues to *implicitly* structure discourse. For example, and as noted, her reliance on a binary model of sexual difference, wherein each sex must be either "masculine" or "feminine", leads Irigaray to dismiss the possibility of neutrality – as found in Heidegger's and Merleau-Ponty's phenomenological approaches: "For everyone claims neutrality without noticing that he is talking about *one* neuter, *his* neuter, and not an absolute neutrality."[45] There is no neutral position; only a masculine one masquerading as neutral to cover over and perpetuate its dominance. As a consequence, she concludes that the "neuter . . . does not solve the problem of the hierarchy observed by the male and female genders, of the injustices this hierarchy perpetuates or the pathogenic neutralization of languages and values that results".[46]

This historic dependence on and affirmation of a masculinist perspective demonstrates, so Irigaray claims, the phallocentrism of Western representation. While claiming to represent reality, Irigaray maintains that this logic is actually defined

> by the constitution of a *logos*, a language obeying rules such as those of self-identity, of non-contradiction, etc., which . . . have been designed to ensnare the totality of the real in the nets of language, and thus to remove it from sensible experience, from the ever in-finite contiguity of daily life.[47]

Language does not then describe being *per se*, but creates a parallel "world" divorced from the sensible one. Irigaray goes further by explaining that the logic of representation constructed from this divorce recognises the sexual difference – in so far as it is structured around distinct roles for males and females – but "lift[s] one of the two terms . . . [which is] constituted as 'origin,' as that by whose differentiation the other may be endangered and brought to light".[48] For Irigaray, it has been the masculine that has been privileged in Western symbolic systems, with the consequence that everything else, including the feminine, has been defined by and from this originary masculine position "[o]r else carried back into mere extrapolation, into the infinity of some capital letter: Sexuality, Difference, Phallus, etc".[49] which acts as a placeholder for the originary point".[50] Rather than thinking of the sexual difference in terms of difference, Western representation has made sexual difference "a derivation of the problematics of sameness [to be] determined with the project, the projection, the sphere of representation, of the same".[51]

Although Irigaray recognises that this logic distorts "man",[52] she downplays this, if only because the masculine is somewhat compensated because he is privileged within the established logic. In contrast, woman is both distorted *and* degraded. The former because "she" is thought through or from those characteristics or modes of expression attributed to "masculinity"[53] and, as a consequence, is made to express and define herself through a logic that "leaves [her] sex aside".[54] The latter because she is held to be inferior to "man" and, as a consequence, is reduced to "the little structured margins of a dominant ideology, as waste, or excess".[55] Rather than being a full, individual partner, woman is reduced to an objectified appendage of the dominant masculine perspective. She is not then represented on her own terms, but is portrayed as a devalued other to the privileged male. Because "she" is other to him, she becomes what he is not, forever linked with mystery, to become, what Irigaray calls, "La mysterérique".[56]

However, somewhat paradoxically, it is precisely because woman is excluded and distorted in this manner that Irigaray finds a moment of solace. After all, woman's status as an outsider within the patriarchal system of representation presents her with the space from that system to do other than demanded by it:

> Her sex is heterogeneous to this whole economy of representation, but it is capable of interpreting that economy precisely because it has remained 'outside.' Because it does not postulate oneness, or sameness, or reproduction, or even representation. Because it remains somewhere else than in that general repetition where it is taken up only as *otherness of sameness*.[57]

Her heterogeneous relationship to the system of patriarchal representation ensures that "[p]rovided that she does not will to be their equal . . . she does not enter into a discourse whose systematicity is based on her reduction into sameness".[58] As an "excess",[59] woman cannot be fully reduced to the sameness of masculinity or delineated by the signifying patriarchal system. Rather than clear and objective, woman becomes that which "cannot be expressed in words".[60] She comes across as "fuzzy",[61] "beyond all pairs of opposites, all distinctions between active and passive or past and future".[62] Of course, this means that when she is conceptualised by the patriarchal signifiying regime, she is distorted and turned into that which she is not: the devalued opposite of the masculine. But again, her excess from that system ensures that she is always a disquieting figure, always pointing to an otherness that cannot be reincorporated into the same. With this, Irigaray moves from describing woman's status within Western systems of representation to prescribing what needs to occur for that system (and, by extension, the way "woman" is represented) to be altered. This however first requires a word on a topic that quickly marked the reception of Irigaray's early critique of patriarchy: the question of essentialism.

Overcoming Patriarchy and the Problem of Essentialism

In a 1998 debate with Drucilla Cornell, Elizabeth Grosz, and Pheng Cheah, Judith Butler admitted that when they first read Irigaray in the early 1980s, their reaction was one of dismissal: "I was not interested in [Irigaray's] work at all because she seemed to be an essentialist and that was a term we used quite easily then, when we thought we knew what it meant."[63] This assessment is premised on the claim that Irigaray's notion of sexual difference is constructed around a binary masculine/feminine division, and, crucially, that both are defined by definitive, *a priori* characteristics, exclusive to each sex. Only by implicitly proceeding in this way was it thought that Irigaray could then evaluate whether the Western system of representation accurately represents "woman". As Toril Moi argues, however, this leaves Irigaray in a problematic situation. After all, on Irigaray's own terms, "[a]ny attempt to formulate a general theory of femininity will be metaphysical".[64] Therefore, "having shown that so far femininity has been produced exclusively in relation to the logic of the same",[65] Moi argues that Irigaray "falls for the temptation to produce her own positive theory of femininity",[66] which by "defin[ing] 'woman' is necessarily to essentialize her".[67] For this reason, Carolyn Burke rhetorically asks:

> Does [Irigaray's] writing manage to avoid construction of another idealism to replace the 'phallocentric' system that she dismantles? Do her representations of a *parler femme*, in analogy with female sexuality, avoid the centralizing idealism with which she taxes Western conceptual systems?[68]

For these commentators, the fundamental problem with Irigaray's thinking is that, although it claims critical force, it implicitly depends upon a number of ontological assumptions that seem to re-enforce phallogocentrism. Although Irigaray clearly inverts the privileged term in the binary oppositions constitutive of the logic of patriarchy so that it is the feminine not the masculine aspect that is affirmed, she continues to think that both terms can be defined, which appears to depend upon each "possessing" definitive characteristics. As such, Irigaray's critique depends upon and re-enforces the same logic of ahistoric essence as the regime to be overcome. Indeed, by often parroting the attributes given to "woman" by the system of patriarchal representation – for example, when she defines "woman" as mysterious – Irigaray appears to simply re-enforce those representations. As a consequence, her thinking was understood to contribute little to the project of female emancipation.

In the 1990s, however, Irigaray's thinking was subject to substantial re-evaluation that aimed to show that her earlier critics had fundamentally misunderstood her project. Rather than simplistically adopt the essentialist language of the patriarchal system to be overcome, Irigaray was understood to be engaged in a far more complicated and subtle critique of phallogocentrism that, crucially, was aware of the substantial pitfalls involved in this undertaking. Rather than simply attributing an alternative conception of essence to woman and affirming that as the "true" nature of woman over the "false" one found in phallogocentrism, Irigaray was understood to be doing something far more nuanced. As she notes, the tradition

> cannot simply be approached head on, nor simply within the realm of the philosophical itself. Thus it was necessary to deploy other languages – without forgetting their own debt to philosophical language – and even to accept the condition of silence, of aphasia as a symptom – historico-hysterical, hysterico-historical – so that something of the feminine as the limit of the philosophical might finally be heard.[69]

Instead of simply affirming a fundamental *rupture* from patriarchal representation – an affirmation that would establish a binary opposition between patriarchy and a privileged alternative that would, inadvertently, re-instantiate the logic of binary oppositions that structures patriarchy[70] – Irigaray was reread as claiming that "[o]ne cannot alter symbolic meaning by *fiat*, one cannot simply step outside phallogocentrism, simply reverse the symbolism or just make strident or repetitive claims that women are in fact rational".[71] Thought is embedded within and conditioned by its historical situation. Any attempt to simply leave that tradition behind will most likely merely continue to *implicitly* affirm its premises, not least of which by implicitly establishing a binary opposition between "phallogocentrism" and "post-phallogocentrism". Overcoming phallogocentrism has then to depend upon a far more sophisticated *transitional* model of change that occurs from *within* and passes *through* the parameters of that to be overcome. It is for this reason that Irigaray explains that she works "to go back through the masculine imaginary, to interpret the way it has reduced [woman] to silence, to muteness or mimicry [of masculinity], and I am attempting, from that starting-point and at the same time, to (re)discover a possible space for the feminine imaginary".[72]

Furthermore, her defenders pointed out that the early essentialist reading of her work was underpinned by a problematic literal hermeneutical strategy. Not only were Irigaray's comments on "woman" taken as representing her actual views, but, by insisting that her statements could only be interpreted in a unitary fashion, her critics were, somewhat ironically, charged with subjecting her thought to a masculinist logic that valued literality and a single answer. In other words, whereas her critics charged Irigaray with continuing to depend upon the logic of patriarchy, her defenders turned that criticism against her critics to argue that they only arrived at this conclusion because they themselves were the ones who were locked within the logic of patriarchy and, as a consequence, interpreted her comments in accordance with its dependence on literality and a unitary truth. However, as Ping Xu points out, this literal, essentialist reading misses fundamental aspects of Irigaray's early work, such as her affirmation of "mimicry".[73] Once this is taken into account, we see that, rather than simply affirming the logic of patriarchy, Irigaray merely *temporarily* adopts the language of the feminine as outlined in the phallocentric tradition "to exercise a resistance from within [that] discourse",[74] one that brings attention to the absurdity of that discourse, all the while showing the absence of any justification for it.

Irigaray's aim then is not so much to simply step away from the logic of patriarchy to an alternative "truth", but to "[t]urn everything upside down, inside out, back to front"[75] as a means of "jamming the theoretical machine".[76] Simply affirming another truth-system opposed to the patriarchal one would simply re-instantiate the logic of domination inherent in that logic. Only passing through the patriarchal logic in a particular way, one that uses its rules, terms, and logic, is it possible to confuse that logic to deactivate it. Repeating its tropes does not then simply repeat them as if they are accepted as true, but, in a sense, plays with them by ensuring that the repetition is slightly "off":

> The 'subject' sidles up to the truth, squints at it, obliquely, in an attempt to gain possession of what truth can no longer say. Dispersing, piercing those metaphors – particularly the photological ones – which have constituted truth by the premises of Western philosophy: virgin, dumb, and veiled in her nakedness, her vision still naively 'natural,' her viewpoint still resolutely blind and unsuspecting of what may lie beneath the blindness.[77]

Instead of simply abandoning the identity imposed on women by the phallogocentric system, Irigaray adopts it to pass through it.

This occurs through, at least, three strategies. First, rather than appeal to formal logic to expose the flaws within the patriarchal model – a logic that depends upon a singular truth reached by a linear path and so returns us to the foundationalism and linearity inherent in that model – Irigaray insists on the need to use an alternative model of representation based around "riddles, allusions, hints, parables"[78] and "curl(s), helix(es), diagonal(s), spiral(s), roll(s), twirl(s), revolution(s), pirouette(s)".[79]

Second, as noted, she appeals "to an initial phase . . . the one historically assigned to the feminine: that of *mimicry*".[80] She recognises however that this can take two forms: "*mimesis* as production",[81] which she associates with the spontaneous production of music, and "*mimesis* . . . already caught up in a process of *imitation* . . . and *reproduction*".[82] Having noted that the later has been historically dominant and has led "woman" to reproduce herself through the masculine point of reference, Irigaray suggests that it is the first form of mimesis that holds out possibilities for women. Rather than conform to a prior model of action, women must find ways to spontaneously mimic the patriarchal logic in ways that subtly undermine it. This, however, is "complex" because it requires that it be possible to "*copy* anything at all . . . *without appropriating them to oneself, and without adding anything*".[83] There is no singular model for this. Irigaray's own method takes place through an engagement with the philosophical tradition, wherein she undertakes "a fling with the philosopher"[84] to highlight aspects of his thought that remain out of sight to him. This requires that she appear to affirm his position, all the while holding something back, which requires that she have such an intimate knowledge of that position that it appears to be her own. Only then can she take it to the limit, all the while continuing to remain divorced from it in the way that mimicry permits and demands.[85] This duplicity allows her to make statements, perfectly in line with the logic of his position, but which, by coming to it from a different angle, reveal the absurdity of the position rejected. So, by affirming the essentialist traits given to women by the patriarchal system, Irigaray is led to statements that strike the reader as simplistic and naive. Because these statements are perfectly in keeping with the logic of patriarchy historically dominant, the revelation of her supposed naivety also betrays the simplisticity and naivety of the patriarchal system. Crucially, it does so from *within* the premises of that logic, rather than from an external competing "truth" and, as such, disarms the logic of domination inherent in phallogocentrism.

Third, Irigaray complements these strategies with an exhortation to swap the ethic of seriousness inherent in phallogocentrism with one orientated around and from laughter. Rather than react with outrage at the attributes given to her – a response that aims to reverse the position affirmed, but which by meeting it head on merely depends upon and so reiterates the phallogocentric privileging of a logic of domination – woman must learn that the best way to disarm the absurdity of that logic is to laugh at it. This is not to trivialise its content, but to empty its meaning of content *from within*.[86] In so doing, the aim is not to offer a theory of "woman" or even to annihilate masculinity *per se*. "Its function [is] to *cast phallogocentrism, phallocratism*, loose from its moorings in order to return the masculine to its own language, leaving open the possibility of a different language. Which means that the masculine would no longer be 'everything.'"[87] Only once this is achieved and a space for the feminine opened from it can the sexual difference be thought as difference, rather than as the reduction of one sex to another, which, in turn, will allow *both* sexes to exist through the specificity of their respective sexualities.

Irigaray's early work on phallogocentrism is then far subtler than the early essentialist reading of her thinking recognises or permits, in so far as she does not simply depend upon an essentialised theory of woman to oppose the one affirmed by phallogocentrism; she intentionally "carrie[s] out an inversion of the femininity imposed upon [her] in order to try to define the female corresponding to my gender: the in-and-for-itself of my female nature".[88] Overcoming the phallogocentric tradition is not achieved, on Irigaray's telling, by simply affirming an alternative "truth" about "woman" to that of the tradition; such a manoeuvre would not only repeat the phallogocentric discourse of power, dominance, and single truth, but also raise the question of what justifies one conception over another. Instead, she (temporarily) adopts the premises of phallogocentrism to undermine it from within. However, while this strategy may jam the theoretical tenets of phallogocentrism, such disarming appears, as noted, to be both temporary and local. It not only needs to be continuously redone, but, as her critics point out, requires a subtlety that can all too easily go awry. As a consequence, Irigaray came to accept that "[d]econstructing the patriarchal tradition is certainly indispensable, but [it] is hardly enough. It is necessary to define new values directly or indirectly suitable to feminine subjectivity and to feminine identity."[89] It is to this that I now turn.

From Political to an Ontology of Expressive Essentialism

Alison Stone suggests that this "positive" project finds expression in Irigaray's later works, wherein Irigaray foregoes her earlier dependence on a temporary and intentional adoption of the essentialist traits attributed to woman by the phallogocentric tradition to depend upon a full-blown realist essentialism. For Stone, Irigaray's later realist essentialism affirms

> the view that we can know about the world as it is independently of our practices and modes of representations. I therefore understand a realist form of essentialism to consist in the view that male and female bodies can be known to have essentially different characters, different characters which exist, independently of how bodies are represented and culturally inhabited. According to realist essentialism, natural differences between the sexes exist, prior to our cultural activities.[90]

Stone's position is premised on the claim that having disarmed or jammed the phallogocentric theoretical machine in her earlier works through the temporary and mimetic adoption of its essentialist premises, Irigaray subsequently moves to the positive project of describing a non-patriarchal form of sexual relation that respects the sexual difference; an endeavour that depends upon being able to identify what "man" and "woman" entail. In other words, Irigaray moves from a political or strategic engagement with phallogocentrism to an ontological description of the sexes and, by extension, sexual relations that depends upon identifying the defining criteria of each sex.

For this reason, Irigaray rejects the notion that sexual difference is *merely* socially constructed or the consequence of cultural representation. In her later works, she repeatedly insists that sexual difference is biologically pre-given, existing "before" any form of symbolic, social, or cultural construction. For example, in *In the Beginning, She Was*, published in 2013, Irigaray states that "The human species is composed of two genders."[91] In *The Way of Love*, from 2002, we are told that "[t]he difference between man and woman already exists, and it cannot be compared to a creation of our understanding";[92] while in the 1996 interview "Thinking Life as Relation", Irigaray maintains that "[s]exual difference is a given of reality",[93] which reinforces her statement in the previous year that "[m]en and women are corporeally different. This biological difference leads to others: in constructing subjectivity, in connecting to the world, in relating."[94] Furthermore, in *To be Two*, from 1994, Irigaray explains that her "work is based on the recognition of sexual difference, of the irreducibility between man and woman, men and women; an irreducibility which should be treated as a civil and cultural value, and not only as a natural reality to be overcome in culture and in community".[95]

However, it is important to note that, for Irigaray, the notion that sexual difference cannot and should not be reduced to a symbolic or cultural construction does not mean that we should simply fall back on a straight-forward form of biological determinism. Irigaray's thinking on what it is to "become-woman" is composed of a complex and ongoing dialectical relationship between woman's sexually conditioned biological parameters and cultural norms. We will shortly see that this depends upon a particular rethinking of biology in terms of processes rather than substance, but her claim that there are biological differences between the sexes that must be realised socially is the fundamental reason why she rejects Simone de Beauvoir's famous claim that "[o]ne is not born, but rather becomes, woman":[96] it places too much emphasis on a cultural becoming and not sufficient focus on the biological corporeality of woman. Instead of operating through a binary opposition wherein either biology or culture is determinate, Irigaray insists that there is a particular biological–culture dynamic at play in the process of becoming-woman, one nicely summed up by her statement that "I am a woman, but I must still become this woman that I am by nature."[97]

Irigaray therefore accepts that there are biological conditions to the sexes that exist "outside" of cultural representation and, indeed, are the conditions through which any cultural becoming takes place. As a consequence, we have to return to that biological dimension to rethink it in a way that is appropriate to sexual difference. The problem of course is that, on her telling, historical appeals to biology have been "interpreted in terms more masculine than feminine",[98] with the consequence that female corporeality has been ignored or reduced to the masculine body. Instead of repeating this gesture, Irigaray claims that we need to develop a conception of biology based in "the reality of [womans's] biological economy".[99]

As Stone recognises, however, this not only appears to have as its aim a theory of woman that Irigaray had previously rejected,[100] but also seems to reduce "woman" to biologically essential characteristics, which seems to give credence to the early essentialist reading of her work. If she is not to fall back into the reaffirmation of the essentialist thinking that marks the phallogocentric tradition she rejects, Irigaray must find some way to define what distinguishes the sexes without falling into phallogocentric essentialist thinking. Stone suggests that it is with the publication of *An Ethics of Sexual Difference*, in 1983, that Irigaray takes on this project to "elaborat[e] a picture of what material bodies are really like and of how those bodies really relate to the world around them".[101]

Before proceeding, however, a quick word is necessary on Stone's hermeneutical strategy, in so far as it depends upon and, indeed, introduces a fundamental chasm within Irigaray's *oeuvre* between the early critical works, such as *Speculum of the Other Woman* and *The Sex which is Not One*, and her later work, starting with *An Ethics of Sexual Difference*, that Irigaray explicitly rejects. For example, in a 1995 interview, Irigaray explains that her work has been conditioned by three (not two) different but intertwined phases: "The first a critique, you might say, of the auto-mono-centrism of the western subject; the second, how to define a second subject; and the third phase, how to define a relationship, a philosophy, an ethic, a relationship between two different subjects."[102] More importantly, Irigaray also rejects the notion that *An Ethics of Sexual Difference* marks any sort of fundamental rupture in her *oeuvre*, instead explaining that this text is the link that binds her first critical phase with the attempt to redefine female subjectivity on its own terms in the second phase.[103] As a consequence, Irigaray's self-assessment questions Stone's claim that Irigaray's *oeuvre* is marked by a fundamental rupture between an early deconstructive moment and a later reconstructive one. For this reason, I understand that all periods of her writing are orientated to the critique of phallogocentrism and, more importantly, an affirmation of sexual difference as and from difference. The changes in emphasis and orientation are simply the consequence of her addressing the same problematic from different, but complementary, directions.

Nevertheless, I do think that Stone's interpretation of Irigaray's "later" positive conception of sexual difference is not only plausible, but also one of the most sophisticated contemporary readings[104] that allows us to clearly see how Irigaray refocuses thinking on sexuality away from the question of symbolic representation to that of biology. Crucially, Stone shows that Irigaray does so by thinking sexual difference not from an ahistoric essential substance as in the phallogocentric tradition, but from a rethought "natural" ground premised on the notion of "active bodies".[105] In so doing, Stone shows that Irigaray offers a particularly powerful and innovative corrective to Lacan's supposed symbolic account of sexuality that, as we will see in the next chapter, also provides a stimulating contrast to Judith Butler's gender theory. Without claiming that it is an exhaustive account of Stone's reading of Irigaray's "later" work or, indeed, Irigaray's rethinking of sexual difference, the following overview of some aspects of that rethinking will identify the main trajectories of Irigaray's positive conception of sexual difference in a way that also contributes to the development of the historical trajectory of thinking of sexuality in the late twentieth century.

Stone's fundamental claim is that Irigaray grounds her rethinking of sexual difference from a particular philosophy of nature, which, rather than being thought as a static object to be used – a conception found within the phallogocentric tradition that sees "nature" as an object for man's use[106] – is re-conceptualised as a continuous organic becoming that supports and nurtures that which it expresses. Importantly, this becoming is autopoietic based on the notion that nature is always "at least two",[107] with the interaction of both parts being responsible for its continuing existence. As a consequence, Irigaray insists on a fundamental natural duality, thereby undermining the monosexuality of the phallogocentric tradition, and claims that each aspect of this fundamental duality expresses and is defined by "rhythms"[108] specific to each manifestation. The crucial defining aspect of each sex is not then its genitalia[109] nor some ahistoric substantial essence, but its particular "energy",[110] "style",[111] or "spirit"[112] that must be realised individually and culturally. As Stone explains,

> [Irigaray] believes that there is an essential difference between men and women which exists independently of – indeed, is the necessary precondition of – our interpretation of it. This essential difference arises at the level of rhythms which regulate the percipient fluids composing male and female bodies.[113]

For example, in *Sex and Genealogies*, Irigaray claims that "[w]omen do not obey the same sexual economy as men . . . [w]omen have different relations to fluids and solids, to matter, to form, to touch, to symmetry, to repetition, etc. . . . They have a much stronger internal regime, which keeps them in a constant and irreversible pattern of growth."[114] Moreover, "[t]his female temporality is hormonally complex and in turn has consequences for the organization and general equilibrium of the body".[115] For this reason, "time in a woman's life is particularly irreversible, and that, compared to men's time, it is less suited to the repetitive, entropic, and largely non-progressive, nullifying economy of our present environment".[116] Whereas male temporality is linear, female temporality is conditioned by twists, turns, and flows and, as a consequence, "[f]emale sexuality does not correspond to the same economy [as men's]. It is more related to becoming, more attuned to the time of the universe."[117] With this, Irigaray links (female) bodily rhythms of the sexes to the cycles and flows of nature, which are reduced by phallogocentrism to the linearity suited to the masculine body. Although this action also distorts the multiple rhythms defining "man", Irigaray maintains that "[w]oman suffer more grievously from the rupture with cosmic checks and balances"[118] and so calls for a reconstruction of the female body in accordance with its particular "rhythms of nature".[119]

However, it is important to note that the fundamental difference in kind between masculine and feminine bodily rhythms does not mean that *all* woman and men are conditioned by the same rhythm. Each exists within the rhythmic parameters that define their sex, but within those parameters each exists on a continuum through which each moves as they age. Thus,

> [a] woman's life is marked by irreversible events that define the stages of her life. This is true for puberty (which boys also experience), losing her virginity, becoming pregnant, being pregnant, childbirth, breastfeeding – events

that can be repeated without repetition: each time, they happen differently: body and spirit have changed, physical and spiritual development is taking place ... During all this time, a woman experiences menstruation, her periods, as continuously related to cosmic time, to the moon, the sun, the tides, and the seasons. Finally, menopause marks another stage in the becoming of a female body and spirit, a stage characterized by a different hormonal equilibrium, another relation to the cosmic and the social.[120]

Women do not all move through these bodily alterations at the same time or in the same way. "Woman" is marked by a particular corporeal style – one distinct from that which marks "man" – which is grounded in the constantly changing corporeal alterations that are unique to each female body.

Extrapolating from this, we can say that Irigaray's basic point is that the sexes are defined by distinct natural parameters that define the "being" of each sex, although, crucially, following Heidegger, the being of each sex must be understood as becoming. In contrast to Heidegger, however, Irigaray maintains that the becoming of each sex is not open-ended; it is constrained within the parameters of the rhythms that define each sex. There can be and is plenty of heterogeneity *within* each sex, but the discussion must start from and recognise that this heterogeneity occurs within the "universal"[121] conditions that define each one. As such, each individual is both singular and universal, in so far as he or she is a particular, and changing, manifestation of the universal conditions structuring their sex. The possibilities of the sexes change and develop historically, but there is and always will be a fundamental and irreducible difference between the corporeal rhythms of the sexes.

According to Stone, it is here that the strangely troubling aspect of Irigaray's appeal to natural rhythms comes to the fore because "[a]lthough Irigaray explicitly denies being an essentialist, her later view that men and women have natural characters which need and strive for expression is identifiably essentialist".[122] While not essentialist in the sense of affirming and depending upon an ahistoric substance to think "man" and "woman" as her early critics charged, Irigaray is essentialist in attributing distinct and irreducible conditions to both sexes. The key difference is that these conditions are fluid, individually expressive, and rhythmic; at no point do they turn into a static ground, substance, or identity. The conditions underpinning the two sexual positions are defined as a "groundless ground":[123] the former because the parameters of the absolute division defining "woman" or "man" are not static and fixed but fluid and moving; the later because this fluid becoming is the condition that defines the ways in which an individual's sexuality can be expressed. It also ensures that, whereas an individual's sexuality (understood as the rhythm that marks his or her sexual being) can and does change temporally, he or she cannot change his or her "natural" sex. There is significant flexibility *within* each sex, but the difference between them is absolute; a conclusion that, as we will shortly see, raises questions about the heteronormativity inherent in Irigaray's schema.[124]

Conclusion

Therefore, having worked to jam the theoretical machine underpinning the logic of patriarchy to offer a space to rethink sexual difference in non-hierarchal terms, Irigaray's rethinking depends upon and reintroduces a natural or biological essentialism to the discussion of sexuality, albeit one that departs from the substantial, ahistoric essentialism underpinning the historically dominant essentialist-patriarchal model of sexuality. She walks something of a fine, but nevertheless highly original, line, wherein she appeals to natural conditions that exist outside of representation and, in so doing, reaffirms that the sexes are defined by distinct essences, but does so without falling into the (substantive type of) essentialist thinking that has marked Western thinking on sexuality and that has been used to defend the logic of patriarchy that Irigaray rejects. In short, Irigaray not only offers a far more sophisticated engagement with the logic of patriarchy than the other thinkers engaged with so far, but also brings to our attention the heterogeneous nature of "essentialism" to, in so doing, complicate our understanding of "it". Challenging us to re-engage with and rethink the notion of "essentialism" more specifically and the unitary meanings attributed to historically dominant concepts more generally is one of the ways in which Irigaray's analysis remains both interesting and relevant.

Nevertheless, Irigaray's thinking contains a number of highly problematic aspects. In the first instance, there is the issue of her reduction of the history of Western philosophy to a single logic. While there is no doubt that this logic is a particularly dominant one historically, to say that it is the only logic or that there has only been one logic is deeply reductive; indeed, it seems to smack of the masculinist privileging of unity that she otherwise rejects. Now, of course, it could be objected that this book is also structured around the claim that Western philosophy has been structured around one model of sexuality, which I have termed the essentialist-patriarchal model, and so also falls foul of this criticism. However, I have only argued that this model is a particularly *dominant* one within Western philosophy, I do not make the stronger claim, which I take Irigaray to make, that it is the only one. As such, there is no attempt to cling to or ensure that all positions are bound to the same logic. One logic is overwhelmingly dominant, but that does not mean that it has had absolute status.

Irigaray is able to reduce this tradition to a single logic because her definition of what counts as patriarchal is particularly wide, encompassing not only any explicit privileging of masculinity over femininity, but also positions that affirm neutrality or a third term, while her conflation of thought with sex means that, strictly speaking, she must hold that any man who thinks is necessarily patriarchal because he can only ever think from the perspective of his sex. As such, Irigaray is implicitly committed to the claim that any thinking that comes from a "man" is necessarily exclusionary of woman and so patriarchal. This, however, is conceptually reductive and politically problematic, in so far as to say that thought is necessarily sexed to the extent that it is not possible to think of the other makes it difficult to see how the shared world that Irigaray affirms can be created.

This links to the second problem with Irigaray's thinking: her expansive notion of patriarchy means that it is not clear that her privileging of sexual difference is not itself patriarchal. Although she claims that her privileging of sexual difference over other forms of difference is due to the universality of the sexual difference, in structuring differences in this manner Irigaray creates a hierarchy between the different forms of difference. This is problematic because she associates hierarchy with phallogocentrism and insists that overcoming phallogocentrism requires a reconfiguration of logic away from verticality towards horizontality where each position is understood to be different from, rather than subordinate to, other positions.[125] However, for her to privilege sexual difference continues to give primordial importance to a form of difference over others and, indeed, she grounds those other differences in sexual difference. It therefore depends upon and re-instantiates the logic of hierarchy that she explicitly rejects. Irigaray would defend herself by claiming that the sexual difference is both universal and the condition of all privileging, meaning that her focus is not the consequence of any privileging on her part but a consequence of accurately understanding "reality", but it is difficult to see *why* we must follow her on this point. It appears that she simply starts from that premise and asks that we follow her based on trust in her insight or because such a position is taken to be obvious and clear. If the former, Irigaray is guilty of turning herself into a singular font of truth and so perpetuating phallogocentrism's affirmation of a single unified truth. If the latter, her theory is premised on empirical observation of phallogocentric society and so ends up taking a historical division for ontological "fact". In either case and on her terms, her privileging of sexual difference does not undermine phallogocentrism, but actually implicitly affirms it.

The third issue relates to the binary nature of her conception of sexual difference, and in particular the implicit claim that sexuality must initially be structured around "men" and "women". With this, Irigaray's schema forecloses sexuality within two possibilities and so is marked by a fundamental inability to discuss alternative forms of sexuality. While she certainly admits different types of male and female sexuality, her conception of sexual difference is limited to masculine and feminine forms. It is therefore simply incapable of considering, for example, the notion of "intersex", where individuals are neither clearly one nor the other. Indeed, Irigaray is explicitly hostile to the possibility of a non-binary sexual division, as evidenced by her rejection of sexual androgyny and her claim that it ultimately depends upon the binary sexual difference.[126] She even claims that "[i]f you are asexuate, I have nothing to say to you".[127] Starting from a binary sexual division means that the discussion must *always* be brought back to that division; it is the "foundational" point from which all subsequent discussion result. Its binary nature must therefore structure all subsequent divisions. As a consequence, and although Irigaray's affirmation of sexual difference may aim to open up thinking on feminine sexuality long devalued, it does so by perpetuating alternative exclusions simply by foreclosing sexuality as either male or female.

A further consequence of the binary nature of Irigaray's conception of sexual difference is its heteronormative nature. This issue has generated significant debate in the literature with commentators split. Those who defend Irigaray tend to take one of two strategies: on the one hand, Tina Chanter[128] and Gail Schwab[129] seek to dissolve the charge by arguing that the problem that Irigaray address is not heteronormativity but the question of sexual difference and, in particular, the way that women have been devalued within the West's phallogocentrism.[130] On this telling, it is therefore unfair to ask of Irigaray something that her thinking never aims to offer.

The problem with this line of reasoning is however twofold. First, it significantly reduces the scope and applicability of Irigaray's thinking, in so far as "it" must be understood only in relation to a very specific issue – phallogocentrism – and cannot be transported to or used to enquire into other related issues. Furthermore, this defence does nothing to undermine the charge of heteronormativity; it simply states that it is not Irigaray's key concern. But even if this is so, it merely means that while her thinking might resolve one issue (sexual difference), it does so at the expense of another (heteronormativity). Again, its applicability would be severely restricted.

As a consequence, other commentators have offered a stronger defence of Irigaray. Ofelia Schutte, for example, claims that the sexual difference is only exclusionary "from the standpoint of a masculinist logic",[131] with the implication that once woman is accorded her "proper" place and status, it will encompass and rectify all exclusions. The problem, of course, is that it is not clear why this would occur. In particular, it is not clear why readdressing the role and status of women would necessarily overcome exclusions based on race or class, let alone how that would necessarily permit non-heteronormative forms of sexuality to be included. This latter point is addressed by Pheng Cheah and Elizabeth Grosz, who claim that Irigaray maintains that biological sexual determinations are "oddly contentless",[132] which, when combined with her claim that sexual becoming has a biological *and* cultural component, means that her thinking "permits great room for singularity and variability"[133] and "does not militate against queer forms of desire".[134] In other words, Irigaray's thought may start from a binary biological division, but it can subsequently take on multiple forms once it "mixes" with the cultural aspect. While this recognises that Irigaray can maintain mulitiple forms of sexuality, it is not clear that it undermines the criticism that her thinking starts from and so is locked within a binary heterosexual biological division. After all, as Alison Stone points out,

> Irigaray's assignation of ontological priority to sexual difference directly implies that heterosexual relationships have greater value than any other forms of relationship. Since heterosexual relationships demand openness to someone who is other at the most fundamental level, such relationships are the most complex and challenging, conferring a proportionately enhanced level of moral worth upon those who negotiate them. For Irigaray, heterosexuality confers greater merit on its practitioners than [other] forms of sexuality can.[135]

Therefore, for those who wish to apply Irigaray's insights to non-heterosexual forms of sexual relations, it seems that they must simply re-enact Danielle Poe's hermeneutical strategy of disregarding Irigaray's own comments to read her in the desired way. Only in this way can Poe claim that despite "Irigaray's own interpretation of sexual difference, I read the cultivation of sexual difference as inclusive of transsexual and transgender experience".[136] There is however, strictly speaking, no textual support for such a reading, with the consequence that it is unclear whether Irigaray's thinking can actually sustain such an interpretation. Indeed, if it can, the result would be a "Irigaray plus X" amalgamation rather than anything that actually can be attributed to Irigaray *per se*.[137]

Given this, I agree with those who claim that, because Irigaray starts from a binary biological division between men and women, regardless of how this is subsequently expressed, her thinking is foreclosed within a binary heteronormative opposition. As Judith Butler puts it, "[Irigaray] is not willing to challenge the divide of the human race into two. The state both expresses and reinforces the truth of how we should be actualized in our sexual identities, male/female."[138] Because Irigaray's sexual difference is structured around a biological binary heteronormative division, Butler charges that Irigaray's thinking remains foreclosed within that division, even as she insists on the fluid becoming of its sexual expression. Overcoming this cannot, on Butler's telling, be achieved by rethinking "sexuality" to unmoor it from ontological determinations to in so doing free up its possible expressions. As we have seen in previous chapters, this is the approach taken by proponents of psychoanalytic, phenomenological, and feminist theories, each of which has either undermined a straightforward essentialism at the expense of depending upon a logic of patriarchy or undermined patriarchy but foreclosed sexuality within (a form of) essentialism. According to Butler, the problem with these approaches is not so much that they employ the correct critical conceptual paradigm but implement it wrongly, but, more seriously and problematically, that they use the wrong conceptual apparatus to try to undermine the essentialist-patriarchal model of sexuality. If sexuality is not to be foreclosed within predetermined schemas, a far more radical conceptual alteration was held to be necessary; one that moved the terms of the debate away from a primordial questioning of sexuality towards that of gender. It is to this that we now turn.

Notes

1. There is, of course, substantial debate regarding the relationship between "structuralism" and "poststructuralism". Without entering into these debates, I note that the definitive history of these "movements" – one that collapses them into "structuralism" – is François Dosse, *History of Structuralism, Volume 2: The Sign-Sets, 1967–Present*, trans. Deborah Glassman (Minneapolis: University of Minnesota Press, 1997). On the continuing relevance of poststructuralism, see the essays collected in Gavin Rae and Emma Ingala (eds), *Historical Traces and Future Pathways of Poststructuralism: Aesthetics, Ethics, and Politics* (Abingdon: Routledge, 2021).
2. See, for example, Jacques Derrida, "Structure, Sign, and Play in the Discourse of the Human Sciences", in *Writing and Difference*, trans. Alan Bass (Abingdon: Routledge, 1978), pp. 351–370.
3. I am of course simplifying dramatically here for narrative effect. It goes without saying that the affirmation of difference was (appropriately) itself differentiated within poststructuralist thought. For a discussion of this, see Gavin Rae, *Poststructuralist Agency: The Subject in Twentieth-Century Theory* (Edinburgh: Edinburgh University Press, 2020).
4. Jacques Lacan, *Seminar XIX: . . . Or Worse*, edited by Jacques-Alain Miller, trans. A. R. Price (Cambridge: Polity, 2018), from 1971–1972; and Jacques Lacan, *Seminar XX: On Feminine Sexuality, The Limits of Love and Knowledge, 1972–1973*, edited by Jacques-Alain Miller, trans. Bruce Fink (New York: W. W. Norton, 1999).

5. Lacan, *Seminar XIX*, p. 6.
6. Lorenzo Chiesa, *The Not-Two: Logic and God in Lacan* (Cambridge, MA: The MIT Press, 2016); Joan Copjec, *Read my Desire: Lacan Against the Historicists* (London: Verso, 2015); Tim Dean, *Beyond Sexuality* (Chicago, IL: University of Chicago Press, 2000); Patricia Gherovici, *Transgender Psychoanalysis: A Lacanian Perspective on Sexual Difference* (Abingdon: Routledge, 2017); Alenka Zupančič, *What is Sex?* (Cambridge, MA: The MIT Press, 2017). For a critical discussion of this line of interpretation, see Gavin Rae "Questioning the Phallus: Jacques Lacan and Judith Butler", *Studies in Gender and Sexuality*, vol. 21, n. 1, 2020, pp. 12–26.
7. Lacan, *Seminar XX*, p. 72.
8. Ibid., p. 73.
9. Ibid., p. 74.
10. Luce Irigaray, *An Ethics of Sexual Difference*, trans. Carolyn Burke and Gillian C. Gill (Ithaca, NY: Cornell University Press, 1993), p. 5.
11. Luce Irigaray, *Speculum of the Other Woman*, trans. Gillian C. Gill (Ithaca, NY: Cornell University Press, 1985), p. 13.
12. Ibid., p. 167n8.
13. Irigaray, *Speculum of the Other Woman*, p. 133.
14. Luce Irigaray, *Marine Lover of Friedrich Nietzsche*, trans. Gillian C. Gill (New York: Columbia University Press, 1991).
15. Luce Irigaray, *The Forgetting of Air in Martin Heidegger*, trans. Mary Beth Mader (Austin, TX: University of Texas Press, 1999).
16. The most extended narrative overview of this history is found in Luce Irigaray, *In the Beginning, She Was* (London: Bloomsbury, 2013).
17. Irigaray, *Speculum of the Other Woman*, p. 141.
18. Space constraints mean that I will not discuss this aspect of her thinking, but for a recent discussion see Laura Roberts, *Irigaray and Politics: A Critical Introduction* (Edinburgh: Edinburgh University Press, 2019).
19. Luce Irigaray, "The Question of the Other", trans. Noah Guynn, *Yale French Studies*, vol. 87, 1995, pp. 7–19 (p. 8).
20. Interestingly, Irigaray sent Beauvoir a copy of *Speculum of the Other Woman* upon its publication, only to be met with silence. While admitting that this non-response made her "quite sad" (Luce Irigaray, "Equal or Different?", trans. David Macey, in *The Irigaray Reader*, edited by Margaret Whitford [London: Wiley–Blackwell, 1991], pp. 30–34 [p. 31]), Irigaray later realised that the reason for it was most likely her own fault, springing from her adoption and affirmation of "woman's" status as "other", a concept that Beauvoir's *The Second Sex* explicitly rejects. Irigaray concludes that "I must have offended her without wishing to. I had read the 'Introduction' to *The Second Sex* well before I wrote *Speculum*, and could no longer recall what was at stake in the problematic of the *other* in de Beauvoir's work. Perhaps, for her part, she didn't understand that for me my sex or gender [*genre*] were in no way 'second,' but that sexes or genders are *two*, without being first or sex" (Irigaray, "The Question of the Other", pp. 9–10).

21. Irigaray, "Equal or Different?", p. 32.
22. Ibid., p. 32.
23. Carolyn Burke, "Irigaray through the Looking Glass", *Feminist Studies*, vol. 7, n. 2, 1981, pp. 288–306 (p. 302); Judith Butler, Pheng Cheah, Drucilla Cornella, and Elizabeth Grosz, "The Future of Sexual Difference: An Interview with Judith Butler and Drucialla Cornell", *Diacritics*, vol. 28, n. 1, 1998, pp. 19–42 (p. 19); Toril Moi, *Sexual–Textual Practices: Feminist Literary Theory* (London: Methuen, 1985), p. 139.
24. Margaret Whitford, *Luce Irigaray: Philosophy in the Feminine* (Abingdon: Routledge, 1991), pp. 70–71; Ping Xu, "Irigaray's Mimicry of the Problem of Essentialism", *Hypatia*, vol. 10, n. 4, 1995, pp. 76–89 (pp. 77–78).
25. Luce Irigaray, *This Sex which is Not One*, trans. Catherine Porter with Carolyn Burke (Ithaca, NY: Cornell University Press, 1985), p. 78.
26. Alison Stone, *Luce Irigaray and the Philosophy of Sexual Difference* (Cambridge: Cambridge University Press, 2006), pp. 4–5, 29, 45, 105–106.
27. See, for example, Irigaray, *Speculum of the Other Woman*, p. 134.
28. Irigaray, *An Ethics of Sexual Difference*, p. 5.
29. Luce Irigaray, "Thinking Life as Relation", trans. Stephen Pluhacek, Heidi Bostic, and Luce Irigaray, in *Why Different?: A Culture of Two Subjects*, edited by Luce Irigaray and Sylvère Lotringer, trans. Camille Collins (New York: Semiotext(e), 2000), pp. 145–169 (p. 166).
30. Luce Irigaray, "Introduction", in *Why Different?: A Culture of Two Subjects*, edited by Luce Irigaray and Sylvère Lotringer, trans. Camille Collins (New York: Semiotext(e), 2000), pp. 7–13 (p. 5).
31. Irigaray, *This Sex which is Not One*, p. 142.
32. Irigaray, "Thinking Life as Relation", pp. 166–167.
33. Luce Irigaray, "The Civilization of Two", in *Why Different?: A Culture of Two Subjects*, edited by Luce Irigaray and Sylvère Lotringer, trans. Camille Collins (New York: Semiotext(e), 2000), pp. 71–80 (p. 72).
34. Luce Irigaray, "The Teaching of Difference", in *Why Different?: A Culture of Two Subjects*, edited by Luce Irigaray and Sylvère Lotringer, trans. Camille Collins (New York: Semiotext(e), 2000), pp. 121–126 (pp. 121–122).
35. Irigaray, "The Civilization of Two", p. 72.
36. Irigaray, *An Ethics of Sexual Difference*, p. 6.
37. Irigaray, *Speculum of the Other Woman*, p. 133.
38. Ibid., p. 133.
39. Ibid., pp. 133–134.
40. Ibid., p. 136.
41. Luce Irigaray, *Sexes and Genealogies*, trans. Gillian C. Gill (New York: Columbia University Press, 1993), p. 17.
42. Ibid., p. 17.
43. Irigaray, *This Sex which is Not One*, p. 23.
44. Ibid., p. 70.
45. Irigaray, *Sexes and Genealogies*, p. 117.

46. Ibid., pp. 172–173.
47. Irigaray, "Thinking Life as Relation", p. 154.
48. Irigaray, *Speculum of the Other Woman*, p. 21.
49. Ibid., p. 21.
50. Ibid., p. 21.
51. Ibid., pp. 26–27.
52. Irigaray, *This Sex which is Not One*, p. 128. See also, Irigaray, *In the Beginning She Was*, p. 151. For a discussion of this, see Britt-Marie Schiller, "The Incomplete Masculine: Engendering the Masculine of Sexual Difference", in *Thinking with Irigaray*, edited by Mary C. Rawlinson, Sabrina L. Hom, and Serene J. Khader (Albany, NY: State University of New York Press, 2011), pp. 131–151.
53. Irigaray, *Speculum of the Other Woman*, pp. 140–141.
54. Irigaray, *This Sex which is Not One*, p. 149.
55. Ibid., p. 30.
56. Irigaray, *Speculum of the Other Woman*, p. 191. In a translator's note, Gillian Gill explains that "la mystérique" is a neologism of the French words for mysticism, hysteria, mystery, and the femaleness; all of which have been historically attributed to "woman" to paint her as irreducibly other to the attributes taken to define masculinity (ibid., p. 191). For a discussion of the role(s) that mysticism plays in Irigaray's thinking, see Amy Hollywood, *Sensible Ecstacy: Mysticism, Sexual Difference, and the Demands of History* (Chicago, IL: University of Chicago Press, 2002), pp. 187–210.
57. Irigaray, *This Sex which is Not One*, p. 152.
58. Ibid., p. 152.
59. Irigaray, *Speculum of the Other Woman*, p. 230.
60. Ibid., p. 230.
61. Ibid., p. 230.
62. Ibid., p. 230.
63. Butler, Cheah, Cornell, Grosz, "The Future of Sexual Difference", p. 19.
64. Moi, *Sexual–Textual Practices*, p. 139.
65. Ibid., p. 139.
66. Ibid., p. 139.
67. Ibid., p. 139.
68. Burke, "Irigaray through the Looking Glass", p. 202.
69. Irigaray, *This Sex which is Not One*, pp. 149–150.
70. Ibid., pp. 33, 129.
71. Whitford, *Luce Irigaray*, p. 70.
72. Irigaray, *This Sex which is Not One*, p. 164.
73. Xu, "Irigaray's Mimicry of the Problem of Essentialism", p. 77.
74. Ibid., p. 78.
75. Irigaray, *Speculum of the Other Woman*, p. 142.
76. Irigaray, *This Sex which is Not One*, p. 78.
77. Irigaray, *Speculum of the Other Woman*, p. 136.
78. Ibid., p. 143.

79. Ibid., p. 238.
80. Irigaray, *This Sex which is Not One*, p. 76.
81. Ibid., p. 131.
82. Ibid., p. 131.
83. Ibid., p. 151.
84. Ibid., p. 151.
85. Ibid., p. 152.
86. Ibid., p. 163.
87. Ibid., p. 80.
88. Luce Irigaray, *I Love to You: Sketch of a Possible Felicity in History*, trans. Alison Martin (Abingdon: Routledge, 1996), p. 63.
89. Irigaray, "Introduction", p. 10.
90. Alison Stone, "From Political to Realist Essentialism: Rereading Luce Irigaray", *Feminist Theory*, vol. 5, n. 1, 2004, pp. 5–53 (p. 6).
91. Irigaray, *In the Beginning, She Was*, p. 52.
92. Luce Irigaray, *The Way of Love*, trans. Heidi Bostic and Stephen Pluháček (London: Continuum, 2002), p. 106.
93. Irigaray, "Thinking Life as Relation", p. 166.
94. Luce Irigaray, "The Time of Difference", in *Why Different?: A Culture of Two Subjects*, edited by Luce Irigaray and Sylvère Lotringer, trans. Camille Collins (New York: Semiotext(e), 2000), pp. 95–99 (p. 95).
95. Luce Irigaray, *To be Two*, trans. Monique M. Rhodes and Marco F. Cocito-Monoc (London: Athlone, 2000), pp. 66–67.
96. Simone de Beauvoir, *The Second Sex*, trans. Constance Borde and Sheila Malovany-Chevallier (New York: Vintage, 2011), p. 294.
97. Irigaray, *I Love to You*, p. 107.
98. Irigaray, "Thinking Life as Relation", p. 150.
99. Ibid., p. 151.
100. Irigaray, *Sex which is Not One*, pp. 122, 159.
101. Stone, *Luce Irigaray and the Philosophy of Sexual Difference*, p. 39.
102. Luce Irigaray, Elizabeth Hirsch, and Gary A. Olson, "'Je–Luce Irigaray': A Meeting with Luce Irigaray", trans. Elizabeth Hirsch and Gaëton Brulotte, *Hypatia*, vol. 10, n. 2, 1995, pp. 93–114 (p. 97).
103. Ibid., p. 97.
104. Irigaray's later work has led to heterogeneous interpretations. Besides Stone's "realist" reading, Penelope Deutscher (*A Politics of Impossible Difference: The Later Work of Luce Irigaray* [Ithaca, NY: Cornell University Press, 2002]) focuses on the question of Irigaray's privileging of sexual difference and the long-standing charge that this downplays other differences, such as race and class, to show how Irigaray's thinking can contribute to debates regarding multiculturalism. In contrast, Virpi Lehtinen (*Luce Irigaray's Phenomenology of Feminine Being* [Albany, NY: State University of New York Press, 2015]) argues that the question of Irigaray's essentialism is best engaged with by tying her thought to the phenomenological tradition and, in particular, its thinking of

embedded corporeality. While Deutscher's text is interesting, it is orientated to a question that is distinct from the one motivating this study. Lehtinen's has more in common with the topic motivating this study – the question of sexuality – but she thinks Irigaray through the phenomenological tradition and so, strictly speaking, offers a hybrid interpretation of Irigaray's thinking. Stone, in contrast, focuses on the question of sexuality to, in contrast to Lehtinen, advance a "realist" conception of sexual difference that is based on detailed readings of Irigaray's later texts.

105. Stone, *Luce Irigaray and the Philosophy of Sexual Difference*, p. 41.
106. Irigaray, *Speculum of the Other Woman*, p. 150; Luce Irigaray, "Different but United through a New Alliance", in *Why Different?: A Culture of Two Subjects*, edited by Luce Irigaray and Sylvère Lotringer, trans. Camille Collins (New York: Semiotext(e), 2000), pp. 113–119 (p. 117).
107. Irigaray, *I Love to You*, p. 35.
108. Stone, *Luce Irigaray and the Philosophy of Sexual Difference*, p. 99.
109. Irigaray, *Sex which is Not One*, p. 142.
110. Irigaray, *To be Two*, p. 55.
111. Irigaray, *Sexes and Genealogies*, p. 169.
112. Irigaray, *I Love to You*, p. 25.
113. Alison Stone, "The Sex of Nature: A Reinterpretation of Irigaray's Metaphysis and Political Thought", *Hypatia*, vol. 18, n. 3, 2003, pp. 60–84 (p. 77).
114. Irigaray, *Sexes and Genealogies*, p. 200.
115. Ibid., p. 200.
116. Irigaray, Hirsch, Olson, "'Je–Luce Irigaray'", p. 108.
117. Ibid., p. 108.
118. Irigaray, *Sexes and Genealogies*, p. 201.
119. Ibid., p. 200.
120. Irigaray, Hirsch, Olson, "'Je–Luce Irigaray'", pp. 108–109.
121. Irigaray, *I Love to You*, pp. 39, 51.
122. Stone, *Luce Irigaray and the Philosophy of Sexual Difference*, p. 6.
123. Irigaray, *I Love to You*, p. 107.
124. Although I will not engage with it, Stone subjects her reading of Irigaray's "realist essentialism" to critique, focusing on its (1) biological determinism, (2) historical narrative, (3) privileging of sexual difference, and (4) heteronormativity (*Luce Irigaray and the Philosophy of Sexual Difference*, pp. 46–49). In relation to the latter, it is interesting to note that Stone appeals to the work of Karen Barad (ibid., pp. 36–37), who I will return to in Chapter 8, to develop an alternative ontology which she terms "realist non-essentialist" (Stone, "From Political to Realist Essentialism", p. 18), wherein the continuous becoming of each being, including "its" sexuality, is based on non-anthropocentric processes of materialisation that are not defined by or pre-constrained within a binary heteronormative division. In so doing, Stone aims to provide a space to think non-binary forms of sexuality; an endeavour that she claims is excluded by Irigaray's schema.

125. Irigaray, *Sex which is Not One*, p. 146; see also Irigaray, *An Ethics of Sexual Difference*, p. 17.
126. Irigaray, *Sexes and Genealogies*, p. 123.
127. Irigaray, *To be Two*, p. 104.
128. Tina Chanter, *Ethics of Eros: Irigaray's Rewriting of the Philosophers* (Abingdon: Routledge, 1995), p. 44.
129. Gail Schwab, "Sexual Difference as Model: An Ethics for the Global Future", *Diacritics*, vol. 28, n. 1, 1998, pp. 76–92 (p. 82).
130. Irigaray herself makes this point in the 1995 interview "'Je–Luce Irigaray'": "Mine is an *oeuvre* that concerns the relations of sexual difference; its not necessary to demand that I create the work of others" (p. 112).
131. Ofelia Schutte, "A Critique of Normative Heterosexuality: Identity, Embodiment, and Sexual Difference in Beauvoir and Irigaray", *Hypatia*, vol. 12, n. 1, 1997, pp. 40–62 (p. 52).
132. Pheng Cheah and Elizabeth Grosz, "Of Being-Two: Introduction", *Diacritics*, vol. 28, n. 1, 1998, pp. 3–18 (p. 13).
133. Ibid., p. 13.
134. Ibid., p. 13.
135. Stone, "The Sex of Nature", p. 79.
136. Danielle Poe, "Can Luce Irigaray's Notion of Sexual Difference be Applied to Transsexual and Transgender Narratives?", in *Thinking with Irigaray*, edited by Mary C. Rawlinson, Sabrina L. Hom, and Serene J. Khader (Albany, NY: State University of New York Press, 2011), pp. 111–128 (p. 116).
137. Judith Butler makes the same point in relation to Pheng Cheah and Elizabeth Grosz's claim that Irigaray's thinking permits an affirmation of relations between the same sex: "But you are the one to provide that supplement, and God bless you, as it were, for doing that, but then let's claim it as the Liz Grosz–Pheng Cheah supplement to Irigaray" (Butler, Cheah, Cornell, Grosz, "The Future of Sexual Difference", p. 29).
138. Ibid., p. 25. To overcome this, Shannon Winnubst claims that Irigaray must be read in conjunction with Foucault's genealogical methodology to bring "Irigaray's insistence on sexual difference as the primary axis of subjectivity into a historical field where other differences affect how sexual difference gets articulated [and, in so doing,] further dispel the insidious possibility of Irigaray's reinscribing the economy of the Same in her articulations of sexual difference" ("Exceeding Hegel and Lacan: Different Fields of Pleasure within Foucault and Irigaray", *Hypatia*, vol. 14, n. 1, 1999, pp. 13–37 [pp. 29–30]).

Part III

Gender Theory and Queer Materialities

CHAPTER 7

Butler and Performativity: Thinking Sex through Gender

The turn to Judith Butler's thinking on gender introduces a number of important alterations within our study specifically and twentieth-century critical thinking on sexuality more generally. *Historically*, we move to the end of the twentieth century; *culturally* we move from thinkers located in France and Germany to one located in America; *linguistically*, English now becomes the language through which the question of sexuality is engaged with, an alteration that introduces a distinct *conceptual* apparatus, in so far as we move from the focus on the question of sexuality that has marked all previous chapters, to one that emphasises the "foundational" importance of *gender*. This "concept" is absent from the conceptual apparatus of Freud, Heidegger, Merleau-Ponty, Lacan, and, as I argued, Beauvoir, and while a number of translators of Irigaray's works have translated the French *"genre"* as "gender", Irigaray herself maintains that the two do not exactly overlap conceptually.[1] Irigaray's suspicion seems to be based on the conclusion that gender is (1) too indeterminate, and (2) linked to cultural constructions that all too easily risk re-enforcing phallogocentrism.[2] Overcoming this requires, on her telling, a more determinate bedrock that cannot be constructed away; namely, the "biological" differences between the sexes. As we saw, however, this ensures that her thinking is foreclosed within a heteronormative schema. It also seems to implicitly depend upon a biology/culture division.

In contrast, in this chapter, I will show that Butler holds that overcoming the logics of essentialism, patriarchy, and heteronormativity cannot be done by tweaking the categories of thought that have previously been used. Rather, we need a fundamental alteration in the logic shaping such thinking so that sexuality is understood to be a way of acting that is inherently and fully "constructed" rather than pre-given and limited by predefined logics or categories. In so doing, Butler *explicitly* criticises both aspects of the essentialist-patriarchal model to question and undermine any foreclosing of sexual/gender expression, while, in so doing, also bringing to the fore an explicit critical questioning of heteronormativity – that is, the idea that sexual identity and relations are necessarily defined by a masculine/feminine division and/or that this form of division should be affirmed as the model for all others forms of sexual relations – to open up and respect non-heteronormative forms of gender sexuality.

To outline this, I focus on Butler's *Gender Trouble*,[3] published in 1990, and *Bodies that Matter*[4] (published in 1993), while utilising other texts as and when necessary to support a point therein. Although Butler's thinking has developed substantially from this, especially in the new millennium where they[5] have published a plethora of works that focus on concepts such as vulnerability,[6] precarity, and precariousness,[7] Butler's early work on gender remains both the "foundation" of their later works[8] and, not surprisingly, that which is most directly applicable to a rethinking of sexuality. For this reason, I will focus on Butler's analyses of the relationship between sex and gender, performativity, and embodiment, to defend three fundamental arguments. First, Butler's turn to gender is premised on the attempt to undermine *any* form of biological essentialism. Instead, Butler insists that gender "grounds" sex. This depends upon a further sub-argument that takes us to the heart of contemporary debates regarding the status and place of pre- or non-discursive forms of matter. In contrast to the view – outlined by, for example, Beauvoir and, on a certain reading, Irigaray – that there is an originary bodily sexuality that is expressed culturally, Butler follows the far more radical (Lacanian) line that the human world is intimately structured by the symbolic realm of language and meaning. As such, not only is the biological world underpinned by symbolic meaning, but, crucially, perceiving of a biological/symbolic division is itself a consequence of a particular symbolic configuration. However, in contrast to Lacan's insistence that sexual positions are constructed from the anchoring point of the (masculine) phallus, Butler claims that their symbolic construction is unrestricted, with the consequence that the construction of gender is also open-ended and heterogeneous.

Second, when Butler claims that gender is constructed, they mean it in a very specific way based on their notion of "performativity". I argue that the fundamental difference between "constructivism" and "performativity" is concerned with the role of intentional agency, in so far as Butler argues that the former is premised on a passive subject that is moulded by the social environment, whereas the latter is based on the notion that the subject arises as a consequence of particular social processes that it also actively participates in. With this, Butler holds that the question of gender onto-genesis cannot be resolved through the binary opposition that pitches a founded, passive, and socially conditioned subject who has its gender defined by others against a voluntarist position wherein a subject simply wilfully chooses its gender. Instead, Butler maintains that the process is an immanent one, where a socially conditioned subject also participates in the creation of itself as a gendered self.

Third, I take up the question of the role of the body in Butler's gender theory by engaging with the long-standing claim that it reduces gender to a symbolic construction that is unable to account for non-discursive forms of materiality.[9] To defend Butler, I first show that they respond to this specific criticism in *Bodies that Matter* by arguing that it cannot be resolved by thinking it through a straightforward signification/materiality opposition, where one is held to be foundational for the other. Instead, Butler argues for a particularly innovative position that insists on the fundamental importance of symbolic meaning for our understanding of embodiment, all the while rejecting linguistic foundationalism by recognising that there is always a material excess to symbolic construction. Although it might be argued that this is susceptible to the charge that Butler makes against their critics – namely that the affirmation of an excess to the symbolic is itself a symbolic statement and so affirms the primacy of the symbolic – Butler argues that this only holds if we examine the issue through the lens of a logic of binary symbolic/materiality opposition wherein one of these positions must be foundational for the other. Instead, Butler suggests that what this issue really points to is the complexity inherent in the materiality–signification relation, in which neither grounds the other but they instead exist in a relation of asymmetric dialectical entwinement: materiality has to be symbolised to pass into human existence and the symbolic is, as a consequence, always tied to materiality, without the latter being reducible to the symbolic. There is then a bodily dimension to the symbolic construction of gender, but the symbolic signification of gender cannot capture all aspects of material being. Rather than being defined by a predetermining essence, structure, or relation, gender-sexual identity is a constant process of social-symbolic-embodied creation that occurs without predefinition or foreclosure and, for this reason, never takes definitive finished form or corresponds to pre-existing structures.

Sex as Gender Performativity

Butler's *Gender Trouble* offers a radical critique of feminist thinking on sexuality, as a precursor to reconfiguring such thinking around the notion of gender. Butler starts by noting that feminist theory had tended to be premised on a particular notion of identity: "For the most part, feminist theory has assumed that there is some existing identity, understood through the category of woman, who not only initiates feminist interests and goals within discourse, but constitutes the subject for whom political representation is pursued."[10] Butler's problem with this is that *"politics* and *representation* are controversial terms"[11] in so far as *"representation* serves as the operative term within a political process that seeks to extend visibility and legitimacy to women as political subjects",[12] while also describing "the normative function of a language which is said either to reveal or to distort what is assumed to be true about the category of woman".[13] In other words, Butler's problem with this feminist strategy is that identity is not *a priori*, but a normative construction. "Feminist identity" is not, then, an apolitical bedrock which can act as the foundation for political activity; it is inherently political and hence changeable precisely because it is normatively constituted.

While Butler admits that recent (for them) theory has started to take this issue on board to abandon any straightforward appeal to an *a priori* stable identity, Butler complains that these tend not to go far enough because they are orientated around obtaining political recognition for a subject that is in control of the process. This does not engage with the processes through which such a subject is created.[14] To correct this, Butler notes that their gender theory takes aim at three dominant strands within (feminist thinking) on sexuality. First, the essentialist problem where sexuality is tied to and thought from *a priori* stable forms of identity. Second, a heteronormative problem, where gender has often been restricted to a straightforward masculine/feminine division; one that has "often [had] homophobic consequences".[15] Third, the logic of patriarchy, wherein sexuality is reduced to or thought from a heterosexual relation/framework structured from a privileging of the masculine position. This can be either *explicit* or *implicit* entailing a far subtler dependence upon a privileged foundational point. For example, Butler argues that the heteronormativity that has tended to mark feminist theory is a consequence of a continuing form of phallogocentrism, in so far as such thinking has tended to affirm a binary sexual difference that implicitly takes heteronormative relations to be foundational for all other forms and, in so doing, continues to depend upon the logic of hierarchy sustaining phallogocentrism. Alternatively, if feminist theory depends upon a stable ontological (feminine) identity, it simply repeats the same logic of hierarchy and the reduction of difference to unity found in phallogocentrism. Furthermore, merely inverting the privileged term does not undermine the logic shaping that relation. For this reason, Butler explains that feminist thought has to re-evaluate its conceptual apparatus "to understand how the category of 'woman,' the subject of feminism, is produced and restrained by the very structures of power through which emancipation is sought".[16]

From this, Butler, somewhat paradoxically, rejects the notion that the question of "sexuality" can and should be orientated around "sexuality". Instead, Butler follows Gayle Rubin[17] in distinguishing between sex and gender, to claim that the latter is determinate for the former. Whereas sex refers to biology or embedded sexual attributes, gender refers to the socially constructed norms and values delineating what each sex entails and the appropriate norms of each. That gender is premised on open-ended construction and is determinate for sex means that if taken "to its logical limit, the sex/gender distinction suggests a radical discontinuity between sexed bodies and culturally constructed genders".[18] The great benefit of introducing the culturally constructed notion of gender into the conceptual matrix is that it opens up the ways in which sexuality can be exhibited: "If gender is the cultural meanings that the sexed body assumes, then a gender cannot be said to follow from a sex in any one way."[19] Indeed, "[a]ssuming for the moment the stability of binary sex, it does not follow that the construction of 'men' will accrue exclusively to the bodies of males or that 'women' will interpret only female bodies . . . [T]here is also no reason to assume that genders ought also to remain as two".[20] After all,

> [w]hen the constructed status of gender is theorized as radically independent of sex, gender itself becomes a free-floating artifice, with the consequence that *man* and *masculine* might just as easily signify as female body as a male one, and *woman* and *feminine* a male body as easily as a female one.[21]

The problem that arises at this point relates to the relationship between sex and gender. So far it might be thought that sex is a biological pre-given and gender a cultural construct, with the former grounding the later. Butler's innovation is to question the innateness of biological determinations:

> Can we refer to a 'given' sex or a 'given' gender without first inquiring into how sex and/or gender is given, through what means? And what is 'sex' anyway? Is it natural, anatomical, chromosomal, or hormonal, and how is a feminist critic to assess the scientific discourses which purport to establish such 'facts' for us? Does sex have a history? Does each sex have a different history, or histories? Is there a history of how the duality of sex was established, a genealogy that might expose the binary options as a variable construction? Are the ostensibly natural facts of sex discursively produced by various scientific discourses in the service of other political and social interests?[22]

Butler's argument is that "biology", including what it entails, is not an *a priori* given, but a historical *conceptual* construct: "If the immutable character of sex is contested, perhaps this construct called 'sex' is as culturally constructed as gender; indeed, perhaps it was always already gender, with the consequence that the distinction between sex and gender turns out to be no distinction at all."[23] As such, sex is not something fixed and determining, but a category that is both created and capable of resignification. Whereas Irigaray maintains a biological sexual difference that is realised and given meaning culturally, Butler argues that the former is itself a consequence of (socially-performative) discourse and so concludes that it makes "no sense ... to define gender as the cultural interpretation of sex, if sex itself is a gendered category".[24] For this reason, "[g]ender ought not to be conceived merely as the cultural inscription of meaning on a pregiven sex (a juridical conception); gender must also designate the very apparatus of production whereby the sexes themselves are produced".[25] As such, "gender is not to culture as sex is to nature; gender is also the discursive/cultural means by which 'sexed nature' or 'a natural sex' is produced and established as 'prediscursive,' prior to culture, a politically neutral surface *on which* culture acts".[26]

With this, Butler reaffirms their disagreement with Irigaray by implicitly claiming that Irigaray's notion of sexual difference as a biological given distinct from culture does not, as Irigaray maintains it does, describe "sex" *per se*, but is a consequence of a particular culturally inscribed form of thinking about sex. Indeed, on a related note, Butler claims that Irigaray's distinction between "pre-discursivity" (= biological sexual difference) and "discursivity" (= cultural production) fails to recognise that the "production of sex as the prediscursive ought to be understood as the effect of the apparatus of cultural construction designated by *gender*".[27]

That sex is constructed by gender, which is open-ended, means that gender is not foreclosed within a predetermining schema; its forms of expression are open. While it may take a heteronormative form, this outcome is not predetermined; it is a consequence of a particular heteronormative form of construction that, crucially, cannot, despite its own claims to the contrary, be considered definitive. The afoundationality inherent in the notion of power underpinning Butler's description of the normalising process of cultural construction means that gender structures, meanings, and relations result from the changing configurations of norms and power relations constitutive of each cultural production. These are in constant movement, as are, therefore, their effects, including gender and, by extension, sex.

However, it is important to clarify that in maintaining that sex is a consequence of gender construction, Butler does not claim that gender somehow overcomes or over-codes an already existing body: "'the body' is itself a construction, as are the myriad 'bodies' that constitute the domain of gendered subjects. Bodies cannot be said to have a signifiable existence prior to the mark of their gender."[28] Rather than a straightforward hierarchal binary model, wherein either (biological) sex grounds (culturally constructed) gender or vice versa, Butler collapses both into "gender", before arguing that *if* the notion of "sex" is retained, it does so as a consequence of a particular configuration of "gender" not as "something" necessarily opposed to or foundational for gender.

It is for this reason that Geoff Boucher misses the radicality of Butler's position when he complains that Butler works with a particularly reductionist conception of "sex" that conflates "'sexuality' in the sense of sexual preference towards a particular gender, and 'sexuality' in the biological sense of the structure of the reproductive organs".[29] His argument is that, although Butler's affirmation of gender may apply to the former, it simply ignores the latter, which Boucher holds to exist independently to gender. As I have argued, however, Butler's point is far subtler, in so far as they maintain that (1) sexuality as orientation is a consequence of gender construction (= performativity), wherein each individual learns, accepts, and comports itself in accordance with the social norms that define what that particular society holds to be appropriate for each sexual identity, and (2) "biology" is not simply an *a priori* pre-discursive foundation for gender; what biology is and its place in relation to knowledge is a social construct. For Boucher to think of biology and, by extension, sexuality in the manner that he does reveals not a "truth" about sexuality *per se*, but the normative schema that marks Boucher's conception of sexuality. The issue then, for Butler, would be to ask Boucher for the justification for his claim that we can say anything about the content of the pre-discursive form of discourse; a question that can only be responded to discursively and from the perspective of a culturally specific symbolic system, thereby recuperating Boucher's affirmation of a "pre"-discursive biological form of sexuality into symbolic construction (= gender). For this reason, Boucher's critique simply misses the points that Butler is making about the constructed "nature" of gender, the symbolic "nature" of our epistemic categories, and the body–signification/nature–culture/materiality–language relations.

The key aspect of Butler's proposal is that gender construction is not a one-time process after which "gender" is fixed, but a constant one, with the consequence that gender never coalesces into a fixed thing:

> Gender is a complexity whose totality is permanently deferred, never fully what it is at any given juncture in time. An open coalition, then, will affirm identities that are alternately instituted and relinquished according to the

purposes at hand; it will be an open assemblage that permits of multiple convergences and divergences without obedience to a normative telos of definitional closure.[30]

If gender ever appears or is affirmed to entail a closed, fixed identity, it is only because it has been constructed and affirmed in that configuration.

Crucially, however, the construction does not need to take a particular form. With this, we see that the roles traditionally assigned to the genders are disrupted, undermined, and open-ended: masculinity is not necessarily singular or tied to the phallus,[31] while the lack of any *a priori* identity means that "femininity" is not a "thing" to be correctly conceived, but a "category [that] serve[s] as a permanently available site of contested meanings".[32] It must also be remembered that the creation of any form of gender identity is problematic, according to Butler, because it is necessarily premised on (an) exclusion(s), in so far as it affirms one form of gender over others without being able to justify that privileging because of the afoundationalism inherent in the process of gender construction.

The Performativity of Gender

The question of how gender is constructed ties into another issue motivating Butler's thinking; namely, that of agency. Traditionally, modern Western philosophy has premised individual action on a foundational subject who is understood to intentionally and freely choose or will his or her activities and self. Butler, however, rejects this conception of the subject to instead claim that the subject is an effect of social processes and norms.[33] Rather than being something fixed and determinate, gender is brought forth by the norms of society. The result is a conception of gendered subjectivity as socially embedded, rather than socially unencumbered; founded, rather than foundational; and constituted, rather than constituting. It also ensures that gender construction is an inherently normative process.

Importantly, Butler clarifies that "normativity" has, at least, two senses, in so far as it can be used "to describe the mundane violence performed by certain kinds of gender ideals"[34] or it can pertain "to ethical justification, how it is established, and what concrete consequences proceed thereform".[35] In other words, the normative process entails both a certain privileging of a particular normative schema over others *and* some attempt to provide a rationale to justify that schema. Rather than *a priori*, both aspects are constructions from within the premises of the affirmed normative schema. From this, each schema produces the forms and norms through which gender can be expressed as well as the punishments for violating the approved norms. In so doing and

> [t]o the extent the gender norms (ideal dimorphism, heterosexual complementarity of bodies, ideals and rule of proper and improper masculinity and femininity, many of which are underwritten by racial codes of purity and taboos against miscegenation) establish what will and will not be intelligibly human, what will and will not be considered to be 'real,' they establish the ontological field in which bodies may be given legitimate expression.[36]

Ontological categories are not then fixed, determined, or *a priori*, but result *a posteriori* from the social norms created from and through social interactions. Ontology, for Butler, does not then describe fixed substances; it describes an ongoing, open-ended process through which bodies become without, strictly speaking, becoming anything determinate. This is not a one-time movement, but a continuous process that occurs without fixed foundation and takes place through the social norms and processes of normalisation inherent in social existence.

Crucially, a social norm is "not the same as a rule, and it is not the same as a law".[37] Whereas rules and laws are predetermined and formal, "[a] norm operates within social practices as the implicit standard of *normalization*".[38] These norms are not created by the subject, but pre-exist the subject's appearance; indeed, the subject is born into and created from the norms supporting it. As such,

> [w]e come into the world on the condition that the social world is already there, laying the ground for us. This implies that I cannot persist without norms of recognition that support my persistence: the sense of possibility pertaining to me must first be imagined from somewhere else before I can begin to imagine myself.[39]

The subject is not then self-constituting; it is a consequence of the norms governing and creating social practices through which "it" expresses itself. Furthermore, the subject only becomes a subject by virtue of being recognised socially; a process that requires acceptance of and conformity to the accepted norms. For this reason, the subject almost instantly is subjected to a normalisation process that brings it into the paradigm delineating the acceptable forms of behaviour, appearance, and thought of its society. It is through this process that the "subject" becomes subjugated into a gendered subject who is subject to the "norms, ideas and ideals [that] hold sway over embodied life [to] provide coercive criteria for normal 'men' and 'women'".[40]

Language plays a fundamental role in both the instantiation and transmission of social norms/practices. There is not a linear process to this, where, for example, first come norms then language or vice versa; rather, language and norms are co-constituting. In turn, this co-constitution founds the subject by conceiving of "it" in a particular way to bring the subject forth in a way that is socially acceptable, while what is considered to be socially acceptable depends upon and changes with and through subjective actions. Butler makes this point by appealing to Althusser's notion of *"interpellation"*[41] – the process through which a subject is created by responding to being hailed in a particular way – to show how it works in relation to the creation of gender. Butler's point is that the subject is not gendered and then goes out to the world; such a view risks re-instantiating the foundational subject. The gendered subject is created through the use of language, which, in turn, reflects and re-enforces social norms.

To show this, Butler points to "the medical interpellation which (the recent example of the sonogram not withstanding) shifts an infant from an 'it' to a 'she' or a 'he,' and in that naming, the girl is 'girled,' brought into the domain of language and kinship through the interpellation of gender".[42] This is not a one-time event; "th[e] founding interpellation is reiterated by various authorities and throughout various intervals of time to reinforce or contest naturalized effect. The naming is at once the setting of a boundary, and also the repeated inculcation of a norm."[43] The gender naming does not simply produce a label, but attributes an entire set of norms to dictate activities and practices that must be continually enacted to remain viable. As such, Butler explains that "[t]o the extent that the naming of the 'girl' is transitive, that is, initiates the process by which a certain 'girling' is compelled, the term or, rather, its symbolic power, governs the formation of a corporeally enacted femininity that never fully approximates the norm".[44]

Importantly, there is always a "gap" between the norm-demand and its realisation through bodily practices. This ensures that the "girl" is never "girly" enough, in so far as she can never fully live up to the normative ideal even though she remains under constant pressure to do so. Butler's conclusion is that "[f]emininity is . . . not the product of a choice, but the forcible citation of a norm, one whose complex historicity is indissociable from relations of discipline, regulation, punishment".[45] Through a complex and ongoing network of social practices, a particular normative framework is constructed and "imposed" onto the subject to ensure that "it" acts in a particular way.

Again, however, rather than pre-existing or transcending this social field, the subject is both immersed in the social field and, indeed, constructed immanently from and through it: "th[e] citation of the gender norm is necessary in order to qualify as a 'one,' to become viable as a 'one,' where subject-formation is dependent on the prior operation of legitimating social norms".[46] For this reason, "[t]he sign, understood as a gender imperative – 'girl!' – reads less as an assignment than as a command and, as such, produces its own insubordinations".[47] Because the "imposition" constructs the subject, the limitations inherent in it – in so far as the subject is channelled towards one ideal at the expense of alternatives – are also, somewhat paradoxically, the conditions through which the subject can bend, alter, or undermine those same norms to create possibilities and opportunities for itself. As Butler puts it, "by being called a name, one is also, paradoxically, given a certain possibility for social existence, initiated into a temporal life of language that exceeds prior purposes that animate that call".[48]

Importantly, social norms are not simply external to and imposed onto subjects in a linear process. The norm–subject relation is far more complicated and dialectically entwined. While the subject is an effect of social norms, social norms themselves only exist because they are adopted and re-enacted by the subjects they create. Gender norms are not then determinate for the subject constructed nor are they "a set of free-floating attributes".[49] "[G]ender is always a doing, though not a doing by a subject who might be said to pre-exist the deed".[50] Instead the subject is brought to existence through those norms and, indeed, in the same "act" of being brought forth also perpetuates those norms through the actions perpetuated from them. So, to reiterate, gender is not the consequence of and does not entail the representation of a prior identity; "[t]here is no gender identity behind the expressions of gender",[51] "identity is performatively constituted by the very 'expressions' that are said to be its results".[52] Instead of being representational, gender is expressive, but rather than expressing a predetermined form of identity it is a non-foreclosed, immanent expression of the social norms that create the subject but depend for their expression on the subject's reiteration of them. As such, gender construction entails "acts, gestures, enactments, generally construed, [that are] *performative* in the sense that the essence or identity that they otherwise purport to express are *fabrications* manufactured and sustained through corporeal signs and other discursive means".[53]

The construction that gives rise to gender is then of a particular form; rather than "construction" in the sense of a social imposition onto a passive body, "performativity" points to the notion that "the gendered body ... has no ontological status apart from the various acts which constitute its reality".[54] Gender is performatively constituted through the practical doing of the social norms that bring the subject to exist and only through the way it practices the social norms does the subject come to exist. For this reason, Joris Vlieghe explains that

> [t]he existence of a social order and the destruction of different identities and hierarchal positions within that order are thus wholly dependent upon the constant repetition or even better re-enactment of specific roles and their consolidated meanings: performing those roles again and again, a social agent gets reproduced.[55]

There is no predetermined roadmap for how this will play out; "nothing determines me in advance – I am not formed once and for all but continually and repeatedly. I am still being formed as I form myself in the here and now. And my own self-formative activity . . . becomes part of that ongoing formative process. I am never simply formed, nor I am ever fully self-forming."[56]

With this, Butler rejects any notion of a fixed foundation to social norms *and* subjective identity: social norms create the subject but only exist because they are performatively reiterated by the subjects they create; in turn, subjects are grounded in social norms, but, because norms are a consequence of the actions and practices of all other subjects constitutive of and supporting social norms, the subject is also constituted through and as a process of ongoing social becoming. Rather than stability and order, there is only ever, at both the social and subjective levels, flux and the continuous construction–destruction of norms and identities. Indeed, this ties into Butler's preference for the pronouns "they/them" instead of "she/her", which, generally speaking, (1) supports Butler's insistence regarding the constituting role that language plays in "constructing" material reality, (2) highlights the multidimensionality of gender, (3) undercuts the traditional heteronormative gender binary opposition, and (4) performs a remaking of the norms that define both the parameters of gender assignment and the forms of gender that are considered to be socially acceptable.

However, while the notion of "performativity" is fundamental to Butler's gender theory, they latterly came to admit that "[i]t is difficult to say precisely what 'performativity' is not only because my own views on what 'performativity' might mean have changed over time, most often in response to excellent criticisms, but because so many others have taken it up and give it their own formulations".[57] Nevertheless, in the 2010 essay "Performative Agency", Butler identifies four aspects to it. First, "performativity seeks to counter a certain kind of positivism according to which we might begin with already delimited understandings of what gender, the state, and the economy are".[58] With this, Butler rejects the notion of a static predetermined identity, a position that depends upon and re-enforces their anti-essentialism. Second, "performativity works, when it works, to counter a certain metaphysical presumption about culturally constructed categories, and to draw our attention to the diverse mechanism of construction".[59] Third, "performativity starts to describe a set of processes that produce ontological effects, that is, that work to bring into being certain kinds of realities or, fourthly, that lead to certain kinds of socially binding consequences".[60]

Crucially, these normalising procedures condition but do not determine gender expression. Subjects "come into the world on the condition that the social world is already there, laying the groundwork for us",[61] but the norms through which the subject comes to be also need to be re-instantiated through the practical actions of the subjects created from them, which, as noted, are conditioned but not determined by previous instantiations of those norms. However, contra Lois McNay,[62] reiteration is never simply a mechanical reproduction of the same. Although "gender is a kind of doing, an incessant activity performed, in part, without one's knowing and without one's willing, it is not for that reason automatic or mechanical. On the contrary, it is the practice of improvisation within a scene of constraint."[63] The subject can always practise its constituting gender norms in a multitude of different ways that are constantly open to revision.

Furthermore, because performativity is practice-based, it is intimately tied up with and dependent upon the body; indeed, Butler calls gender "the repeated stylization of the body [through] a set of repeated acts within a highly rigid regulatory frame that congeal over time to produce the appearance of substance, of a natural sort of being".[64] The body is not however preformed as if there were something divorced from it doing the performing, nor is there anything like "a pure body"[65] devoid of signification and social norms; the body is always a consequence of the performative gender practices learnt and perpetuated as the subject is formed by and negotiates the social norms constitutive of the social body.

With this, Butler points to a particular conception of subjective intentional agency that rejects voluntarism, wherein the foundational subject simply chooses and wills its activity and ends. The subject is always embedded within and an effect of social norms, but it is not *determined* by those norms. Instead, Butler points to a specific conception of power to explain that agency is always possible but only from "within" the contours that define the expression of power relations.[66] Rather than simply being impositional on a pre-existing subject, Butler follows Foucault in holding that power is constitutive of reality, an ongoing becoming, and fundamentally creative.[67] There is no such thing as escaping from power altogether, nor is power something possessed. Power is constituted by productive relations that express a world including subjects. The key point, however, is that the expression of power (through social norms for example) happens "to" subjects and, at the same time, depends upon being reiterated by those "same" subjects. Social norms need to be reiterated by those subjects and are kept alive when subjects act in accordance with them. It is in the momentary change that takes place from being subjected by power to acting through power that Butler locates agency. At the moment of reiteration, the subject acts as a relay for the expression of power relations and so can "choose" how to perpetuate them; a "choice" that has the potential to push them in different directions.[68] For this reason, Butler explains that

> [p]erformativity describes th[e] relation of being implicated in that which one opposes, this turning of power against itself to produce alternative modalities of power, to establish a kind of political constestation that is not a 'pure' opposition, a 'transcendence' of contemporary relations of power, but a difficult labor of forging a future from resources inevitably impure.[69]

The Question of the Body

Butler's gender theory therefore decentres the subject from the foundational status it has long had within Western philosophy to embed "it" within constantly changing networks of social-symbolic relations. Holding that sexuality is a consequence of the socio-culturally constructed performative practices that generate and sustain social norms undercuts any notion of substantive essentialism and any foreclosing of sexuality within predetermined schemas. In so doing, Butler challenges the dependence on and appeal to restrictive logical parameters that limit sexuality to certain normative schemas at the expense of others. Instead, focusing on gender opens up the parameters through which sexuality can be thought and expressed. Given the lack of foundation to justify a particular series of norms, Butler actively resists the temptation to affirm one form of sexual identity or normative schema; doing so would simply affirm a unitary sexual identity and so repeat the error to be overcome. The aim is to remove obstacles to sexual (gender) expression so that individuals are liberated from the violence and restrictions that have traditionally accompanied sexual norms.[70]

However, while the influence of Butler's gender theory has been substantial, there is one issue that has continued to plague its reception, in so far as it has long been concluded that tying sexuality to the cultural production of gender norms creates a free-floating form of sexual identity that distorts or simply annihilates the material body by reducing it to an idealistic symbolic creation. Susan Bordo, for example, objects that in Butler's gender theory "language swallows everything up",[71] Lois McNay complains that it "tends to valorize the action of resignification *per se*",[72] and Seyla Benhabib[73] and Patricia Clough[74] conclude that it is simply unable to adequately account for the material body. Even when it is accepted that Butler does not affirm linguistic idealism, Butler's account of materiality is still rejected or found to be too language-orientated: Vicki Kirby, for example, charges that Butler offers an analysis of the materiality of textuality and not a "materiality of matter",[75] which leads Veronica Vasterling to conclude that it "has negative consequences for a feminist and queer theory of the body".[76]

These conclusions are premised on two main assumptions. First, there is an idealism/materialism distinction underpinning Butler's schema, with language tied to the former and the body to the latter. And, second, Butler's gender theory is premised on a simple act of symbolic resignification, with the consequence that Butler's critics conclude that Butler affirms a "mere" idealistic analysis that ignores or, worse, rejects, the importance of materiality. In what follows, however, I defend Butler against these charges by first showing that Butler does not reduce performativity to a linguistic activity; performativity is a *social practice* with a linguistic component and is therefore premised on the actions and interactions of socially-induced bodies. I then argue that the charge that Butler operates through a binary opposition attributes to Butler's thinking a position that Butler explicitly rejects. Rather than simply accepting and operating through a linguistic/materialism opposition, Butler works to show that the two are entwined; a conclusion that means that any linguistic alteration has material significance and vice versa.

To reiterate then, according to Butler, the body is not predefined by a natural sex/gender; the body is the site where and through gender performativity immanently takes place and, indeed, is that which is shaped and reshaped by such gender performance. Gender signifies an entire way of being; one that is never fixed or determined but always reconstructed in each act. Butler calls it *"a corporeal style"*[77] and explains that "[g]ender is the repeated stylization of the body, a set of repeated acts within a highly rigid regulatory frame that congeals over time to produce the appearance of substance, of a natural sort of being".[78] Importantly, while "there are individual bodies that enact these significations by becoming stylized into gendered modes, this 'action' is a public action [with] temporal and collective dimensions".[79] This social aspect regulates the ways in which gender identities and performance can be expressed within a particular milieu.

However, as noted, rather than an individual who acts within a society or a society that determines individual habits, Butler's notion of the individual–society relation is a complex one wherein each is entwined and conditions, without determining, the other. There is no straightforward opposition between them nor is the relationship structured from a foundational logic where one simply grounds the other. Given the complexity of the multiple "parts" (social, symbolic, psychic, and so on) coalescing through it, Butler explains that the body is never singular; rather, "'the body' is itself a construction, as are the myriad 'bodies' that constitute the domain of gendered subjects. Bodies cannot be said to have a signifiable existence prior to the mark of their gender."⁸⁰ As such, the question becomes: "To what extent does the body *come into being* in and through the mark(s) of gender?"⁸¹

Butler's initial response in *Gender Trouble* was, as noted, often taken to be problematic because it seems to fold the body into the symbolic construction inherent in gender. After all, the notion of "sex" and, with it, considerations of biology, seem to disappear from the equation to be replaced with or collapsed into gender (re-)significations. Such a conclusion is however based on the notion that Butler's analysis operates through a binary (sex/gender, essence/constructivist) opposition that simply inverts the privileged term so that the latter options ground the former. In contrast, Butler maintains that "performativity" cannot be constrained within a binary opposition; thinking of gender/sex, culture/nature in terms of a binary opposition is itself the result of a symbolic construction that constrains the debate within those terms and that logic. Butler's notion of performativity undermines this presupposition by showing that each term and the relation between them is constructed through its entwinement with the other.

To clarify their position, Butler returns to the question of performativity in *Bodies that Matter* to insist that if we are to think the body as constructed then such action "demands a rethinking of the meaning of construction itself".⁸² In so doing, Butler more closely examines the "nature" of performativity to show the ways in which performativity is nexal, operating at the intersection of the psyche, the social, and the symbolic. This, in turn, requires renewed focus on the question of embodiment to identify how it both "constructs" and constrains performativity.

There are, at least, two key issues to this. First, Butler rejects the notion that materiality describes an inert substance or "a site or surface".⁸³ For this reason, the claim that Butler starts from the notion of a passive body is simply mistaken.⁸⁴ Materiality, and hence embodiment, is/are never passive according to Butler; it always entails *"a process of materialization that stabilizes over time to produce the effect of boundary, fixity, and surface we call matter"*.⁸⁵ This stabilisation process is never completed. Rather than a passive "thing", materiality refers to a process; a verb not a noun.

Second, materialisation always has to be thought through its immanent relationship to regulatory powers that shape and alter its expression: "[embodiment] is part of a regulatory practice that produces the bodies it governs, that is, whose regulatory force is made clear as a kind of productive power; the power to produce – demarcate, circulate, differentiate – the bodies it controls".⁸⁶ Returning to the notion of "sex" in *Gender Trouble*, Butler explains that "'sex' is an ideal construct which is forcibly materialized through time. It is not a simple fact or static condition of a body, but a process whose regulatory norms materialize 'sex' and achieve this materialization through a forcible reiteration of those norms."[87] Importantly, not only do "bodies never quite comply with the norms by which their materialization is impelled",[88] but it is precisely because they do not, and indeed materialisation must be continuously reiterated, that the body multiplies and changes and alternative possibilities for material expression constantly open up.

This brings forth a number of revisions in Butler's gender theory. First, it demands "the recasting of the matter of bodies as the effect of a dynamic of power, such that the matter of bodies will be indissociable from the regulatory norms that govern their materialization and the signification of those material effects".[89] Second, performativity must be understood "not as the act by which a subject brings into being what she/he names, but, rather, as that reiterative power of discourse to produce the phenomena that it regulates and constrains".[90] Third, "the construal of 'sex' [must] no longer [be thought] as a bodily given on which the construct of gender is artificially imposed, but as a cultural norm which governs the materialization of bodies".[91] Fourth, there must be "a rethinking of the process by which a bodily norm is assumed, appropriated, taken on as not, strictly speaking, undergone *by a subject*, but rather that the subject, the speaking 'I,' is formed by virtue of having gone through such a process of assuming a sex".[92] And, finally, this process must be linked to "the question of *identification*, and ... the discursive means by which the heterosexual imperative enables certain sexed identifications and forecloses and/or disavows other identifications".[93] It is here that Butler's use of Althusser's notion of "*interpellation*"[94] once more enters the scene to reaffirm Butler's point that signification "physically" creates the one being signified. Specifically, and as noted, Butler identifies the ways in which newborn babies are gendered by being designated as "boy" or "girl", with this shifting the "'it' to a "she' or a 'he,' and [where] in that naming, the girl is 'girled,' brought into the domain of language and kinship through the interpellation of gender".[95] Through this, signification (the name) becomes material (it literally creates the girl with all the expectations and norms that this entails for that signifying regime), while matter gains signification and comes to matter (the "it" becomes a "girl" with all the significance that entails for that particular socio-symbolic system).

According to Butler, therefore, the material–signification relationship has onto-epistemic importance: *ontologically*, signification and matter become what they are through each other; neither pre-exists the relation, which means that, second, *epistemologically*, what a thing is depends, in a very strong sense, on how it is signified. Butler warns, however, that this does not reduce matter to signification: "To claim that discourse is formative is not to claim that it originates, causes, or exhaustively composes that which it concedes; rather it is to claim that there is no reference to a pure body which is not at the same time a further formation of the body."[96] Instead of operating through a binary opposition between a material body and an immaterial signifier, body and signifier are entwined. As Butler explains in the 1995 essay "Contingent Foundations", "the options for theory are not exhausted by *presuming* materiality, on the one hand, and *negating* materiality, on the other".[97] Deconstructing the binary opposition between materiality and signification shows the performative entwinement of both and "does not freeze, banish, render useless, or deplete of meaning the usage of the term [bodies]; on the contrary, it provides the conditions to *mobilize* the signifier in the service of an alternative production".[98] Crucially, however, Butler clarifies that "[t]his is not to say that the materiality of bodies is simply and only a linguistic effect which is reducible to a set of signifiers. Such a distinction overlooks the materiality of the signifier itself"[99] and "also fails to understand materiality as that which is bound up with signification from the start".[100]

Whereas Dorothea Olkowski finds this circularity "frustrating"[101] and demands an analytic that will "unravel these terms",[102] Butler's point is that the foundationalism that such a demand depends upon ignores the relationality through which meaning and by extension "things" are generated: materiality cannot be thought devoid of signification, while signification, in literally "constructing" being, is inherently material. Neither term can be, strictly speaking, divorced from or collapsed into the other to affirm a foundational materiality or signification. Although different, materiality and signification have to be thought through their constitutive entwinement. This is difficult and is why Butler confesses that "I am not a very good materialist. Every time I try to write about the body, the writing ends up being about language."[103] While it might be thought that this confirms the charge that Butler is a linguistic idealist, Butler quickly clarifies that "[t]his is not because I think the body is reducible to language; it is not".[104] Such a conclusion arises from fallaciously thinking of the relationship in terms of a binary opposition that fails to appreciate the entwinement of matter and signification wherein "[l]anguage emerges from the body, constituting an emission of sorts. The body is that upon which language falters, and the body carries its own signs, its own signifiers, in ways that remain largely unconscious."[105] While signification is material and materiality is revealed through signification, they are not two parts that join to form a whole. Rather, Butler insists that "it must be possible to claim that the body is not known or identifiable apart from the linguistic coordinates that establish the boundaries of the body – *without* thereby claiming that the body is nothing other than the language by which it is known".[106] What this looks like is necessarily left open, namely because "it" will take different forms, but Butler's conclusion is that "[a]lthough the body depends on language to be known, the body also exceeds every possible linguistic effort of capture".[107]

The problem, of course, is that, on Butler's telling, this "pre-discursive body" can never be known – an action that requires signification – and so, strictly speaking, cannot be posited as that which is distinct from discursivity. After all, it is only by passing into language that "a certain social existence of the body first becomes possible".[108] Whereas this appears to posit two bodies – one "pre"-discursive and another that is socio-discursive – Butler is quick to point out that this thought of "a body that has not yet been given social definition [is] an impossible scene"[109] for it asks us to signify something that cannot be signified. Nevertheless, Butler maintains that this pre-discursive body must be posited to avoid the charge of (1) linguistic idealism and/or (2) foundationalism: the materiality of the signifier points to an excessive material "sphere" other than signification, but yet this "other" cannot be symbolised to ground signification; "it" is purely other. Yet, as Butler notes, this pure otherness is immediately undermined by its positing, which returns "it" to signification: "To posit a materiality outside of language is still to posit that materiality, and the materiality so posited will retain that positing as its constitutive condition."[110] Again, while this may be thought to affirm the primacy of signification, signification is, as she previous noted, always conditioned by a material excess that, paradoxically, cannot be signified but yet in being posited is always tied (without being reduced) to signification. What might be thought to be a relatively simple choice between affirming signification or affirming materiality proves to be far more complex: the simple affirmation of either option actually reveals its paradoxical entwinement with the "other" to, in so doing, unmask the often unappreciated complexity of the materiality–signification relationship.

Concluding Remarks

With this, Butler's gender theory marks an important movement in contemporary critical interrogations into sexuality that alters the terms of the debate away from "sexuality" *per se* – that is, sexuality as a pre-existing "thing" to be studied – to a discussion of the ways in which sexuality is assembled socially, symbolically, and psychically through the performative construction of *gender*. Indeed, Butler's thinking is something of the "hinge" upon which contemporary engagements with the constructed nature of sexuality are premised; that is, Butler's gender theory is either affirmed or the ground from which alternatives are developed.

This is fundamentally because Butler goes further than the other thinkers that I have engaged with in undermining the foreclosure of sexuality within predetermined schemas. By arguing that sexuality is a consequence of (gender) cultural performativity, Butler rejects any appeal to an essential pre-given biological form of sexuality, claiming that such a description does not capture a pre-existing reality to be accurately represented but unjustifiably imposes one constructed model of sexuality as the only one. With this, Butler also rejects representational models of becoming – where ontological becoming is conditioned by and constrained within a prior ahistoric model – to instead affirm a model of immanent expressive becoming. As such, there is no prior existing form of sexuality that grounds individual action or being and must be accurately represented symbolically. Instead, sexuality is held to be nothing other than a symbolic construction, in so far as what sexuality *is* depends upon how it is constructed socially and performatively. Any claim to stable and static essential sexual characteristics is premised on a "false" ontology that fails to recognise that there is no pre-existing reality, only the construction of an ever-changing reality that is taken to be "reality". While this leads to the psychoanalytic question of *why* that particular symbolic construction is valued over others, Butler's more general point is that, as symbolic constructions, there are no *a priori* categories or schemas through which this *has* to take place. Sexuality is never necessarily foreclosed within predetermining categories.

With this, Butler, second, argues that sexuality is a normative social-symbolic construct rather than a biological pre-given one. Because symbolic systems are open-ended, the norms generated by them cannot ever be closed, determinate, or fixed. They are and must be constantly re-enforced through the actions and interactions of the subjects they create. The moment of reiteration is the moment when those norms can be altered; a process that can be explicit or subtle. As a consequence, individuals never relate to and perform gender norms in exactly the same way. Such norms are always capable of being subverted and altered and, crucially, that possibility is integral to the functioning of gender norms themselves. For Butler, this ensures that sexuality is not a predefined form of being, but a process in which we are taught what is and is not socially acceptable. The afoundationality of that normalisation process calls into question any definitive response, all the while reminding us that alternative normalisation possibilities are also available.

By claiming that the onto-genetic field is indeterminate, Butler, third, not only rejects any foreclosing of sexuality within predetermined schemas, but, in so doing, also undermines the logic of patriarchy that has long dominated Western thinking on the topic. Because sexuality is performatively constructed without *a priori* foundations, not only do the sexual positions have to be created but there is no reason why (1) the masculine should be valued over the feminine, thereby undermining any *a priori* affirmation of patriarchy, or, crucially, (2) why sexuality and sexual relations need to be limited to a masculine/feminine binary opposition. With this, Butler introduces a conceptual innovation to the historical debate, in so far as, while the other thinkers I have engaged with have called into question aspects of the essentialist-patriarchal model of sexuality but have tended to continue to affirm one aspect while doing so, Butler not only explicitly rejects both the logics of essentialism and patriarchy, but also demonstrates that there is a "third" problem that accompanies this critique but which has been almost completely ignored by the philosophical tradition: the question of heteronormativity, which occurs when sexuality is reduced to a masculine/feminine division that is taken to be the only appropriate and legitimate form of sexual relation. Whereas the other critical commentators we have examined never discuss this explicitly, instead appearing to take it for granted that sexuality is principally structured around a heteronormative matrix, Butler points out that, if sexuality is a form of gender construction without *a priori* forms that foreclose "it", then there is no reason to think that sexuality must be structured around the masculine/feminine division *or* that this division should be privileged over others.

This is important because it explicitly questions the privileging of heteronormativity to accept the validity of alternative forms of sexuality, and, in so doing, calls attention to the elasticity of gender expressions and, by extension, sexuality. However, it does not simply point to the validity of homosexuality; doing so would risk reducing sexuality to hetero- and homosexual forms. Butler empties the conceptual space from predeterminations to open up the possibilities for gender/sexual expression to include intersex, trans*, and, more generally, gender fluidity wherein individuals move throughout and across sexual identities, which will become increasingly important as thinking on sexuality moves towards queer theory and the abandonment of *any* form of determinate (sexual) identity.

These developments do however depend upon a certain critical appropriation of and distancing from Butler's thinking, particularly regarding the relationship between symbolic construction and materiality. As noted, a number of critics charged Butler's thinking with linguistic reductionism that was unable to take into consideration the materiality of embodiment.[111] I defended Butler against this charge by showing Butler is are aware of this criticism and explicitly rejects it by rethinking the way in which materiality and signification work together to create "the body" – the body can only be known through signification, but yet cannot be held to be reducible to signification; there is always an excessive unknowable aspect to this materiality–signification construction – but Butler's point does lead to something of an admitted paradox, in so far as the claim that the body cannot be reduced to signification is itself a statement from a particular system of signification and so returns us to the fundamental importance of signification. In other words, Butler's affirmation of a pre-discursive material excess to evade the charge of linguistic idealism results, somewhat paradoxically, in the recuperation of this excess into the symbolic realm in a way that seems to reaffirm the foundationality of the symbolic linguistic realm.

Butler engages with this paradox and indeed resolves to leave it open to force us to think it in all its contradictions, but others have not been so keen on such a strategy, instead claiming that the recuperation of the material excess into the symbolic reveals Butler's continuing privileging of the linguistic over the material. I have argued that this is only so if Butler's thinking on the materiality–symbolic relation is thought from a foundationalist logic of binary opposition so that each aspect is held to be distinct from the other with one grounding the relation – both positions which are explicitly rejected by Butler – but the perceived failure of Butler's gender theory to adequately account for the material excess that escapes every symbolic construction contributed to the renewed focus on materiality that has marked the new millennium.

For Butler, this risks re-instantiating the binary materiality/signification logic of oppositions to be overcome, but for representatives of this "new materialism"[112] – a term that groups together a heterogeneous group of thinkers[113] – focusing on "materiality" and thinking it in terms of emergent, non-binary processes (1) shows the fallacy inherent in any appeals to static forms of identity, and (2) undermines the anthropocentrism inherent in Butler's gender theory, wherein norms affirming a fixed sexual identity are only overcome through an act of *human* symbolic construction. Indeed, whereas Butler's gender theory seems to accept that some form of gender identity is inevitable and even largely unproblematic as long as we also recognise that such identity is never fixed or determinate, proponents of the materialist turn are guided by the stronger claim that no form of identity is acceptable because it has no basis in reality given that materiality is defined by an ongoing process of emergent non-binary becoming. They agree with Butler that there is no foundational identity or schema to constrain gender, but argue that this is not because individual action deconstructs a symbolic system that holds this to be the case; it is because of the emergent, non-binary processes inherent in matter's ontological constitution, a position that rejects the existence, at any stage, of a clear-cut singular sexual or gender identity. The following chapter takes this up through the agential realism of Karen Barad; a development that moves critical thinking on sexuality from gender performativity to queer materialities.

Notes

1. See, for example, Luce Irigaray, *Sexes and Genealogies*, trans. Gillian C. Gill (New York: Columbia University Press, 1993).
2. In an important endnote in the 1991 essay "A Bridge between Two Irreducible to Each Other" (in *Why Different?: A Culture of Two Subjects*, edited by Luce Irigaray and Sylvère Lotringer, trans. Camille Collins (New York: Semiotext(e), 2000), pp. 57–62), Irigaray explains that "I often use the word 'sex' for the sexed identity. This doesn't designate the sexual *per se*, in particular genitality, rather the woman being and the man being. The word 'gender' is often understood as already codified by language and culture; it thus runs the risk of perpetuating the existing hierarchy between men and women" (p. 59n14).
3. Judith Butler, *Gender Trouble: Feminism and the Subversion of Identity*, Second edition (Abingdon: Routledge, 1999).
4. Judith Butler, *Bodies that Matter: On the Discursive Limits of 'Sex'* (Abingdon: Routledge, 1993).
5. As explained in the Introduction, Butler identifies as "they/their" rather than "she/her". This (1) ties into Butler's insistence on the important role that language plays in "constructing" material reality, (2) highlights the multidimensionality of gender, (3) undercuts the traditional heteronormative gender binary opposition, and (4) performs a remaking of the norms that define gender expression.
6. Judith Butler, *Precarious Life: The Powers of Mourning and Violence* (London: Verso, 2006), pp. 19–49.
7. Judith Butler, *Frames of War: When Life is Grievable?* (London: Verso, 2009), p. 10.
8. This issue has been somewhat controversial within the literature. For example, Bonnie Honnig (*Antigone Interrupted* [Cambridge: Cambridge University Press, 2013], pp. 43–46) and Catherine Mills ("Normative Violence, Vulnerability, and Responsibility", *differences: A Journal of Feminist Cultural Studies*, vol. 18, n. 2, 2007, pp. 133–156), have insisted on a fundamental rupture between Butler's early work on gender and later work on ethics. In contrast, Emma Ingala ("From Hannah Arendt to Judith Butler: The Conditions of the Political", in *Subjectivity and the Political: Contemporary Perspectives*, edited by Gavin Rae and Emma Ingala [Abingdon: Routledge, 2018], pp. 35–54) and also Butler (*Giving an Account of Oneself* [New York: Fordham University Press, 2005], p. 3) reject such a division.
9. Seyla Benhabib, "Subjectivity, Historiography, and Politics", in Seyla Benhabib, Judith Butler, Drucilla Cornell, and Nancy Fraser, *Feminist Contentions: A Philosophical Exchange* (Abingdon: Routledge, 1995), pp. 107–126 (p. 109); Susan

Bordo, *Unbearable Weight, Feminism, Western Culture, and the Body* (Berkeley, CA: University of California Press, 1993), p. 291; Patricia Ticineto Clough, "Introduction", in *The Affective Turn: Theorizing the Social*, edited by Patricia Ticineto Clough and Jean Halley (Durham, NC: Duke University Press, 2007), pp. 1–33 (p. 8); Lois McNay, "Subject, Psyche, and Agency: The Work of Judith Butler", *Theory, Culture, and Society*, vol. 16, n. 2, 1999, pp. 175–193; Vicki Kirby, "When All That is Solid Melts into Language: Judith Butler and the Question of Matter", *International Journal of Sexuality and Gender Studies*, vol. 7, n. 4, 2002, pp. 265–280 (p. 269); Veronica Vasterling, "Butler's Sophisticated Constructivism: A Critical Assessment", *Hypatia*, vol. 14, n. 3, 1999, pp. 17–38 (p. 19).
10. Butler, *Gender Trouble*, p. 2.
11. Ibid., p. 2.
12. Ibid., p. 2.
13. Ibid., p. 2.
14. Ibid., p. 2.
15. Ibid., p. viii.
16. Ibid., p. 4.
17. Gayle Rubin, "Thinking Sex: Notes for a Radical Theory of the Politics of Sexuality", in *Pleasure and Danger: Exploring Feminist Sexuality*, edited by Carol S. Vance (Abingdon: Routledge, 1984), pp. 267–319 (p. 308).
18. Butler, *Gender Trouble*, p. 9.
19. Ibid., p. 9.
20. Ibid., p. 9.
21. Ibid., p. 9.
22. Ibid., p. 9.
23. Ibid., pp. 9–10.
24. Ibid., p. 10.
25. Ibid., p. 10.
26. Ibid., p. 10.
27. Ibid., p. 10.
28. Ibid., p. 12.
29. Geoff Boucher, "Judith Butler's Postmodern Existentialism: A Critical Analysis", *Philosophy Today*, vol. 48, n. 4, 2004, pp. 355–369 (p. 358).
30. Butler, *Gender Trouble*, p. 22.
31. Ibid., p. 18.
32. Ibid., p. 21.
33. Judith Butler, "Contingent Foundations", in Seyla Benhabib, Judith Butler, Drucilla Cornell, and Nancy Fraser, *Feminist Contentions: A Philosophical Exchange* (Abingdon: Routledge, 1995), pp. 35–58 (p. 36).
34. Butler, *Gender Trouble*, p. xx.
35. Ibid., p. xxi.
36. Ibid., p. xxv.
37. Judith Butler, "Gender Regulations", in *Undoing Gender* (Abingdon: Routledge, 2004), pp. 40–56 (p. 41).
38. Ibid., p. 41.

39. Judith Butler, "Beside Oneself: On the Limits of Sexual Autonomy", in *Undoing Gender* (Abingdon: Routledge, 2004), pp. 17–39 (p. 32).
40. Judith Butler, "The Question of Social Transformation", in *Undoing Gender* (Abingdon: Routledge, 2004), pp. 204–231 (p. 206).
41. Louis Althusser, "Ideology and Ideological State Apparatus (Notes Toward an Investigation)", in *Lenin and Philosophy and Other Essays*, trans. Ben Brewster (New York: Monthly Review Press, 2001), pp. 85–126 (p. 118).
42. Butler, *Bodies that Matter*, p. xvii.
43. Ibid., p. xvii.
44. Ibid., p. 177.
45. Ibid., p. 177.
46. Ibid., p. 177.
47. Ibid., p. 181.
48. Judith Butler, *Excitable Speech: A Politics of the Performative* (Abingdon: Routledge, 1997), p. 2.
49. Butler, *Gender Trouble*, p. 34.
50. Ibid., p. 34.
51. Ibid., p. 34.
52. Ibid., p. 34.
53. Ibid., p. 185.
54. Ibid., p. 185.
55. Joris Vlieghe, "Foucault, Butler, and Corporeal Experience: Taking Social Critique beyond Phenomenology and Judgement", *Philosophy and Social Criticism*, vol. 40, n. 10, 2014, pp. 1019–1035 (p. 1022).
56. Judith Butler, "Introduction", in *Senses of the Subject* (New York: Fordham University Press, 2015), pp. 1–16 (p. 6).
57. Butler, *Gender Trouble*, p. xv.
58. Judith Butler, "Performative Agency", *Journal of Cultural Economy*, vol. 3, n. 2, 2010, pp. 147–161 (p. 147).
59. Ibid., p. 147.
60. Ibid., p. 147.
61. Butler, "Beside Oneself", p. 32.
62. McNay, "Subject, Psyche, and Agency", p. 102.
63. Judith Butler, "Introduction: Acting in Concert", in *Undoing Gender* (Abingdon: Routledge, 2004), pp. 1–16 (p. 1).
64. Butler, *Gender Trouble*, p. 45.
65. Butler, *Bodies that Matter*, p. xix.
66. Butler, *The Psychic Life of Power: Theories in Subjection* (Stanford, CA: Stanford University Press, 1997), pp. 1–18.
67. Michel Foucault, *A History of Sexuality: Volume 1*, trans. Robert Hurley (New York: Vintage, 1990), pp. 92–102.
68. Butler, *Bodies that Matter*, p. 167. For a critical discussion of Butler's account of agency, see Gavin Rae, *Poststructuralist Agency: The Subject in Twentieth-Century Theory* (Edinburgh: Edinburgh University Press, 2020), chapter 5.
69. Butler, *Bodies that Matter*, p. 184.

70. For a discussion of Butler's views on the violence–normativity relation, see Emma Ingala, "Judith Butler: From a Normative Violence to an Ethics of Non-Violence", in *The Meanings of Violence: From Critical Theory to Biopolitics*, edited by Gavin Rae and Emma Ingala (Abingdon: Routledge, 2019), pp. 191–208.
71. Bordo, *Unbearable Weight, Feminism, Western Culture, and the Body*, p. 291.
72. McNay, "Subject, Psyche, and Agency", p. 187.
73. Benhabib, "Subjectivity, Historiography, and Politics", p. 109.
74. Clough, "Introduction", p. 8.
75. Kirby, "When All That is Solid Melts into Language", p. 269.
76. Vasterling, "Butler's Sophisticated Constructivism", p. 19.
77. Butler, *Gender Trouble*, p. 190.
78. Ibid., p. 45.
79. Ibid., p. 191.
80. Ibid., p. 12.
81. Ibid., p. 12.
82. Butler, *Bodies that Matter*, p. x.
83. Ibid., p. xviii.
84. Dorothea Olkowski, "Materiality and Language: Butler's Interrogation of the History of Philosophy", *Philosophy and Social Criticism*, vol. 23, n. 1, 1997, pp. 37–53.
85. Butler, *Bodies that Matter*, p. xviii.
86. Ibid., p. xii.
87. Ibid., p. xii.
88. Ibid., p. xii.
89. Ibid., p. xii.
90. Ibid., p. xii.
91. Ibid., p. xii.
92. Ibid., p. xii–xiii.
93. Ibid., p. xiii.
94. Althusser, "Ideology and Ideological State Apparatus (Notes Toward an Investigation)", p. 118. Butler further discusses this concept in *The Psychic Life of Power*, pp. 106–131.
95. Butler, *Bodies that Matter*, p. xvii.
96. Ibid., p. xix.
97. Butler, "Contingent Foundations", p. 51.
98. Ibid., pp. 51–52.
99. Butler, *Bodies that Matter*, p. 6.
100. Ibid., p. 6.
101. Olkowski, "Materiality and Language", p. 39.
102. Ibid., p. 39.
103. Judith Butler, "The End of Sexual Difference", in *Undoing Gender* (Abingdon: Routledge, 2004), pp. 174–203 (p. 198).
104. Ibid., p. 198.
105. Ibid., p. 198.

106. Judith Butler, "How Can I Deny that these Hands and this Body are Mine?", in *Senses of the Subject* (New York: Fordham University Press, 2015), pp. 17–35 (p. 20).
107. Ibid., pp. 20–21.
108. Butler, *Excitable Speech*, p. 5.
109. Ibid., p. 5.
110. Butler, *Bodies that Matter*, p. 37.
111. This is a charge that has long plagued symbolic accounts of sexuality, having been previously levelled against Lacan. See, for example: Eve Tavor Bannet, *Structuralism and the Logic of Dissent* (Urbana, IL: University of Illinois Press, 1989), p. 20; Mikkel Borch-Jacobsen, *Lacan: The Absolute Master*, trans. Douglas Brick (Stanford, CA: Stanford University Press, 1991), p. 195; Jean-Luc Nancy and Philippe Lacoue-Labarthe, *The Title of the Letter: A Reading of Lacan*, trans. François Raffoul and David Pettigrew (Albany, NY: State University of New York Press, 1992), p. 62; Jacques Derrida, "For the Love of Lacan", in *Resistances of Psychoanalysis*, trans. Peggy Kamuf, Pascale-Anne Brault, and Michael Naas (Stanford, CA: Stanford University Press, 1998), pp. 39–69 (p. 60). In contrast, recent scholarship has affirmed the materiality of Lacan's thinking, with this pitching those, such as Alain Badiou (*Theory of the Subject*, trans. Bruno Bosteels [London: Continuum, 2009], pp. 133, 188) and Slavoj Žižek (*The Fragile Absolute or, Why is the Christian Legacy Worth Fighting For?* [London: Verso, 2000], p. 92), who insist on a division between an "early" idealist Lacan (orientated around the affirmation of the primary importance of the symbolic) and a latter "materialist" one where the "real" comes to the fore, against others, including Adrian Johnston (*Badiou, Žižek, and Political Transformations: The Cadence of Change* [Evanston, IL: Northwestern University Press, 2009], pp. 122–123) and Tom Eyers ("Lacanian Materialism and The Question Of The Real", *Cosmos and History: The Journal of Natural and Social Philosophy*, vol. 7, no. 1, 2011, pp. 155–166), who argue against that division and conclude that his thought was always materialist.
112. For a discussion of "new materialism" and its relationship to sexuality, see Myra J. Hird, "Feminist Matters: New Materialist Considerations of Sexual Difference", *Feminist Theory*, vol. 5, n. 2, 2004, pp. 223–232.
113. For a discussion of this heterogeneity, see Diana Coole and Samantha Frost (eds), *New Materialisms: Ontology, Agency, and Politics* (Durham, NC: Duke University Press, 2010).

CHAPTER 8

Barad, Agential Realism, and Queer Theory

Although it is hard to overestimate the impact that Butler's gender theory has had on discussions of sexuality, it was almost immediately subjected to significant and ongoing critique. As noted in the previous chapter, this was in part to do with Butler's treatment of the body. Underestimating the subtlety of Butler's position on the materiality–signification relation led a number of commentators to insist that Butler simply affirms signification over materiality; a position that, so it was maintained, had to be rectified through a privileging of material processes. While I defended Butler against these criticisms, the affirmation of the fundamental importance of materiality "over" signification was part of a wider theoretical trend at the turn of the new millennium.

A number of interlinked reasons can be identified to help account for this materialist turn. First, there was a growing aversion to the so-called "linguistic turn" that had long been acknowledged to be fundamental to twentieth-century philosophy.[1] Although it is most often associated with the development of "analytic" philosophy, the turn to language was also fundamental to "continental" philosophy, in particular the work of Jacques Derrida, Martin Heidegger, Jürgen Habermas, and, of course, Jacques Lacan and Judith Butler. Although it is questionable whether the turn to language within these thinkers does actually entail a commitment to idealism, there was a general sense that focusing on language was to the detriment of materiality and, as such, needed to be corrected.

This feeds tangentially into and brings to the fore an issue that, while often subterranean, marks twentieth-century thinking on sexuality and pits those, such as Lacan and Butler, who were taken to explicitly affirm the importance of symbolic categories to the designation of "sexuality", against others, including Merleau-Ponty, Beauvoir, and Irigaray, who were taken to focus on the primacy of material embodiment. Again, while it is questionable whether the so-called symbolic account of sexuality downplays or ignores materiality to the extent charged, the perception that it did was sufficient to stimulate the debate and, indeed, points to something of a fault line through late twentieth-century thinking on the topic.

Second, commentators increasingly came to worry that symbolic accounts of sexuality were but a historically contingent issue, consequent of a much deeper and broader problem within Western philosophy itself. With this, the parameters of the diagnosis were widened away from local debates regarding how sexuality could and should be thought materially to the question of how materiality has been treated and designated historically. From this, the symbolic turn's supposed degradation of the material body was understood to be but the latest manifestation of Western philosophy's abandonment of the body. Elizabeth Grosz, for example, charges Western philosophy with "a profound somatophobia",[2] Elizabeth Wilson complains about the "antibiologism"[3] inherent in contemporary feminist discussions of the body, which itself emanates from a profound "biophobia",[4] and Somer Brodribb ties this "anti-matter"[5] position to the logic of patriarchy to conclude that continuing to repeat this "anti-physis approach is to repeat patriarchal ideology".[6] Brodribb's position is dependent on a number of theoretical assumptions relating to the nature of patriarchy and, indeed, the issue of whether simply turning to "materiality" alone is sufficient to undermine phallogocentrism that, as noted, have proven to be problematic, but her basic point criticises the coordinates that are held to have been dominant in Western philosophy and warns that while feminist thinking may aim to overcome patriarchy, the opponent is a tricky one. It is, despite best intentions, all too easy to *implicitly* repeat the logic sustaining that to be overcome. To correct this anti-materialist bias requires not simply a reaffirmation of materiality over idealist or linguistic premises, but a fundamental re-engagement with the Western philosophical tradition, including its logic and categories, as a precursor to reinvigorating "it" through a renewed focus and thinking of a reconceived conception of materiality.

Third, these developments were tied to and accompanied by a profound rejection of the status of "poststructuralism" within Anglo-American academic philosophy. Whereas those figures who came to be associated with "poststructuralism" had radically disrupted the French philosophical scene in the 1960s and 1970s and, indeed, the Anglo-American one in the 1980s, by the middle of the 1990s there was a growing strand of thinking, at least in those predisposed to so-called continental philosophy, that held that "poststructuralism" was the problem to be overcome. This was generally because of a tendency to reduce poststructuralist thought to a linguistic foundationalism or idealism, which was often supported by repetition of Jacques Derrida's (mistranslated and misunderstood) claim that "*[t]here is nothing outside of the text*".[7] Although Derrida was often taken to be the focus of critique, namely because of the role that Derridean deconstruction played in introducing "poststructuralist" thinking to American academia, it is a serious mistake to reduce "poststructuralism" to Derrida's thinking, reduce Derrida's thinking to one statement, and, indeed, conclude that his statement means that everything is reducible to (the immateriality of) language.[8] Nevertheless, such a hermeneutical strategy fed into and supported the critique of the linguistic turn that was gradually taking hold in the name of a renewed materialism and the rejection of poststructuralist thought that was often held to be necessary to permit this.[9]

Somewhat ironically, however, those who insisted on the need to move beyond poststructuralist thought to affirm and renew a privileging for materialism were aided, often implicitly, by developments within "poststructuralist" thought itself; namely, but not exclusively, by the growing popularity of the differential ontology of Gilles Deleuze at the turn of the new millennium within Anglo-American academia, and, in particular, the emphasis it places on the fundamental importance of anonymous, open-ended becomings thought from pre-personal differential relations.[10] The gradual diffusion of the logic underpinning this position brought to the fore the notion that bodies are manifestations of the ongoing differential relations subtending them. Rather than focus on the body or hold that individuals are self-founding, the emphasis moved to engaging with the material (ontological) processes that generate individual bodies. In turn, this depended upon and contributed to (1) a growing tendency to see matter in non-anthropocentric, inherently dynamic, emergent, expressive, and autopoietic terms, and (2) the incorporation of scientific insights into philosophical discussions as a means of adequately describing these processes.[11]

These historical modifications, though not definitive, help to account for the genesis of the materialist turn that has marked contemporary theory since around the turn of the new millennium. The rejection of linguistic idealism, the focus on the primary importance of matter, the rethinking of matter in terms of dynamic, pre-personal, emergent processes, the critique of (Butler's) poststructuralist thought, and the appeal to scientific insights – namely those of quantum physics – finds its clearest and most sophisticated expression in the thought of Karen Barad.[12] The guiding contention of Barad's analysis is that "[l]anguage has been granted too much power. The linguistic turn, the semiotic turn, the interpretative turn, the cultural turn: it seems that at every turn lately every 'thing' – even materiality – is turned into a matter of language or some other form of cultural representation."[13]

From this, Barad focuses on Butler's performative gender theory to conclude that, although it recognises that matter is an ongoing process of becoming, Butler places too much emphasis on language, does not sufficiently outline the becoming of materiality, and is anthropocentric, in so far as Butler focuses on humans and is unable to consider how matter itself becomes regardless of human intention.[14]

In contrast, Barad takes over the emphasis that Butler places on performativity, but reinscribes it in terms of (1) practices rather than, as Barad maintains that Butler does, citational iterability, and (2) the non-intentional becoming of matter rather than intentional human endeavours.[15] Barad subsequently turns away from Butler to science and technology studies and utilises the quantum theory of Niels Bohr to offer an account of the "entanglements"[16] that result from and constitute the autopoietic processes that materialise matter "in-itself". Instead of discrete, monadic entities existing in relation to one another, Barad develops the notion of "intra-action"[17] to argue that there is no clear-cut boundary between entities; each is intimately and ontologically bound up with others, impacting and shaping its becoming. This ensures that there is no foundational point driving the becoming of matter, nor do humans have a privileged role to play in this ongoing endeavour. Matter is defined through a continuous, open-ended, random process of entwined emergence, which Barad terms "agential realism":[18] the former because matter is constantly changing; the latter because matter is mind-independent.

Although principally an ontology, referring to the fundamental structures of Being, Barad's agential realism has important implications for the questioning of human sexuality. Affirming the continuous entanglement of matter undermines any possibility for clear-cut distinctions wherein attributes are taken to delineate discrete entities. There is only a fundamental blurring of conceptual categories that makes it impossible to attribute an identity, however ephemeral, to an entity. Rather than "masculine" or "feminine", there is only ever a continuous hybrid becoming, specific to each entity that cannot be grouped under universal or fixed terms. The result is a *queer* conception of sexuality that mirrors and is an effect of the queerness of matter itself.[19] Whereas Butler's gender theory also aims to undermine the notion of a determinate gender identity, there is a sense in which Butler's thinking – in part because of its Hegelian background[20] – permits the claim that adopting a gender identity is acceptable and/or necessary as long as it is not taken to be definitive. In contrast, when we move from Butler's gender theory to Barad's queer theory, all vestiges of identity are ontologically undermined to instead "leave" a continuous autopoietic material process of differential becoming.

With this, I argue that Barad's agential realism takes to its logical limits the questioning of the premises supporting the essentialist-patriarchal-heteronormative model of sexuality. Not only is there no fixed essence, but the binary division that sustains patriarchy is rejected, while the fluidity of matter means that heterosexuality is not the only or, indeed, the primary form of sexual expression. While this appears to support the conclusion that it is with Barad's agential realism that contemporary thinking on sexuality finally overcomes any foreclosing of sexual expression within predefined categories and, in so doing, fully opens it up to individual, ongoing forms of expression, by way of conclusion I identify a number of problems within Barad's account that undermine its explanatory force and, in so doing, reopen the question of sexuality.

Situating the Debate

Barad's agential realism is orientated from and against the conceptual and philosophical coordinates that they maintain have intertwined to structure Western thinking. The first is "Cartesian",[21] which Barad uses as a catch-all term for a logic of binary oppositions. This logic is tied epistemologically to "representationalism",[22] which describes "the belief in the ontological distinction between representations and that which they purport to represent; in particular, that which is represented is held to be independent of all practices of representing".[23] Representationalism, in turn, is dependent upon a mind-independent world composed of individuated entities. Barad calls this "individualism"[24] and explains that, on this model, "beings exist as individuals with inherent attributes, anterior to their representation".[25] Although Barad does not make this move, I argued that these premises underpin the essentialist-patriarchal(-heteronormative) model of sexuality, in so far as it is premised on the notions that the sexes are divided in two, each of which is defined by inherent (essential) attributes, which do not change, and must be accurately represented to be known. Therefore, although Barad rarely mentions "sexuality" *per se*, their critique of representationalism also criticises the logical schema supporting the model that has historically dominated discussions of the topic. Indeed, this critique forms the basis for the move beyond human sexuality to queer materialities.

Barad is, however, aware that Cartesian representationalism has already been the subject of philosophical critique, most notably from poststructuralist thinkers. Although Barad rarely explicitly mentions who they have in mind with this nomenclature, instead tending to talk problematically about "poststructuralism" as if it were a unified school of thought with a definitive programme, when Barad does identify a poststructuralist figure it is Butler's gender theory that acts, in many respects, as the lodestone for Barad's thinking: it is the one that Barad moves towards to subsequently depart from to develop their own position.

Barad recognises that "Butler does not deny the materiality of the body whatsoever"[26] and, indeed, brings to our attention that "[m]atter, like meaning is not an individually articulated or static entity"[27] nor is "[m]atter... immutable or passive".[28] Indeed, Butler is praised for reminding us that "[m]atter is always already an ongoing historicity".[29] However, despite these positives, Barad concludes that Butler continues to give priority to the symbolic realm when thinking materiality, with the consequence that Butler is charged with privileging discourse over materiality. This charge has strong and weak versions. The former states that "Butler's theory ultimately reinscribes matter as a passive product of discursive practices rather than as an active agent participating in the very process of materialisation".[30] On this telling, Butler is unable to account for the activity inherent in the processes that generate materiality because Butler reduces materiality to discursive practices and so is guilty of linguistic foundationalism.

However, no sooner has Barad made this charge than they backtrack on it: "I want to carefully distinguish my critique from a host of accusations against Butler that incorrectly accuse her [sic] of idealism, linguistic monism, or a neglect or even erasure of 'real flesh-and-blood bodies.'"[31] To do so, Barad offers a weaker critique of Butler's treatment of materiality, which insists that while Butler "*does* provide us with an insightful and powerful analysis of some *discursive* dimensions of the materialisation of real flesh-and-blood bodies",[32] Butler's "analysis of materialization ... leaves out critical components".[33] The problems inherent in Butler's account are held by Barad to be the consequence of Butler's (1) reliance on Foucault's notion of power, which Barad understands to be exclusively focused on the ways in which social norms structure discourse,[34] and (2) failure "to recognize matter's dynamism".[35] Regarding the former, Barad claims that focusing on social norms is simply too indeterminate: "[s]urely it is the case ... that there are 'natural,' not merely "social,' forces that matter".[36] In turn, the latter is held to be a consequence of Butler's focus on Foucault's analysis of power and Barad's claim that Butler thinks materiality from symbolic discourse.

In the previous chapter, I questioned whether Butler's thinking on materiality is actually premised on such a materiality (= passive)/symbolic (= active) opposition; after all, while Butler (and Lacan) maintain that *any* knowledge about materiality must pass through and so be shaped by discursive/symbolic structures, with the consequence that what is meant by "materiality" is an effect of those structures, they both reject the notion that this reduces materiality to the symbolic to instead claim that they are entwined, albeit with this entwinement always marked by a posited material excess that escapes symbolisation. Nevertheless, Barad bases their critique on the notion that Butler utilises a binary materiality/discursive opposition, before concluding that this re-instantiates a latent Cartesianism that needs to be corrected by holding that the two are actually entwined. This does not reduce either to the other because materiality exists regardless of discourse, although discourse is necessary to reveal the ongoing processes inherent in materialisation.

However, Butler would be able to respond that, although Barad appears to insist on the entanglement of materiality and discourse, Barad actually starts from a (theoretical) presupposition regarding the structure and "nature" of materiality, including its relationship to discourse, to subsequently not only use this presupposition to judge alternative theories but also look for and adopt a particular discourse that corresponds to and affirms Barad's prior assumption. In other words, rather than engage with the complicated ways in which materiality and discourse are co-implicated to show how the latter limits knowledge of the former, Barad's realist position simply adopts a particular conception of materiality as a first principle and subsequently looks to construct arguments to support that presupposition and its relationship to a particular notion of discourse that preserves the "independence" of materiality. This is why Barad appeals to our "best"[37] scientific, social, and philosophical theories, without ever explaining why they attain that status: it is simply assumed because they confirm Barad's prior assumption about the nature of materiality. As a consequence, a Butlerian critique would be that Barad ends up in the highly problematic situation of claiming to offer an analysis of the processes of materialisation that structure and give rise to matter, all the while actually constructing a conception of materiality as a dynamic process from a particular symbolic discourse; namely, Niels Bohr's quantum physics.[38] Not only does this unjustifiably privilege the epistemic validity of one discursive system over others, but it also means that the disclosure of materiality depends upon the parameters of that discursive system; a dependency that reduces materiality to the (abstraction, on Barad's terms) of that discourse.

In turn, Barad's response would be to push back against what they take to be the fundamental, but latent, anthropocentrism inherent in Butler's thinking. Although Butler decentres the subject from the foundationalism role inherent in Western post-Cartesian thinking, Barad claims that Butler continues to orientate the analysis around human being and so fails to realise that human being is not the centre of existence or indeed integral to it.[39] To correct this, Barad takes over Bohr's claim regarding the role that the observer plays in the interpretation and generation of data, but, based on both a metaphysical realist position and a rejection of the anthropocentrism inherent in his account, claims that this does not reduce knowledge to human being. Instead, Barad maintains that ontology and epistemology are entwined, but cannot be reduced to either aspect, meaning that while the nature of materiality is only known through human cognition, it cannot be reduced to human knowledge. However, while this decentres human being from the foundational role given to it by Cartesian thought, Barad insists that this does not mean that agential realism is anti-humanist. This conclusion simply re-instantiates a humanist/anti-humanist binary opposition and so, by extension, the binary logic of Cartesianism. Instead, Barad insists on the need for a "posthumanist"[40] account that does not operate through a nature/culture division nor does it "presume that man is the measure of all things".[41]

Butler also decentres the subject from its long-held foundational role but insists that human knowledge is symbolically grounded, with the consequence that the limitations of the symbolic feed through into the limitations of our knowledge of materiality. In contrast, Barad's posthumanist account "tak[es] issue with [all notions of] human exceptionalism while [continuing to be] accountable for the role we play in the differential constitution and differential positioning of the human among other creatures (both living and nonliving)".[42] The human is an effect of pre-personal processes of materialisation and so cannot be the focus of study; a position that has dramatic implications for the question of agency, which is no longer tied to human being exclusively, but is thought in terms of the movement inherent in the ongoing materialisation of matter. According to Barad, this "makes evident a much larger space of possibilities for change".[43]

For Butler and symbolic accounts more generally, however, this risks incoherence because, on the one hand, Barad's anti-anthropocentric position makes human action a determined effect of pre-personal material processes, but, on the other hand, their own theory necessarily emanates from a human focal point, with the consequence that, in a particular sense, it is anthropocentric; an issue that brings to mind Tim Hayward's criticism that supposedly non-anthropocentric positions are often premised on a number of conceptual slippages. Specifically, Hayward insists that those who try to overcome anthropocentrism often fail to appreciate that the analysis must always be based on the human perspective and so is premised on a certain form of anthropocentrism. Hayward does, however, recognise that it does not follow that the resultant analysis has to privilege the human perspective. Instead, he insists that those who argue against human exceptionalism or anthropocentrism must continue to offer an analysis that is *anthropocentric* because it is necessarily premised on and undertaken from the human perspective, but do not have to fall foul of *speciesism* that hierarchises or discriminates between species or *human chauvinism* that affirms the human over other species; indeed, we might also add over other forms of materiality more generally.[44]

While these distinctions arguably help to bridge the gulf that appears to exist between (Barad's reading of) Butler's thinking and the problems thrown up by Barad's agential realist critique of anthropocentrism, Barad's metaphysical realism means that they appear to reject the notion that a remnant of any form of anthropocentrism must remain; the existence of a world beyond human being is taken for granted and needs to and, indeed, can be explained. Indeed, Barad's anti-anthropocentrism and claim that discourse is tied up with materiality means that any knowledge of materiality actually expresses what materiality "really" is; it is not an anthropocentric construct. Butler's symbolic account would however question how knowledge of that is possible: how can a human being (Barad) question and respond to that which Barad claims exists beyond human cognition – i.e. non-human beings and non-discursive materiality – without reducing this to either the human perspective or the parameters of a discursive system?

Again, for Barad's realist account, there simply is a material world and knowledge of it is possible as long as the discursive system accurately expresses the dynamic becoming inherent in materiality. For Butler, however, this means that any knowledge that Barad "gains" about materiality is still tied, in some way, to human being. This is not to say that the human being is central or foundational to knowledge – Butler also rejects this – but that the epistemic role of human cognition cannot be evaded or downplayed. Somewhat confusingly, Barad would not necessarily have a problem with this; as a material being, humans express the agency inherent in all materiality and so have a role to play in the (discursive) expression of materiality, although, as we will see, Barad is quiet on what precisely that role is. As a consequence, Barad allows that the human contributes to the expression of materiality without identifying how this takes place. In contrast, for Butler, human cognition is symbolically structured and so is dependent upon the limitations inherent in every symbolic system. As such, it is not possible to claim to have captured "the" nature of materiality; all that can be claimed is that we understand materiality based on the parameters of a particular symbolic system. For Barad, however, this reduces materiality to discourse. To avoid that, Barad simply affirms that discourse does not prevent the revelation of materiality because the two are intertwined: one cannot be revealed without the other; or, put differently, studying one reveals the other. The key is to find a discursive system that is capable of doing justice to the dynamic expressionism of the process that give rise to materiality. This does not reduce materiality to discourse, but reveals materiality as it is.

Butler, however, could respond that such a position is where the coordinates of Barad's position problematically clash, in so far as Barad claims that materiality and discourse are entwined, while also claiming that discourse can reveal the "nature" of materiality despite the latter always exceeding the former. On a Butlerian telling, Barad is, despite their protestations to the contrary, either guilty of offering a discursive analysis dressed up as a materialist one, or simply assuming that they can know about materiality independently of discourse without explaining how this is possible; a position that problematically bypasses the role of human cognition in the generation of knowledge and re-enforces the charge that Barad is guilty of offering a discursive analysis dressed up as a non-discursive materialist one. Barad's response would presumably be that this charge is simply incapable of recognising that materiality and knowledge of it are not fundamentally discursive or anthropocentric; they are based on ongoing processes of emergent materialisation. The discussion therefore returns to and revolves around the relationship between materiality and discursivity, including what is meant by each.

Although this attempt to bring Barad and Butler together does not aim or claim to be definitive, it does bring to the fore the question of whether Barad's treatment of Butler is sufficiently nuanced to do justice to the subtleties and "depth" of Butler's position, especially on the question of materiality and its relationship to discursivity. This is important because of the ambiguity in Barad's position regarding Butler's thinking: it is unclear whether agential realism is premised on the strong critique that holds that Butler reduces materiality to discourse and so ends up in linguistic idealism or whether it is premised on the weak version that maintains that Butler does not sufficiently account for the processes of materialisation. The former leads to the conclusion that Barad aims to depart from Butler's thinking to correct its perceived idealism; the latter that it merely aims to complement Butler's thinking with one that more fully brings to light the processes of materialisation that are pointed to but not fully explicated in Butler's gender theory. This ambiguity means that it is not entirely clear what the specific target of Barad's critique is, which in turn generates difficulties regarding the question of whether Barad's agential realism resolves problematic issues identified therein.

Nevertheless, bringing Barad and Butler together, however briefly, does bring to light some of the ways in which symbolic and realist accounts (of sexuality) are dependent on fundamentally distinct ontological, epistemological, and metaphysical premises. In turn, those premises lead to heterogeneous conclusions regarding the issues generated from them. The disagreement between Butler's gender theory and Barad's theory of queer materialities is not then a superficial one; it depends upon the responses given to a number of subtle but fundamental disagreements regarding the nature of reality, the nature of being, the role of human being in the world and knowledge generation specifically, and the relationship between thought and being. For Barad, however, the fundamental issue that unlocks all others is the relationship between materiality and discursivity; a topic that requires that the focus be on the former aspect to respond to the questions of "how *discourse* comes to matter . . . [and] how *matter* comes to matter".[45]

Iterative Performativity, Infra-action, and Agency

To do so, Barad affirms a new ontology of "entanglements".[46] Rather than starting with pre-existing, predefined individuated entities with definitive characteristics and attributes that subsequently come into contact with one another, materiality is held to be entangled, with no clear-cut divisions, and where each part is intimately bound to the others. As Barad puts it, "[t]o be entangled is not simply to be intertwined with another, as in the joining of separate entities, but to lack an independent, self-contained existence. Existence is not an individual affair".[47] This not only undercuts the central premise of the individualism that Barad diagnoses as lying historically at the foundation of Western thought, but, in so doing, rejects the premises of representationalism and Cartesian binarism.

To develop and defend this, Barad focuses on the quantum physics of Niels Bohr because "he . . . call[s] into question an entire tradition in the history of Western metaphysics: the belief that the world is populated with individual things with their own independent sets of determinate properties".[48] Indeed, Barad goes on to claim that Bohr's quantum theory is important because it is "inherently less androcentric, less Eurocentric, more feminine, more postmodern, and generally less regressive than the masculinist and imperializing tendencies found in Newtonian physics".[49] The reasoning behind this statement is never made explicit, but Barad seems to base the assessment on a number of conceptual conflations in which Newtonian physics is premised on a similar ontology and metaphysics to that which underpins Cartesian representationalism.[50] In turn, Cartesian representationalism is, as we have seen, premised on an essentialist ontology and a logic of binary oppositions that can turn into hierarchies that have supported all sorts of exclusions, including patriarchy and heteronormativity. To counter this, Bohr is understood to reject two central premises of Newtonian physics: (1) "the world is composed of individual objects with individually determined boundaries",[51] and (2) "measurements involve continuous determinable interactions such that the values of the properties obtained can be properly assigned to the premeasurement properties of objects as separate from the agencies of observation".[52] In combination, Bohr rejects the ways in which Newtonian physics is premised on "representationalism (the independently determinate existence of words and things), the metaphysics of individualism (that the world is composed of individual entities with determinate boundaries and properties), and the intrinsic separability of knower and known".[53]

Barad does, however, note that while they will draw on Bohr's thinking, they will not aim to explicate what he says, but will "use Bohr's writings for thinking about these issues"[54] and will select the appropriate parts based on a judgement about "what makes sense for developing a coherent account".[55] Barad's appropriation of Bohr's quantum theory does not then pretend to be wholly consistent with his writings. Instead, Barad develops their argument from a particular reading of Bohr's theory – one shorn of "his unexamined humanist commitments"[56] – in combination with insights from "current scholarship in science studies, the philosophy of science, physics, and various interdisciplinary approaches that might be collectively be called 'critical social theories' (e.g. feminist theory, critical race theory, queer theory, postcolonial theory, (post-)Marxist theory, and poststructuralist theory)".[57] Through this heterogeneous combination, Barad engages with the question "what does 'material' mean?"[58]

The guiding premise is that materiality is not a static pre-existent thing, but a continuous autopoietic, immanent, and emergent process of becoming. Importantly, this "[m]attering is simultaneously a matter of substance and significance, most evidently perhaps when it is the nature of matter that is in question, when the smallest parts of matter are found to be capable of exploding deeply entrenched ideas and large cities".[59] Rather than a distinction between substance and significance, Barad binds them relationally to make each dependent upon the other. Getting a handle on this requires a discussion of the emergent processes that generate matter, the discursive practices contributing to this, and the relation between materiality and discourse.

To start, Barad dispels several misconceptions that result from the historical dominance of the Cartesian representationalist model. This is necessary because the Cartesian model has led to materiality being associated with passive substance, while relationality is understood in terms of a relation between two preformed opposing entities, with language tacked on top and used to represent each one. Instead, Barad claims that

> Material conditions matter, not because they 'support' particular discourses that are the actual generative factors in the formation of bodies but rather because matter comes to matter through the iterative intra-activity of the world in its becoming. The point is not merely that there are important material factors in addition to discursive ones; rather, the issue is the conjoined material-discursive nature of constraints, conditions, and practices.[60]

With this, Barad distinguishes their position from (what is taken to be) Butler's over-reliance of a symbolic model, wherein gender performativity is structured from and around the construction of linguistic and social norms. As noted, for Barad, this is simply too linguistically reductionist, in so far as it does not consider or explain either the nature of materiality or the relationship between materiality and linguistic construction, and, indeed, appears to implicitly slip into a materiality/language (Cartesian) opposition with the former grounded in the latter. Overcoming this requires, on Barad's telling, that both aspects are thought to be entangled and engaged in an emergent process of ongoing becoming, but where, somewhat paradoxically, the emphasis is on the material aspect. Thus, as we will see, discourse is not a linguistic or ideational activity; it is reconfigured as a material practice that contributes to the movement and alteration of the (components of the) material world.

To do so, Barad reiterates that it is necessary to reject and move beyond the notion that entities are individuated. While their individuation might seem to be obvious – "At first glance, the outside boundary of the body may seem evident, indeed incontrovertible. A coffee mug ends at its outside surface just as surely as people end at their skins"[61] – Barad appeals to physics to explain that "edges or boundaries are not determinate either ontologically or visually".[62] The problem is that the inner/outside division, while appearing to be obvious, is actually dependent upon a particular ontology of vision and epistemology based on a particular form of empiricism that have long been questioned and rejected: "[w]hen it comes to the 'interface' between a coffee mug and a hand, it is not that there are x number of atoms that belong to a hand and y number of atoms that belong to the coffee mug".[63] Barad further explains that vision is also not constructed around clear-cut boundaries: "it is a well-recognized fact of physical objects that if one looks closely at an 'edge,' what one sees is not a sharp boundary between light and dark but rather a series of light and dark bands – that is, a diffraction pattern".[64] Rather than being definitive and predetermined, perceiving of objects in terms of clear-cut boundaries is, like all perception, "a result of the repetition of (culturally and historically) specific bodily performance".[65]

Initially, this may be thought to give rise to the claim that, because perception is socio-culturally derived, what is perceived is also fundamentally socio-cultural. Barad, however, rejects this. Falling back on a metaphysical realist position, Barad maintains that regardless of how it is perceived, materiality never actually conforms to clear-cut boundaries but is always entwined and entangled. As a consequence, there is a form of "objectivity" inherent in Barad's analysis, in so far as materiality, regardless of perception, takes on certain emergent characteristics. It is not however entirely clear how this feeds into the claim that materiality and discursivity are entangled, for it appears to mean that, regardless of what the discourse says, materiality simply always takes on certain characteristics.

Nevertheless, Barad warns that although matter is differentiated and differentiating, materiality is fundamentally univocal: "there is no need to postulate different materialities (i.e., materialities that are inherently of different kinds)".[66] *All* that exists is, by definition, material, with the consequence that each thing, whether physical or not, shares the same fundamental ontological character. It is for this reason that each thing can interact with, shape, and form all the others; for this to happen requires that each thing be composed of the "same" fundamental ontological character, which is obviously not to say that each thing is the same. With this, Barad claims to have overcome one of the fundamental problems that marks Butler's account; namely, how the discursive and materiality relate to one another. On Barad's telling, they are able to do so because they are expressions of the "same" fundamental ontological "stuff": matter.

Crucially, however, matter is only ever defined by a continuous process of materialisation. To explain this process in accordance with the rejection of ontological monadism and affirmation of ontological entanglement, Barad distinguishes between "interaction, which assumes that there are separate individual agencies that precede their interaction",[67] and "intra-action [which] recognizes that distinct agencies do not precede, but rather emerge through, their intra-action".[68] The notion of intra-action is fundamental to Barad's agential realism and responds "to the question of the making of differences, of 'individuals,' rather than assuming their independent or prior existence".[69] Through it, Barad is also able to explain that materialities come to be what they are through particular forms of relationality wherein they are also tied to and emerge through others, who, in turn, only emerge through their relationality. There is no foundation to this relationality, with the consequence that the existence of both positions in the relation is dependent upon and changes with the relation sustaining them.

With the notion of intra-action, Barad proposes a particular relational ontology, wherein it is not just the meaning but the being of materiality that is relationally generated. If it were just the meaning of the entities that was relational, they would pre-exist the relation but gain meaning from each other. However, Barad claims that "[i]t is not enough to simply assert that identity is a relation, if the relation in question is between or among entities that are understood to precede their relation".[70] Barad's more radical proposal – albeit one that was also made by Lacan – is that both the being and the meaning of materiality is relational: the sheer existence of each materiality emanates relationally from another. As a consequence, materiality is not static but is dependent on constant dynamic processes of materialisation.

Importantly, Barad claims that relations are not composed of symmetrical aspects. If they were, there would be a fixed, ordered, and predictable becoming. Instead, materialisation is inherently random, disjointed, and unpreditable. There is no way to identify how matter will be materialised or where it will lead to. For this to occur requires an asymmetric relation that, in turn, is dependent upon a random, unpredictable, but ever possible "spark" that generates the process of materialisation. To explain this, Barad once more turns to quantum theory and its notion of a quantum which describes a "bit of a hitch, a tiny disjuncture in the underlying continuum".[71] With this random jerk, the

> tiny disjuncture, existing in neither space nor time, torques the very nature of the relation between continuity and discontinuity to such a degree that the nature of change changes from a rolling unravelling stasis into a dynamism that operates at an entirely different level of 'existence,' where 'existence' is not simply a manifold of being that evolves in space and time, but an iterative becoming of spacetimemattering.[72]

Rather than being static or ordered, "[t]he world is an open process of mattering through which mattering itself acquires meaning and form through the realization of different agential possibilities".[73] This process generates "[t]emporality and spatiality"[74] while "[r]elations of exteriority, connectivity, and exclusion are reconfigured".[75] Indeed, Barad claims that "[t]he changing topologies of the world entail an ongoing reworking of the notion of dynamics itself".[76] In other words, nothing pre-exists the materialisation process; all becomes what it is through these processes and, indeed, continues to become based on the vagaries of that becoming, itself expressed through and from the peculiarities of the quantum. As such, "the world's radical aliveness comes to light in an entirely nontraditional way that reworks the nature of both relationality and aliveness (vitality, dynamism, agency)".[77]

One of the ways in which the world comes alive and expresses itself is through discourse. To counter the linguistic turn, Barad distinguishes between "language", which is reduced to ideas or words, and "discourse" which describes material practices: "Discursive practices are not speech acts, linguistic representations, or even linguistic performances, bearing some unspecified relationship to material practices".[78] Discursive practices express and emanate from the intra-actions inherent in the processes of materialisation. They are, as a consequence, "not ideational but ... actual physical arrangements".[79] Discursive production is then intra-actively constitutive of the processes inherent in materialisation. It is not tied to or dependent on individuals but is "an ongoing performance of the world in its differential dance of intelligibility and unintelligibility".[80]

Studying these discursive practices is, however, difficult. They constantly change, are changed by the attempt to understand them, and, indeed, are the condition for intelligibility, thereby ensuring that their existence conditions how they will be conceptualised. Nevertheless, Barad claims that it is through specific agential intra-actions, called "apparatus"[81] that the "boundaries and properties of the 'components' of phenomena become determinate and that particular embodied concepts become meaningful".[82] Importantly, however, apparatus are not "inscription devices"[83] that precede or over-code material intra-actions, nor are they "neutral probes of the natural world or structures that deterministically impose some particular outcome".[84] Apparatuses

> are dynamic (re)configurings of the world, specific agential practices/intra-actions/performances through which specific exclusionary boundaries are enacted. Apparatuses have no inherent 'outside' boundary. This indeterminacy of the 'outside' boundary represents the impossibility of closure – the ongoing intra-activity in the iterative recon-figuring of the apparatus of bodily production. Apparatuses are open-ended practices.[85]

More specifically, apparatuses are "material-discursive practices"[86] that "produce differences that matter [in so far] as they are boundary-making practices that are formative of matter and meaning, productive of, and part of, the phenomena produced".[87] This is because "apparatuses are material configurations/dynamic reconfigurings of the world"[88] and, indeed, "are themselves . . . constituted and dynamically reconstituted as part of the ongoing intra-activity of the world".[89] They "are not located in the world but are material configurations or reconfigurations of the world that re(con)figure spatiality and temporality as well as (the traditional notion of) dynamics (i.e., they do not exist as static structure, nor do they merely unfold or evolve in space and time)".[90]

Apparatus achieve this through "*agential cut[s]*"[91] which slice up the originary "phenomenon of the inherent ontological (and semantic) indeterminacy"[92] to create (the appearance of) distinct entities. They therefore contrast forcibly with "the more familiar Cartesian cut which takes this distinction for granted".[93] The "agential separability"[94] effected is, however, intra-active, with the consequence that the agential cut is not something that transcends that intra-action; it is the condition through which the ontological entanglement appears as and through discrete intra-active entities. It is, however, important to note that "the 'distinct' agencies are only distinct in a relational, not an absolute, sense, that is, *agencies are only distinct in relation to their mutual entanglement; they don't exist as individual elements*".[95] They can and are constantly remade based on the intra-actions conditioning the agential cut.

Barad's "quantum ontology"[96] is then *realist* because, as we have seen, materiality exists independently of the human mind and is *agential* because matter is nothing other than an ongoing process of intra-active becoming. However, whereas "agency" has historically been tied to the notion of a foundational human subject who rationally and reflectively intends or wills a particular action and/or end, Barad explains that agency "is an enactment, not something that someone or something has".[97] So, although Barad accepts that, as materialities, "human subjects do have a role to play, indeed a constitutive role"[98] in shaping and perpetuating the intra-actions inherent in materialisation, Barad is also clear that "[a]gency is not aligned with human intentionality or subjectivity. Nor does it merely entail resignification or other specific kinds of moves within a social geometry of antihumanism".[99] By moving the terms of the debate away from the (intentional, willed) agency of human being, which is understood to be an effect of the larger processes of agency inherent in materiality, Barad aims to show that conceptual schemas that have long claimed to be based on naturally *determined* parameters are premised on a number of incorrect assumptions that perpetuate significant conceptual exclusions that are actually undermined by the ongoing agency inherent in the "natural" processes they claim to affirm. Recognising this and properly understanding the open-ended intra-actions inherent in materiality will, so Barad claims, permit a range of issues that have long been foreclosed within predetermined fixed categories to be opened, including the question of sexuality. It is to this that we now turn.

Queer Theory

Barad's agential realism offers then a radical critique of the ontological essentialism, Cartesian dualism, and epistemic representationalism that has long marked Western thought. Although Barad's critique is primarily pitched at the ontological level – and, as such, shares similarities with Heidegger's thinking in this regard, although agential realism's "flat" ontology departs from the transcendence inherent in his ontological difference – it has substantial implications for the ways in which the agency inherent in the immanent processes that give rise to materialities find expression. Given the topic and argument of this book, I will limit the discussion to its consequences for (1) the essentialist-patriarchal(-heteronormative) model of sexuality, and (2) the question of sexuality more generally.

The key to both issues is Barad's notion of intra-action, which, it will be remembered, rejects the notion that entities exist in individuated form prior to coming into contact with one another. Instead, materialities are ontologically entangled, coming to be what they are only through their relationality and, indeed, the intra-action of the agential cut. With this, Barad rejects the fundamental premise of "essentialism" by claiming not only that objects do not have an individuated essence, but also that each only is what it is through its ongoing entanglement with others. As this relationality alters, in particular due to the irregularities inherent in the quantums subtending materiality, so too will each aspect of it, including the structure and "nature" of the relation itself. Intra-action also undermines the fundamental premises of the logic of patriarchy because, by calling into question the notion that materialities are defined by clear-cut boundaries, it rejects the straightforward masculine/feminine division upon which patriarchy depends. The intra-active, ongoing emergent "nature" of materiality means that there simply is no male/female opposition, with the consequence that it is not possible to privilege one over the other. Because it purposefully undermines the privileging of the masculine position inherent in the logic of patriarchy, Barad claims that "[a]gential realism is a feminist intervention".[100]

However, as Butler showed, undermining the premises supporting sexual essentialism and patriarchy does not guarantee that sexuality will not continue to be foreclosed within certain structures. In particular, Butler identifies a problematic heteronormativity that has also marked Western critical thinking on the topic. As such, the essentialist-patriarchal model is also intimately, if not always explicitly, tied to the question of heteronormativity, with the consequence that to prevent the foreclosure of sexuality within pre-established boundaries, Barad needs to show that their agential realist account undermines sexual essentialism, patriarchy, *and* heteronormativity.

Barad takes up this issue through the question of, what they call, "moralism",[101] an issue that is tied to the notion of "human exceptionalism, and, in particular, human superiority [that props] up the specific moral injunction against 'unnatural' human behaviors".[102] Barad's point is that the latent privileging of heteronormativity is premised on a particular conception of "nature", itself dependent upon an essentialist ontology and logic of binary opposition. As Barad explains, however, "if the crime is against Nature herself – the whole of Nature, that is, if the act is so egregious as to go 'against all that is natural' – then it must have been committed by some agent who is outside of Nature, presumably a human agent, one cognizant of his sins".[103]

Two problems result. First, "if the act is against Nature, and the actor is not of Nature, but outside it, then all acts committed by this actor must be . . . 'unnatural', by definition".[104] In other words, the problem becomes not the *act* but the entire being of the individual committing it. That, however, sets up a binary opposition between "good" and "bad" beings that runs counter to the entangled nature of materiality.

Second, and at the same time, "if the moral injunction is against 'unnatural' human behaviors, including acting like a beast, then this is because one is acting like nature – performing 'natural' acts".[105] The claim that non-hetero forms of sexuality and sexual relations are somehow un-natural undermines itself because it relies upon that which it rejects; namely the possibility that humans (= civilisation), while being held to be ontologically distinct from nature (= non-civilisation), are, in fact capable of acting in accordance with "nature" through the "uncivilised" "bestial" actions of homosexuality. The heteronormative critique is then premised on a paradoxical conception of humanity as being both a natural being and somehow not being such a being, with this ambiguity undermining the supposed "purity" that is taken to define human being. As Barad puts it, "the (il)logic at work trips over the very divide – the nature/culture divide – it seeks to secure. In fact, it is the law itself – in fashioning some human acts as bestial in nature – that breeches the sacred divide, opening up the possibility of humans engaging in nonhuman acts".[106] In other words, moralist heteronormativity undermines itself immanently because it holds two contradictory positions: (1) the human, as a natural being, commits natural acts, and (2) the human is fundamentally other-than nature. The latter, however, disqualifies the former. Either the moralist critique must go and non-heteronormative forms of sexuality are accepted as natural or the human must be accepted as a natural being, which brings forth the question of the "nature" of nature. While the moralist position explicitly insists that nature is fixed and unidimensional, with the consequence that only certain predeterminable actions are permitted for humans – "the discourse on 'crimes against nature' always already takes liberty in the confidence that Nature is herself a good Christian, or at least traffics in a kind of purity that the human has been excluded from ever since the Edenic fall of man"[107] – Barad points out that an alternative ethics arises once it is accepted that "nature" is not fundamentally singular or unchanging, but, as Barad's intra-active ontology points out, "is a commie, a pervert, or a queer[.]"[108]

By claiming that nature is queer and that sexuality is inherently material, Barad sets the scene for an important conceptual innovation with regards to gender theory. Whereas Butler's gender theory is held to be premised on a symbolic form of construction, with the consequence that it usurps binary oppositions by simply constructing symbolic systems not constrained by them, Barad's focus on materiality leads to the claim that Butler's proposal is too superficial, in so far as it threatens to make "sexuality" a non-material construction that depends upon the contingent intentional actions of individuals. If, however, individuals do not intentionally construct a non-binary symbolic system, there appears to be nothing in Butler's schema that permits a critique of that action. After all, it is the symbolic system that generates the parameters of a critique and, given the afoundationality of Butler's symbolic account, there appears to be no way to claim that one schema is "better" than another. There is, in other words, no foundation from which to ground Butler's critique of essential, patriarchal, and heteronormativity. Bared aims to get round this problem by grounding critique on the "bed-rock" of non-human material processes to insist that, regardless of the discursive system in place or individual action, nature *never* supports the premises of the essentialist-patriarchal-heteronormative schema. The quantum nature of materiality means that "there is something inherently queer about the nature of matter".[109]

By queer, Barad does not simply mean strange or out of the ordinary. With quantum theory there is no such thing as "ordinary"; things are far stranger to the extent that they cannot be referenced through "the ordinary":

> The point in referring to them as 'queer' is not to use an eye-catching term when 'odd' or 'strange' would have sufficed, nor is it to make a case that these critters engage in queer sexual practices (though some do, at least on some countings), but rather to make the point that their very 'species being,' as it were, makes explicit the queering of 'identity' and relationality.[110]

Appealing to "queer" is then part of Barad's rejection of all forms of identity: "What is needed ... is a way of thinking about the nature of differentiating that is not derivative of some fixed notion of identity or even a fixed spacing."[111]

To do so, Barad returns to quantum theory and its notion of "quantum leaps".[112] These jerks in the continuum that subtend and generate materiality "are not simply strange because a particle moves discontinuously from one place here now to another place there, but [because] the fundamental notions of trajectory, movement, space, time, and causality are called into question".[113] More specifically, "unlike any ordinary experience of jumping or leaping, when an electron makes a 'quantum leap' it does so in a discontinuous fashion (belying the very notion of a 'leap'): in particular, the electron is initially at one energy level and then it is at another without having been anywhere in between!"[114] But things are even stranger than this because, strictly speaking, a quantum leap is "not just any discontinuous movement, but a particularly queer kind that troubles the very dichotomy between discontinuity and continuity. Indeed, quantum dis/continuity troubles the very notion of dichotomy – the cutting into two – itself (including the notion of 'itself'!)."[115] In other words, at no stage of the process can materialisation be said to conform to a straightforward linear movement or, indeed, anything straightforward generally. Not only does this ensure that "[q]ueer is a radical questioning of identity and binaries, and quantum physics, like queerness, displaces a host of deeply-held foundational dualisms",[116] but it also undermines certain notions of intelligibility because it is simply not possible to determine the trajectory of quantum leaps and, by extension, the becoming of materiality.

For this reason, "[q]uantum entanglements are not the intertwining of two (or more) states/entities/events, but a calling into question of the very nature of two-ness, and ultimately of one-ness as well. Duality, unity, multiplicity, being are undone."[117] Rather than a static foundation, there is only ever constant disruption that never takes on determinate form. Barad instead uses the imaginary of "slime"[118] because it points to a form of materialisation that constantly changes to take on different forms but in which the form that takes cannot be predetermined. Of course, the forms this will take cannot be predetermined or anticipated in advance because of the quantum leaps at its "heart", but the point is to try to conjure up an imaginary to permit us to reconceive ontology away from the clear-cut boundaries that have historically structured Western thinking. As a consequence, rather than start from a determinate ground, one premised on pre-existing divisions, Barad rhetorically asks us to consider what would happen "if the very ground, the 'foundation' for judging right from wrong, is a flaming queen, a faggot, a lesbo, a tranny, or gender-queer?"[119] Not only would the essentialist-patriarchal(-heteronormative) model lose the coordinates that structure it, but the options for sexual/gender/queer expression would be completely opened, even in ways that we cannot currently conceive.

Although it is tempting to try to tame such queer madness, and, indeed, the history of Western philosophy has generally tried to achieve this through its affirmation of a fixed single sexual identity, Barad rejects such an approach. Attempts to do so are counter-productive because they are based on a strategy that cannot possibly win (you cannot after all go against the processes of materialisation), with the consequence that the failure to quarantine the queerness of nature risks turning it into something to be anxious about or even feared. If that were to happen, we would be in the queer position of being afraid of what we actually are.[120] Instead of trying to control or constrain the ways in which the queer becomings of nature are expressed, Barad proposes that we remain open to their queerness. Only this will ensure that we are able to account for all of the ways in which materiality expresses itself and, in so doing, remain "true" to all the possible configurations and practices that result.

We have then to abandon the idea that there are *a priori* or, indeed, universal categories or forms of sexuality: "The point is to make plain the undoing of universality, the importance of the radical specificity of materiality as iterative materialisation."[121] Because sexuality is held to be an expression of the chaos that defines materiality, gender-queerness is always unique and singular, but, at the same time, multiple, fluid, and changing in unexpected ways. There cannot be a single right form of sexuality nor can there be "'acts against nature'";[122] any form of sexuality that exists emanates from the quantum leap of nature and so is "natural". Indeed, Barad posits that quantum theory allows us to think of nature as "an ongoing questioning of itself – of what constitutes naturalness . . . In other words, nature itself is an ongoing deconstructing of naturalness."[123] Given the constant and wild experimentation inherent in and emanating from the intra-activity of materiality, "perversity and monstrosity lie at the core of being – or rather, it is threaded through them",[124] with the consequence that far from being simple or straightforward,

> [e]ach 'individual' always already includes all possible intra-actions with 'itself' through all possible virtual others, including those (and itself) that are noncontemporaneous with itself . . . Indeterminacy is an un/doing of identity that unsettles the very foundations of non/being.[125]

Sexuality is never simple or clearly defined; it is multidimensional, fluid, and always radically singular in each moment. Instead of fighting "nature" by clinging to clear-cut sexual categories or, indeed, identity in general, Barad pushes us to embrace all the weird and wonderful (sexual) possibilities opened up by this to appreciate and affirm the power and differentiation inherent in the "[p]olymorphous perversity"[126] of materially "queer/trans'formations".[127]

Concluding Remarks

With this, Barad draws our attention to a number of important insights regarding sexuality. First, sexuality has no determinate essence. Indeed, in a sense, Barad "completes" the deconstruction of sexual essentialism started by Freudian psychoanalysis by purposefully and fully aiming to remove any and all foreclosings to the queer expressions of matter. Sexuality is never pure or clear-cut; it is queer, composed of multiple non-binary entangled moving "parts" that constantly break out and are exhibited in distinct and unknowable or unexplainable ways. Rather than these being intentionally chosen by individuals, they are premised on the quantum becoming of matter itself, and so are inherently and fundamentally material (= natural). For this reason, queerness cannot be held to be the result of individual choice; it is matter expressing itself through "individuals" based on the quantum leaps inherent in materiality. In turn, sexuality is inherently fluid and changing, meaning that it is not only more complex than traditionally thought but also far more monstrous, expressing itself in distinct and surprising forms and fashions.

Barad therefore rejects the notion that sexuality is substantive and essentialist and claims that it is natural (= material) rather than (symbolically) constructed. By also holding that nature is queer, "nature" is reconfigured in terms of open-ended processes of quantum becoming rather than fixed categories. Indeed, Barad's notion of intra-action undermines the binary divisions that support patriarchy, while the insistence that nature is queer prevents any single form of sexuality from claiming a privileged status. Heteronormativity is also undermined and, in its place, a completely indeterminate notion of sexuality is affirmed; one which is never constrained within definitive or universal categories and which takes on new and unexpected, thoroughly individual, forms in each moment.

However, for all the insights provided, there is a strong sense in which Barad achieves this only because their queer account of sexuality relies upon or simply bypasses a number of problems inherent in or resulting from the presuppositions supporting the agential realist position. While the agential realist position is, no doubt, theoretically innovative, and, I would argue, also *practically* important in so far as it calls into question any attempt to foreclose sexual expression based on fixed (naturalist) premises, it is built on a number of assumptions that undermine its (theoretical) validity or that need to be developed to fully provide conceptual support for its important practical implications.

In the first instance, Barad's account is orientated from and against a particularly reductionist reading of the history of Western philosophy as evidenced, most obviously, by the insistence on the foundational importance of Cartesian representationalism, the problematic treatment of "poststructuralism", including its reduction to a (partial) reading of Judith Butler's gender theory, and the claim that agential realism offers a unique materialist account that corrects the idealism constitutive of Western philosophy. As Han Thomas Adriaenssen[128] points out, the question and indeed critique of representationalism long precedes Descartes, in so far as it was a fundamental issue in the Middle Ages, with the consequence that "representationalism" is far more diverse than Barad appears to appreciate. While Barad might identify and counteract a particular form of "representationalism", it is not clear that this overcomes all its historical variants.

Indeed, I have already noted that this tendency to appeal to reductionist readings of the positions that Barad attacks is inherent in Barad's treatment of both poststructuralism and Butler's thinking, but it is also found in Barad's treatment of "materialism". As Elizabeth Grosz points out, materialism has a long history in Western philosophy (and, indeed, post-Cartesian philosophy specifically) – Grosz focuses on the Stoics, Spinoza, Nietzsche, Deleuze, and Simondon – with the consequence that Western philosophy offers a variety of different forms of materialism, many of which are explicitly orientated against Cartesian representationalism.[129] Barad does not engage with any of these and so operates against a rather narrow conception of materialism that subsequently permits them to make bold claims about the originality of agential realism that might not stand if a more nuanced and subtle appreciation of the history of materialism was offered. Of course, Barad might respond that their theory is somehow different because it is grounded in contemporary scientific theories, but Grosz points to the work of Raymond Ruyer who also develops a materialist account from those premises (albeit not Bohr's quantum theory). A significant question mark remains therefore over whether Barad depends upon and counter-acts something of a straw (wo)man to claim for the agential realist account a unique position that is not justified because Barad's treatment of the question of materialism in Western philosophy is so truncated and reductionist.

Although this does not necessarily invalidate Barad's conclusions – it is, after all, quite possible that if Barad were to go through all the variants of materialism found within Western philosophy, the uniqueness of the agential realist position would still be affirmed – there are also issues with the theory itself. Specifically, while it is strong at showing that materiality is queer and, as such, cannot and does not ever attain a fixed identity, it is weak at explaining or even engaging with the issue of why, despite this, we have historically thought in terms of essential sexual identities or heteronormative frameworks. If these simply do not exist at the ontological level and all that exists is fundamentally an expression of the quantum processes inherent in materiality, it is difficult to see how this has been possible. It seems to demand that "something" be in some minimal way independent of the processes generating materiality to act against them. This, however, is precisely what Barad's theory of intra-active entanglement explicitly rejects. Barad therefore appears to construct their analysis against an opponent that their theory explicitly rejects as being possible.

The fundamental reason for this is, I want to suggest, that Barad appears to commit a sort of naturalist fallacy where ethics and epistemology are bound to and, in a sense, reduced to ontology, so that ethics and epistemological categories are expressions of the becomings of matter. There does not seem to be a way to counteract the processes of materiality, nor, given her critique of anthropocentrism, can human beings (or any other materialities for that matter) actively or intentionally counteract those processes; they are, after all, its effects. Sexual queerness is then an expression of materiality (= nature) and so natural. This is liberating, in so far as it justifies the existence of those sexualities and sexual practices/relations that have long been discriminated against, but, at the same time, it collapses ethics into ontology to claim that what is, as an expression of materiality, is always "natural" and so justified. Again, this is perfectly in keeping with Barad's celebration of the monstrous and perverse queerness of nature, but it does not answer and, indeed, seems to bypass the question of those forms of sexual expression that cause unwanted pain or suffering. Barad might respond that this is where their notion of responsibility comes in, but (1) this collapses ethics into ontology to claim that ethics relates not to individual action but material becomings;[130] and (2) responsibility does not describe the "*response*(ability)" to be given to the other but the (response) *ability* to act, with this being a consequence of the specific material configuration.[131] By limiting the discussion to the question of *whether* individuals can respond and failing to discuss *what* is the response necessitated by and permitted by (response)*ability*, it is difficult to see how individual forms of sexual expression can be sanctioned or prohibited and, at worst, appears to provide ontological support for *all* forms of sexual activity no matter what they entail or against whom they are perpetrated.

This is a direct consequence of Barad's critique and rejection of anthropocentrism and Barad's theory of agency, which is synonymous with impersonal material changes rather than intentional human endeavour. Although accepting that humans have a role to play, Barad does not spell out what this is and, indeed, appears to actively undermine it as a possibility because of the "discontinuity" of the quantum leaps constitutive of materiality and the rejection of (human) intentionality, will, and choice. It seems then that humans are simply at the mercy of pre-personal ontological forces beyond their control. While we are effects of those processes and contribute to their becoming, we cannot influence them.

Ironically, this charge has long been made against poststructuralist thought – that from which Barad often distinguishes their theory due to poststructuralism's perceived linguistic reductionism – with proponents of a variety of theoretical positions charging that its decentring of the foundational subject leaves no way to account for intentional agency to affect political change. I have elsewhere explored this issue to defend a number of poststructuralist thinkers against this charge by showing that rather than simply deconstructing the foundational subject to make it an effect of pre-personal forces, they also aim to reconstruct the constituted subject in a way that permits intentional agency.[132] However, in critiquing poststructuralist thought on this score, Barad, somewhat ironically, falls into the trap that is often erroneously thrown at poststructuralist thought; namely, that its decentring of the subject leaves no possibility of intentional agency. Again, although Barad says that we have a role to play, Barad is, at best, evasive regarding what humans can do to shape material becoming and certainly does not explain the mechanisms through which it takes place. Having rejected those mechanisms – will, intention, choice – that the Christian West has long relied on, Barad challenges us to come up with alternatives, but Barad's radical critique of anthropocentrism seems to cut off the means to permit this.

For this reason, Gill Jagger's claim that we can "operationalise" Barad's thinking "through intervening in the boundary-making process to reconfigure the material-discursive apparatus of bodily production through which phenomena such as sexed bodies are constituted"[133] not only ignores Barad's claim that the agential cut that generates boundary-making processes is not and cannot be grounded in human action, in so far as it constitutes the condition for the expression of (relatively) distinct materialities, but also implicitly depends upon and demands the type of intentional action that is explicitly rejected by Barad's critique of anthropocentric intentional will.

Interestingly, in a recent interview, Barad was asked to respond to this issue – that is, the question of agency – through the mediation of the issue of invention, to which, in the first instance, Barad responded by reaffirming that it is absolutely not "an 'I' that is doing the thinking, because to assume that would be to reinscribe the Cartesian notion of the thinking subject as the human individual, closely aligned with representationalism",[134] before going on to question the notion of the "new" because it risks downplaying historical or transitional processes of becoming and is problematically tied up with individualistic legal representations of ownership such as copyright and patents. However, rather than then go on to respond to the question of what this means for the question of who/what invents and/or how this occurs, Barad concludes that "these enactions are not merely enactions by the human as such, as 'the human' is always already the product of a constitutive discursive practice that needs to be accounted for in its materialization".[135] For this reason, "the question is rather what *thinking* is. Who/what is doing the thinking and with what and whom is thinking happening (because it never happens alone)?"[136] However, although this may challenge long-held anthropocentric positions, especially those relating to the "self" and "identity", it not only seems to reduce agency to thought but also does not get us very far in terms of responding to the issue of who acts and how this is possible given the agential realist ontology. Despite Barad's insistence on the fundamental importance of material agency, the agential realist critique of anthropocentrism and insistence that agency is implicated at the level of matter itself empties out the possibility of intentional agency to the extent that humans appear as mere effects of material changes rather than being capable of purposeful action to affect those processes of onto-genesis. We are, as a consequence, left in a somewhat strange situation: on one level, we are inherently agential, in so far as we are material beings that constantly change, but, on another level, we lack (intentional) agency, with the consequence that we are passive effects of the changes inherent in the processes of materialisation that constitute us.

In turn, this is tied to and reveals what is arguably the most problematic aspects of Barad's agential realist account: its treatment of the *political-juridical* and *ethical-normative* dimensions of material expression and, by extension, sexuality. There has obviously always been political intent behind Barad's agential realist theory, but this has tended to be implicit rather than explicit. Barad has however tried to rectify this in a number of recent works by tying quantum field theory, upon which the agential realist account (of sexuality) depends, to the political domain through an analysis of (1) the relation between quantum theory and the atomic bomb, which is also tangentially tied to questions of colonialism and militarism,[137] and (2) quantum field theory's notion of time upon which much Western thought – including its conceptions of historical memory – depends.[138] Importantly, these discussions are conducted at the ontological level in so far as they are orientated to outlining the constitution of matter itself. By linking politics to ontology in this manner, Barad is able to maintain that politics is imbricated into the very fabric of matter to the extent that "[m]atter is political all the way down".[139]

The problem, however, is that although this intends to entangle the political with the material, there is no discussion, however tentative, within Barad's analyses of what constitutes the "political", nor, despite Barad's claim that "[s]pecificity is everything – and everything *is* specific",[140] is the political dimension of matter explored in its actual specificity; that is, what the political means for actual specific events or configurations, such as how it might apply to the realm of sexuality, which would also require, amongst other aspects, an analysis of the symbolic and juridical dimensions of sexual expression to explore what is culturally, normatively, and legally permitted sexually and how this is supported by or contradicts the agential realist ontology.

Part of this lack of emphasis on the political is methodological, in so far as Barad warns that we cannot approach the political dimension as if it were distinct from physics or matter; that is, we cannot "assume each exists in and answers questions about wholly separate epistemic and ontic domains, and from this assumption analyze if and how physics has been infiltrated by the political".[141] Instead,

> it is necessary in thinking quantum physics and social-political theories together to switch optics: rather than using one as a lens for examining the other in their assumed separateness, to diffractively read their insights through one another in order to understand them *in their inseparability* – that is, to be able to trace the entanglements across all temporal and spatial scales, or rather, more to the point to rethink the assumed natures of space and time, and indeed, *scale* itself.[142]

This is an interesting point, in so far as it aims not to affirm or simply adopt the position of quantum physics as the foundation for thinking through the political, but insists on the entanglement of both; an endeavour that, as Barad notes, means that it is necessary to "open up the notion of 'the physics,' as well as the political, to being reworked".[143] However, in the actual implementation of this methodology, Barad's theorising is far stronger at reworking the former than the latter. Barad is honest enough to recognise this, admitting that they are more comfortable working in the language of quantum mechanics,[144] but this does not lessen the problems that result, in so far as it continuously leads Barad to implicitly downplay the political dimension. For example, having noted that it is necessary to rework both "physics" and "the political", Barad immediately ignores the latter to explain that it is "no small task: to work with and rework the physics".[145] There is no mention of what it means to rework the political. Furthermore, Barad goes on to explain that they offer a *"political physics"*;[146] a formulation that, however inadvertent, betrays a continuing privileging of physics in which politics is thought of as a dimension of physics. Even when Barad tries to rebalance the relationship by reminding us that agential realism is developed from "crucial insights from critical social and political theories, including feminist, queer, postcolonial, decolonial, and critical race theories",[147] there is a sense in which those insights are used in the service of the development of the quantum ontology underpinning agential realism rather than actual detailed engagements with the various theories or the politics permitted by them. In sum, despite recognising the importance of the political dimension and insisting it is tied up with the ontological, Barad's discussion of the former always quickly returns to develop the onto-epistemological arena (tied to quantum theory) or shows how the political event or theory supports the onto-epistemological position underpinning agential realism. Not only is the actual discussion of these supposedly political events underdeveloped, but the quick movement back to the onto-epistemological focus of agential realism means that, rather than entwined, there continues to be a privileging of the ontological over the political.

When we turn to the ethical dimension of Barad's agential realism, it must be admitted that it is much stronger. This is perhaps not surprising given that agential realism aims to be *"ethico-ontoepistemology"*.[148] To develop this, Barad has latterly drawn on and sought to extend Jacques Derrida's work on hospitality to show that the relationality underpinning the quantum ontology of agential realism does not simply "operate" at the individual level but offers the possibility to reconceive of *materiality* in terms of "an ongoing transmutation, an undoing of self, of identity, where the 'other' is always already within".[149] Barad's conclusion is that the relational ontology of quantum theory is the moment wherein the question of justice arises, which is understood not in terms of a definite thing to be realised, but as "the lived possibility of difference/differencing without exclusion, a differencing that undoes exclusions through the dynamism by which that which is constitutively excluded becomes a constitutive part of the self, precisely in an undoing of Self/Other (as well as the Self)".[150] Importantly, this does not occur at the level of the individual or individual relations or questions of moral comportment, but is a constitutive feature of matter itself. There is a "yearning for justice that is written into the world, into the very nature of matter itself, in an undoing of itself, of essence, of kind".[151]

Barad warns however that tying matter to justice "is not [to] say that the world is always already just by its very nature";[152] it simply means that matter always expresses

> an invitation to a practice of *radical hospitality* – an opening up to all that is possible in the thickness of the Now in rejecting practices of a-voidance, taking responsibility for injustices, activating and aligning with forces of justice, and welcoming the other in an undoing of the colonizing notion of selfhood rather than as a marker of not us, not me.[153]

In other words, *"a force of justice is available with-in every moment, every place, every bit of matter"*.[154] But this doesn't mean that "justice" will or indeed can ever be achieved: "Justice is always to-come, and always a matter of an incalculable number of entanglements. But just because it is infinite it doesn't mean that we don't engage in it. We must engage with it, even knowing that it is infinite and we will never arrive, finally."[155] While there is obviously liberatory intent behind this, in so far as it always offers the possibility of a more just world which we should strive to create, it also brings us back to the troubling question of agency and the issue of "who" or "what" the "we" is that Barad maintains is capable of interjecting into the quantum becoming of matter to direct it towards a more just formation. As noted, Barad rejects both anthropocentrism – which is tied to the idea that humans can control matter – and the notion of agency tied to an intentional ego. Instead, "[a]gency is a matter of intraacting: it is an enactment",[156] with the consequence that agency occurs at the level of matter itself.

Again, however, it is unclear what enacts the intra-action; that is, whether it is possible to identify the impetus or spark that brings forth alterations "in" matter. Barad tries to clarify the issue by linking it to questions of *political* agency by claiming that

> when people come together en mass to protest injustices, to articulate their demands and desires for justice, this is *political agency in its enactment, in its multiply expressed desirings for being in connection and collectively reworking the material condition of human and nonhuman lives as well as reworking the very possibilities for change.*[157]

Indeed, Barad gives the example of the tactics used by the Hong Kong pro-democracy protestors of 2019–2020, wherein months into the protests, and with an awareness that police violence was escalating, the protestors "shifted to a form of creative resistance that belies the expected atomistic engagement: rather than masses of people showing up at one given location, like a particle (which occupies a given position), they started thinking of movement in terms of being (like) water – that is, like waves rather than particles".[158] This is a different kind of movement from the movement of discrete individuals; it "is to be fluid, formless, and shapeless, to surge up in one spot, quickly dissipate, only to reemerge with intensity elsewhere a short time later – protest making and moving as waves diffracting. This movement was not a form of chaos but rather a decentralized well-coordinated effort."[159]

Although Barad is trying to point to a different form of agency from that which is premised on individual, monadic will, the example is problematic because it does not explain "how" the protestors were able to shift their creative resistance, if indeed it was the protestors that did this. Barad's discussions of the agency of masses explains *that* a mass has coalesced for a particular end and the possibilities that arise from that formation, but again it does not explain *how* that occurred. It might be objected that this is provided through Barad's insistence on the performative entwinement of matter and activity, thereby indicating that material becoming occurs through the material beings "composing" it, but that would require a far more detailed explanation of the mechanisms in and through which individuals act than is provided by Barad's discussion. Barad's theory is stronger at showing that matter itself structures agents, without demonstrating how the performative acts of those agents subsequently impact upon the becoming of matter.

Admittedly, Barad notes that developing the agential realist position is a "continuing project of working to bring forward the radical possibilities for living-being otherwise that are always already with-in quantum physics (itself)",[160] but returning to the question of sexuality, we see that, as it stands, Barad's agential reason purposefully rejects or, at least, sidesteps the question of the ways in which (1) individuals intentionally construct or contribute to their sexual expressions, and/or (2) individuals and communities intentionally construct (exclusionary) normative ideals to permit, constrain, or punish forms of sexuality, despite, as Barad's queer theory affirms, there being no "natural" basis for those prohibitions. In other words, Barad's ontological focus undercuts the notion that sexuality is universal, fixed, determined, and binary, and, in so doing, opens up sexuality to the queerness of matter. Because materiality is queer, so too are its expressions, including sexuality. This ensures that the *binary* sexual opposition that has dominated Western thought actually contradicts the queerness of material reality. In contrast, *non-binary* forms of sexuality, so long held to be contrary to nature, actually express the queerness of matter. It is queer forms of sexuality and not binary forms that are natural. This opens up sexual expression to queer forms, all the while grounding those expressions in the reality of "matter" as opposed to the supposedly immaterial (social) constructions of the symbolic realm found in poststructuralist thought.

However, by collapsing material expressions, including individual sexuality, into pre-personal material becomings to show that sexuality never actually is fixed or universal, Barad's agential realism is unable to both adequately explain how individuals can contribute to the realisation of their sexuality and/or consider or explain how fixed (binary) conceptions of sexuality have (and do) continue to dominant and structure the ethico-political-juridical spheres of existence despite, as demonstrated by Barad's agential realist theory, them not having any basis in materiality. For example, Barad's theory seems unable to explain how there can exist laws that explicitly outlaw homosexuality and/or queer sexualities, when such sexualities are a possible expression of the queerness of materiality, or, put differently, when such exclusions contradict the queerness of matter. Either those laws must be an expression of material becoming, with the consequences that matter is not (always) so queer and it is not clear how Barad can criticise them *or* it is possible that such laws exist but do so in a way that contradicts the queerness of materiality despite being an expression of the queermess of materiality. That either means that such laws are not grounded in the queer structures of materiality, which contradicts the ontology underpinning the agential realist position, or they are grounded in queer materiality but there is some way in which it is possible that entities (in this case laws) may contradict their own material grounding, which not only requires explanation but also brings us back to the issue of "who" is the agent that affects such a disjunction. In short, Barad's queer theory is strong at undermining the notions of fixed sexual identity and essentialism by showing that sexuality is "grounded" in moving material becomings, but it does not explain how, despite this, (certain) sexual identities are nevertheless adopted and affirmed, both by individuals and societies, to foreclose – and indeed justify that foreclosure – sexual expression in the first place.

Rectifying this would require a much clearer and extensive consideration and explanation of (1) the socio-political-communitarian dimensions of meaning-formation and sexual expression, including the way(s) in which the intentional actions and interactions of "individual" material-beings facilitate and contribute to this; (2) how socio-political-juridical structures affirm and support particular (binary) conceptions of sexuality to the detriment of others despite this normative-juridical affirmation of certain sexualities and sexual practices contradicting the queerness of materiality that grounds them; (3) how exclusionary forms of sexuality, such as those inherent in the essentialist-patriarchal-heteronormative model, can exist despite contradicting the open material queerness that they both depend upon and express; and (4) the relationship between material being and the symbolic realm to explain how the latter can contradict the former despite, on Barad's telling, the material and symbolic being constitutively and intimately entwined. Such an analysis would presumably require a far stronger and more extensive discussion of the symbolic realm that recognises that the symbolic, while entwined with the material, is not so entangled that it cannot contradict the material conditions underpinning and sustaining it. Barad is wary of providing such an account, despite claiming that the symbolic is tied to materiality, because it would presumably risk reaffirming the importance of the symbolic "over" materiality; a position that Barad associates with the poststructuralist linguistic reductionism that agential realism aims to correct. However, without that discussion of the ways in which the symbolic (itself tied to questions of ethics, politics, and law) can depart from the conditions of material becoming that sustain it, to, in so doing, create conceptions of sexuality that do not accurately reflect the queer becoming of matter, Barad's agential realist account, for all its insights and liberatory intent, is ultimately unable to explain how it is and has been possible for the essential-patriarchal-heteronormative model of sexuality, against which agential realism sets itself, to not only come into existence in the first place, but to also be able to dominate discussions of the topic for so long, and, indeed, to be held to be "natural", despite, as Barad points out, it actually having no material basis.

Barad's agential realist account leaves us then in a problematic position, in which we are given the conceptual tools to rethink sexuality in terms of the absolute openness of material queerness, without being able to explain how the alternative, exclusionary forms of sexuality can actually exist in the first place. Without that explanation, the agential realist account (1) risks its own redundancy, in so far as it claims to fight an opponent – in the form of exclusionary models of sexuality – that it is unclear can actually exist based on the premises of agential realism; namely, due to its grounding in the open-ended queer becoming of matter; and/or (2) inadvertently risks downplaying the dangers of such exclusionary models of sexuality because the affirmation of non-intentional queer material becoming appears to forestall both the need to and the possibility of actively and intentionally combating them; all that "we" must do is await their undermining through the agency of matter itself, an undermining that is always taking place and/or has already taken place because materiality is (always) queer. For all its promise, innovation, and originality, Barad's agential realist account returns us to and, in so doing, reopens the question(ing) of sexuality. How to do so is taken up in the conclusion.

Notes

1. See, for example, Michael Losonsky, *Linguistic Turns in Modern Philosophy* (Cambridge: Cambridge University Press, 2006).
2. Elizabeth Grosz, *Volatile Bodies: Toward a Corporeal Feminism* (Bloomington, IN: Indiana University Press, 1994), p. 5.
3. Elizabeth A. Wilson, *Neural Geographies: Feminism and the Microstructure of Cognition* (Abingdon: Routledge, 1998), p. 14.
4. Sarah Ahmed, "Some Preliminary Remarks on the Founding Gestures of the 'New Materialism'", *European Journal of Women's Studies*, vol. 15, n. 1, 2008, pp. 23–39 (p. 28).
5. Somer Brodribb, *Nothing Mat(t)ers: A Feminist Critique of Postmodernism* (New York: New York University Press, 1992), p. 24.
6. Ibid., p. 133.

7. Jacques Derrida, *Of Grammatology: Corrected Edition*, trans. Gayatri Chakravorty Spivak (Baltimore, MD: The Johns Hopkins University Press, 1997), p. 158. This a mistranslation of "*il n'y a pas de hors-texte*": "there is no outside-text".
8. For a recent critical discussion of Derrida's materialism, see Clayton Crockett, *Derrida after the End of Writing: Political Theology and New Materialism* (New York: Fordham University Press, 2017).
9. For a discussion of (1) what has come to be known as "new materialism", see the essays collected in Diana Coole and Samantha Frost (eds), *New Materialisms: Ontology, Agency, and Politics* (Durham, NC: Duke University Press, 2010); and (2) how theory moved beyond poststructuralism, see Rosi Braidotti (ed.), *After Poststructuralism: Transformations and Transitions* (Abingdon: Routledge, 2013).
10. Gilles Deleuze, *Difference and Repetition*, trans. Paul Patton (New York: Columbia University Press, 1994). For a critical discussion of Deleuze's ontology, see Gavin Rae, *Ontology in Heidegger and Deleuze* (Basingstoke: Palgrave Macmillan, 2014).
11. See, for example, the essays collected in Sarah Ellenzweig and John H. Zammito (eds), *The New Politics of Materialism: History, Philosophy, Science* (Abingdon: Routledge, 2017).
12. In personal correspondence with the author, Karen Barad expressed a desire to use the pronouns they/their (instead of she/her) to describe themselves. Regardless of the personal reasons for such a choice, conceptually speaking, it (1) supports the theoretical claim of agential realism that sexuality is multiple and fluid, and (2) undercuts the theoretical assumptions of the essential-patriarchal-heteronormative model. For these reasons, I use those pronouns when referring to Barad.
13. Karen Barad, *Meeting the Universe Halfway: Quantum Physics and the Entanglement of Matter and Meaning* (Durham, NC: Duke University Press, 2007), p. 132.
14. Ibid., pp. 34–35.
15. Ibid., p. 133.
16. Ibid., p. ix.
17. Ibid., p. 33.
18. Ibid., p. 26.
19. Karen Barad, "Nature's Queer Performativity", *Kvinder, Køn & Forskning*, vol. 1–2, 2012, pp. 25–53; Karen Barad, "Transmaterialities: Trans*/Matter/Reality and Queer Political Imaginings", *GLQ: A Journal of Lesbian and Gay Studies*, vol. 21, n. 2–3, 2015, pp. 387–422.
20. Butler traces the Hegelian influences shaping twentieth-century French thinking in *Subjects of Desire: Hegelian Reflections in Twentieth-Century France* (New York: Columbia University Press, 1999). For Hegel, identity and difference are dialectically entwined: identity is never singular but is always composed of and dependent upon an ongoing process of differential becoming, whereas difference always takes on an identity to the extent that even "non-identity" takes on the identity of "lacking" identity. Hegel's entire *oeuvre* can be read as explicating this point, but the most developed formal discussion of the identity–difference

relationship is found in chapter 2A of Book Two: The Doctrine of Essence in *The Science of Logic*, trans. George di Giovanni (Cambridge: Cambridge University Press, 2010), pp. 356–365. For a discussion of (1) how the identity–difference relation plays out throughout Hegel's thinking generally but especially in relation to the question of human being, see Gavin Rae, *Realizing Freedom: Hegel, Sartre, and the Alienation of Human Being* (Basingstoke: Palgrave Macmillan, 2011); and (2) the forms of identity that can continue to adhere to ontologies that are affirmative of pure difference, see Gavin Rae, "Traces of Identity in Deleuze's Differential Ontology", *International Journal of Philosophical Studies*, vol. 22, n. 1, 2014, pp. 86–105.
21. Barad, *Meeting the University Halfway*, p. 48.
22. Ibid., p. 48.
23. Ibid., p. 46.
24. Ibid., p. 46.
25. Ibid., p. 46.
26. Ibid., p. 61.
27. Ibid., p. 150.
28. Ibid., p. 151.
29. Ibid., p. 151.
30. Ibid., p. 151.
31. Ibid., p. 192.
32. Ibid., p. 192.
33. Ibid., p. 192.
34. Ibid., p. 64.
35. Ibid., p. 64.
36. Ibid., p. 66.
37. Ibid., p. 30.
38. Ibid., p. 23.
39. Ibid., p. 34.
40. Ibid., p. 136.
41. Ibid., p. 136. The notion of "posthumanism" is heterogeneous (for a good overview, see Cary Wolfe, *What is Posthumanism?* [Minneapolis, MN: Minnesota University Press, 2010]), but I have elsewhere argued that posthumanist theory is premised around a critique of anthropocentrism that can be traced back to an implicit and often unacknowledged dependence on the critique of metaphysics inherent in Heidegger's fundamental ontology. See Gavin Rae, "Heidegger's Influence on Posthumanism: The Destruction of Metaphysics, Technology, and the Overcoming of Anthropocentrism", *History of Human Sciences*, vol. 27, n. 1, 2014, pp. 51–69.
42. Barad, *Meeting the Universe Halfway*, p. 136. For a general overview of the problem of anthropocentrism, see Gavin Rae, "Anthropocentrism", in *Encyclopaedia of Global Bioethics*, edited by Henk ten Have (Dordrecht: Springer, 2014), pp. 1–12.
43. Ibid., p. 35. Ironically, Butler has frequently been charged with being unable to account for human agency because Butler is held to reduce agency to determined

effects of pre-personal structures and processes. Whereas Butler has developed a sophisticated account of human agency to counter this criticism, Barad revels in the charge and, indeed, doubles-down on it by explicitly claiming that agency is inherently and fundamentally non-human. Butler's most sophisticated account of agency is found in *The Psychic Life of Power: Theories in Subjection* (Stanford, CA: Stanford University Press, 1997). For a critical discussion of Butler's theory of agency, see Gavin Rae, *Poststructuralist Agency: The Subject in Twentieth-Century Theory* (Edinburgh: Edinburgh University Press, 2020), chapter 5.

44. Tim Hayward, "Anthropocentrism: A Misunderstood Problem", *Environmental Ethics*, vol. 6, n. 1, 1997, pp. 9–63 (pp. 52–55).
45. Barad, *Meeting the Universe Halfway*, p. 192.
46. Ibid., p. ix.
47. Ibid., p. ix.
48. Ibid., p. 19.
49. Ibid., p. 67.
50. Ibid., p. 106.
51. Ibid., p. 107.
52. Ibid., p. 107.
53. Ibid., p. 107.
54. Ibid., p. 69.
55. Ibid., p. 69.
56. Ibid., p. 27.
57. Ibid., p. 26.
58. Ibid., p. 22.
59. Ibid., p. 3.
60. Karen Barad, "Posthumanist Performativity: Toward an Understanding of How Matter Comes to Matter", *Signs: Journal of Women in Culture and Society*, vol. 28, n. 3, 2003, pp. 801–831 (p. 823).
61. Barad, *Meeting the Universe Halfway*, p. 155.
62. Ibid., p. 156.
63. Ibid., p. 156.
64. Ibid., p. 156.
65. Ibid., p. 155.
66. Ibid., p. 211.
67. Ibid., p. 33.
68. Ibid., p. 33.
69. Karen Barad and Adam Kleinman, "Intra-actions", *Mousse*, vol. 34, summer, 2012, pp. 76–81 (p. 77).
70. Barad, "Nature's Queer Performativity", p. 33.
71. Barad, *Meeting the Universe Halfway*, p. 233.
72. Ibid., p. 234.
73. Ibid., p. 141.
74. Ibid., p. 141.
75. Ibid., p. 141.

76. Ibid., p. 141.
77. Ibid., p. 33.
78. Barad, "Posthumanist Performativity", p. 820.
79. Ibid., p. 820.
80. Ibid., p. 820.
81. Ibid., p. 816.
82. Ibid., p. 815.
83. Ibid., p. 816.
84. Ibid., p. 816.
85. Ibid., p. 816.
86. Barad, *Meeting the Universe Halfway*, p. 146.
87. Ibid., p. 146.
88. Ibid., p. 146.
89. Ibid., p. 146.
90. Ibid., p. 146.
91. Ibid., p. 140.
92. Ibid., p. 140.
93. Ibid., p. 140.
94. Ibid., p. 140.
95. Ibid., p. 33.
96. Barad, "Nature's Queer Performativity", p. 45.
97. Barad, *Meeting the Universe Halfway*, p. 214.
98. Ibid., p. 172.
99. Ibid., p. 235.
100. Karen Barad, "Agential Realism: Feminist Interventions in Understanding Scientific Practices", in *Science Studies Reader*, edited by Mario Biagioli (Abingdon: Routledge, 1999), pp. 1–11 (p. 7).
101. Barad, "Nature's Queer Performativity", p. 28.
102. Ibid., p. 28.
103. Ibid., p. 28.
104. Ibid., p. 28.
105. Ibid., p. 29.
106. Ibid., p. 29.
107. Ibid., p. 29.
108. Ibid., p. 29.
109. Ibid., p. 39.
110. Ibid., p. 33.
111. Ibid., p. 32.
112. Karen Barad, Malou Juelskjær, and Nete Schwennesen, "Intra-active Entanglements: An Interview with Karen Barad", *Kvinder, Køn & Forskning*, vol. 1–2, 2012, pp. 10–24 (p. 19).
113. Ibid., p. 19.
114. Barad, "Nature's Queer Performativity", p. 39.
115. Karen Barad, "Quantum Entanglements and Hauntological Relations of Inheritance: Dis/continuities, SpaceTime Enfoldings, and Justice-to-Come", *Derrida*

Today, vol. 3, n. 2, 2010, pp. 240–268 (p. 246). Indeed, what Barad finds so remarkable "about quantum physics is how astonishingly queer it is – it is so queer that it queers queer, keeping it in motion . . . Not only specific binaries are destabilized, but even the cuts are iteratively cross-cut" (Barad, Juelskjær, Schwennesen, "Intra-active Entanglements", p. 19).
116. Barad, Juelskjær, Schwennesen, "Intra-active Entanglements", p. 18.
117. Barad, "Quantum Entanglements and Hauntological Relations of Inheritance", p. 246.
118. Barad and Kleinman, "Intra-actions", p. 80.
119. Ibid., p. 80.
120. Barad, "Nature's Queer Performativity", p. 45.
121. Barad, "Transmaterialities", p. 413.
122. Barad, "Nature's Queer Performativity", p. 47.
123. Ibid., p. 412.
124. Ibid., p. 401.
125. Ibid., p. 401.
126. Ibid., p. 399.
127. Ibid., p. 399.
128. Han Thomas Adriaenssen, *Representation and Scepticism from Aquinas to Descartes* (Cambridge: Cambridge University Press, 2019).
129. Elizabeth Grosz, *The Incorporeal: Ontology, Ethics, and the Limits of Materialism* (New York: Columbia University Press, 2017).
130. Barad, *Meeting the Universe Halfway*, p. 393.
131. Barad and Kleinman, "Intra-actions", p. 81.
132. Rae, *Poststructuralist Agency*.
133. Gill Jagger, "The New Materialism and Sexual Difference", *Signs: Journal of Women in Culture and Society*, vol. 40, n. 2, 2015, pp. 321–342 (p. 338).
134. Karen Barad and Daniela Gandorfer, "Political Desirings: Yearnings for Mattering (,) Differently", *Theory & Event*, vol. 24, n. 1, 2021, pp. 14–66 (p. 29).
135. Ibid., p. 29.
136. Ibid., p. 28.
137. Karen Barad, "No Small Mattter: Mushroom Clouds, Ecologies of Nothingness, and Strange Topologies of Spacetimemattering", in *Arts of Living on a Damaged Planet: Ghosts and Monsters of the Anthropocene*, edited by Anna Tsing, Nils Bubandt, Elaine Gan, and Heather Swanson (Minneapolis, MN: Minnesota University Press, 2017), pp. 103–120; Karen Barad, "After the End of the World: Entangled Nuclear Colonialisms, Matters of Force, and the Material Force of Justice", *Theory & Event*, vol. 22, n. 3, 2019, pp. 524–550.
138. Karen Barad, "Troubling Time/s and Ecologies of Nothingness: Re-turning, Re-membering, and Facing the Incalculable Atomic Bomb", *New Formations*, n. 92, September 2017, pp. 56–86.
139. Barad and Gandorfer, "Political Desirings", p. 29.
140. Ibid., p. 28.
141. Ibid., p. 21.
142. Ibid., p. 22.

143. Ibid., pp. 22–23.
144. Ibid., p. 34.
145. Ibid., p. 23.
146. Ibid., p. 23.
147. Ibid., p. 23.
148. Ibid., p. 39.
149. Barad, "After the End of the World", p. 543. Derrida outlines his thinking on hospitality across a variety of works, but the most succinct discussion is found in *Of Hospitality: Anne Dufourmantelle Invites Jacques Derrida to Respond*, trans. Rachel Bowlby (Stanford, CA: Stanford University Press, 2000). For an extended discussion of Derrida's thinking on hospitality, see Judith Still, *Derrida and Hospitality: Theory and Practice* (Edinburgh: Edinburgh University Press, 2010).
150. Barad and Gandorfer, "Political Desirings", p. 46.
151. Ibid., p. 46.
152. Barad, "After the End of the World", p. 544.
153. Ibid., p. 545.
154. Ibid., p. 544.
155. Barad and Gandorfer, "Political Desirings", p. 33.
156. Ibid., p. 59.
157. Ibid., p. 59.
158. Ibid., p. 54.
159. Ibid., pp. 54–55.
160. Barad, "After the End of the World", p. 540.

Conclusion: Sexuality as Constellation

The preceding chapters have been guided by the contention that the history of Western philosophical thinking on the question of sexuality has been marked by one dominant logic, termed here the "essentialist-patriarchal" model, which morphed into the essentialist-patriarchal-heteronormative model. Although it has been expressed in different ways, thinkers from Ancient Greece, early Christianity through to modern philosophy, German Idealism, and the nineteenth century tended to foreclose the nature and meaning of sexuality (including sexual relations) within the coordinates of this model. Western thinking has then tended to be premised on a binary division between "men" and "women", both of which are designated as such because they are held to "possess" a number of definitive and mutually exclusive essential ontological characteristics which, in turn, have been accompanied by a privileging of the masculine position over the feminine and heterosexual relations over alternatives. The place, status, and possibilities for each sex and, indeed, sexual relations generally have then tended to be heavily prescribed and foreclosed within pre-established boundaries.

This model was the subject of substantial critique within twentieth-century thought, as thinkers from distinct methodologies and traditions questioned its insistence that the meaning of sexuality is fixed or predetermined. Although this did not generate agreement, what it did demonstrate was that the question of sexuality depends upon a whole assortment of ontological, metaphysical, epistemological questions, the responses to which generate distinct conceptions of sexuality and, indeed, juridical-political-moral frameworks that support and re-enforce them. For example, with regards to the essentialist-patriarchal model, it tends to justify itself through appeal to theological scripture, a particular version of nature and what is natural, understood in ahistoric, determinate terms, and/or the assumptions driving specific juridical-political-ethical frameworks regarding the division of social space or how the sexes should act that, in turn, are tied to questions of language, history, and cultures. What appears to be a relatively simplistic model is then actually revealed to be a complex and heterogeneous one.

Rather than simply abandon the premises of the essentialist-patriarchal model to affirm an alternative from the perspective of formal logic or abstract system-building, proponents of, amongst others, psychoanalytic, phenomenological, and feminist theories purposefully insisted on the need to undertake a historically informed analysis that recognises and takes seriously the way(s) in which "sexuality" has been previously thought. The basic premise driving these endeavours is that altering the dominant conceptual apparatus cannot occur in abstraction from history but must pass through it to twist open alternative pathways. As such, the critical perspectives engaged with in the previous chapters have tied their analyses to the concrete history of the topic as this has been defined by the dominant logic structuring the debate historically, at least as this has been thought within Western society, to highlight the exclusions that have marked it. The result has been a fertile and ongoing, if, at times, subterranean but also increasingly radical, engagement with the historically dominant essentialist-patriarchal model of sexuality specifically and question of sexuality more generally.

Starting at the dawn of the twentieth century, Freudian psychoanalytic theory aimed to move the discussion of "sexuality" away from the essentialist ontologies of substance historically dominant, to a developmental model of sexuality based on psychic mechanisms. Not only does Freud go on to insist on the important role that sexuality plays at all stages of human being – it does not simply adhere to adulthood – he also goes to great lengths to explain and demonstrate that the form this takes alters throughout an individual's life. As a consequence, sexuality is held to be an inherent aspect of human being and one that is far more complex than the essential-patriarchal model recognises, in so far as it is historic, indeterminate, and dependent on an ongoing developmental process that is always subtended by an originary bisexuality.

Despite the importance of Freud's critique of ontological essentialism, his rethinking of sexuality is however marked by two problems: not only does it continue to depend upon a logic of patriarchy, but, importantly, sexual expression is foreclosed within binary structures, both in terms of the originary *bi*sexuality from which individual sexuality develops and the binary heteronormative nature of what he considered to be "healthy" individuals. In contrast, Martin Heidegger engaged with the ontological understanding subtending Freud's thinking to move the terms of the debate from the psychic to the ontological level to "ground" sexuality in the response given to the question of the meaning of Being. By tying the question of Being to time, Heidegger insisted, *pace* Freud, that sexuality is not structured from an originary bisexuality; it is orientated from an originary ontological indeterminacy that, through a process of autopoietic differentiation, is expressed in multiple factical forms that continue to find expression through a process of open-ended becoming. However, while this undermines the binary logic subtending patriarchy, Heidegger focuses on placing the question of sexuality in relation to the question of the meaning of Being, rather than in developing any ontic, or empirical, conception of sexuality *per se*. Although we can extrapolate from his ontological analysis, the ontic level was not his concern, with the consequence that his thinking is particularly weak regarding it.

This changed as Husserlian-inspired phenomenology was transported from Germany to France in the 1930s and 1940s, with the material embodied basis of sexuality coming to the fore. Indeed, for the next fifty years or so, the question of sexuality and, in particular, the rejection of the essentialist-patriarchal model of sexuality occupied much French thinking as it grappled with whether sexuality is structured from the material body or symbolic structures; a debate that took us from phenomenology to feminist theory by way of poststructuralism and a particular return to Freudian psychoanalysis. Although this reveals the ways in which the questioning of the essentialist-patriarchal model traverses distinct theoretical perspectives, the significant interest in the question of sexuality in France from the mid-1940s onwards, but not Germany after Heidegger – despite the considerable attention to the issue in the German-speaking world up to the start of Nazism – also points to the culturally grounded nature of any questioning of sexuality. This became further evident with the movement to gender theory and queer theory later in the century, which moved from thinkers based in France to those located in America (albeit who were influenced by much French thinking) and gave rise to a distinct conceptual apparatus through which to engage with the problem.

While a variety of French phenomenologists took up the question of sexuality, often in direct confrontation with Heidegger, I argued that the most sophisticated response was provided by Maurice Merleau-Ponty in his early work on the sexed body. Merleau-Ponty agrees with Heidegger on the need to adopt Husserl's phenomenological reduction to bracket presuppositions regarding sexuality, but they differ in terms of how to implement this. Merleau-Ponty insists, contra Heidegger, that the analysis must be conducted from, through, and with specific focus on the human body rather than from a prior ontological analysis that brackets the question of (bodily) facticity. This brings to the fore the fundamental, but not foundational, role that sexuality plays in embodied experience, as a precursor to insisting on the ambiguous nature of sexuality: although part of human embodied being, "sexuality" does not have a separate existence but is bound up with the entire existence of each body. The consequences of this are debated, but its main contribution is to highlight and set in motion a conceptual bond between sexuality and the lived body that reverberates throughout subsequent thought.

To this point, Freud, Heidegger, and Merleau-Ponty were shown to hold a common problematisation of the ontological essentialism inherent in Western thinking on sexuality, but left untouched the patriarchal aspect. This changed with Simone de Beauvoir, who purposefully and explicitly engages with the question of essentialism but focuses more on the role that "woman" plays in Western thought. In so doing, she outlines the problem of patriarchy and, based on her insistence that sexuality is a cultural construct, proposed a forceful critique of it. While it appears that Beauvoir's critique continues to insist on a binary heteronormative opposition between "man" and "woman", to examine the cultural status of the latter, I argued that her notion of ambiguity and comments on the biology–culture relationship not only complicate that assessment but also led her thinking to be an important point of reference for future analyses. Indeed, it became a subterranean point of reference for the symbolic/material division that would structure subsequent debates.

This division came to the fore with the structuralist eclipse of phenomenology that took place in 1950s France, a movement that gave rise to several conceptual innovations. Jacques Lacan's return to Freud reinvigorated psychoanalytic thinking by insisting on the fundamental importance of the differential relations subtending symbolic meaning. This not only made "sexuality" a relational concept, thereby continuing the rejection of ontological essentialism inherent in Freudian and phenomenologically inspired accounts, but also brought to the fore the centrality of the problem of language. Lacan, at least in his writings and teachings throughout the 1950s, did, however, continue to think the sexual positions from a predetermined anchor point – the phallus – to foreclose sexual expression within fixed boundaries. Although ultimately ambiguous regarding the role and function of the phallus – a position that, on one reading, binds his thinking on sexuality to Merleau-Ponty and Beauvoir who also emphasise the ambiguous "nature" of the phenomena – it appears to either systematically downgrade the feminine position to secondary status or dissolve the problem of sexuality within the question of the structure of the symbolic and, specifically, whether the symbolic requires a foundational anchor point. As a consequence, and although it rejects ontological essentialism and, indeed, insists on the symbolic construction of sexuality, to appear to remove any and all foreclosings, Lacan, nevertheless, once again confines sexuality within a patriarchal logic.

Lacan's work in the 1950s was influential, not only in psychoanalytic theory, but also in relation to the development of poststructuralist thinking on sexuality generally. This, however, brought forth another set of conceptual alterations to structure the debate – some of which drew on Lacan's later work on the real – the most important of which was the rejection of the notion that the symbolic system is anchored in and by a point of reference. By undercutting the logical foundationalism that was understood to support (Lacan's dependence on) the logic of patriarchy, the idea was to remove all ways in which one sexual position could be privileged over another. Indeed, by recuperating the overtly materialist positions proposed by Merleau-Ponty and Beauvoir, Luce Irigaray went further by claiming that, contra Lacan, symbolic systems are grounded in the material differences between the sexes. So, having worked to disarm the logic of patriarchy from within its own premises and, in so doing, demonstrating the historically grounded nature of her critique, Irigaray supplemented this with a reconfiguration of the sexes based on the unique differences inherent in the natural rhythms of each. In so doing, she moved the discussion away from the symbolic sphere to the natural, material one, while also reconfiguring this in terms of processes and flows rather than substances as has traditionally been the case. Her thinking is then an important corrective to Lacan's symbolic account that also brings to the fore the fault line running through the two approaches. However, as noted, Irigaray is somewhat unique in relation to the thinkers discussed because while they tend to undermine ontological essentialism without questioning the logic of patriarchy, she combats the latter by depending on a particular ontological essentialism, albeit one thought in terms of flows and rhythms rather than fixed substances. Although this reveals the heterogeneity inherent in the notion of "essence", it also means that, for all her conceptual innovation, Irigaray continues to think within the essentialist logic – that she also shows is far more heterogeneous than often appreciated – governing the essentialist-patriarchal model of sexuality.

Importantly, Irigaray's structuring of sexual difference around a binary masculine/feminine division brought to the fore the issue of heteronormativity; that is, the way in which the Western tradition has foreclosed sexuality within a masculine/feminine structure and/or taken this structure as the model for all others. This was often ignored or simply uncritically accepted by those who otherwise criticised the essentialist-patriarchal model, but the importance of heteronormativity to the essentialist-patriarchal model extends our understanding of the exclusions and foreclosings inherent in that model and, by extension, the parameters against which any critique of it must pass. If the foreclosure inherent in the essentialist-patriarchal model is to be overcome, the heteronormativity that has also accompanied it – but which has long been ignored – must also be overcome. Doing so required a specific conceptual innovation borne of a geographical alteration from France to America and a linguistic one from French to English.

In particular, Judith Butler insists that it depends upon a particular conceptual alteration away from a direct engagement with the nature of "sexuality" *per se*, to that of gender, which is held to support and generate the former. By claiming that gender is based on an ongoing performative construction, Butler reiterates Lacan's symbolic orientation while criticising Lacan's continuing phallogocentrism. Instead of insisting that the construction of gender is structured from the symbolic phallus, Butler maintains that it is based on an open-ended performative construction through and from the iteration of discursive practices and social norms. Importantly, this does not conform to nor is it predefined by a prior model; gender performativity is afoundational and constructed through its doing, with the consequence that its expression is always open.

However, although I argued that Butler explicitly rejects ontological essentialism, the logic of patriarchy, and binary sexual oppositions, and goes on to provide a subtle response to the question of embodiment and materiality, Butler's supposed reliance on social-linguistic performativity brought forth the charge – often based on a reductionist reading – that they give too much weight to socio-linguistic processes to the detriment of material ones. As such, it was held to fall into abstraction. From this premise, Karen Barad insists on the need to ground gender construction, not in symbolic performativity, but on the processes of materialisation understood through Niels Bohr's quantum theory. By showing that materiality is nothing other than a constant queer becoming, in so far as it lacks any identity and moves through random intra-active material jerks, Barad not only rejects the scaffolding supporting any form of ontological essentialism and, indeed, any form of identity, sexually or otherwise, but also calls into question the West's conceptual dependence on logical and materially clear-cut boundaries by insisting on their entangled status. This, in turn, undermines the logic that supports the logic of patriarchy – there simply are no such things as "masculinity" and "femininity" – by pointing to the hybrid and ever-changing nature of sexual expression and, by extension, any privileging of heteronormativity, or, indeed, distinct forms of normativity.

For Barad, each queer form of sexual expression is natural, in so far as it is an expression of the processes inherent in the materialisation of matter, and, importantly, is inherently individual and single. This is not, however, to say that individuals have a single form of sexuality or even that individuals choose their queerness; it makes the stronger claim that because "individuals" are effects of differentiating material processes, they are composed of multiple and queer "sexualities" that are subject to constant change and alteration. It is not possible then to make universal or general(isable) statements about sexuality; it is always queer, expressing itself in distinct and unpredictable ways based on the quantum leaps constituting the material processes subtending "it". Rather than constraining or foreclosing this within predetermined parameters, Barad insists that the queerness of matter must be respected and adhered to, with the consequence that they push us to accept and celebrate the multidimensionality and queerness of sexuality, including our own.

Although this moves us a long way from the fixed predetermined ontological certainties of the essentialist-patriarchal model and, indeed, Freud's initial attempt to break it down by positing an originary ontological bisexuality, the celebration of radical indeterminacy and unpredictability inherent in Barad's quantum queer theory does contain one glaring problem: it deconstructs all foreclosures of sexuality to show that they cannot be supported materially but has nothing to say on why, nevertheless, Western thought has (been able to) insist(ed) on such foreclosings. I argued that this was a consequence of Barad's privileging of the ontological level to the relative lack of any engagement with the normative, political, and juridical dimensions of sexuality that would explain how exclusionary forms of sexuality and sexual expression can be created and sustained despite contradicting their own queer material grounding. Barad's queer theory rejects the foreclosure of sexual expression and, indeed, the attempt to describe sexual expression through any form of identity – a position that, paradoxically, undermines the importance of "sexuality"; after all, there is, strictly speaking, no such "thing" to focus on – to, in so doing, open it up to forms of expression that have long been rejected or excluded. But it achieves this by simply bypassing a number of associated issues or proposing solutions that conflict with a number of its other aspects. For all its deconstructive power, it is therefore marked by lacunae that undermine its explanatory force.

Of course, it could be objected that this is perfectly in keeping with and, indeed, a direct consequence of Barad's insistence on the queer nature of sexual expression; it is so indeterminate, changing, singular, and unpredictable, that it must contain such lacunae. I do not necessarily want to deny that conclusion nor do I want to simply re-instantiate a unitary normative framework to engage with sexuality. One of the great benefits of the move to gender and beyond that to queer is that it removes all foreclosings of sexuality to remind us of its material indeterminancy, fluidity, and indeed inherent singularity. However, although I have much sympathy for this approach, it is also problematic because it threatens to turn sexuality into an effect of anonymous material processes that fails to recognise and so is unable to take into consideration or engage with the collective political and juridical dimensions that affirm socially acceptable forms of sexuality and sexual expression. These are part of the socio-political-ethico-juridical processes through which a collective defines itself, in so far as it outlines the rules and norms by which individuals must live and express themselves in accordance with. Not only does Barad's agential realism appear to deny intentional agency to individuals but it also seems to be unable to explain how the norms, rules, and juridical laws that are conditions of social existence may actually, and potentially necessarily, foreclose sexuality and sexual expression within restrictive (binary) parameters despite such foreclosure contradicting its supposed grounding in and expression of the open-ended queer becoming of matter.

Barad's agential realism leaves us in this position because, despite insisting that sexuality is an expression of multiple material entanglements, which should therefore bring forth a rich engagement with distinct aspects (social, normative, political, juridical, and so on) of sexuality and sexual expression, there is an overwhelming tendency to affirm a fundamentally ontological explanation for sexuality. As such, it tends to reduce sexuality to an ontological phenomenon and, in so doing, continues to affirm a singular approach to "it". Ironically, such a position contains and threatens to reaffirm many of the exclusions that it claims to want to undermine. By grounding sexuality in ontology, Barad's agential realism reminds us that sexuality is open-ended, fluid, wholly singular, and queer, but is unable to adequately explore the political, social, normative, and juridical dimensions of sexuality and sexual expression that shape how sexuality is symbolically created through social codes that delineate acceptable sexual expressions and also, by extension, create sexual (binary) exclusions that contradict the expressive queerness of matter itself. It is, in other words, caught between celebrating and affirming the open-ended material queerness of sexuality, while being unable to adequately explain how such processes have given rise to the exclusionary social, political, normative, and/or juridical discourses on sexuality that have historically dominated.

Moving Forward

The question arising at this point refers to where we go from here. How to respect and stay "true" to the fundamental lesson that has arisen from the historical trajectory charted throughout the previous chapters regarding the absolutely indeterminate, open-ended, singular, expressive becoming of sexuality, all the while recognising the important role that sexuality plays in existence and doing so in a way that does not simply reduce it to one dimension? If there is no fixed foundation to ground sexuality – one of the reasons for the substantial debate that has arisen around "it" – and the issue is, as we have seen, fundamentally multidimensional, constantly moving across different parts which are themselves in constant movement, how are we to engage with the question of sexuality? Indeed, from the previous chapters, it appears that we are caught in something of an antinomy between, on the one hand, insisting that the problem of sexuality is a real one and promising that while previous attempts to capture "it" have been flawed, if we only continue to engage with it and indeed continue to empty it of any determinations we will eventually find the correct answer, one not based on prior exclusions; or, on the other hand, insisting that the long history of failed attempts to get a handle on the issue point to the conclusion that it is a problem without solution or, put differently, a "false" problem – whether because of its inherent complexity or because it simply does not exist as a "thing" to be conceptualised – that must forever evade our conceptual grasp. The optimism of the first option depends upon the possibility that a single answer – even one which claims that sexuality is non-determined – can be given to the question, while the latter option simply abandons the topic, thereby ignoring the fact that the concept exists and so presumably delineates "something" and, indeed, has played a fundamental role in shaping Western thinking and culture.

Although it might be tempting to impale ourselves on the horns of this dilemma, my suggestion – one in keeping with the critique of binary oppositions outlined in previous chapters – is that there is another, far more satisfactory, option that navigates through the Charybdis of foundationalism and the Scylla of abandonment by respecting the afoundationalism, heterogeneity, and complexity that the previous chapters have revealed to surround the problem of sexuality, all the while continuing to treat sexuality as a "real" problem to be engaged. In the first instance, however, this requires a bit of a detour through methodological issues as to how to engage with the question of what it is that we engage with when we talk of "sexuality". That is, it requires that we first turn away from a direct study of sexuality to focus on the question of how to think about sexuality.

Despite their heterogeneity and the differences between them, what unites the various figures discussed throughout the previous chapters is an implicit assumption that "sexuality" is something identifiable that can be studied and conceptualised. Even those claiming that it is open-ended make a definitive claim about sexuality that applies univocally across all its manifestations.

This is not to say that all have agreed on the fundamental characteristic of sexuality, but all have agreed that there is *a* fundamental principle or characteristic that allows us to grasp what sexuality is: bisexuality for Freud, indeterminacy for Heidegger, body for Merleau-Ponty and Beauvoir, the symbolic for Lacan, natural rhythms according to Irigaray, and gender performativity or queer materiality for Butler and Barad respectively. Although these all aim to explicitly undercut the notion that sexuality is fixed, their solutions continue to implicitly operate around a particular conceptual lodestone that has the unintended consequence of shepherding the analysis into a particular conceptual corral. In other words, the attempt to affirm openness and heterogeneity is undermined by the insistence that, regardless of the manifestation, sexuality is undermined by a particular universality: it is *fundamentally* queer, or performative, or ontologically neutral, or bisexual, and so on. This generates substantial philosophical discussion, but my argument is that it continues to be based on a misguided assumption as to what the concept "sexuality" is, tries to do, and by extension what we can say about "it". This approach can, at best, provide certain insights into aspects of a particular configuration of sexuality, but it remains partial because it continues to insist that there is always only one way to approach the issue.

Instead of continuing to try to identify what "sexuality" fundamentally is, as if it could be reduced to a universal feature, my suggestion is that we re-problematise the issue away from the assumption that sexuality delineates a *uni*-versal phenomenon or characteristic defined by a singular approach and, by extension, response, towards one in which "sexuality" is best understood as the concept that collects and so acts as the entry point into a heterogeneous and continuously changing field of distinct vectors, dimensions, concepts, and questions. To start to outline what I have in mind and what this might look like, I take off from an unusual source: the early critical theory of Walter Benjamin. Although not a figure normally associated with questions of sexuality, if only because Benjamin does not directly discuss this issue, in his famous "Epistemo-Critical Forward" to his *Origin of German Trauspiel*,[1] Benjamin does engage with the question of presentation or representation (*Darstellung*) in philosophy – that is, how philosophy is to properly present or represent an issue – to offer us a highly original analysis of concepts as constellations that I will suggest can be used to rethink how we approach the question of sexuality. It is to this, admittedly, highly abstract analysis that I now briefly turn, before returning to tie it to the question(ing) of sexuality.

Benjamin and Ideas as Constellations

For Benjamin, philosophy is unique in that its mode of presentation is an issue for it. Other disciplines tend not worry about how to present their findings because there tends to be a predefined way to do so. Scientific presentation, for example, is premised on and orientated around and from the question of closure, in so far as it aims to present a doctrine outlining the truth of the issue and does so based on the closed and restricted relationship between the premises of its argument and the conclusion generated; a procedure that is also conducted in a sterile, formal, or technical language that aims to avoid any recognition of the complexities and ambiguities of language. Indeed, mathematics explicitly formulates its arguments in technical terms and formal mathematical symbols to avoid the ambiguities of language and, in so doing, supposedly be more precise.[2] In contrast, philosophy is both dependent upon "historical codification"[3] and is intimately connected to the question of language. It is therefore always problematised and opened up. Benjamin's conclusion is that this is because philosophy and science have different ends: whereas the presentation of science is orientated around didactic requirements – with the consequence that it aims to remove ambiguity from the equation – "method in philosophical projects is not just absorbed in their didactic implementation".[4] Philosophical projects do not just aim to present the objective dimension of information about a phenomenon, but are guided by and aim to express "an esoteric dimension [that] inheres in them, a dimension they are incapable of shedding, forbidden to disown – and which, were they ever to boast of it, would condemn them".[5] While scientific forms of presentation aim to offer a systematic analysis of an issue, the system is premised on simply combining elements that present themselves to thought. Scientific doctrine constantly expands itself to bring into the fold "more" bodies and aspects, but it does so in the vain attempt to grasp or identify a "truth" that lies through these external connections. In contrast, Benjamin relies upon a particular ontology to insist that objects cannot be reduced to that which appears or presents itself. There is another "hidden" or implicit dimension to objects that evades conceptual (scientific) thought, but which is fundamental to revealing the "truth" of the object. By avoiding this esoteric dimension, scientific enquiry can provide us with knowledge of the object, but never its truth. Philosophical thought, on the contrary, aims to capture the esoteric "spirit" or dimension that inheres throughout each phenomenon so as to describe its truth, but, by definition, must struggle to do so conceptually. For this reason, philosophy is forced to pay attention to its method of presentation.

Historically, this esoteric dimension has linked philosophy to theological analysis and the mode of presentation occurring through a "'tractatus,' [which] contains a reference, however latent, to those objects of theology without which truth cannot be thought".[6] While the tractatus may have presented a formal doctrine, it was premised on the idea that the fundamental spirit defining the issue, its esoteric dimension, cannot be captured objectively nor can it be presented through a process of formal logic deduction. These texts aim to capture an exuberance that cannot be expressed formally or conceptually, but is that on which such formal conceptuality depends. As such, their tone may be doctrinal, but "in their inmost disposition they are denied the conclusiveness of instruction that could maintain itself, like doctrine, on its own authority".[7] This is not presented like a mathematical proof that aims to prove a particular point because the text is not informative, it is "educative".[8] It aims to change how we think about something. For this reason, the mode of presentation is not incidental or predetermined, but is specific to the material, how it is understood, and how the reader is to receive the underlying message. In turn, this feeds into the issue of how to think; it must be thought about in such a way that its presentation permits the underlying esoteric message to appear. Rather than appearing directly as if the issue were clearly delineated and fully transparent, this dimension appears indirectly. As such, the attempt to educate is premised on and requires a particular mode of presentation: "Method is indirection. Presentation as indirection, as the roundabout way – this, then, is the methodological character of the tractatus."[9] Philosophical presentation renounces "the unbroken course of intention"[10] and "constantly begins anew".[11] It does not unfold through a continuous process, but is constituted by an "intermittent rhythm".[12] In other words, philosophical enquiry does not proceed mechanically to produce a deduced or straightforward direct description of a phenomenon. It is orientated by and around a continuous struggle to grasp and express the phenomenon; a struggle that arises from its endeavour to educate and not simply inform. Rather than a linear movement of progress, philosophical presentation is defined by a stop-start rhythm as it tries to grapple with and express the esoteric dimension that escapes conceptuality.

The obvious difficulty here is that the conceptuality of writing struggles to grasp what is non-conceptual. Speaking overcomes this, in so far as the "speaker makes use of voice and facial expressions to underscore individual sentences – even where they cannot stand on their own – and fuses them into an often fluctuating and vague train of thought".[13] Written presentation does not have that luxury, however. Instead, it struggles to capture and express that which does not lend itself to conceptuality. For Benjamin, this ensures that there is a particular rhythm to philosophical presentation; it cannot be formal or informative, but nor does it have as its goal the desire to "enthrall or excite enthusiasm".[14] Philosophical presentation is orientated, not around entertainment or information, but "reflection".[15] It aims to bring the reader to a point where he/she is brought to reflect on the issue, an activity that again reopens it. This is very distinct from scientific presentation which aims to close thought by capturing the correct answer. By aiming to capture the esoteric dimension and returning to it in different ways and directions, philosophical presentation aims to educate us in how to reflect.

For this reason, philosophy is not concerned with objective phenomena *per se*, but "has ideas as its object".[16] This does not mean that philosophy is divorced from material reality; for Benjamin, materiality and ideality are intimately connected. It simply means that philosophical presentation is concerned with the "presentation of ideas".[17] Even when a philosopher claims to be discussing material being or becoming, the discussion is always concerned with an *idea* of material being or becoming. Those that aim to discuss *pure* materiality, divorced from an ideational component, either fail to recognise their dependence on ideas or reduce philosophy to a scientific form of informational exchange. In either case, however, the stimulus for educative reflection inherent philosophical presentation is absent.

With this, Benjamin introduces an important distinction between "Truth, actualized in the round dance of presented ideas",[18] and "knowledge".[19] "Knowledge is a having",[20] and "[i]ts object is determined by the very fact that it must be held within consciousness – even if it be transcendental consciousness".[21] The object is possessed by knowledge and through such possession it is possible to know it and inform about it. There is a distinct gap between knowledge and its object, which permits the former to take possession of the latter. This proceeds through questioning. However, although this may provide us with *information* about the object under investigation, it is, on Benjamin's telling, unable to ascertain its "truth"[22] because truth is not revealed through questioning. The details behind this claim are rather abstract and technical, but the basic point is that, according to Benjamin, *knowledge* "is oriented to the particular, but not in an unmediated way to its unity".[23] In other words, knowledge orientates itself towards a particular (example) and aims to study that in its particularity. Rather than focus on the wholeness or unity of the object, which would require an engagement with questions of history, language, socio-cultural embeddedness, and so on, and how they intra-relate that would, strictly speaking, extend beyond the parameters of the physical object being studied, knowledge seeks to understand the particular object as it appears in that particular moment and form, which it takes to be the "entire" object. Although he cannot discount the possibility that there exists such a thing as the "unity of knowledge"[24] – that is, that continuous questioning will eventually allow us to know all aspects of the phenomenon – Benjamin claims that this would not actually reveal the "truth" of the object because it would simply be premised on the interconnection of "distinct pieces of knowledge and, to an extent, on their alignment and balancing"[25] which would fail to grasp its esoteric truth. Even if it were possible to collect information about all aspects of the object, such a process would be formal and mechanical and so unlikely to ever reveal the "organic" totality.

While (thought as) *knowledge* is orientated towards disclosure and information about the object, (thought as) *truth* is a very different beast. Truth is orientated, not to the particularities of a thing (its dimensions, qualities, features, and so on), but to the thing itself; or, as Benjamin calls it, its esoteric dimension. Whereas knowledge focuses on a particular object and seeks to understand that object in its particularity, "truth in its essence is determined as a unity in a thoroughly unmediated and direct manner".[26] Its direct access to that unity allows truth to *comprehend* what the thing is immediately. Crucially, however, in distinction to knowledge, "[w]hat is peculiar to this determination as something direct is that it cannot be ascertained through questioning".[27] The reasoning behind this claim is, again, highly abstract, but Benjamin claims that while knowledge exists at a distance from being – it is this that permits thought as knowledge to question its object – truth is intimately connected to being; it is the immediate comprehension of what the thing is (the "eureka" moment if you will). Importantly, Benjamin maintains that as a moment of comprehension, truth is tied to and occurs through ideas. When we comprehend something, we obtain an instant idea of what the thing actually is. For this reason, whereas the relationship between knowledge and being is mediated by concepts and questioning, truth has an unmediated relation to being. With truth, thought and being correspond; there is no gap between them. Because of this, ideas are different to concepts and so truth (tied to the comprehension of ideas) cannot be ascertained conceptually or by extension through questioning – "[T]ruth is beyond all questioning"[28] – which, for Benjamin, depends upon a distance from Being to permit a questioning of Being. But if this is so, how do we ascertain the truth?

Benjamin responds that we need to distinguish between *concepts* that "arise out of the spontaneity of understanding"[29] and *ideas* which "are given to contemplation".[30] Knowledge is tied to concepts that are orientated around the understanding. Truth, however, is not orientated around concepts or the understanding, but is tied to ideas that are comprehended. With this, Benjamin sets up an important distinction between ideas and concepts, in which "[i]deas are something given in advance".[31] Prior to conceptually analysing an object to obtain knowledge about it, there is an idea, or comprehension, about what the object is. That comprehension establishes the parameters for the conceptual investigation. How ideas are comprehended and then conceptualised forms the basis for the different philosophical systems. For this reason, "Plato proposed . . . his theory of ideas, Leibniz . . . his monadology, and Hegel . . . his dialectic".[32] They are distinguished, not at the level of concept, but at the level of the ideas that they each try to impart conceptually.

Benjamin's overall point is that truth is not primarily concerned with concepts or a conceptual level of analysis that aims to inform about an object; truth is concerned with the immediate comprehension of the idea of the thing. That idea, in turn, creates the non-conceptual parameters that delineate the framework through which the object is conceptualised. The key, however, is that the idea does not emanate from the object of study; the object of study is only ever the *idea* of the object or the *comprehension* of that object, which provide(s) the horizon that makes possible conceptual thought of it. Philosophical enquiry does not deal with objects *per se*, it deals with the ideas, or comprehension, of objects. Orientated through reflection, thought obtains an immediate comprehension of the truth, or idea, of the object. The comprehension of the object – what the object is, how to think about it, and so on – as manifested through the idea (of it), must however be presented and is, philosophically, through conceptual analysis. However, the difference between the non-conceptuality of ideas and conceptual thought means that the truth (i.e. idea) can never fully appear conceptually. Ideas exist beyond concepts and so, in a sense, their expression requires a contraction of the idea for it to be expressed conceptually. Conceptual thought, however, is not satisfied with such a partial exposition; it aims to gain knowledge of the idea and so wants to capture its truth. To do so, it thinks that it can examine the idea from different perspectives and directions so that the conceptual "presentation of an idea makes that idea manifest as a configuration of concepts".[33]

As noted, however, Benjamin rejects this: it would be a grave mistake to think that by looking at an idea from a variety of different perspectives thought can somehow simply combine them to understand the truth of the object. This accumulative understanding of "truth" is flawed as it focuses only on the relationship between its external components and does not really understand or reveal the "esoteric" dimension of truth, which is the domain of the ideas. Rather than lament the fact that ideas cannot be reduced to a singular conceptual sense or meaning or adopt an accumulative conception of truth, Benjamin affirms an alternative pathway, in which the very nature of conceptuality itself is questioned and altered. Rather than corresponding to or expressing a homogeneous meaning or concept, ideas are "constellations".[34] More specifically, "ideas present themselves not in themselves but solely in a correlation of the elements of things in the concept – indeed, as the configuration of these elements".[35]

To develop this, Benjamin offers the following analogy: "Ideas are to things as constellations to stars."[36] Constellations of stars are constituted in such a way that patterns, while not necessarily existing, can be read into their various positions or relations, thereby giving rise to the appearance of order and meaning. How that order is generated depends upon how the stars are configured in relation to one another and the capacity to see or imagine the connections in such a way that a figure arises. That figure, of course, never strictly speaking exists, but is read through the relations between the stars. Ideas are premised on the same logic. They are not actually anything, but are recognised, if at all, only because their component parts (concepts) are taken to form a particular identity or meaning. Change the perception or the component parts and the idea disappears or takes on an alternative ideational form. For this reason, ideas are "neither their concepts nor their laws"[37] nor "do [they] serve the knowledge of phenomena, and in no way can the latter be the criterion determining the existence of ideas".[38] They are what arises from the perception of the relations between the component pieces. Indeed, the "meaning of phenomena for ideas is exhausted in their conceptual elements".[39] What the phenomenon is depends upon how it is presented, which depends upon how its components are held to relate to one another. There is never simply one concept that can describe the totality of the idea nor is there one way to bind the constellation together because (1) conceptual thought is a contraction of ideas, and (2) ideas are constellations of concepts. Indeed, strictly speaking, for Benjamin, there is not an object that exists apart from the constellation; to study the constellation's parts *is* to study what the object is. Looking ahead, this means that "sexuality" *is* only the term we use to describe a particular combination of concepts.

Because ideas are transmitted through concepts, changing the concept focused on or its relation to others also changes the idea that is to be expressed. If I use the words (concepts) "God" or "light" to describe a higher being (idea), the combination of the two does not bring us closer to describing the same idea; describing the idea as "God" offers a very different idea than if I use the word "light". Put differently, using "God" or "light" describes different ideas; they do not provide different perspectives on the same idea, nor, strictly speaking, am I describing the "same" idea through each. After all, not only are the concepts ("God" and "light") different, but they have different components, histories, contexts, senses, and so on, that impact on how they are understood, which, in turn, shapes the idea that is transmitted through them.

Furthermore, how the constellation is read – the parts that we focus on and how they are conceptualised and joined – impacts on and shapes not just how the idea is conceptualised but also what it actually is. To focus on one part of the constellation means that the constellation takes shape from and around that point; what it is therefore is shaped from that privileging, one that changes if another part of the constellation is emphasised. For this reason, ideas are not uniform or undifferentiated, nor is the idea a meaningful core surrounded by components that when properly constructed, reconstruct or represent the definitive core or meaning of the idea. "The idea can be described as the formation of the nexus in which the uniquely occurring extreme stands with its like."[40] Rather than simple monads that can be described by a single concept, ideas are fields in which "the phenomena are simultaneously divided out and saved".[41] They "constitute an irreducible multiplicity".[42] However, the nexus does not just exist as an empty "virtual arrangement of phenomena".[43] It must be brought to existence and is by being designated and singled out through a name. In the previous example, the name "God" is the term for the nexus point through which a particular constellation of concepts, intent on expressing an idea, is brought forth. It is by being named that the idea comes to exist and exists as a constellation of concepts. "God", the concept, does not then name a being; it names the nexus point of a constellation of concepts that aim to express a particular idea. In the next section, I suggest that "sexuality" fulfils the same function. It is to this that I now turn.

Sexuality as Constellation

Benjamin's analysis of concept-constellations offers us a very different way to think about sexuality than those approaches that are guided, however implicitly, by the assumption that it is "something" that we can attempt to gain knowledge about and/or which attempt to do so by reducing it to a universal characteristic, determination, or approach. In the first instance, his analysis reveals that discussions of sexuality refer not to a particular concrete phenomenon, but to an idea about that phenomenon. For example, the essentialist-heteronormative-patriarchal model does not describe sexuality *per se*, but operates with an *idea* about what sexuality is – sexuality is necessarily defined by a male/female division, where each sex is defined by unchanging essential characteristics, with the male privileged – and then reads phenomena through that idea so that they are interpreted in accordance with that idea. While the authors engaged with in the various chapters are critical of the idea of sexuality supporting the essentialist-heteronormative-patriarchal model, they too are guided by an idea about sexuality that they then seek to outline conceptually.

The problem, however, is that, despite rejecting the fixidity inherent in the essentialist-patriarchal-heteronormative model to open sexuality up to different expressions, each of the authors engaged with in the preceding chapters continues to implicitly privilege one fundamental dimension, property, or characteristic of sexuality. For Freud, all forms of sexuality are fundamentally bisexuality; for Heidegger and Merleau-Ponty, sexuality is fundamentally ontologically neutral "before" being expressed ontically; for Beauvoir, Lacan, and Irigaray, sexuality is always socio-historical, symbolic, or premised on natural differences; while Butler and Barad hold that it is always either a gender performativity or a queer materiality. Admittedly, the thinking of Butler and Barad is far more open to different expressions than that of Freud or even Irigaray, but in each instance the enquiry is implicitly guided by the attempt to determine *what* sexuality is, which leads to the positing of a universal response that claims that, regardless of the actual sexual expression, it is understandable or must be thought about in a singular way; one that accords with the idea about sexuality that subtends the particular thinker's analysis (bisexuality in Freud, symbolic in Lacan, gender for Butler, and so on). I am not necessarily disagreeing with their analyses or the general conceptual movement that occurs across their theories, in which the restrictive parameters of the essentialist-patriarchal-heteronormative model of sexual expression are emptied out and opened up, but I am arguing that these approaches continue to be problematically one-dimensional in so far as they continue to implicitly claim that there is one characteristic or response to the question of sexuality that expresses what "sexuality" fundamentally is across all its expressions. By continuing to insist on one fundamental approach to the topic, they reduce sexual expression to their particular privileged idea of sexuality, all the while insisting on a universality to sexuality.

In contrast, Benjamin's notion of concept-constellations points to the "idea" that the concept "sexuality" describes, not a universal substance, characteristic, or dimension, but a singular point of inflection that collects, binds, and expresses a variety of different issues and questions and indeed responses to them. Rather than a "thing" that corresponds to an actual entity, "sexuality" is the empty lodestone, or the name, through which the constellation of component parts constituting each worldview is revealed to conceptual thought. In other words, "sexuality" describes a nexal function through which the constellation of concepts that support and generate it inflect to reveal themselves. Or, put differently, "sexuality" delineates not a thing to be identified, but a horizontal field across which the constellation of questions and concepts generating what we name as sexuality play out. When we study or investigate "sexuality" we are not then studying a substance, but in a sense are "using" the term "sexuality" to engage with a conglomeration of different parts, including philosophical, juridical, social, ethical, or political concepts and questions, which we can read as coalescing into a worldview that we, for shorthand, call (name) "sexuality".

In terms of sexual expression, this means, rather radically, that there *is* no such thing as "sexuality" *per se*. "Sexuality" is simply the name given to describe a constellation of concepts, and, by extension, a particular notion of "sexuality" is only ever the name given to that particular constellation. "Sexuality" is not distinct from its constellation, but is the name for the constellation. To study "sexuality" therefore is not to engage with "something" that exists apart from its constellating parts; to study "sexuality" is only ever to study its constellating parts. Two consequences result. First, "sexuality" is not distinct from its component parts but is the name for the nexal point through which those constellating parts coalesce to express themselves conceptually. Second, if the constellation is termed "sexuality", and the constellation is by definition composed of relations between different parts which are themselves always changing, then no two constellations and by extension no two forms of "sexuality" can ever be the same. Furthermore, "a" constellation of sexuality is never static. Putting these points together, we see that, in some instances, the constellation may manifest itself bisexually, in others gender performatively, in others still in terms of queerness, others heterosexuality, and so on, while it is equally possible that the constellation may change over the course of a life so that sexual expression changes however ephemerally, while in others it may not. The point is that the meaning of each constellation depends upon how the constellating parts are grouped together and understood, while, in any case, each constellation and by extension expression of sexuality is an absolute fluid multiplicity based on the particular constellation of components parts that generate and sustain it in each moment.

While this indicates how Benjamin's notion of concept-constellation alters how we understand sexual expression, it also has implications for how we investigate "it". Rather than being able to maintain that "sexuality" refers to a universal dimension of (human) existence or entails a singular meaning, Benjamin's notion of concept-constellation indicates that the notion, or name "sexuality", arises from the attempt to give identity to a constellation of concepts. The identity (which itself is premised on conceptuality), however, always fails to express the idea it aims to expound. Furthermore, when we engage with a concept, in this case "sexuality", we tend to do so by focusing on one constellating part; a focus that allows us to get started but which should never be taken to be the end point. Not only does this mean that we need to be wary as to how we read the constellation – Which aspects do we focus on? Is there a privileged point through which we outline it? and so on – so as to not reduce the constellation to our understanding of it, but we should also be wary of reading a constellation of "sexuality" through one lens. For example, it might be thought that the ongoing critique of the essentialist-patriarchal-heteronormative model is premised on the affirmation of sexual equality, whether that is between sexes or sexual practices and expressions. While this might be an aspect of it, so that engaging with the question of "sexuality" through the lens of equality may bring to light aspects of the former, doing so reduces the constellation supporting "sexuality" to the question of equality and most probably one form of equality, such as political or economic or social or equality of identity, and forgets or rather ignores other dimensions that may not be compatible with an equality focus. For example, we could say that a notion of "sexuality" is dependent upon, at a minimum, responses to a constellation of questions including those relating to (1) identity, such as what is the self, how to understand sexual difference, questions of consent and free will, desire; (2) law, such as what are socially acceptable forms of sexual expression, sanctions for breaking those, which are in turn tied to questions of power, right, and so on; (3) economics, to do with distribution of resources and access to resources; (4) culture and history, to do with the values of the society, symbolic structures, means of expression, and so on; (5) politics, regarding self-responsibility (age of consent), reproductive rights, recognition (marriage); and (6) normativity, regarding how we should act. Each one of these may touch on questions of "equality", or, put differently, engaging with the question of sexual equality may bring us to engage with each of these areas, but it does so from the lens of "equality" to give us an understanding of "sexuality" from that constellating point. If, however, we were to focus on the question of (sexual) "identity" (for example), not only would we not necessarily have to reach the question of equality – we would engage the question of "sexuality" differently as we would be constructing and reading the constellation differently – but it would generate a very different conception of "sexuality". For Benjamin, these cannot be accumulated to gradually build up our understanding of "sexuality" *per se*. They only ever give us an understanding of *a* constellation; that is, the constellation "sexuality" read through the constellating point of "equality" provides us with a completely different constellation and hence conception of "sexuality" than one based on "identity". Alterations to one of these complicated, multiple dimensions and questions changes the structure and form of the constellation and by extension the expression of sexuality generated.

Constellations are not then static so that we could enquire into their different aspects to gradually and accumulatively build up an understanding of "sexuality" by individually examining each of their constellating parts. A constellation is not a closed whole but an open-ended field wherein each of its parts is linked to a multiplicity of others. Focusing on one dimension at a time ignores the ways in which that dimension itself is a constellation and so constantly changes, which in turn alters all the constellations it forms. Furthermore, we cannot gradually build up a complete picture of a constellation nor think that each constellation provides insights into the "same" thing, as if they were all orientated to the same phenomenon. We do not just look at something called "sexuality" from a political or social or economic direction and combine them all to better understand "sexuality" as a socio-political-economic "thing".

For this reason, sexuality as constellation contains important differences from Patricia Hill Collins's version of intersectionality.[44] Collins's analysis is interesting and important because it engages with the ontological and epistemological assumptions founding (her conception of) intersectionality to, in so doing, start to engage with and outline its theoretical assumptions. Collins's claim that relationality is fundamental for intersectionality is of particular interest because relationality is also constitutive of sexuality as constellation. This does however bring forth the question of the type of relationality at play. In response, Collins distinguishes between "relationality through addition, articulation, and co-formation"[45] to initially claim that "Relationality through co-formation lies at the heart of intersectionality itself",[46] before ultimately concluding that each form of relationality is a viable option for and so has a role to play in intersectional analyses.[47] Collins appears therefore to leave us in a situation where intersectionality is tied to vastly different forms of relationality. While this opens up the possible ways in which intersectionally can function, it not only calls into question its explanatory force – When, for example, is it legitimate to think in terms of each form of relationality and indeed what legitimises that criteria? – but also its coherency; after all, the forms of relationality that Collins accepts are disjunctive not complementary. For these reasons, sexuality as constellation departs from Collins's position in fundamental ways.

First, while Collins accepts the importance and validity of relationality as additive, sexuality as constellation is not additive. This difference is based on an ontological disagreement. Collins's notion of relationality as additive depends upon a monadic conception of components wherein categories (race, sex, gender, and so on) are added together to build up a more complex understanding of the phenomena. This not only treats categories, such as sex and race, as homogeneous, but it risks reintroducing a foundational logic to the analysis which opens up the question as to the originary starting point from which additional components are added: Is sex the foundational position to which gender and class are subsequently added or is it gender or some other category that founds the others? This not only risks, as Collins recognises, returning the analysis to a singular foundational "master point",[48] but also reduces the additional points to contingent supplements to that originary position. This implicit return to a foundational position seems to contradict one of the core tenets of intersectionality, which I take to be that entities cannot be engaged with in isolation. Collins responds to this issue not by calling into question the logic of addition and its grounding in ontological monadism, but by claiming that, rather than adding all components together at once, it would be better to do so "over time rather than than at one point in time".[49] Her point is that "Theoretically, one can add together gender, race, and class in any order. But practically, the sequence in which one adds a particular category to others matters."[50] This however seems to miss the point. The issue is not how you sequence the categories; the problem is with the notion that the categories can in fact be sequenced. Collins's notion of relational addition is based on a logic of purity which, in turn, is tied to an originary ontological monadism, wherein the categories exist as (homogeneous) monads to be placed in (different) sequence(s). In contrast, the constellation theory developed here rejects that monadic logic; categories are not homogeneous, nor can they simply be picked up and studied or added to others. Categories, such as sex, are not singular monads but are effects of constellations of various "parts", which themselves are constellations. *Pace* Collins, sexuality cannot be understood by simply adding various parts together to gradually build up an analysis; sexuality as constellation is a singular, organic, and constantly changing expression of intra-connected "parts". Sex and class do not constitute separate entities that combine to produce a more complex entity; sex and class, themselves constellations, form a particular constellation that reveals a particular form of sexuality. Separating the parts to study them does not reveal the constellation, it fundamentally changes it and them.

Indeed, Benjamin's notion of concept-constellation teaches us that to look at "sexuality" from a political or social or economic direction is to talk of a fundamentally different "sexuality" each time: enquiries that engage with the constellation "sexuality" through the political constellating point offer a very different account of "sexuality" to those that construct the constellation from a social or economic or juridical one. In turn, a social account of "sexuality" focuses on different dimensions and orders the constellation in a different way to generate a different nexus and hence "sexuality" than does a juridical conception of "sexuality". There may appear to be some overlap between the privileged points so that a social conception of "sexuality" will likely touch on juridical issues, but what the "juridical" means will be different for each constellation. How the "social" perceives the "juridical" will be different to how the "political" does. The way in which the constellation is engaged alters the shape and hence meaning of the constellation and so leads to very different conceptions of "sexuality". With this, the logic of Benjamin's position reveals the fundamental irreducibility of different conceptions of "sexuality"; each is organised through and expresses a unique constellation, even as they commonly name it "sexuality". To examine the constellation through a different lens of that constellation does not lead to or elucidate the same subject or notion of sexuality; each lens into "the" constellation reconstitutes the constellation and so brings forth a different entity, in this case sexuality.

Second, the monadic premises supporting Collins's position come to the fore in her notion of relationality as co-formation. On first glance, this might appear to undermine my claim that Collins depends on an originary monadism; if parts are co-formed, they would appear to necessarily intersect and so form one another mutually. The problem, however, lies in how Collins understands co-formation. This is not based on co-*constitution*, where the being of each category is conditioned by the other in the relation. It is based on the idea that categories pre-exist their relationality as separate entities – as Collins puts it: "It's meaningless to argue that race and gender co-form one another without assuming that they are separate entities"[51] – that subsequently (can) come into contact with one another and, in so doing, affect their (subsequent) *formation*. The co-forming that takes place is of a purely external variety, which is presumably why Collins can also claim that co-formation is consistent with addition. Returning to Barad's distinction between inter-action and intra-action, Collins's position is premised on *inter*-relationality, which depends upon pre-existing entities coming into relation with one another. In turn, this ties into Collins's affirmation of a holism within which each monadic position exists and in which each is brought into relation with one another. In so doing, Collins reveals that the ontology underpinning her position is premised on the parts/whole division.[52]

In contrast, the constellation theory developed here is based on a notion of relationality emanating from Barad's notion of *intra*-action. As outlined in Chapter 8, whereas *inter*-action "assumes that there are separate individual agencies that precede their interaction ... intra-action recognizes that distinct agencies do not precede, but rather emerge through, their intra-action".[53] Rather than existing as monadic entities that subsequently *inter*-act with one another within an overarching holism, *intra*-action shows how things come to be through their ongoing, open-ended ontologically entangled becoming. Sexuality as constellation is not then premised on an originary monadism or a logic of addition, nor is it defined by a parts/whole division; it is premised on *intra*-relationality, which holds that far from being something homogeneous and distinct from other aspects in a way that allows them to subsequently be added together or put in relation, categories such as class, gender, race, and so on, are constantly changing and, indeed, come to be through their open-ended ontological entangled becoming. Based on Barad's distinction between interaction and intraction, Collins's notion of *inter*-sectionality continues to implicitly insist that component pieces pre-exist and so come into contact with one another. In contrast, sexuality as constellation follows Barad's notion of *intra*-action to look at the ways in which the components of each constellation are composed of ontologically entangled becomings that become through one another not simply in relation to one another. The various elements of the constellation are not additive or externally related to one another; they *intra*-act to bring forth the constellation. It is because of the particularity of each ontological becoming that each constellation is unique and changing. In turn, it is because of the particularlity of each ontological becoming that each form of sexuality is unique and changing.

This goes a long way to explaining the heterogeneity of the critical engagements outlined throughout this book: each thinker or perspective focuses on one particular constellating point through which to conduct the enquiry, with the consequence that they not only produce different conceptions of "sexuality", but when they do touch on the "same" issues their reliance on a different conception or reading of the constellation produces fundamental differences. Heidegger's ontological account of "sexuality" is very different to Barad's ontological account. That they focus on the ontological dimension whereas Freud focuses on the psychic dimension again produces different constellations of "sexuality", but, as we saw, even when Freud's psychically-orientated constellation touches on ontological issues, what "ontology" means for him is very different to what it means for Heidegger because the constellation supporting his notion of "ontology" is different, as is the role that they give it in relation to their particular constellation of "sexuality". Benjamin's conception of concepts-as-constellations allows us then to not only explain or engage with the constellation "sexuality" but to also make sense of the contestation and debate that has arisen around "it": the various thinkers discussed previously do not discuss the "same" "thing" – as if "sexuality" were a singular point that they all passed – but different constellations which support and are named "sexuality". As we have seen, this means that what "sexuality" designates for one thinker is not necessarily shared by others.

Benjamin's notion of concept-constellation is radical and important therefore not only because it offers a *critique* of those perspectives that reduce a concept to a unitary dimension, response, or constellation, but also because it provides us with a *hermeneutic meta-tool* to make sense of the substantial *historical* debates that have taken place regarding the "topic". However, his account also has *conceptual* importance, in so far as reading the question of "sexuality" through his notion of concept-constellation means, of necessity, that a questioning of each constellation of "sexuality" must necessarily move beyond itself to shine a light on and bring us to question its constellating points. If "sexuality" is nothing other than its constellating points, focusing on how these dimensions shape and construct an understanding of "sexuality" allows us to both understand that *particular* constellation of "sexuality" and comprehend how the constellating points themselves function to create meaning, life opportunities or exclusions, and so on, in that particular constellation.

Returning to the previous example of "equality" and its relationship to sexuality, Benjamin's analysis insists that the tendency to focus on the question of sexual equality would be problematically reductionist, in so far as it reduces the constellation to one issue. However, by examining a constellation of "sexuality" through the lens of "equality", we can not only say something about the particular constellation being examined, but, of necessity, must also engage with the constellation "equality". To question the constellation "sexuality" through the constellation of "equality" is not then to simply return us to the constellation "sexuality" to enlighten us about "it". It can also bring us to question the constellation that generates and sustains "equality", which in turn will lead us to its constellating parts, and so on. The question of "sexuality" is no longer framed in terms of engaging with "equality" to understand "sexuality"; we also use "sexuality" to examine the constellation "equality." Rather than the first-order question that structures second-order issues – a configuration that has led to a long-standing notion that "sexuality" must be a determined "thing" or foundation for other spheres; for example, the essentialist-patriarchal-heteronormative model is based on the idea that "sexuality" is necessarily bifurcated between "men" and "women" who are defined by definitive characteristics that necessarily require specific responses to questions of ethics, politics, law, and so on, with these responses, in turn, justifying and supporting the originary conception of "sexuality" – "sexuality" becomes a second-order issue dependent upon the responses given to other issues. "Sexuality" is not that to be studied *per se*, but *is* the conceptual lens through which we examine the concepts and philosophical problems upon which it depends. This might include a questioning of how political debate generates meaning, the relationship between political discourse and rights (sexual or otherwise), questions of exclusion and inclusion, issues of distribution of resources, including access to education, free movement, and public access provision, as well as philosophical questions of identity, normative questions relating to social relations, comportment, and questions about what is deemed to be legal, that will also tie into issues of power, culture, language, and so on. As a second-order phenomenon – that is, we only understand "sexuality" once we have a grasp of a host of other issues – "sexuality" is never that which is actually studied. When we study "sexuality" we are actually studying the first-order questions, the constellation, upon which an idea of "sexuality" depends. Benjamin's notion of concept-constellation allows us to recognise this because it conceives that ideas, including "sexuality", are not things but nexus that are organised around and express a particular constellation. Rather than enquiring into something called "sexuality", we only ever engage with its supporting constellation and, from that, bind the constellating parts together in a particular way. "Sexuality" is the name for the nexal point through which the constellation is expressed. There never actually is a questioning of something called "sexuality" *per se*.

Those looking for a universal theory of sexuality to understand "sexuality" will likely be disappointed by both my rejection of such a possible theory and indeed this apparent rather radical downplaying of the problem; after all, sexuality *per se* is no longer the focus as "it" becomes the lens for engaging with its constellating components. Rather than continue to respond to the question of sexuality by conceiving of it as a "thing" to be designated by a universal characteristic or dimension; or, on the other extreme, simply abandoning the question and concept altogether, Benjamin's notion of concept-constellation allows us to maintain the relevance of the question without reducing it to "something" to be determined. Specifically, Benjamin permits us to think of "sexuality" as a complex, moving, multidimensional field. In turn, this requires that we alter the terms of the debate away from the question of what sexuality is to think of it in terms of what it does. By this, I mean that we see the term "sexuality" as fulfilling a role; it does not correspond to an actual thing but operates as (1) a *nexus* that *functions* as the conceptual hinge that contingently binds its subtending constellations of component points, and (2) the lens through which the constellational field that is composed of multidimensional component points (temporally) expresses itself. Reconceived in this way as an empty but "singular" point of inflection that depends upon and brings to the fore a complex field of distinct, often competing, dimensions – at the individual level, these often deal with questions of self-identity and self-expression, and, at the collective level, juridical-political issues regarding, for example, acceptable and ideal forms of sexual expression and social norms, each of which is also tied to a range of ontological, metaphysical, and epistemological questions about what identity is, what we can know, how we should structure social relations, and so on – and the relation between them, that "it" is tied to and, indeed, depends upon, we move beyond the long-standing temptation to frame the question of sexuality in terms of something to be discerned or understood, to a lens that permits us to engage with the raft of issues that support it and, in so doing, open up our understanding of sexuality to its complexity and possibilities. With this, sexuality is in a sense made less important, as it is not actually the focus of study but a proxy for the comprehension of the constellation that sustains and subtends it, while also, somewhat strangely, made more important, as it is used as the proxy through which the comprehension of the constellation supporting it is engaged. Reconceptualising sexuality in this way as a nexal function expressing a constellation opens "it" up by turning "it" into a multidimensional hermeneutic tool that can be used to bring to light and engage with the intricate dynamics of individual and social existence, both independently and in combination, while also reminding us that sexual expression is complex, constantly shifting, and absolutely singular. Ultimately, it is this that provides the question(ing) of sexuality with its ongoing philosophical importance and allure.

Notes

1. Walter Benjamin, *Origin of German Trauspiel*, trans. Howard Eiland (Cambridge, MA: Harvard University Press, 2019), pp. 1–39. Famously, this study was to be Benjamin's *Habilitationsschrift*, the qualification necessary within the German academic system to be permitted to teach at university level, but was rejected – more accurately, Benjamin was recommended to withdraw the study to avoid the embarrassment of rejection – by the University of Frankfurt. Nevertheless, Benjamin published the thesis in 1928 at which time its reputation gradually grew until in the second half of the century it came to be regarded as a highly influential work of philosophical and literary criticism.
2. Ibid., pp. 1–2.
3. Ibid., p. 1.
4. Ibid., p. 2.
5. Ibid., p. 2.
6. Ibid., p. 2.
7. Ibid., p. 2.
8. Ibid., p. 2.
9. Ibid., p. 2.
10. Ibid., p. 3.
11. Ibid., p. 3.
12. Ibid., p. 3.
13. Ibid., pp. 2–3.
14. Ibid., p. 3.
15. Ibid., p. 3.
16. Ibid., p. 4.
17. Ibid., p. 4.

18. Ibid., p. 4.
19. Ibid., p. 4.
20. Ibid., p. 4.
21. Ibid., p. 4.
22. Ibid., p. 5.
23. Ibid., p. 5.
24. Ibid., p. 5.
25. Ibid., p. 5.
26. Ibid., p. 5.
27. Ibid., p. 5.
28. Ibid., p. 5.
29. Ibid., p. 5.
30. Ibid., p. 5.
31. Ibid., p. 6.
32. Ibid., p. 7.
33. Ibid., p. 10.
34. Ibid., p. 10.
35. Ibid., p. 10.
36. Ibid., p. 10.
37. Ibid., p. 10.
38. Ibid., p. 10.
39. Ibid., p. 10.
40. Ibid., p. 11.
41. Ibid., p. 11.
42. Ibid., p. 21.
43. Ibid., p. 10.
44. Patricia Hill Collins, *Intersectionality as Critical Social Theory* (Durham, NC: Duke University Press, 2019). Intersectionality has a juridical origin, in so far as it was coined by Kimberlé Crenshaw in the late 1980s to critique and provide tools to reveal the ways in which US antidiscrimination law, which provided protection against racial discrimination and sexual discrimination, was unable to perceive the specific forms of discrimination that arose when those two categories intersected; in the case examined by Crenshaw that related to the discrimination suffered by black women within a specific working environment. See Kimberlé Crenshaw, "Demarginalizing the Intersection of Race and Sex: A Black Feminist Critique of Antidiscrimination Doctrine, Feminist Theory, and Antiracist Politics", *University of Chicago Legal Forum*, vol. 1989, iss. 1, art. 8, pp. 139–167. Needless to say, interest in and use of intersectional theory has subsequently exploded and, indeed, has moved far beyond the juridical sphere. One consequence of this, however, is that intersectional theory has become extremely heterogeneous. For a history of intersectionality, see Ange-Marie Hancock, *Intersectionality: An Intellectual History* (Oxford: Oxford University Press, 2016).
45. Collins, *Intersectionality as Critical Social Theory*, p. 226.

46. Ibid., p. 244.
47. Ibid., p. 250.
48. Ibid., p. 228.
49. Ibid., p. 229.
50. Ibid., p. 229.
51. Ibid., p. 241.
52. Ibid., pp. 243–244.
53. Karen Barad, *Meeting the Universe Halfway: Quantum Physics and the Entanglement of Matter and Meaning* (Durham, NC: Duke University Press, 2007), p. 33.

BIBLIOGRAPHY

Abbey, Ruth, "Beyond Misogyny and Metaphor: Women in Nietzsche's Middle Period", *Journal of the History of Philosophy*, vol. 34, n. 2, 1996, pp. 233–256.

Adriaenssen, Han Thomas, *Representation and Scepticism from Aquinas to Descartes* (Cambridge: Cambridge University Press, 2019).

Ahmed, Sarah, "Some Preliminary Remarks on the Founding Gestures of the 'New Materialism'", *European Journal of Women's Studies*, vol. 15, n. 1, 2008, pp. 23–39.

Aho, Kevin A., "The Missing Dialogue between Heidegger and Merleau-Ponty: On the Importance of the *Zollikon Seminars*", *Body and Society*, vol. 11, n. 2, 2005, pp. 1–23.

Ainley, Alison, "The Invisible of the Flesh: Merleau-Ponty and Irigaray", *Journal of the British Society for Phenomenology*, vol. 28, n. 1, 1997, pp. 20–29.

Alexander, Anna, "The Eclipse of Gender: Simone de Beauvoir and the *Différance* of Translation", *Philosophy Today*, vol. 41, n. 1, 1997, pp. 112–122.

Althusser. Louis, "Ideology and Ideological State Apparatus (Notes Toward an Investigation)", in *Lenin and Philosophy and Other Essays*, trans. Ben Brewster (New York: Monthly Review Press, 2001), pp. 85–126.

Aquinas. Thomas, *Summa Theologiae*, trans. Fathers of the English Dominican Province (Einsiedeln: Benziger Bros, 1947).

Aristotle, *History of Animals*, trans. d'A. W. Thompson, in *The Complete Works of Aristotle*, edited by Jonathon Barnes (Princeton, NJ: Princeton University Press, 1984), pp. 1702–2174.

——, *Politics*, trans. Ernest Baker, revised by R. F. Stanley (Oxford: Oxford University Press, 1995).

Arp, Kristina, "Beauvoir's Concept of Bodily Alienation", in *Feminist Interpretations of Simone de Beauvoir*, edited by Margaret A. Simmons (University Park, PA: Pennsylvania State University Press, 1995), pp. 161–178.

Ascher, Carol, "Simone de Beauvoir – Mother of Us All", *Social Text*, vol. 6, n. 2, 1987, pp. 107–109.

Augustine, *On the Trinity, Books 8–15*, edited by Gareth B. Mathews, trans. Stephen McKenna (Cambridge: Cambridge University Press, 2002).

Badiou, Alain, *Theory of the Subject*, trans. Bruno Bosteels (London: Continuum, 2009).

Bahovec, Eva D., "Beauviour between Structuralism and 'Aleatory Materialism'", in *A Companion to Simone de Beauvoir*, edited by Laura Hengehold and Nancy Bauer (Oxford: Wiley-Blackwell, 2017), pp. 249–259.

Bailly, Lionel, *Lacan* (London: OneWorld, 2009).

Bannet, Eve Tavor, *Structuralism and the Logic of Dissent* (Urbana, IL: University of Illinois Press, 1989).

Barad, Karen, "Agential Realism: Feminist Interventions in Understanding Scientific Practices", in *Science Studies Reader*, edited by Mario Biagioli (Abingdon: Routledge, 1999), pp. 1–11.

——, "Posthumanist Performativity: Toward an Understanding of How Matter Comes to Matter", *Signs: Journal of Women in Culture and Society*, vol. 28, n. 3, 2003, pp. 801–831.

——, *Meeting the Universe Halfway: Quantum Physics and the Entanglement of Matter and Meaning* (Durham, NC: Duke University Press, 2007).

——, "Quantum Entanglements and Hauntological Relations of Inheritance: Dis/continuities, SpaceTime Enfoldings, and Justice-to-Come", *Derrida Today*, vol. 3, n. 2, 2010, pp. 240–268.

——, "Nature's Queer Performativity", *Kvinder, Køn & Forskning*, vol. 1–2, 2012, pp. 25–53.

——, "Transmaterialities: Trans*/Matter/Reality and Queer Political Imaginings", *GLQ: A Journal of Lesbian and Gay Studies*, vol. 21, n. 2–3, 2015, pp. 387–422.

——, "No Small Mattter: Mushroom Clouds, Ecologies of Nothingness, and Strange Topologies of Spacetimemattering", in *Arts of Living on a Damaged Planet: Ghosts and Monsters of the Anthropocene*, edited by Anna Tsing, Nils Bubandt, Elaine Gan, and Heather Swanson (Minneapolis, MN: Minnesota University Press, 2017), pp. 103–120.

——, "Troubling Time/s and Ecologies of Nothingness: Re-turning, Re-membering, and Facing the Incalculable Atomic Bomb", *New Formations*, n. 92, September 2017, pp. 56–86.

——, "After the End of the World: Entangled Nuclear Colonialisms, Matters of Force, and the Material Force of Justice", *Theory & Event*, vol. 22, n. 3, 2019, pp. 524–550.

Barad, Karen, and Daniela Gandorfer, "Political Desirings: Yearnings for Mattering (,) Differently", *Theory & Event*, vol. 24, n. 1, 2021, pp. 14–66.

Barad, Karen, and Adam Kleinman, "Intra-actions", *Mousse*, vol. 34, summer, 2012, pp. 76–81.
Barad, Karen, Malou Juelskjær, and Nete Schwennesen, "Intra-active Entanglements: An Interview with Karen Barad", *Kvinder, Køn & Forskning*, vol. 1–2, 2012, pp. 10–24.
Barbaras, Renaud, *The Being of the Phenomenon: Merleau-Ponty's Ontology*, trans. Ted Toadvine and Leonard Lawler (Bloomington, IN: Indiana University Press, 2004).
Bartky, S. L., "Originative Thinking in the Later Philosophy of Heidegger", *Philosophy and Phenomenological Review*, vol. 30, n. 3, 1970, pp. 368–381.
Bauer, Nancy, "Beauvoir's Heideggerian Ontology", in *The Philosophy of Simone de Beauvoir: Critical Essays*, edited by Margaret A. Simons (Bloomington, IN: Indiana University Press, 2006), pp. 65–91.
——, "Simone de Beauvoir on Motherhood and Destiny", in *A Companion to Simone de Beauvoir*, edited by Laura Hengehold and Nancy Bauer (Oxford: Wiley-Blackwell, 2017), pp. 146–159.
Beauvoir, Simone de, "Jean-Paul Sartre", in *Philosophical Writings*, edited by Mary Beth Marder (Urbana, IL: University of Illinois Press, 2004), pp. 229–234.
——, *The Second Sex*, trans. Constance Borde and Sheila Malovany-Chevallier (New York: Vintage, 2011).
——, *The Ethics of Ambiguity*, trans. Bernard Frechtman (New York: Open Road, 2018).
Benhabib, Seyla, "Subjectivity, Historiography, and Politics", in Seyla Benhabib, Judith Butler, Drucilla Cornell, and Nancy Fraser, *Feminist Contentions: A Philosophical Exchange* (Abingdon: Routledge, 1995), pp. 107–126.
Benjamin, Walter, *Origin of German Trauspiel*, trans. Howard Eiland (Cambridge, MA: Harvard University Press, 2019).
Björk, Ulrika, "Paradoxes of Femininity in the Philosophy of Simone de Beauvoir", *Continental Philosophy Review*, vol. 43, n. 1, 2010, pp. 39–60.
Borch-Jacobsen, Mikkel, *Lacan: The Absolute Master*, trans. Douglas Brick (Stanford, CA: Stanford University Press: 1991).
Bordo, Susan, *Unbearable Weight, Feminism, Western Culture, and the Body* (Berkeley, CA: University of California Press, 1993).
Boucher, Geoff, "Judith Butler's Postmodern Existentialism: A Critical Analysis", *Philosophy Today*, vol. 48, n. 4, 2004, pp. 355–369.
Braddock, Matthew, "A Critique of Simone de Beauvoir's Existential Ethics", *Philosophy Today*, vol. 51, n. 3, 2007, pp. 303–311.
Braidotti, Rosi (ed.), *After Poststructuralism: Transformations and Transitions* (Abingdon: Routledge, 2013).

Brennan, Teresa, *The Interpretation of the Flesh: Freud and Femininity* (Abingdon: Routledge, 1992).
Brodribb, Somer, *Nothing Mat(t)ers: A Feminist Critique of Postmodernism* (New York: New York University Press, 1992).
Burke, Carolyn, "Irigaray through the Looking Glass", *Feminist Studies*, vol. 7, n. 2, 1981, pp. 288–306.
Butler, Judith, "Sex and Gender in Simone de Beauvoir's *Second Sex*", *Yale French Studies*, vol. 72, 1986, pp. 35–49.
——, "Sexual Ideology and Phenomenological Description: A Feminist Critique of Merleau-Ponty's Phenomenology of Perception", in *The Thinking Muse: Feminism and Modern French Philosophy*, edited by Jeffner Allen and Iris Marion Young (Bloomington, IN: Indiana University Press, 1989), pp. 85–100.
——, *Bodies that Matter: On the Discursive Limits of "Sex"* (Abingdon: Routledge, 1993).
——, "Contingent Foundations", in Seyla Benhabib, Judith Butler, Drucilla Cornell, and Nancy Fraser, *Feminist Contentions: A Philosophical Exchange* (Abingdon: Routledge, 1995), pp. 35–58.
——, *Excitable Speech: A Politics of the Performative* (Abingdon: Routledge, 1997).
——, *The Psychic Life of Power: Theories in Subjection* (Stanford, CA: Stanford University Press, 1997).
——, *Gender Trouble: Feminism and the Subversion of Identity*, Second edition (Abingdon: Routledge, 1999).
——, *Subjects of Desire: Hegelian Reflections in Twentieth-Century France* (New York: Columbia University Press, 1999).
——, "Beside Oneself: On the Limits of Sexual Autonomy", in *Undoing Gender* (Abingdon: Routledge, 2004), pp. 17–39.
——, "Gender Regulations", in *Undoing Gender* (Abingdon: Routledge, 2004), pp. 40–56.
——, "Introduction: Acting in Concert", in *Undoing Gender* (Abingdon: Routledge, 2004), pp. 1–16.
——, "The End of Sexual Difference", in *Undoing Gender* (Abingdon: Routledge, 2004), pp. 174–203.
——, "The Question of Social Transformation", in *Undoing Gender* (Abingdon: Routledge, 2004), pp. 204–231.
——, *Giving an Account of Oneself* (New York: Fordham University Press, 2005).
——, *Precarious Life: The Powers of Mourning and Violence* (London: Verso, 2006).
——, *Frames of War: When Life is Grievable?* (London: Verso, 2009).
——, "Performative Agency", *Journal of Cultural Economy*, vol. 3, n. 2, 2010, pp. 147–161.

———, "How Can I Deny that these Hands and this Body are Mine?", in *Senses of the Subject* (New York: Fordham University Press, 2015), pp. 17–35.

———, "Introduction", in *Senses of the Subject* (New York: Fordham University Press, 2015), pp. 1–16.

Butler, Judith, Pheng Cheah, Drucilla Cornella, and Elizabeth Grosz, "The Future of Sexual Difference: An Interview with Judith Butler and Drucialla Cornell", *Diacritics*, vol. 28, n. 1, 1998, pp. 19–42.

Carmen, Taylor, *Merleau-Ponty* (Abingdon: Routledge, 2008).

———, "Between Empiricism and Intellectualism", in *Merleau-Ponty: Key Concepts*, edited by Rosalyn Diprose and Jack Reynolds (Abingdon: Routledge, 2014), pp. 44–56.

Cartwright, David E., *Schopenhauer: A Biography* (Cambridge: Cambridge University Press, 2010).

Cerda-Rueda, Alejandro, "Introduction", in *Sex and Nothing: Bridges from Psychoanalysis to Philosophy*, edited by Alejandro Cerda-Rueda (London: Karnac, 2016), pp. xi–xx.

Changfoot, Nadine, "Transcendence in Simone de Beauvoir's *The Second Sex*: Revisiting Masculinist Ontology", *Philosophy and Social Criticism*, vol. 35, n. 4, 2009, pp. 391–410.

Chanter, Tina, *Ethics of Eros: Irigaray's Rewriting of the Philosophers* (Abingdon: Routledge, 1995).

———, "The Problematic Normative Assumptions of Heidegger's Ontology", in *Feminist Interpretations of Martin Heidegger*, edited by Nancy J. Holland and Patricia Huntington (University Park, PA: Pennsylvania State University Press, 2001), pp. 73–108.

———, *Gender* (London: Continuum, 2006).

Chasseguet-Smirgel, Janine, "Freud and Female Sexuality: The Consideration of Some Blind Spots in the Exploration of the 'Dark Continent'", *International Journal of Psychoanalysis*, vol. 57, 1976, pp. 275–286.

Cheah, Pheng, and Elizabeth Grosz, "Of Being-Two: Introduction", *Diacritics*, vol. 28, n. 1, 1998, pp. 3–18.

Chiesa, Lorenzo, *The Not-Two: Logic and God in Lacan* (Cambridge, MA: The MIT Press, 2016).

Clack, Beverley, *Misogyny in the Western Philosophical Tradition* (Basingstoke: Palgrave Macmillan, 1999).

Clark, Judith (ed.), *Feminist Interpretations of Augustine* (University Park, PA: Pennsylvania State University Press, 2007).

Clough, Patricia Ticineto, "Introduction", in *The Affective Turn: Theorizing the Social*, edited by Patricia Ticineto Clough and Jean Halley (Durham, NC: Duke University Press, 2007), pp. 1–33.

Cohler, Bertram J., and Robert M. Galatzer-Levy, "Freud, Anna, and the Problem of Female Sexuality", *Psychoanalytic Inquiry*, vol. 28, n. 1, 2008, pp. 3–26.
Collins, Patricia Hill, *Intersectionality as Critical Social Theory* (Durham, NC: Duke University Press, 2019).
Coole, Diana, *Merleau-Ponty and Modern Politics after Anti-Humanism* (Lanham, MD: Rowman & Littlefield, 2007).
Coole, Diana, and Samantha Frost (eds), *New Materialisms: Ontology, Agency, and Politics* (Durham, NC: Duke University Press, 2010).
Copjec, Joan, *Read my Desire: Lacan against the Historicists* (London: Verso, 2015).
Crenshaw, Kimberlé, "Demarginalzing the Intersection of Race and Sex: A Black Feminist Critique of Antidiscrimination Doctrine, Feminist Theory, and Antiracist Politics", *University of Chicago Legal Forum*, vol. 1989, iss. 1, art. 8, pp. 139–167.
Crockett, Clayton, *Derrida after the End of Writing: Political Theology and New Materialism* (New York: Fordham University Press, 2017).
Daigle, Christine, "Unweaving the Threads of Influence: Beauvoir and Sartre", in *A Companion to Simone de Beauvoir*, edited by Laura Hengehold and Nancy Bauer (Oxford: Wiley-Blackwell, 2017), pp. 260–270.
Davidson, Arnold I., *The Emergence of Sexuality: Historical Epistemology and the Formation of Concepts* (Cambridge, MA: Harvard University Press, 2001).
Dean, Tim, *Beyond Sexuality* (Chicago, IL: University of Chicago Press, 2000).
DeCrane, Susanne, *Aquinas, Feminism, and the Common Good* (Washington, DC: Georgetown University Press, 2004).
Deleuze, Gilles, *Difference and Repetition*, trans. Paul Patton (New York: Columbia University Press, 1994).
Derrida, Jacques, "Structure, Sign, and Play in the Discourse of the Human Sciences", in *Writing and Difference*, trans. Alan Bass (Abingdon: Routledge, 1978), pp. 351–370.
——, *Of Grammatology: Corrected Edition*, trans. Gayatri Chakravorty Spivak (Baltimore, MD: The Johns Hopkins University Press, 1997).
——, "For the Love of Lacan", in *Resistances of Psychoanalysis*, trans. Peggy Kamuf, Pascale-Anne Brault, and Michael Naas (Stanford, CA: Stanford University Press, 1998), pp. 39–69.
——, *Of Hospitality: Anne Dufourmantelle Invites Jacques Derrida to Respond*, trans. Rachel Bowlby (Stanford, CA: Stanford University Press, 2000).
——, "*Geschlecht I*: Sexual Difference, Ontological Difference", trans. Ruben Bevezdivin and Elizabeth Rottenberg, in *Psyche: Inventions of the Other, volume 2*, edited by Peggy Kamuf and Elizabeth Rottenberg (Stanford, CA: Stanford University Press, 2008), pp. 7–26.

Descartes, René, "Meditations on First Philosophy", in *Discourse on Method and Meditations on First Philosophy*, Fourth edition, trans. Donald A. Cress (Indianapolis, IN: Hackett, 1998), pp. 59–103.

Deutscher, Penelope, *A Politics of Impossible Difference: The Later Work of Luce Irigaray* (Ithaca, NY: Cornell University Press, 2002).

DeVun, Leah, *The Shape of Sex: Nonbinary Gender from Genesis to the Renaissance* (New York: Columbia University Press, 2021).

Dillon, Martin C., "Merleau-Ponty on Existential Sexuality: A Critique", *Journal of Phenomenological Psychology*, vol. 11, n. 1, 1980, pp. 67–81.

——, *Merleau-Ponty's Ontology*, Second edition (Evanston, IL: Northwestern University Press, 1998).

Direk, Zeynep, "Simone de Beauvoir's Relation to Hegel's Absolute", in *A Companion to Simone de Beauvoir*, edited by Laura Hengehold and Nancy Bauer (Oxford: Wiley-Blackwell, 2017), pp. 198–210.

Dosse, François, *History of Structuralism, Volume 2: The Sign-Sets, 1967–Present*, trans. Deborah Glassman (Minnesota, MN: University of Minnesota Press, 1997).

Ellenzweig, Sarah, and John H. Zammito (eds), *The New Politics of Materialism: History, Philosophy, Science* (Abingdon: Routledge, 2017).

Escudero, Jesus Adrian, "Heidegger and the Hermeneutics of the Body", *International Journal of Gender and Women's Studies*, vol. 3, n. 1, 2015, pp. 16–25.

Eyers, Tom, "Lacanian Materialism and The Question of The Real", *Cosmos and History: The Journal of Natural and Social Philosophy*, vol. 7, n. 1, 2011, pp. 155–166.

Fausto-Sterling, Anne, *Sexing the Body: Gender, Politics, and the Construction of Sexuality* (New York: Basic Books, 2000).

Fine, Cordelia, *Delusions of Gender: The Real Science behind Sex Differences* (London: Icon, 2010).

Fink, Bruce, *Lacan on Love: An Exploration of Lacan's Seminar VIII, Transference* (Cambridge: Polity, 2015).

Finzi, Daniela, and Herman Westerink (eds), *Dora, Hysteria, and Gender: Reconsidering Freud's Case Study* (Leuven: Leuven University Press, 2018).

Føllesdal, Dagfinn, "Husserl's Reductions and the Role They Play in His Phenomenology", in *A Companion to Phenomenology and Existentialism*, edited by Hubert L. Dreyfus and Mark A. Wrathall (Oxford: Wiley-Blackwell, 2006), pp. 105–113.

Foucault, Michel, *A History of Sexuality: Volume 1*, trans. Robert Hurley (New York: Vintage, 1990).

Freedland, Cynthia (ed.), *Feminist Interpretations of Aristotle* (University Park, PA: Pennsylvania State University Press, 1998).

Freud, Sigmund, "Femininity", in *The Standard Edition of the Complete Psychological Works of Sigmund Freud: Volumes 22*, edited and translated by James Strachey (New York: W. W. Norton, 1989), pp. 139–167.

——, *The Outline of Psycho-Analysis: The Standard Edition of the Complete Psychological Works of Sigmund Freud: Volume 23*, edited and translated by James Strachey (New York: W. W. Norton, 1989).

——, *The Question of Lay Analysis*, in *The Standard Edition of the Complete Psychological Works of Sigmund Freud, Volume 20*, edited and translated by James Strachey (New York: W. W. Norton, 1990), pp. 177–258.

——, *Three Essays on Sexuality: The Standard Edition of the Complete Psychological Works of Sigmund Freud: Volume 3*, edited and translated by James Strachey (New York: Basic Books, 2000).

——, "Female Sexuality", in *The Standard Edition of the Complete Psychological Works of Sigmund Freud: Volume 21*, edited and translated by James Strachey (London: Vintage, 2001), pp. 223–243.

——, "Some Psychical Consequences of the Anatomical Distinction between the Sexes", in *The Standard Edition of the Complete Psychological Works of Sigmund Freud: Volume 19*, edited and translated by James Strachey (London: Vintage, 2001), pp. 248–258.

Froese, Katrin, "Bodies and Eternity: Nietzsche's Relation to the Feminine", *Philosophy and Social Criticism*, vol. 26, n. 1, 2000, pp. 25–49.

Fullbrook, Edward and Kate Fullbrook, *Sex and Philosophy: Rethinking de Beauvoir and Sartre* (London: Continuum, 2008).

Gallagher, Shaun, "Merleau-Ponty", in *Consciousness and the Great Philosophers: What Would They have Said About our Mind–Body Problem?*, edited by Stephen Leach and James Tartaglia (Abingdon: Routledge, 2016), pp. 235–243.

Galster, Ingrid, "'The Limits of the Abject': The Reception of *Le Deuxième Sexe* in 1949", in *A Companion to Simone de Beauvoir*, edited by Laura Hengehold and Nancy Bauer (Oxford: Wiley-Blackwell, 2017), pp. 37–46.

Gherovici, Patricia, "Where Have the Hysterics Gone?: Lacan's Reinvention of Hysteria", *English Studies in Canada*, vol. 40, n. 1, 2014, pp. 47–70.

——, *Transgender Psychoanalysis: A Lacanian Perspective on Sexual Difference* (Abingdon: Routledge, 2017).

Glazebrook, Trish, "Heidegger and Ecofeminism", in *Feminist Interpretations of Martin Heidegger*, edited by Nancy J. Holland and Patricia Huntington (University Park, PA: Pennsylvania State University Press, 2001), pp. 221–251.

Godelier, Maurice, *Claude Lévi-Strauss: A Critical Study of his Thought* (London: Verso, 2018).

Gómez Ramos, Antonio, "Hegel's Ethical Life and Heidegger's They: How Political is the Self?", in *Subjectivity and the Political: Contemporary Perspectives*, edited by Gavin Rae and Emma Ingala (Abingdon: Routledge, 2018), pp. 197–219.

Gothlin, Eva, "Reading Simone de Beavoir with Martin Heidegger", in *The Cambridge Companion to Simone de Beauvoir*, edited by Claudia Card (Cambridge: Cambridge University Press, 2003), pp. 45–65.

Grimwood, Tom, "Re-Reading *The Second Sex's* 'Simone de Beauvoir'", *British Journal for the History of Philosophy*, vol. 16, n. 1, 2008, pp. 197–213.

Groenhout, Ruth, "Beauvoir and the Biological Body", in *A Companion to Simone de Beauvoir*, edited by Laura Hengehold and Nancy Bauer (Oxford: Wiley-Blackwell, 2017), pp. 73–86.

Grosz, Elizabeth, "Merleau-Ponty and Irigaray in the Flesh", *Thesis Eleven*, n. 36, 1993, pp. 37–59.

——, *Volatile Bodies: Toward a Corporeal Feminism* (Bloomington, IN: Indiana University Press, 1994).

——, *The Incorporeal: Ontology, Ethics, and the Limits of Materialism* (New York: Columbia University Press, 2017).

Guenther, Lisa, "Merleau-Ponty and the Sense of Sexual Difference", *Angelaki*, vol. 16, n. 2, 2011, pp. 19–33.

Hancock, Ange-Marie, *Intersectionality: An Intellectual History* (Oxford: Oxford University Press, 2016).

Harper, Kyle, *From Shame to Sin: The Christian Transformation of Sexual Morality in Late Antiquity* (Cambridge, MA: Harvard University Press, 2013).

Hass, Lawrence, *Merleau-Ponty's Philosophy* (Bloomington, IN: Indiana University Press, 2008).

Hatab, Lawrence, "Nietzsche on Women", *The Southern Journal of Philosophy*, vol. 19, n. 3, 1981, pp. 333–345.

Hayward, Tim, "Anthropocentrism: A Misunderstood Problem", *Environmental Ethics*, vol. 6, n. 1, 1997, pp. 9–63.

Hegel, Georg W. F., *Elements of the Philosophy of Right*, edited by Allen W. Wood, trans. H. B. Nisbet (Cambridge: Cambridge University Press, 1991).

——, *The Science of Logic*, trans. George di Giovanni (Cambridge: Cambridge University Press, 2010).

Heidegger, Martin, *Being and Time*, trans. John Macquarrie and Edward Robinson (Oxford: Blackwell, 1962).

——, *Letter on Humanism*, trans. Frank A. Capuzzi in collaboration with J. Glenn Gray, in *Basic Writings*, edited by David Farrell-Krell (London: Harper Perennial, 1977), pp. 217–266.

——, *The Metaphysical Foundations of Logic*, trans. Michael Heim (Bloomington, IN: Indiana University Press, 1984).

——, *Zollikon Seminars: Protocols–Conversations–Letters*, edited by Medard Boss, trans. Franz Mayr and Richard Askay (Evanston, IL: Northwestern University Press, 2001).

Heinämaa, Sara, "What is a Woman?: Butler and Beauvoir on the Foundations of the Sexual Difference", *Hypatia*, vol. 12, n. 1, 1997, pp. 20–39.

——, *Toward a Phenomenology of Sexual Difference: Husserl, Merleau-Ponty, Beauvoir* (Lanham, MD: Rowman & Littlefield, 2003).

——, "Simone de Beauvoir's Phenomenology of Sexual Difference", in *The Philosophy of Simone de Beauvoir: Critical Essays*, edited by Margaret A. Simons (Bloomington, IN: Indiana University Press, 2006), pp. 20–41.

Hekman, Susan, "Simone de Beauvoir and the Beginnings of the Feminine Subject", *Feminist Theory*, vol. 16, n. 2, 2015, pp. 137–151.

Hird, Myra J., "Feminist Matters: New Materialist Considerations of Sexual Difference", *Feminist Theory*, vol. 5, n. 2, 2004, pp. 223–232.

Holdcroft, David, *Saussure: Signs, System, and Arbitrariness* (Cambridge: Cambridge University Press, 2008).

Hollywood, Amy, *Sensible Ecstasy: Mysticism, Sexual Difference, and the Demands of History* (Chicago, IL: Univerity of Chicago Press, 2002).

Holveck, Eleanor, "Can a Woman be a Philosopher? Reflections from a Beauvoirian Housemaid", in *Feminist Interpretations of Simone de Beauvoir*, edited by Margaret A. Simmons (University Park, PA: Pennsylvania State University Press, 1995), pp. 67–78.

Honnig, Bonnie, *Antigone Interrupted* (Cambridge: Cambridge University Press, 2013).

Horrocks, Roger, *Freud Revisited: Psychoanalytic Themes in the Postmodern Age* (Basingstoke: Palgrave Macmillan, 2001).

Hübscher, Angelika, "Schopenhauer und 'die Weiber'", *Schopenhauer-Jahrbuch*, 1977, pp. 187–203.

Huntington, Patricia, *Ecstatic Subjects, Utopia, and Recognition: Kristeva, Heidegger, Irigaray* (Albany, NY: State University of New York Press, 1998).

——, "Introduction I – General Background History of the Feminist Reception of Heidegger and a Guide to Heidegger's Thought", in *Feminist Interpretations of Martin Heidegger*, edited by Nancy J. Holland and Patricia Huntington (University Park, PA: Pennsylvania State University Press, 2001), pp. 1–42.

Husserl, Edmund, *The Crisis of European Science and Transcendental Phenomenology*, trans. David Carr (Evanston, IL: Northwestern University Press, 1970).

——, *Ideas pertaining to a Pure Phenomenology and to a Phenomenological Philosophy, First Book*, trans. F. Kersten (Dordrecht: Kluwer, 1983).

—, *Logical Investigations: Volume One*, trans. J. N. Findlay (Abingdon: Routledge, 2001).

Hutchins, Kimberley, "Beauvoir and Hegel", in *A Companion to Simone de Beauvoir*, edited by Laura Hengehold and Nancy Bauer (Oxford: Wiley-Blackwell, 2017), pp. 187–197.

Ingala, Emma, "From Hannah Arendt to Judith Butler: The Conditions of the Political", in *Subjectivity and the Political: Contemporary Perspectives*, edited by Gavin Rae and Emma Ingala (Abingdon: Routledge, 2018), pp. 35–54.

—, "Judith Butler: From a Normative Violence to an Ethics of Non-Violence", in *The Meanings of Violence: From Critical Theory to Biopolitics*, edited by Gavin Rae and Emma Ingala (Abingdon: Routledge, 2019), pp. 191–208.

—, "Not just *a* Body: Lacan on Corporeality", in *Historical Traces and Future Pathways of Poststructuralism: Aesthetics, Ethics, Politics*, edited by Gavin Rae and Emma Ingala (Abingdon: Routledge, 2021), pp. 143–159.

Irigaray, Luce, *Speculum of the Other Woman*, trans. Gillian C. Gill (Ithaca, NY: Cornell University Press, 1985).

—, *This Sex which is Not One*, trans. Catherine Porter with Carolyn Burke (Ithaca, NY: Cornell University Press, 1985).

—, "Equal or Different?", trans. David Macey, in *The Irigaray Reader*, edited by Margaret Whitford (Oxford: Wiley-Blackwell, 1991), pp. 30–34.

—, *Marine Lover of Friedrich Nietzsche*, trans. Gillian C. Gill (New York: Columbia University Press, 1991).

—, *An Ethics of Sexual Difference*, trans. Carolyn Burke and Gillian C. Gill (Ithaca, NY: Cornell University Press, 1993).

—, *Sexes and Genealogies*, trans. Gillian C. Gill (New York: Columbia University Press, 1993).

—, "The Question of the Other", trans. Noah Guynn, *Yale French Studies*, vol. 87, 1995, pp. 7–19.

—, *I Love to You: Sketch of a Possible Felicity in History*, trans. Alison Martin (Abingdon: Routledge, 1996).

—, *The Forgetting of Air in Martin Heidegger*, trans. Mary Beth Mader (Austin, TX: University of Texas Press, 1999).

—, "A Bridge between Two Irreducible to Each Other", in *Why Different?: A Culture of Two Subjects*, edited by Luce Irigaray and Sylvère Lotringer, trans. Camille Collins (New York: Semiotext(e), 2000), pp. 57–62.

—, "Different but United through a New Alliance", in *Why Different?: A Culture of Two Subjects*, edited by Luce Irigaray and Sylvère Lotringer, trans. Camille Collins (New York: Semiotext(e), 2000), pp. 113–119.

——, "Introduction", in *Why Different?: A Culture of Two Subjects*, edited by Luce Irigaray and Sylvère Lotringer, trans. Camille Collins (New York: Semiotext(e), 2000), pp. 7–13.

——, "The Civilization of Two", in *Why Different?: A Culture of Two Subjects*, edited by Luce Irigaray and Sylvère Lotringer, trans. Camille Collins (New York: Semiotext(e), 2000), pp. 71–80.

——, "The Teaching of Difference", in *Why Different?: A Culture of Two Subjects*, edited by Luce Irigaray and Sylvère Lotringer, trans. Camille Collins (New York: Semiotext(e), 2000), pp. 121–126.

——, "The Time of Difference", in *Why Different?: A Culture of Two Subjects*, edited by Luce Irigaray and Sylvère Lotringer, trans. Camille Collins (New York: Semiotext(e), 2000), pp. 95–99.

——, "Thinking Life as Relation", trans. Stephen Pluhacek, Heidi Bostic, and Luce Irigaray, in *Why Different?: A Culture of Two Subjects*, edited by Luce Irigaray and Sylvère Lotringer, trans. Camille Collins (New York: Semiotext(e), 2000), pp. 145–169.

——, *To be Two*, trans. Monique M. Rhodes and Marco F. Cocito-Monoc (London: Athlone, 2000).

——, *The Way of Love*, trans. Heidi Bostic and Stephen Pluháček (London: Continuum, 2002).

——, *In the Beginning, She Was* (London: Bloomsbury, 2013).

Irigaray, Luce, Elizabeth Hirsch, and Gary A. Olson, "'Je-Luce Irigaray': A Meeting with Luce Irigaray", trans. Elizabeth Hirsch and Gaëton Brulotte, *Hypatia*, vol. 10, n. 2, 1995, pp. 93–114.

Jagger, Gill, "The New Materialism and Sexual Difference", *Signs: Journal of Women in Culture and Society*, vol. 40, n. 2, 2015, pp. 321–342.

Johnston, Adrian, *Badiou, Žižek, and Political Transformations: The Cadence of Change* (Evanston, IL: Northwestern University Press, 2009).

Kant, Immanuel, *Critique of Pure Reason*, edited and translated by Paul Guyer and Allen Wood (Cambridge: Cambridge University Press, 1998).

——, *Anthropology from a Pragmatic Point of View*, edited and translated by Robert B. Louden (Cambridge: Cambridge University Press, 2006).

Kirby, Vicki, "When All That is Solid Melts into Language: Judith Butler and the Question of Matter", *International Journal of Sexuality and Gender Studies*, vol. 7, n. 4, 2002, pp. 265–280.

Kofman, Sarah, *Women in Freud's Writings*, trans. Katherine Porter (Ithaca, NY: Cornell University Press, 1985).

Kruks, Sonia, "Gender and Subjectivity: Simone de Beauvoir and Contemporary Feminism", *Signs: Journal of Women in Culture and Society*, vol. 18, n. 1, 1992, pp. 89–110.

——, "Simone de Beauvoir: Teaching Sartre about Freedom", in *Feminist Interpretations of Simone de Beauvoir*, edited by Margaret A. Simmons (University Park, PA: Pennsylvania State University Press, 1995), pp. 79–96.

——, "Merleau-Ponty and the Problem of Difference in Feminism", in *Feminist Interpretations of Maurice Merleau-Ponty*, edited by Dorothy Olkowski and Gail Weiss (University Park, PA: Pennsylvania State University Press, 2006), pp. 25–48.

Lacan, Jacques, *Seminar I: Freud's Papers on Technique*, edited by Jacques-Alain Miller, trans. John Forrester (New York: W. W. Norton, 1991).

——, *Seminar II: The Ego in Freud's Theory and in the Technique of Psychoanalysis*, edited by Jacques-Alain Miller, trans. Sylvana Tomaselli (New York: W. W. Norton, 1991).

——, *Seminar III: The Psychoses*, edited by Jacques-Alain Miller, trans. Dennis Porter (New York: W. W. Norton: 1993).

——, *Seminar XX: On Feminine Sexuality, The Limits of Love and Knowledge, 1972–1973*, edited by Jacques Alain-Miller, trans. Bruce Fink (New York: W. W. Norton, 1999).

——, "Guiding Remarks for a Convention on Female Sexuality", in *Écrits*, trans. Bruce Fink in collaboration with Héloïse Fink and Russell Grigg (New York: W. W. Norton, 2006), pp. 610–620.

——, "Introduction to Jean Hyppolite's Commentary on Freud's 'Verneinung'", in *Écrits*, trans. Bruce Fink in collaboration with Héloïse Fink and Russell Grigg (New York: W. W. Norton, 2006), pp. 308–317.

——, "Position of the Unconscious", in *Écrits*, trans. Bruce Fink in collaboration with Héloïse Fink and Russell Grigg (New York: W. W. Norton, 2006), pp. 703–721.

——, "Presentation and Transference", in *Écrits*, trans. Bruce Fink in collaboration with Héloïse Fink and Russell Grigg (New York: W. W. Norton, 2006), pp. 176–185.

——, "Response to Jean Hyppolite's Commentary on Freud's 'Verneinung'", in *Écrits*, trans. Bruce Fink in collaboration with Héloïse Fink and Russell Grigg (New York: W. W. Norton, 2006), pp. 318–333.

——, "The Function and Field of Speech and Language in Psychoanalysis", in *Écrits*, trans. Bruce Fink in collaboration with Héloïse Fink and Russell Grigg (New York: W. W. Norton: 2006), pp. 197–268.

——, "The Instance of the Letter in the Unconscious, or Reason since Freud", in *Écrits*, trans. Bruce Fink in collaboration with Héloïse Fink and Russell Grigg (New York: W. W. Norton, 2006), pp. 412–441.

——, "The Signification of the Phallus", in *Écrits*, trans. Bruce Fink in collaboration with Héloïse Fink and Russell Grigg (New York: W. W. Norton, 2006), pp. 575–584.

——, *Seminar VIII: Transference*, edited by Jacques-Alain Miller, trans. Bruce Fink (Cambridge: Polity, 2015).
——, *Seminar XXIII: The Sintome*, edited by Jacques-Alain Miller, trans. A. R. Price (Cambridge: Polity, 2016).
——, *Seminar V: Formations of the Unconscious*, edited by Jacques-Alain Miller, trans. Russell Grigg (Cambridge: Polity, 2017).
——, *Seminar XIX: . . . Or Worse*, edited by Jacques-Alain Miller, trans. Adrian Price (Cambridge: Polity, 2018).
Laqueuer, Thomas, *Making Sex: Body and Gender from the Greeks to Freud* (Cambridge, MA: Harvard University Press, 1990).
Le Doeuff, Michèle, "Simone de Beauvoir: Falling into (Ambiguous) Line", in *Feminist Interpretations of Simone de Beauvoir*, edited by Margaret A. Simmons (University Park, PA: Pennsylvania State University Press, 1995), pp. 59–66.
Lehtinen, Virpi, *Luce Irigaray's Phenomenology of Feminine Being* (Albany, NY: State University of New York Press, 2015).
Léon, Céline T., "Beauvoir's Woman: Eunuch or Male?", in *Feminist Interpretations of Simone de Beauvoir*, edited by Margaret A. Simmons (University Park, PA: Pennsylvania State University Press, 1995), pp. 137–161.
Levinas, Emmanuel, *Time and the Other*, trans. Richard A. Cohen (Pittsburgh, PA: Duquesne University Press, 1987).
Losonsky, Michael, *Linguistic Turns in Modern Philosophy* (Cambridge: Cambridge University Press, 2006).
Low, Douglas, "Merleau-Ponty's Criticism of Heidegger", *Philosophy Today*, vol. 53, n. 3, 2009, pp. 273–293.
Luft, Sebastian, "Husserl's Theory of the Phenomenological Reduction: Between LifeWorld and Cartesianism", *Research in Phenomenology*, vol. 34, n. 1, 2004, pp. 198–234.
McConnell Graybeal, Jean, *Language and "the Feminine" in Nietzsche and Heidegger* (Bloomington, IN: Indiana University Press, 1990).
McGowan, Todd, "The Signification of the Phallus", in *Reading Lacan's Écrits: From "Signification of the Phallus" to "Metaphor of the Subject"*, edited by Stijn Vanheule, Derek Hook, and Calum Neill (Abingdon: Routledge, 1999), pp. 1–20.
McMullin, Irene, *Time and the Shared World: Heidegger on Social Relations* (Evanston, IL: Northwestern University Press, 2013).
McNay, Lois, "Subject, Psyche, and Agency: The Work of Judith Butler", *Theory, Culture, and Society*, vol. 16, n. 2, 1999, pp. 175–193.
McWeeny, Jennifer, "Beauvoir and Merleau-Ponty", in *A Companion to Simone de Beauvoir*, edited by Laura Hengehold and Nancy Bauer (Oxford: Wiley-Blackwell, 2017), pp. 211–223.

Marrato, Scott, *The Intercorporeal Self: Merleau-Ponty on Subjectivity* (Albany, NY: State University of New York Press, 2013).
Merleau-Ponty, Maurice, *Phenomenology of Perception*, trans. Colin Smith (Abingdon: Routledge, 1962).
——, "In Praise of Philosophy", in *In Praise of Philosophy and Other Essays*, trans. John Wild and James M. Edie (Evanston, IL: Northwestern University Press, 1963), pp. 3–70.
——, *Signs* (Evanston, IL: Northwestern University Press, 1964).
——, *The Visible and the Invisible*, edited by Claude Lefort, trans. Alphonso Lingis (Evanston, IL: Northwestern University Press, 1968).
Mill, John Stuart, *On the Subjection of Women*, in *The Collected Works of John Stuart Mill, Volume XXI*, edited by John Robson (Toronto: University of Toronto Press, 1985), pp. 259–340.
Mills, Catherine, "Normative Violence, Vulnerability, and Responsibility", *differences: A Journal of Feminist Cultural Studies*, vol. 18, n. 2, 2007, pp. 133–156.
Mirvish, Adrian, "Simone de Beauvoir's Two Bodies and the Struggle for Authenticity", *Journal of French and Francophone Philosophy*, vol. 13, n. 1, 2003, pp. 78–93.
Mitchell, Juliet, "Introduction – I", in *Feminine Sexuality: Jacan Lacan and the école freudienne*, edited by Juliet Mitchell and Jacqueline Rose, trans. Jacqueline Rose (London: Macmillan, 1982), pp. 1–26.
Moi, Toril, *Sexual–Textual Practices: Feminist Literary Theory* (London: Methuen, 1985).
——, *Simone de Beauvoir: The Making of an Intellectual Woman*, Second edition (Oxford: Oxford University Press, 2008).
Moya, Patricia, and Maria Elena Larrain, "Sexuality and Meaning in Freud and Merleau-Ponty", *The International Journal of Psychoanalysis*, vol. 97, n. 3, 2016, pp. 737–757.
Nancy, Jean-Luc, and Philippe Lacoue-Labarthe, *The Title of the Letter: A Reading of Lacan*, trans. François Raffoul and David Pettigrew (Albany, NY: State University of New York Press, 1992).
Nietzsche, Friedrich, *Human, All too Human*, trans. R. J. Hollingdale (Cambridge: Cambridge University Press, 1996).
——, *Beyond Good and Evil*, edited by Rolf-Peter Horstmann and Judith Norman, trans. Judith Norman (Cambridge: Cambridge University Press, 2002).
Nussbaum, Martha, "Plato and Affirmative Action", *New York Review of Books*, 12 April 1984: https://www.nybooks.com/articles/1985/01/31/plato-affirmative-action/
Okin, Susan Moller, *Women in Western Political Thought* (Princeton, NJ: Princeton University Press, 2013).

Oksala, Johanna, "Female Freedom: Can the Lived Body be Emancipated?", in *Feminist Interpretations of Maurice Merleau-Ponty*, edited by Dorothy Olkowski and Gail Weiss (University Park, PA: Pennsylvania State University Press, 2006), pp. 209-228.

Oliver, Kelly, and Marilyn Pearsall (eds), *Feminist Interpretations of Nietzsche* (University Park, PA: Pennsylvania State University Press, 1998).

Olkowski, Dorothea, "Materiality and Language: Butler's Interrogation of the History of Philosophy", *Philosophy and Social Criticism*, vol. 23, n. 1, 1997, pp. 37-53.

Oppel, Frances Nesbitt, *Nietzsche on Gender: Beyond Man and Woman* (Charlottesville, VA: Virginia University Press, 2005).

Pagdens, Anthony, *The Enlightenment and Why it Still Matters* (Oxford: Oxford University Press, 2013).

Parker, Emily Anne, "Becoming Bodies", in *A Companion to Simone de Beauvoir*, edited by Laura Hengehold and Nancy Bauer (Oxford: Wiley-Blackwell, 2017), pp. 87-98.

Peden, Knox, *Spinoza contra Phenomenology: French Rationalism from Cavaillès to Deleuze* (Stanford, CA: Stanford University Press, 2014).

Petronella Foultier, Anna, "Language and the Gendered Body: Butler's Early Reading of Merleau-Ponty", *Hypatia*, vol. 28, n. 4, 2013, pp. 767-783.

Phillips, Kim M. and Barry Reay, *Sex before Sexuality: A Premodern History* (Cambridge: Polity, 2011).

Plato, *Phaedo*, trans. G. M. A. Grube, in *Complete Works*, edited by John M. Cooper (Indianapolis, IN: Hackett Publishing, 1997), pp. 50-100.

——, *Republic*, trans. G. M. A. Grube and Rev. C. D. C. Reeve, in *Complete Works*, edited by John M. Cooper (Indianapolis, IN: Hackett Publishing, 1997), pp. 971-1223.

——, *Timaeus*, trans. Donald J. Zeyl, in *Complete Works*, edited by John M. Cooper (Indianapolis, IN: Hackett Publishing, 1997), pp. 1225-1291.

Poe, Danielle, "Can Luce Irigaray's Notion of Sexual Difference be Applied to Transsexual and Transgender Narratives?", in *Thinking with Irigaray*, edited by Mary C. Rawlinson, Sabrina L. Hom, and Serene J. Khader (Albany, NY: State University of New York Press, 2011), pp. 111-128.

Preester, Helena de, "Merleau-Ponty's Sexual Schema and the Sexual Component of Body Integrity Identity Disorder", *Medical Healthcare and Philosophy*, vol. 16, n. 2, 2013, pp. 171-184.

Rae, Gavin, *Realizing Freedom: Hegel, Sartre, and the Alienation of Human Being* (Basingstoke: Palgrave Macmillan, 2011).

——, "Being and Technology: Heidegger on the Overcoming of Metaphysics", *Journal of the British Society for Phenomenology*, vol. 43, n. 3, 2012, pp. 305-325.

—, "Sartre on Authentic and Inauthentic Love", *Existential Analysis: Journal of the Society for Existential Analysis*, vol. 23, n. 1, 2012, pp. 75–88.

—, "Overcoming Philosophy: Heidegger on the Destruction of Metaphysics and the Transformation to Thinking", *Human Studies*, vol. 36, n. 2, 2013, pp. 235–257.

—, "Anthropocentrism", in *Encyclopaedia of Global Bioethics*, edited by Henk ten Have (Dordrecht: Springer, 2014), pp. 1–12.

—, "Heidegger's Influence on Posthumanism: The Destruction of Metaphysics, Technology, and the Overcoming of Anthropocentrism", *History of Human Sciences*, vol. 27, n. 1, 2014, pp. 51–69.

—, *Ontology in Heidegger and Deleuze* (Basingstoke: Palgrave Macmillan, 2014).

—, "Traces of Identity in Deleuze's Differential Ontology", *International Journal of Philosophical Studies*, vol. 22, n. 1, 2014, pp. 86–105.

—, *Evil in the Western Philosophical Tradition* (Edinburgh: Edinburgh University Press, 2019).

—, *Poststructuralist Agency: The Subject in Twentieth-Century Theory* (Edinburgh: Edinburgh University Press, 2020).

—, "Questioning the Phallus: Jacques Lacan and Judith Butler", *Studies in Gender and Sexuality*, vol. 21, n. 1, 2020, pp. 12–26.

—, "The 'New Materialisms' of Jacques Lacan and Judith Butler", *Philosophy Today*, vol. 65, n. 3, 2021, pp. 655–672.

Rae, Gavin, and Emma Ingala (eds), *Historical Traces and Future Pathways of Poststructuralism: Aesthetics, Ethics, and Politics* (Abingdon: Routledge, 2021).

Reineke, Martha J., "Lacan, Merleau-Ponty, and Irigaray: Reflections on a Specular Drama", *Auslegung*, vol. 14, n. 1, 1987, pp. 67–85.

Reineke, Sandra, "The Intellectual and Social Context of *The Second Sex*", in *A Companion to Simone de Beauvoir*, edited by Laura Hengehold and Nancy Bauer (Oxford: Wiley-Blackwell, 2017), pp. 28–36.

Roberts, Laura, *Irigaray and Politics: A Critical Introduction* (Edinburgh: Edinburgh University Press, 2019).

Robinson, Patricia Murphy, "The Historical Repression of Women's Sexuality", in *Pleasure and Danger: Exploring Female Sexuality*, edited by Carol S. Vance (Abingdon: Routledge, 1984), pp. 251–266.

Rose, Jacqueline, "Introduction – II", in *Feminine Sexuality: Jacques Lacan and the école freudienne*, edited by Juliett Mitchell and Jacqueline Rose (London: Macmillan, 1982), pp. 27–58.

Rousseau, Jean-Jacques, *Emile, or On Education*, trans. Alan Bloom (New York: Basic Books, 1979).

Rowley, Hazel, *Tête-à-Tête: The Tumultuous Lives and Loves of Simone de Beauvoir and Jean-Paul Sartre* (New York: Harper, 2006).
Rubin, Gayle, "Thinking Sex: Notes for a Radical Theory of the Politics of Sexuality", in *Pleasure and Danger: Exploring Feminist Sexuality*, edited by Carol S. Vance (Abingdon: Routledge, 1984), pp. 267–319.
——, "The Traffic in Women: Notes on the 'Political Economy' of Sex", in *The Second Wave: A Reader in Feminist Theory*, edited by Linda Nicholson (Abingdon: Routledge, 1997), pp. 27–62.
Russell, Matheson, "Phenomenological Reduction in Heidegger's *Sein Und Zeit*: A New Proposal", *Journal of the British Society for Phenomenology*, vol. 39, n. 3, 2008, pp. 229–248.
Sanders, Mark, "Merleau-Ponty and the Ethics of Engagement", in *Ethics and Phenomenology*, edited by Mark Sanders and J. Jeremy Wisnewski (Lanham, MD: Lexington, 2013), pp. 103–116.
Sandford, Stella, "Contingent Ontologies: Sex, Gender, and 'Woman' in Simone de Beauvoir and Judith Butler", *Radical Philosophy*, vol. 97, September/October, 1999, pp. 18–29.
——, *Plato and Sex* (Cambridge: Polity, 2010).
——, "Beauvoir's Transdisciplinarity: From Philosophy to Gender Theory", in *A Companion to Simone de Beauvoir*, edited by Laura Hengehold and Nancy Bauer (Oxford: Wiley-Blackwell, 2017), pp. 15–27.
Sartre, Jean-Paul, *Being and Nothingness: An Essay on Phenomenological Ontology*, trans. Sarah Richmond (Abingdon: Routledge, 2018).
Saussure, Ferdinand de, *Course in General Linguistics*, edited by Charles Bally, Albert Sechehaye, and Albert Riedlinger, trans. Roy Harris (Chicago, IL: Open Court, 1986).
Schiller, Britt-Marie, "The Incomplete Masculine: Engendering the Masculine of Sexual Difference", in *Thinking with Irigaray*, edited by Mary C. Rawlinson, Sabrina L. Hom, and Serene J. Khader (Albany, NY: State University of New York Press, 2011), pp. 131–151.
Schopenhauer, Arthur, "On Women", in *Parerga and Paralipomena, volume 2*, trans. E. F. J. Payne (Oxford: Clarendon Press, 1974), pp. 614–626.
Schott, Robin (ed.), *Feminist Interpretations of Kant* (University Park, PA: Pennsylvania State University Press, 2007).
Schutte, Ofelia, "A Critique of Normative Heterosexuality: Identity, Embodiment, and Sexual Difference in Beauvoir and Irigaray", *Hypatia*, vol. 12, n. 1, 1997, pp. 40–62.
Schwab, Gail, "Sexual Difference as Model: An Ethics for the Global Future", *Diacritics*, vol. 28, n. 1, 1998, pp. 76–92.
Smith, Joel, "Merleau-Ponty and the Phenomenological Reduction", *Inquiry*, vol. 48, n. 6, 2005, pp. 553–571.

Still, Judith, *Derrida and Hospitality: Theory and Practice* (Edinburgh: Edinburgh University Press, 2010).

Stoller, Silvia, "Reflections on Feminist Merleau-Ponty Skepticism", *Hypatia*, vol. 15, n. 1, 2000, pp. 175–182.

Stone, Alison, "The Sex of Nature: A Reinterpretation of Irigaray's Metaphysis and Political Thought", *Hypatia*, vol. 18, n. 3, 2003, pp. 60–84.

——, "From Political to Realist Essentialism: Rereading Luce Irigaray", *Feminist Theory*, vol. 5, n. 1, 2004, pp. 5–53.

——, *Luce Irigaray and the Philosophy of Sexual Difference* (Cambridge: Cambridge University Press, 2006).

Sullivan, Shannon, "Domination and Dialogue in Merleau-Ponty's Phenomenology of Perception", *Hypatia*, vol. 12, n. 1, 1997, pp. 1–19.

Tertullian, *On the Apparel of Women*, 16 August 2003: http://www.tertullian.org/anf/anf04/anf04-06.htm

Tidd, Ursala, *Simone de Beauvoir* (Abingdon: Routledge, 2004).

Toulalan, Sarah, and Kate Fisher (eds), *The Routledge History of Sex and the Body: 1500 to the Present* (Abingdon: Routledge, 2013).

Vasterling, Veronica, "Butler's Sophisticated Constructivism: A Critical Assessment", *Hypatia*, vol. 14, n. 3, 1999, pp. 17–38.

Versaldi, Giuseppe Cardinal, and Archbishop Angelo Vincenzo Zani, *Male and Female He Created Them: Towards a Path of Dialogue on the Question of Gender Theory in Education* (Vatican City: 2019): http://www.educatio.va/content/dam/cec/Documenti/19_0997_INGLESE.pdf

Vintges, Karen, "*The Second Sex* and Philosophy", in *Feminist Interpretations of Simone de Beauvoir*, edited by Margaret A. Simmons (University Park, PA: Pennsylvania State University Press, 1995), pp. 45–48.

Vlieghe, Joris, "Foucault, Butler, and Corporeal Experience: Taking Social Critique beyond Phenomenology and Judgement", *Philosophy and Social Criticism*, vol. 40, n. 10, 2014, pp. 1019–1035.

Watson, Eve, "Some Guiding Remarks for a Convention on Female Sexuality", in *Reading Lacan's Écrits: From "Signification of the Phallus" to "Metaphor of the Subject"*, edited by Stijn Vanheule, Derek Hook, and Calum Neill (Abingdon: Routledge, 1999), pp. 66–91.

Whitford, Margaret, *Luce Irigaray: Philosophy in the Feminine* (Abingdon: Routledge, 1991).

Wilson, Elizabeth A., *Neural Geographies: Feminism and the Microstructure of Cognition* (Abingdon: Routledge, 1998).

Winnubst, Shannon, "Exceeding Hegel and Lacan: Different Fields of Pleasure within Foucault and Irigaray", *Hypatia*, vol. 14, n. 1, 1999, pp. 13–37.

Wolfe, Cary, *What is Posthumanism?* (Minneapolis, MN: Minnesota University Press, 2010).

Wollstonecraft, Mary, *A Vindication of the Rights of Woman* and *A Vindication of the Rights of Men*, edited by Janet Todd (Oxford: Oxford University Press, 2009).

Xu, Ping, "Irigaray's Mimicry of the Problem of Essentialism", *Hypatia*, vol. 10, n. 4, 1995, pp. 76–89.

Young, Iris Marion, "Throwing Like a Girl: A Phenomenology of Feminine Body Comportment Motility and Spatiality", *Human Studies*, vol. 3, n. 2, 1980, pp. 137–156.

Young, Julian, "Nietzsche and Women", in *The Oxford Handbook of Nietzsche*, edited by Ken Gemes and John Richardson (Oxford: Oxford University Press, 2013), pp. 46–62.

Zahavi, Dan, *Husserl's Phenomenology* (Stanford, CA: Stanford University Press, 2003).

Žižek, Slavoj, *The Fragile Absolute or, Why is the Christian Legacy Worth Fighting For?* (London: Verso, 2000).

Zupančič, Alenka, *The Odd One In: On Comedy* (Cambridge, MA: The MIT Press, 2008).

——, *What is Sex?* (Cambridge, MA: The MIT Press, 2017).

INDEX

absence, 135–7, 142, 165
absurdity, 157, 165–7
agency, 194, 199, 210–13, 221–2, 224, 228, 230, 238–40, 243, 246–9
  human, 248–9
  political, 243
agential realism, 13, 209, 214–51
ambiguity, 3, 9, 13, 16–18, 76, 78, 90, 92, 103, 108, 112–16, 118, 122–3, 125, 127–8, 223, 263
  ontological, 118
anthropocentrism, 208, 217, 220–3, 238–40, 243, 248–9
apparatus, 34, 192, 229
Aquinas, St Thomas, 5, 24, 108, 251
Aristotle, 3–5, 21–2, 24, 108, 156

Barad, Karen, 11, 14, 19–20, 25, 182, 209, 214–5, 247–52, 258–9, 262, 270, 276, 281
Beauvoir, Simone de, 11–12, 14, 16, 18, 25, 74, 92–3, 101–29, 178, 181, 183, 187–8, 256–57, 262

being, 70–5, 93–4, 106–7, 119–23, 131–2, 134–7, 139–42, 146–7, 158–62, 171–2, 194, 196–206, 217–18, 224, 226–8, 232, 234–8, 240–1, 243–6, 255, 266, 268–9, 275
  human, 24, 104, 115, 129, 238, 248
  -in-the-world, 65, 75, 89
belief, 22, 218, 224
Benjamin, Walter, 262–8, 272, 278–9
binary oppositions, 10, 12–13, 15, 72–3, 75–7, 88–90, 111–12, 142, 144–6, 157–8, 163–4, 202, 204, 207–9, 218, 221, 224, 231–3
biological
  differences, 43, 113–14, 122, 135, 168–9, 187
  division, 158, 176
  essentialism, 103, 136, 173, 188
  sex, 1, 34, 101, 120, 132
biology, 32, 59, 106, 108–9, 113–14, 120, 135, 147, 159, 169–70, 191–3, 202, 256
birth, 36, 78, 113

bisexuality, 15, 38, 40, 46, 262, 270
  initial, 32, 36, 38–9
  ontological, 259
  physical, 34–5
body, 2, 16, 19, 23–4, 36–7, 77–86, 88–9, 94, 102, 110–13, 119–22, 137, 149, 168–9, 171–2, 188–9, 191–3, 195, 199–205, 208–16, 225–6, 262–3
  active, 111, 170
  gendered, 75, 83, 93, 197
  human, 85, 111, 255
  individual, 15, 91, 201, 216
  neutral, 16, 80, 84
  passive, 112, 197, 202
  pre-discursive, 205
  sexed, 16, 74–97, 103, 191, 239, 255
  sexualized, 158
  situated, 103, 121, 123
  woman's, 40, 80, 113, 120
Butler, Judith, 11, 13–14, 18–19, 25, 82–3, 95, 119–21, 125–6, 128–9, 132–3, 149, 176–80, 183, 187–214, 216–17, 219–23, 231–3, 248–9, 258, 270

castration, 42–5, 136
categories, 12, 41, 75, 92, 104, 121, 146, 187–8, 191–2, 194, 215, 273–6, 280
child, 7–9, 36–8, 41, 47, 110, 143–5
children, 1, 3–4, 6, 9, 36, 105
  sexuality of, 36
Christianity, 3, 5–6, 29
constellation, 14, 20, 114, 253, 262, 267–79

construction, 13, 16, 18, 105–6, 108, 119–20, 122, 163, 169, 191–4, 197–8, 201–2, 206, 226, 232
  cultural, 168, 187, 192
  gender, 120, 122, 188, 192–4, 197, 207, 258
critique, 7, 11, 15, 31–2, 54–5, 58–9, 64–5, 103, 155–6, 182–3, 216, 219–20, 233, 257–8, 261, 276, 280
culture, 126, 133, 156, 158, 168–9, 179, 181–2, 192, 209–10, 249, 251, 254, 261, 272, 277

Dasein, 53, 55, 57–68, 72
Derrida, Jacques, 12, 25, 53, 70, 177, 213–14, 216, 247, 250, 252
differences, 6, 8, 16, 18, 64, 84–5, 91, 96, 115, 135, 137, 154–6, 158–61, 167–8, 170, 173–4, 177, 181, 183, 247
  essential, 11, 171
  natural, 168, 270
discourse, 33, 94, 116, 135, 151, 162, 165, 177, 190, 192–3, 203–4, 220, 222–8, 232
discursive
  practices, 219, 225, 228–9, 258
  system, 220, 222, 233
dreams, 79, 130

education, 6, 21–2, 108, 277
Enlightenment, 3, 5, 22
entities, 53, 56–7, 59–61, 64–5, 67, 69, 112, 159, 217, 225–7, 230–1, 245, 274–5
equality, 8, 16, 18, 115, 156, 272, 277

essentialist-patriarchal model, 11, 13–19, 31, 47, 54, 63, 122, 134, 148, 173, 177, 188, 253–5, 257–9
ethics, 6, 60, 93, 103, 112–13, 149, 166, 170, 177, 183, 209, 238, 245, 251
excess, 19, 162, 189, 208
experience
 lived, 16–17, 85, 103, 118, 121
 transgender, 176
expression, 15, 18, 20, 62–3, 197, 199–200, 202, 216, 218, 227, 230, 235, 237–39, 244–5, 255, 258–60, 267, 269–70, 272

facticity, 58–9, 62–3, 70, 102, 107, 256
family, 4, 8–9, 101
father, 22, 42–3, 45, 143–5, 150
 function, 144, 146
female
 body, 82–3, 119–20, 168, 171–2, 191
 sexuality, 31, 48, 50, 131, 142, 149, 153, 155, 157, 163, 175
feminine, 3–5, 8, 11–12, 23, 29–51, 66–7, 74, 104–5, 131–3, 141–2, 157–8, 160–1, 163–7, 169, 171, 190–1, 217
 position, 133, 140, 142, 256
 sexuality, 30, 48, 149, 175, 177
femininity, 15, 17, 31, 35, 39–41, 43–5, 47–8, 50, 75, 125, 128, 131, 135–6, 140, 142, 163, 194–5
 nature of, 39, 47
fluid, 38, 40, 89, 91–2, 103, 109, 114, 118, 121, 123, 171–2, 177, 235–6, 243, 247

foreclosure, 2, 13, 200, 206, 245, 258–60
freedom, 8, 62–3, 102, 106–7, 110, 120–1, 123, 125
Freud, Sigmund, 15, 29–50, 52, 101, 103, 130, 135–6, 149–51, 154, 156, 160, 254, 256, 259, 262, 270, 276
function, 5, 17, 34–7, 41, 130, 134, 138, 142–4, 148–9, 151, 256, 269, 273, 277–8
 phallic, 139, 142
fundamental ontology, 15, 52–73, 248

gender, 12–13, 18–19, 23–5, 34, 64–5, 67, 117, 119–21, 123, 125–6, 128–9, 167–8, 177–8, 187–94, 196–203, 205–6, 208–9, 258–59, 270–1, 273–4
 identity, 194, 197, 201, 208–9, 217
 ideology, 1, 21
 interpellation of, 196, 203
 norms, 195–7, 199–200, 206
 performativity, 18, 189, 194, 201, 209, 226, 258, 262, 270
 and subjectivity, 126–7
genitals, 29, 31, 33, 36–8, 43, 158

Hegel, G. W. F., 8–9, 23–4, 102, 106, 108, 129, 156, 247–8, 266
Heidegger, Martin, 12, 14–16, 24–5, 52–74, 94, 102–3, 108, 115, 117, 122, 124, 156–8, 161, 172, 247–8, 254–6, 276
heteronormativity, 13, 18, 20, 43, 173, 175, 182, 187–8, 190, 224, 231, 233, 236, 257–8

heterosexuality, 176, 218, 271
history, 5, 10–11, 60, 66, 84, 87–8, 153, 157, 178, 180–1, 191, 247, 253–4, 265, 268, 272
homosexuality, 207, 232
hospitality, 242, 252
human
  cognition, 7, 221–3
  sexuality, 217–18
Husserl, Edmund, 52–3, 70, 74–5, 85, 92–4, 102

ideas, 75, 81, 130, 137, 188, 195, 225, 228, 235, 257, 262–3, 265–71, 275, 277–8
identity, 14–15, 20, 25, 114, 154, 190, 193, 197–8, 207–9, 217–18, 233–5, 240, 242, 247–8, 258–9, 271–2, 277–8
imaginary, 131, 133, 140, 144, 234
individuals, 30, 33–5, 38, 61, 64, 108, 113, 118, 216, 218, 227, 229, 233, 235–6, 238, 244–5, 259–60
inequality, 6, 105–6
intersectionality, 273–4, 280
intra-actions, 19, 217, 227–31, 236, 243, 249, 251, 275–6
Irigaray, Luce, 11–12, 14, 18, 25, 93–4, 97, 155–83, 187–8, 192, 209, 214, 257, 262, 270

judgement, 8, 52, 85–6, 90–1, 107, 211, 225
justice, 3, 9, 44, 84, 156, 222–3, 242–3, 251

Kant, Immanuel, 7–9, 24, 156

Lacan, Jacques, 14, 17–18, 93, 123, 130–45, 147–55, 160, 170, 177–8, 183, 187, 213–14, 219, 256–8, 262, 270
language, 84, 130, 132, 134, 136–8, 148–9, 151, 161, 164–5, 167, 187–8, 190, 195–8, 204–5, 209–10, 212, 214, 216–17, 254, 263
laws, 134, 143, 195, 232, 244–5, 268, 272, 277
  symbolic, 133–4, 143–6
life, 36, 47, 82, 85, 87, 90, 106, 109, 171, 209, 271
lived body, 12, 80, 86, 89, 96, 102, 108, 112, 121, 123, 256
  pre-reflective, 86, 89
logic, 12, 15, 17, 19–20, 24–5, 47, 72–3, 104, 106, 115–16, 118, 120, 122, 131–2, 146, 148–9, 154–6, 159–67, 173–4, 215
  of foundations, 87–9
  of hierarchy, 174, 190
love, 1, 6, 8, 42, 45, 74, 93, 139–41, 149, 151–2, 168, 177, 181–2
  object, 42–3

masculine, 3–5, 11, 17, 19, 30–1, 34–5, 39–43, 46–7, 66–7, 104–5, 115–17, 132–3, 141–3, 155–8, 160–2, 167, 169, 188, 191, 207
  body, 80, 169, 171
  perspective, 13, 39, 54, 65, 75, 115, 132, 160–1
  phallus, 17, 42, 131, 136, 147, 155
material, 13, 18, 203–4, 208, 216, 222, 225, 227, 232, 236, 239–40, 244–5, 255, 257–8, 264–5

material (*cont.*)
    excess, 189, 205, 208
    existence, 121
    practices, 226, 228
materialisation, 19–20, 182, 202–3, 219–21, 223, 227–30, 234, 240, 258
materialism, 216, 237, 247, 251
    new, 103, 151, 208, 213, 246–7
materiality, 14, 19–20, 189, 200–2, 204–5, 207–8, 213–17, 219–20, 222–8, 230–8, 242, 244–6, 258, 265
    expression of, 20, 222, 238
    and language, 212
    queerness of, 244–5
matter, 9, 13–14, 19–20, 25, 70, 188–9, 201–4, 208–13, 216–21, 224–5, 227–30, 233, 235–6, 238, 240–7, 249, 258–60
mattering, 228, 251
Merleau-Ponty, Maurice, 14, 16–17, 25, 74–87, 89–97, 102–3, 108, 115, 122, 156, 187, 255–7, 262, 270
metaphysics, 53, 68, 71, 73, 224–5, 248
mind/body dualism, 58, 112, 129
mother, 42–3, 45, 104, 126, 136, 143–5
    -hood, 101, 110–11, 127
    pre-Oedipal, 144–5
mysticism, 153, 180

name, 76, 138, 148, 157, 197, 203, 216, 269–71, 275, 278
Name-of-the-Father, 143–4
natural attitude, 52, 75
nature, 2–4, 6–14, 35–6, 121–2, 147, 169–71, 182–3, 192–3, 220, 223–4, 228, 231–6, 238, 241–2, 244, 253–4, 256, 258

neutrality, 54, 60–1, 63–4, 68, 76, 102, 157, 161, 174
    ontological, 63, 68, 122
Nietzsche, Friedrich, 10, 23–4, 71, 156, 237
norms, 2, 8, 25, 83, 109, 118, 151, 191–2, 194–200, 203, 206, 208, 260

object, 34–5, 37–8, 52, 54, 58, 65, 67, 75–9, 81–3, 86, 89, 105, 107, 137–9, 141, 224, 226, 263, 265–8
Oedipus complex, 30, 42, 44, 133–6, 143–5
ontic, 57, 59, 61, 64–5, 68–9, 255
ontological
    difference, 15, 25, 53, 56–7, 68–70, 230
    essentialism, 13, 19, 230, 254, 256–8
    monadism, 227, 274
order, 1, 81, 197–8, 268, 274
    symbolic, 144, 146–7, 151
organs, 37, 40, 79, 87, 138
originary
    bisexuality, 15, 31, 39–40, 46, 69, 254–5
    neutrality, 54, 60, 63, 66–8, 75, 156

paternal, 134, 143–6
    functions, 143–6
    law, 134, 144
    metaphor, 133, 143–4, 146
patriarchal, 13, 55, 76, 143–4, 165, 174, 233
    representation, 162, 164
    societies, 110–11, 117
    system, 18, 158, 162, 164, 166

patriarchy, 9–10, 12–13, 15–18, 31, 46–7, 54–55, 63, 66–7, 103–4, 114–18, 122, 131–2, 134, 148, 155–8, 163–6, 173–4, 207, 215, 231, 256–8
penis, 1, 42–45, 132, 135, 138, 160
perception, 10, 25, 74, 76–8, 81, 83–4, 86, 88–9, 93–7, 143, 215, 226, 268
  erotic, 81, 85
  objective, 78, 81–2, 85, 89
performativity, 13, 187–213, 217
person, 32, 40, 55, 77, 140, 145
phallogocentrism, 129, 163–4, 166–8, 170–1, 174–5, 190, 215
phallus, 17, 39, 42, 115, 131–6, 138–44, 146–9, 151–2, 155–6, 160–1, 178, 188, 194, 256
  signification of the, 149, 152
phenomena, 87, 94, 203, 229, 239, 256, 263–5, 268–9, 273
phenomenal field, 78, 89
phenomenological, 14, 16, 110–11, 116–18, 156, 177, 254
philosophers, 2, 10, 85–6, 125, 183
philosophy, 8–9, 21, 23, 64, 94–6, 106, 112, 124–5, 128, 170, 179, 210–12, 262–3, 265
  Western, 2, 10, 44–5, 66, 108, 156–7, 165, 173, 200, 215, 234, 236–7
physics, 19, 220, 225–6, 241
Plato, 4–6, 21, 24, 108, 156, 266
pleasure, 24, 29, 31, 37–8, 42–3, 49, 65, 78, 183, 210
politics, 3–4, 21–2, 24, 84, 106, 150, 177–8, 209, 211–13, 240–1, 245, 247, 272, 277

power, 17–18, 22, 81, 160, 167, 191, 199–200, 202–3, 209, 211–12, 216, 219, 272, 277
  relations, 192, 199
pregnancy, 110–11
processes, 35–9, 59, 61, 63, 105–7, 122, 169, 189–90, 193–6, 198, 202–3, 206, 216, 227–30, 237–8, 240, 255, 257–8, 260, 264
  boundary-making, 239
  emergent, 216, 225–6
  non-binary, 208
  normative, 194
production, 5, 157, 192, 200
psychoanalysis, 20–1, 27, 30, 35–6, 49–50, 54, 59, 95, 101, 108, 130, 149, 151, 155, 160
puberty, 30–2, 36–9, 41–2, 109–10, 158, 171

quantum, 228, 236, 243
  leaps, 20, 233–6, 238, 259
queer, 14, 20, 91–2, 113, 223, 232–3, 236–7, 241, 244–6, 251, 259–60, 262

race, 7, 64, 67, 158, 160, 176, 181, 273–6, 280
reason, 5–7, 9, 40–1, 55–6, 59–63, 83–4, 86–8, 110, 112–14, 116–17, 135–9, 163–4, 170–71, 188–93, 195–7, 199–200, 207, 239, 263–6, 268–9
representationalism, 160, 218, 224–25, 237, 239
  Cartesian, 218, 224, 236–7
rhythms, 171–2, 257
Rousseau, Jean-Jacques, 6–7, 24

Sartre, Jean-Paul, 24, 72, 74, 93, 102, 108, 117, 124, 129, 248
Saussure, Ferdinand de, 130, 136–7, 148, 151
schemas, 75, 80, 85, 131, 147, 194, 206, 208, 233
Schneider, 77–83
Schopenhauer, Arthur, 9–10, 23–4
self, 67, 72, 112, 194, 240, 242, 272
sexual
  difference, 12, 18, 25, 53, 70, 75, 82–6, 92–3, 125, 130–83, 192, 212–13, 251, 257
  equality, 3–4, 272, 277
  essentialism, 9, 15, 31, 43, 47, 55, 63, 92, 132, 147, 231, 235
  identities, 38, 142, 160, 177, 188, 193, 200, 207, 245
  instinct, 29, 34–8
  life, 32, 38–9, 42, 79–80, 87, 110, 150
  object, 32–4, 37, 79, 85
  relations, 2–4, 10, 18, 139, 141–2, 146, 168, 176, 188, 207, 232, 253
  schema, 16, 76, 80–2, 85–6, 89, 91
sexuality, 1–24, 29–83, 85–92, 94–6, 101–28, 130–6, 138–242, 244–8, 250–80
signification, 17, 119, 131, 137, 199, 201–5, 208, 214
signifiers, 130–2, 136–40, 143–4, 204
situation, 32, 81, 102, 107, 112–13, 116–18, 120–2, 140, 163, 220, 273
  of women, 102, 107

social
  norms, 193, 195–200, 219, 226, 258, 278
  practices, 195–6, 201
species, 2, 6–7, 108–9, 113, 222
structuralism, 99, 123, 129–30, 154, 177, 213
  post-, 123, 149, 154, 177, 215–16, 218, 236–8, 247, 255
subject, 79–81, 102, 104–7, 112, 114–15, 117, 136, 138–9, 142, 160, 179, 181–2, 188–91, 194–200, 203, 206, 209–13, 218, 220–1
  conditioned, 189
  dis-embodied transcendental, 67
  gendered, 193, 195–6, 201
subjectivity, 72, 84–5, 94, 123, 126, 183, 209, 212, 230
symbolic
  construction, 19, 132, 139–40, 188–9, 193, 202, 206–8, 257
  phallus, 17, 130–53, 258

theory
  feminist, 11, 18, 20, 25, 48, 54, 114, 119, 121, 123, 125, 177, 181, 189–90, 254–5
  gender, 14, 18, 21, 114, 118, 125, 190, 206, 232, 255
  intersectional, 280
  quantum, 217, 228, 233, 235, 240, 242
  queer, 12, 14, 18–19, 201, 207, 214–51, 255
transcend, 64, 107, 117–18
transcendence, 64, 106–9, 115, 117, 120–1, 123, 125, 128, 200, 230
transcendens, 56, 65
transcendent, 56, 64–5, 80

transcendental
  condition, 65, 78
  phenomenology, 75, 92
  subjectivity, 84
transformation, 71, 107, 247
transsexual, 176, 183
truth, 2, 9, 70, 73, 102, 106, 165–7, 174, 176, 193, 263, 265–7

unity, 134, 146, 154, 173, 190, 234, 265–6

woman, 3–10, 12, 16–17, 24–5, 33, 40–2, 101–29, 131–2, 135–6, 140, 142, 155–6, 160, 162–9, 171–2, 174–5, 178–80, 182, 191, 256
world, 56, 58–9, 62, 64–5, 67, 78, 80–1, 85–7, 105, 107, 113, 137, 168–9, 195–6, 198–9, 222, 224–5, 228–9, 242–3, 251–2